AUSTRALIA

Tony Duboudin and Brian Courtis

with a major contribution by
Stephen Taylor

The
American
Express
Pocket
Guide

Mitchell Beazley

The Authors

Tony Duboudin is a freelance writer and editor. Formerly chief sub-editor of *The Age*, Melbourne, he has also worked on the foreign desk of *The Times*, London, and from 1983–85 was the *Times* correspondent for Australia. He still covers Victoria for the paper, and has lived and worked in Australia since 1968.

Brian Courtis is a freelance arts and entertainments writer who has lived and worked in Australia since 1969. Formerly television critic for *The Age*, Melbourne, and journalist on the London *Daily Express*, his assorted career has included TV scriptwriting, a period as deckhand on an ocean-going yacht, and working on the media arrangements for the Pope's 1986 visit to Australia.

Contributors

Stephen Taylor (Australian Capital Territory, New South Wales, Queensland)
Kim Lockwood (Northern Territory)

Acknowledgments

The authors would like to thank the State Government Tourist Authorities of the Australian Capital Territory, New South Wales, the Northern Territory, Queensland, South Australia, Tasmania, Victoria and Western Australia for their assistance.

Few travel books are without errors, and no guidebook can ever be completely up to date, for telephone numbers and opening hours change without warning, and hotels and restaurants come under new management, which can affect standards. While every effort has been made to insure that all information is accurate at the time of going to press, the publishers will be glad to receive any corrections and suggestions for improvements, which can be incorporated in the next edition, but cannot accept any consequences arising from the use of the book, or from the information contained herein.

Series Editor David Townsend Jones
Assistant Editor Elizabeth Newman
Project assistants Anderley Moore, Helen Panay
Indexer Richard Bird
Gazetteer Catherine Palmer

Art Editor Nigel O'Gorman
Design assistant Christopher Howson
Illustrator Karen Cochrane
Map Editor David Haslam
Production Peter Phillips, Barbara Hind

Edited and designed by Mitchell Beazley International Limited,
Artists House, 14–15 Manette Street, London W1V 5LB
for the American Express Pocket Travel Guide Series

Maps in 2-colour and 4-colour by Lovell Johns Ltd, Oxford, England
Typeset by Bookworm Typesetting, Manchester, England
Printed and bound in Hong Kong by Mandarin Offset

British Library Cataloguing in Publication Da
Duboudin, Tony
Australia.—(The American Express pocket guide).
1. Australia—Description and travel—1981– —Guide-books
I. Title II. Courtis, Brian III. Taylor, Stephen IV. Series
919.4'0463 DU95

ISBN 0–85533–664–1

Contents

How to use this book

The American Express Pocket Guide to Australia is an encyclopedia of travel information, organized in the sections listed on the previous page. There is also a comprehensive index (pages 231–40), and there are full-colour maps at the end of the book.

For easy reference, each state in the *A to Z* is arranged as far as possible alphabetically. For the organization of the book as a whole, see *Contents*. For places that do not have separate entries in the *A to Z* see the *Index*.

Abbreviations

As far as possible only standard abbreviations have been used. These include months, days of the week, points of the compass (N, S, E and W), street names (Ave., Pl., Sq., St.), Saint (St) rooms (rms), Highway (Hwy), century (C), measurements, and routine contractions of Australian state names.

Bold type

Bold type is used in the text mainly for emphasis, to draw attention to something of special interest or importance. At the same time it picks out places – a winery or a minor museum, for example – that do not have full entries of their own.

Cross-references

Whenever a place or section title is printed in *sans serif italics* (e.g., *Opera House* or *Planning*) in the text, you can turn to the appropriate heading in the book for fuller information. Cross-references in this typeface can refer to other main sections in the book – e.g., *Basic information* or *Planning*. Or they can refer to another entry in the same sub-section – so in Sydney's *Sights*, for example, simply turn to *Opera House* whenever you see the cross-reference. And cross-references to other sub-sections (e.g., *Hotels* or *Nightlife*) are always clearly spelled out – as in ". . . the *Australian Opera* company (see *Nightlife*)", or "See *Australian wine* in *Special information*".

How entries are organized

Circular Quay ★
Map 6B3 🚃 *Explorer Bus.*

If Sydney has a transport nerve-centre, this is it. Once, tall-masted barques and schooners arrived here from the mother country; now, ferry services depart across the harbour for the northern suburbs of *Manly* and Mosman, and numerous bus services terminate here (☎ *29 2622 for bus and ferry inquiries*). The Sydney Explorer Bus and the Harbour Explorer both start here, and the city centre is only a 15min walk away.

For all these reasons Circular Quay is an excellent place to begin your investigation of the city. It is also a good starting point for a number of central walks. Here are two suggested routes.
Walk A
Total distance about 5km (3 miles), broken up by lunch along the way.

Follow **Circular Quay East** to **Bennelong Point**, site of the *Opera House*. Continue walking eastwards along the harbourside cove, through the *Royal Botanic Gardens* to **Mrs Macquarie's Chair**. A road, which also bears the name of this early governor's wife, then runs for approximately 1km (½ mile) s past the

For easy reference, use the running heads (printed at the top corner of each page), which show at a glance what is on every page. Examples: **Planning** (page 40); **NSW**/*Sydney hotels* (page 80); **Victoria**/*Excursions* (page 194).

Map references

Each full-colour map at the end of the book has a page number (2–16) and is divided into a grid of squares, identified vertically by letters (A, B, C, D, etc.) and horizontally by numbers (1, 2, 3, 4, etc.). A map reference identifies the page and square in which the street or place can be found – thus *Sydney Opera House* is located in Map 7B4.

Price categories

Price categories for hotels and restaurants are denoted by the symbols ☐ ☐ ☐ ☐ and ☐ which signify cheap, inexpensive, moderately priced, expensive and very expensive, respectively. These correspond approximately with the following actual ranges of prices, which give a guideline at the time of printing. Prices for hotels vary considerably across each range: pro rata, hotels in Sydney, Melbourne and Canberra are the most expensive, in Perth, Adelaide and Brisbane they are about average, and they are least expensive in Hobart, Launceston, Darwin and Alice Springs; outside these major cities prices are lower. Restaurant prices vary much less. Although actual prices will inevitably increase, the relative price category is likely to remain the same.

Price categories	Corresponding to approximate prices	
	for **hotels** *double room with bath; single rather cheaper*	for **restaurants** *meal for one with house wine or BYO bottle*
☐ cheap	under A$50	under A$15
☐ inexpensive	A$50–80	A$15–20
☐ moderately priced	A$80–120	A$20–45
☐ expensive	A$120–150	A$45–70
☐ very expensive	over A$150	over A$70

— Bold blue type for entry headings.

— Blue italics for address, practical information and symbols. For list of symbols see page 6 or back flap of jacket.

— Black text for description.

— Sans serif italics used for cross-references to other entries or sections.

Bold type used for emphasis.

Entries for hotels, restaurants, shops etc. follow the same organization, and are usually printed across a half column. In hotels, symbols indicating special facilities appear at the end of the entry, in black.

Victoria ♣
215 Little Collins St., Melbourne, Vic., 3000 ☎ *63 0441* IDD ● *31264* ℗ *63 9678. Map* **10C3** ☐ *520 rms*
☐ ☐ ☐ AE ● ● VISA

Location: Very central, between Russell St. and Swanston St. Old-fashioned and staid, but this popular hotel has modern business facilities. Comfortable basic accommodation without frills or fancy decor, and the restaurant serves good, wholesome food. Not all rooms have private facilities, so when booking specify a room with a bath or shower. Just the place for the tourist on a budget.
☐ ☐ ☐

Key to symbols

- ☎ Telephone
- IDD International Direct Dialling (IDD)
- ● Telex
- ℻ Facsimile (fax)
- ★ Recommended sight
- ⌒ Parking
- 🆓 Free entrance
- 🔳 Entrance fee payable
- ♿ Facilities for disabled people
- ⋘ Good view
- 📷 Photography forbidden
- 𝘟 Guided tour
- 🍴 Cafeteria
- ✱ Special interest for children
- 🛏 Hotel
- ✿ Good value
- ☐ Cheap
- ⬛ Inexpensive
- ⬛ Moderately priced
- ⬛ Expensive
- ⬛ Very expensive
- ⌂ Residential terms available

- AE American Express
- ◉ Diners Club
- 💳 MasterCard
- VISA Visa
- ⇌ Swimming pool
- ⌒ Sauna
- ♨ Spa
- ▭ Refrigerator in room
- ⚓ Good beach nearby
- ⚲ Tennis
- ✔ Golf
- ⚓ Fishing
- ♈ Gym/fitness facilities
- 👥 Conference facilities
- ⇌ Restaurant
- ⬛ Good wines
- 💬 A la carte available
- 💬 Set (fixed price) menu available
- ⅄ Bar
- ● Disco dancing
- ♫ Nightclub
- ▦ Temporary membership

6

An introduction to Australia

Sun, sea, a bountiful soil and vast mineral wealth combine with a stable political system to give Australia an unmatched sense of wellbeing and comfort. It is a nation that at times borders on smugness – a land blessed with vast wealth that has rightly earned the title of the "Lucky Country".

Because of its European origins Australia in many ways often resembles the old continent. Europeans are always finding little corners of Australia that remind them of home, be it mountains, plains, or sea. Likewise, American visitors identify the style of life with California, and South Africans equate the vast open spaces of the Outback with the veldt. Australia can be all things to all men. But this is misleading, for Australia's origins go back more than 40,000 years, and recent discoveries suggest that the earliest traces of man may be in Australia.

The continent has virtually every type of scenery. Though rarely beautiful in the picture-postcard sense, it frequently has a grandeur and variety unmatched by other countries. It ranges from the pleasant green pastures of the southern part of the state of Victoria and the island of Tasmania to the vast, forbidding desert and spinifex of the Simpson Desert, which covers parts of three states (Western Australia, South Australia and Queensland) and the Northern Territory. In between those extremes, Australia has tropical wetlands and crocodile-infested areas in the Northern Territory, and some of the wildest, most remote mountain landscape to be found anywhere on earth – areas where people have disappeared without trace – that offer first-class skiing comparable with some of the best Europe has to offer.

The kangaroo, the instantly recognizable national symbol, exemplifies the country's unique wildlife, which has evolved independently for millions of years. This isolation is similarly reflected in the flora of the continent, which has also developed its own unique ways of coping with the harsh climate of the world's driest landmass and vast extremes of temperature.

Visitors arriving in this land of plenty, particularly those who have passed through Asia *en route*, may find the economic contrast stark. Couple this with an unconcern often shown by Australians for their regional neighbours, veering sometimes towards outright hostility, and it is tempting to suppose that the nation is wholly indifferent to the Pacific region.

And in some respects that is true. For Australia is an oddity – an ethnically European nation with a Western democracy, surrounded by non-European nations in a region that has few Westminster-style governments. Other than self-interest, Australia has little in common with its neighbours, and still looks to Europe and the United States for inspiration in most fields.

The stereotype is of a land of hard-bitten, hard-riding, hard-drinking frontiersmen. In fact this is the most urbanized nation in the world – truly the home of the large city. A visit to Australia means exploring one or several cities, for they as much reflect the real Australia as does the laconic sheep or cattle farmer in the Outback lording it over thousands of empty square kilometres. The great cities are generally pleasant, handsomely laid out, functional and clean – certainly much cleaner than London or New York. But outside the city centres they lack soul, seeming to stretch aimlessly for kilometre after kilometre. The average Australian city is the epitome of suburbia – and the ambition of the average Australian still goes not much further than owning his own home on a quarter-acre piece of land. That said,

7

the cities do have much to offer, notably the inner areas of Sydney, like the imaginatively preserved Rocks area, and Melbourne, which has some fine Victorian inner suburbs, such as Carlton and North Melbourne. For modern architecture too the centres of all Australian cities have much of merit.

As a nation Australia takes pride in its achievements and sometimes ignores the costs and mistakes. The childlike pride in having the tallest building or the largest department store in the southern hemisphere, for example, suggests a lack of maturity in a society that still tends to venerate sportsmen ahead of artists.

But it should also be said that Australians are an extremely generous people. They possess a wry sense of humour and a laconic turn of phrase. They have a healthy disregard for authority and a great distaste for exaggeration, showing off and other displays of what they call "side". Putting on "side" is an Australian expression applied to those who have an inflated sense of their importance . . . and there is nothing an Australian likes better than deflating such people. They are a phlegmatic and unemotional lot, and the fact that voting is compulsory is a fair indication of their generally apathetic attitude to politics and, more particularly, politicians, who are usually assumed to be less than honest.

They do have an overwhelming need to be liked and a strong desire for approval, particularly by foreigners. This is the so-called cultural cringe, a belief that anything from outside of Australia must be good and, by definition, anything home-grown must be inferior. Though this attitude is now fading it remains a strong national trait. Thus you are likely to be asked, sometimes within hours of arrival, what you think of this or that local manifestation. Provided you are not too critical, Australians will very quickly warm to you, particularly if you are willing to seek their help.

The Australian lifestyle is relaxed and the tempo easy. Blessed with vast natural wealth, originally through wool and meat and, more recently, mineral resources, Australia has never really had to extend itself to enjoy a good standard of living. Only in the past decade or so have the harsher realities of the outside world begun to impinge, and even now there remains a refreshingly unquenchable optimism in the future.

The richness of the language as it is spoken in Australia is among the cultural surprises awaiting those who think they speak the Queen's (or American) English. For Australians enjoy manipulating and, some might argue, doing great violence to the language. They also love abbreviating names and titles, evolving slang (and keeping existing slang alive) and creating expressions.

In many ways the Australian has taken up the London cockney's tradition of creating and preserving slang. This love of slang has a lot to do with Australia's penal beginnings, for many of the early convicts came from the poorest parts of London. Coupled with a desire to mark themselves apart from the authorities, the injection of some Aboriginal words and the additional spice of Irish phrases and expressions (many of Australia's early guests were political prisoners from the various "troubles" in that unfortunate island), this led to the evolution of the unique and rich Australian phraseology and style of speech.

For the visitor the challenge of understanding can be all part of the fun of a visit to Australia. So if a local, for example, asks if you would like to come down to the rubbidy (pub) tomorrow arvo (afternoon), or come around and rip the scab off a few blueys (open the ring pull on some cans of Fosters lager), you will understand the scale of the challenge.

Before you go

Documents required

Visas are required for all visitors to Australia except those from
New Zealand. Visa applications should be accompanied by a
recent passport photograph signed on the back by the applicant,
and the applicant's passport valid for the duration of his or her stay
in the country. A tourist visa is valid for up to 6mths and precludes
the visitor from taking a job in Australia. There are working-
holiday visas, normally valid for 6mths, intended for young people
aged 18-25 to take occasional jobs while travelling and learning
more about the country. Visitors must pay a departure fee of A$20
as they leave.

Vaccination certificates are not normally required unless you
travel from countries affected by yellow fever, smallpox, cholera or
typhoid.

Visitors can use their valid driving licence in Australia for a
equivalent class of vehicle. The licence must be carried when
driving. International driving licences are recognized in all states.
Those planning an extended stay must obtain a valid licence from
the state licensing authority: inquire at any police station.

Travel and medical insurance

The cost of medical treatment in Australia is high. Except for
certain countries with which Australia has reciprocal agreements,
such as the UK and New Zealand, health care costs are not covered
by the local health system called **Medicare**.

Visitors from the UK are covered under Medicare, which
provides basic hospital care (in public wards) and a percentage
(varying, but about 70–80 percent) of the "common fee" charged
by doctors for a range of services. This fee is based on agreement
between the government and the Australian Medical Association
but is not binding on doctors who may, but rarely do, charge
whatever fee they think fit. The "common fee" is the basis on
which refunds from the government under the Medicare system
are calculated. The reciprocal arrangement only covers treatment
needing to be carried out immediately. It will not necessarily cover
the entire cost of treatment: some medication, for example, will be
charged to you.

Visitors from countries with which no reciprocal agreement
exists and those wanting anything more than the most basic
coverage are strongly advised to take out private insurance. The
policy should cover repatriation: costs are high for special
arrangements to fly a sick person from Australia to the UK.

Health care in Australia is comparable, and in some respects
superior, to that available anywhere else. Visitors intending to stay
longer than 6mths may enrol in the Medicare system.

Money

The unit of currency is the dollar (A$), which is split into 100
cents. There are coins for 1 cent, 2 cents, 5 cents, 20 cents, 50
cents and A$1, and notes for A$1 (being phased out and replaced
by the A$1 coin), A$2, A$5, A$10, A$50 and A$100. There is no
restriction on the amount of currency that can be brought into
Australia, but A$5,000 is the maximum that can be taken out of
the country in cash. Travellers cheques issued by American
Express, Thomas Cook and major international banks are widely
accepted. Banks, including those in the suburbs of the large cities,
have a daily exchange rate for the major world currencies. Make
sure you read the instructions included with your travellers

cheques. It is important to note separately the serial numbers of your cheques and the telephone number to call in case of loss. Specialist travellers cheque companies such as American Express provide extensive local refund facilities through their own offices or agents.

Australians have embraced plastic money wholeheartedly and all the major credit cards such as American Express, Diners Club International, Visa and MasterCard are accepted. Most shops and restaurants accept at least two credit cards and more often three or more. The most widespread credit card is the domestic Bankcard, issued and administered jointly by the major Australian banks. Anyone planning an extended stay can obtain a Bankcard if they open a local bank account. American Express offices will change cardmembers' personal cheques in a foreign currency.

Customs

Visitors can bring in duty-free all personal effects, except tobacco goods, alcoholic drinks and perfume, for use during their stay or to take out of the country when they leave. Receipts may need to be produced for expensive electronic goods such as cameras, video machines, tape recorders and watches.

The duty-free allowances for Australians and visitors are generally similar to most other countries. Only people over the age of 18 are eligible for the duty-free allowance.
Tobacco: 200 cigarettes *or* 250 grams of cigars *or* 250 grams of tobacco.
Alcoholic drinks: 1 litre of wine *or* 1 litre of spirits.
Perfume: 15fl.oz./425g/450cc.
Other goods: Although all goods brought into Australia are subject to customs duty, concessions enable most goods to be landed free or at little charge. However, goods ineligible for concessions attract a high combined rate of duty and sales tax.

Such items as goods made to order and not collected before leaving the country – for example, footwear, clothing and jewellery – attract the full customs and sales tax, as do goods dispatched from shops on the visitor's behalf and goods sent as freight intended to arrive on the same aircraft or ship as the visitor. Usually goods brought for the visitor's personal use or that have been owned or used for 12mths do not attract any sort of duty or sales tax.

Items made from a number of endangered species, such as alligator and crocodile, big cats, snakes and lizards, zebra and rhinoceros, are forbidden as imports into Australia. Further information can be obtained from Australian diplomatic missions.

Quarantine regulations

Australian quarantine regulations are among the world's strictest. As exports of rural produce run to around A$6,000 million a year (Australia's second largest income earner after minerals), the concern with keeping animal diseases at bay is understandable. Australia has never experienced an outbreak of foot-and-mouth disease: on its open ranges, such an outbreak would be a disaster and one difficult to control. There has been only one known case of rabies, in the 19thC, and many other animal diseases are unknown. To maintain this disease-free environment imports are banned of meat cooked or raw, plants or seeds, animals alive or dead, reptiles, fish, birds, any animal product such as semen, biological specimens, and soil.

The penalties for breaking these rules can be severe. Many an Italian or Greek family returning to Australia with their favourite salamis has ended up in court facing heavy fines. Even baby food containing meat must be surrendered at the airport.

Because of Australia's unique flora and fauna, illegal trade in the export of birds, particularly members of the parrot family, is lucrative and the penalties correspondingly severe. The unlicensed export of all flora and fauna is forbidden.

Visitors entering Australia must complete a customs and quarantine form, and all aircraft landing in Australia are sprayed with insecticide. The first-time visitor may be amused or alarmed by the sight of uniformed men, in summer usually wearing shorts, walking down the aisle of an aircraft with aerosol cans in each hand spraying the air, but the danger to Australia's valuable sheep and cattle industries is real, and at least quarantine officers now use a low-irritant spray and warn passengers to cover their noses with a handkerchief.

To protect the fruit and wine industries, it is forbidden to move most fruits and certain plants from one state to another. On some borders, particularly between Victoria and South Australia, Department of Agriculture officials are on hand to ensure compliance with the law, and see that all fruit is dumped. At most state border crossing points notices advise travellers what they can take across.

Getting there

By air: Most international carriers fly into the major Australian state capitals. The national airline Qantas (Queensland and Northern Territory Aerial Services), which flew its first passenger in 1922, operates the Kangaroo Route daily between Australia and Britain and Europe in conjunction with British Airways. The route is the longest in the world. Qantas and British Airways operate services into Sydney, Melbourne, Perth, Adelaide and Brisbane. There are direct flights from Australia to the major capitals of Europe, Asia and the USA.

Airlines operating to Australia include: Qantas, British Airways, Singapore Airlines, Cathay Pacific, KLM, United, Continental, Lufthansa, JAT, Alitalia, Olympic, Japan Air Lines, Garuda, Air New Zealand, UTA, Air Caledonia, Thai International, Malaysian Airline System, Air Canada, Philippine Airlines, Air India, Air Vanuatu and Air Niugini.

Jet lag: One of the unavoidable problems of any journey to Australia is jet lag. For travellers from Europe the problem can be particularly acute, as the minimum time spent in the air is about 24hrs, and quite often nearer 30hrs. For travellers from the West Coast of the USA the journey of around 15hrs is not quite so draining, particularly as westbound travel is less disorientating than eastbound. However, either journey will leave you tired. Several precautions during the flight will minimize the effects of jet lag: drink lots of fluid, avoid alcohol, eat sparingly, at stopovers get out of the plane and walk around, and try to get some sleep, if only a catnap.

One of the best ways to recover rapidly is to stay awake for the first day in Australia and try to adjust as quickly as possible to local time. This is particularly important for European travellers who have lost nearly half a day *en route* and will probably have arrived short of sleep at the start of a new day in Australia. Manage to stay awake for that first day, get to bed at an early hour, and recovery can be quick. Try to resist the temptation to go out and launch at once into your holiday.

By sea: There are no scheduled liner services, although several cruise ships call at Australian ports. The *Queen Elizabeth II* frequently calls on round-the-world cruises, as do several other cruise liners. Passage can be arranged on the few general-cargo, non-container vessels that visit Australia.

Climate

Australia has a wide range of climate from temperate in the s island state of Tasmania to tropical (monsoonal) in the far N of Western Australia, Queensland and the Northern Territory. Two-fifths of the continent lies N of the Tropic of Capricorn, and in some parts the rainfall can exceed 2,500mm (200ins) a year; yet Australia is the driest continent on earth. Paradoxically, every year people are lost in the mountains and frequently die of exposure on cross-country skiing trips. But it is also a land where people can die of exposure in the desert.

The southern part of the country has a temperate, Mediterranean-like climate with four seasons, characterized by cool winters, hot summers (especially in Jan and Feb), and mild springs and autumns. Spring and autumn can be the best times to visit the eastern seaboard and Western Australia. In the tropical N there are two seasons, a hot, wet season, with rain falling mainly in Feb and Mar during the prevailing monsoons, and a warm, dry season with a prevalent SE trade wind blowing.

Clothes

The choice of clothes to take will obviously be governed by the season. For the summer, shorts and short-sleeved shirts for men and light, cotton dresses for women should certainly be included, together with bathing suits. The rules of dress are relaxed, although some first-class hotels expect a collar and tie, if not a jacket, for men and a dress for women to be worn at dinner. In summer it is customary for men at work to wear shorts and long, white walking socks, with a collar and tie.

Summer nights can be cool, particularly in Victoria and Tasmania, so the inclusion of a light sweater even in summer is advisable. For winter, warmer clothes are needed and a raincoat should be included. If planning a winter visit to the mountains of the Great Dividing Range, waterproofs and warm clothes are essential, just as they would be in any mountain region in winter. If planning a journey to the Outback, footwear is important: boots or similar should be worn, not just as a support but also as a sensible precaution against the possibility of stepping on snakes, which have a habit of basking in the sun on clear ground.

Poste restante

Central post offices in the state capitals have poste restante counters where mail can be collected. All post offices, even in the remotest areas, will hold mail for collection. It is customary, but not always requested, for some form of identification, such as a passport or international driving license, to be presented when collecting mail.

Getting around

From airports to cities

Private bus services run from all state capital airports to the city centres. Fares vary according to distance and are payable on boarding the bus. Taxis are available at all state capital and most regional airports. As competition is keen at most large airports there is rarely a shortage.

By and large, unlike some countries, Australian cab drivers do not try to take advantage of newly arrived international travellers. Passengers are not, for example, asked to pay for return fares for the cab to get back to the rank or airport.

Flying

Australia's domestic air services are excellent, extensive, and expensive when compared with, say, those in the USA.

The two major internal airlines – **Ansett**, part of Mr Rupert Murdoch's empire, and **Australian Airlines**, formerly Trans Australia Airlines and government-owned – operate parallel services to most centres. It has been a major criticism of the airlines, which operate under a federal government "two-airline policy", that there is little real competition. Flights by the two airlines frequently take off to the same destination within 10mins of each other, and fares are identical. However, in recent years there has been more competition, and both airlines have introduced a wide variety of incentive and Apex (advance purchase) fares. Both operate, and in some cases own, holiday islands in Queensland off the Great Barrier Reef, and offer package holidays to these islands and to scores of other destinations around the country. And both have special tickets that for a fixed price give a fixed number of kilometres and stopovers on their networks, much as in the USA.

In addition to the two major airlines, **East-West Airlines** has extensive services in NSW, Western Australia and Queensland. It also flies Melbourne-Sydney and Sydney-Perth. Both services have a stopover about halfway, in Albury on the Melbourne-Sydney route, and at Alice Springs on the Sydney-Perth route. East-West also has a range of package holidays.

The other major carrier is the regional airline **Kendell**, which operates feeder services into both Melbourne and Adelaide from outlying centres. Kendell too offers an array of package holidays, specializing in country packages. These range from a weekend out of Melbourne in the Coonawarra wine district of South Australia (with the guarantee of space on the return flight for up to two dozen bottles of wine) to a week at Broken Hill in the Outback of South Australia. Kendell flights can be booked through Ansett.

All major airlines offer standby fares on major trunk routes. These offer savings of 20 percent on regular economy fares. Tickets are issued at the airport and you fly when a seat becomes available as allocated by the standby desk. Standby is best suited to people with a flexible itinerary who can use off-peak flights.

Railway services

Because of intense colonial rivalry, NSW, Victoria and Queensland once all had different gauges. After Federation things improved, but it was not until the early 1960s that it became possible to travel between Melbourne and Sydney without having to change trains at Albury, just over the border in NSW. Today it is possible, by using a number of rail links, to travel from northern Queensland to the SE corner of Western Australia.

Despite the early confusion, Australia today boasts one of the few remaining great train journeys in the world, the **Indian Pacific** linking Sydney and Perth, a journey of nearly 4,000km (2,500 miles) that takes three nights (65hrs) and includes the world's longest stretch of straight railway line across the Nullabor Plain, which runs without a bend for 478km (299 miles). The Indian Pacific service started in 1970 shortly after the completion of the standard-gauge link between Western Australia and the eastern

13

part of the country. It has proved highly successful, with some reservations needed up to 12mths ahead.

The last link in the network of standard-gauge rail lines joining all mainland state capitals was completed in 1982, fulfilling a dream that started at the time of Federation.

Other major sectors are Melbourne to Sydney, with a daylight and an overnight service; Melbourne to Adelaide, overnight; Sydney to Brisbane, overnight; Brisbane to Cairns, overnight; Adelaide to Alice Springs, overnight; Sydney to Canberra, daylight service; Sydney to Alice Springs, two days (47hrs); and Adelaide to Perth, two days (42hrs). Sleeping accommodation is available, for a surcharge, on most of the overnight services. Reservations for seats and sleeping cars are recommended for all major services at all times, especially the Indian Pacific and Queensland services.

Within the states, railway services link most major centres in NSW and Victoria, and narrow-gauge services connect many outlying centres in Queensland. Services in South Australia and Western Australia are not as widespread. Both Melbourne and Sydney have extensive suburban railway services, and morning and afternoon rush-hour travel presents the same problems of overcrowding faced by most commuters in large cities.

Buses

Several nationwide bus companies operate services between the state capitals that are far more economical, if considerably more tiring, than air travel. Not counting the 4½hr Sydney-Canberra route, the shortest is around 10hrs (Melbourne-Adelaide). The Adelaide-Perth journey is a bone-numbing 36½hrs. All inter-capital buses are equipped with toilets and water fountains, and some of the more luxurious double-decker vehicles (operated by, for example, **DeLuxe Coachlines**) screen video films during the journey. The major bus lines operating express inter-capital services are **Ansett Pioneer**, **Greyhound** and DeLuxe.

Though bus travel point-to-point can be wearing, touring by bus can be an excellent way of seeing Australia. The three major inter-capital bus companies operate tours, and several other specialist companies offer a wide variety of package holidays, including some that provide for a bus journey one way and a return journey by air. The bus tours range from two-day outings to a 56-day circumnavigation of Australia.

Most tours feature an informed commentary from the drivers (now known as "coach captains"), with frequent stops and overnight accommodation in motels. Daylight touring is the rule – buses aim to arrive by nightfall, allowing time for a shower and a sightseeing walk.

For the more adventurous there are camping tours and safaris. These are more basic forms of bus travel in the Outback, with overnight stops at camping grounds, equipped with showers and laundry facilities, taking the place of motels. All food, camping gear and sleeping equipment is carried on the bus or 4-wheel-drive vehicle. The duration of such tours can range from 2-38 days, or more. Popular with young people, offering a sense of adventure and a good chance to get to know people quickly and make friends, they can be recommended for the young-in-spirit, though hardly for those addicted to home comforts.

Taxis

Australian cabs are basically standard saloon cars. The great majority are radio-controlled. They can be hailed in the street or hired at cab stands, which are clearly indicated in city streets. At night and at weekends cabs can be hard to find.

Like their counterparts the world over, Australian cab drivers are mines of local knowledge and information. The standard of driving is good and the cab system is well policed and monitored. Cab drivers must display their licence with a photograph and number inside the cab. A single passenger is expected to sit in the front with the driver – all part of the egalitarian spirit of Australia. Drivers do *not* expect to be tipped unless they have rendered a special service. However, drivers do expect you to talk to them about anything and everything: you are considered to be a snob or worse if you fail to enter into a conversation.

Most major state capitals operate a two-tier charge system, with a day rate and a more expensive night rate. The rate is displayed inside the cab; lights on the cab sign on the roof indicate which rate is in operation. During the day a single light indicates the cheaper rate; at night both lights are illuminated to indicate the night rate. Cab drivers can ask one passenger if they would mind sharing the cab and fare with another going in a similar direction. There is no obligation to accept the sharing arrangement, though it is customary to agree.

Fares vary slightly from city to city, but basically there is a flag-fall charge (the standard charge for hiring, which comes into force when the driver turns on the meter) and then a combination of kilometres and time. A national cab credit-charge system called **Cabcharge** issues credit-type cards or a book of credit vouchers to account holders. The system is mainly intended for business people, but, as it operates nationwide, may be worth considering for visitors on extended trips. There is an accounting fee on each monthly bill for the service. Many cabs now accept American Express Cards in payment for fares.

Getting around by car

Behind the wheel of a car, many Australians change from being normally fairly tolerant creatures into something far less attractive. In addition to fast and aggressive driving, they sometimes show a marked reluctance to obey traffic laws and lane discipline, which can be disconcerting for visitors accustomed to motorway driving in Europe or the USA. The result is that Australia has one of the highest accident rates of any country in the world. The national road toll is some 3,000 killed a year out of a population of a little more than 16 million.

Australians drive on the left-hand side of the road. Traffic signs are easy to follow, being mainly self-explanatory and pictorial, and are similar to those used internationally. There are some local specialities, such as the sign warning that kangaroos cross some roads, and another alerting drivers to the possibility of slow-moving koalas or wombats crossing. Speed limits are 60kph (37½mph) in built-up areas and 100kph (62½mph) in non-urban areas, unless speed-limit signs indicate otherwise. Increasingly sophisticated methods are employed to detect drivers breaking the law. Some states use radar speed-checks coupled with cameras, which allow police to detect speeding drivers without having to stop them. A photograph showing the offending car's numberplate provides sufficient evidence and a fine is imposed. Similarly, at some intersections cameras photograph cars that jump red lights; police then prosecute on the evidence of a photograph. The wearing of seat belts by the driver and all passengers is compulsory.

Every state in Australia has its own motoring organization similar to the AA or RAC in Britain, and all operate breakdown services. Membership of one entitles visitors to reciprocal services from those in other states. (Addresses of the various motoring organizations are given under state capitals in the *A to Z*).

Parking meters are as much the bane of people's lives in Australia's major cities as in New York and London, and traffic wardens are as universally unpopular.

Traffic laws are basically the same throughout Australia, but with some local state variations. In Melbourne, for example, trams cannot be overtaken on the right, and at most city crossroads, where two tram tracks cross, right turns must be executed from the left-hand side of the road *after* the traffic lights have changed. This is intended to prevent obstruction of trams by cars turning right. Such intersections have large warnings to alert drivers to the right-turn rule, with a diagram showing how to execute the turn. Again, in some states vehicles turning left are obliged to give way to all other vehicles. Before taking to the road it is advisable to consult the state motoring organization for advice: most provide leaflets explaining local traffic laws.

Australia's main highways are popularly known by name rather than route number, although on many maps route numbers are shown, and often both the route number and the highway's name. In the Outback, distances between filling stations can be great.

Outback touring

For those who want to see the "real Australia" and get off the main roads in the Outback there are certain precautions to take. Always inform someone of where you are going and when you expect to arrive. Always carry ample water, enough for at least three or four days, and note that the radiators of most modern cars now contain a poisonous anti-corrosive agent that precludes using the water for drinking in an emergency. Always carry a few spare parts such as a fan belt, spark plugs, tyre repair kit and spare tyre.

If you should become bogged down or have a breakdown do not leave your car, which provides shade and is more easily spotted both from the air and the ground than a lone human. To help conserve body fluid, do not move about in the heat of the day. Always carry a spade in case you do get bogged down.

To obtain water, dig a hole about 1m (3ft) deep, place a tin or other container in the centre of the hole and firmly pack around it any live vegetable matter you can gather (leaves, spinifex, saltbush etc.). Cover the hole with a sheet of plastic secured firmly at the corners, then place a pebble in the middle of the stretched plastic directly above the container. The heat of the sun will distil moisture from the live vegetable matter, and water will condense on the underside of the plastic sheet, gently run down and drip into the container. Using this method it is possible to distil ½ litre (1pt) of drinkable water in 24hrs, which could mean the difference between life and death.

Renting a car

Most large international car rental companies operate in Australia and have desks at state capital airports and agents at regional airports. The car rental market is extremely competitive, so it is advisable to shop around for the best deal. For example, some rental companies offer discounts to people paying with American Express Cards. Most offer either an unlimited-kilometres flat charge or a free initial distance followed by a charge per kilometre. Compulsory third-party insurance is included with the rental, and additional insurance covering collision damage and personal injury can be taken out for an extra fee.

Basic rentals require the car to be returned to the place of rental but one-way rentals can be arranged, though there may be a fee to cover the cost of returning the car to its base. Both Ansett and Australian Airlines will arrange in-flight for a car to be available at your destination. The major car rental companies operating in Australia are **Avis, Hertz, Budget, National** and **Thrifty**. Several cheaper rental companies offer sound, older cars; they have such names as **Rent a Bomb** or **Rent a Wreck** and can be found in the telephone *Yellow Pages*.

Getting around on foot

The inner areas of most Australian cities lend themselves to walking, but once outside the central area the charm diminishes for walkers. The vast suburban sprawls that grew after the end of World War II were designed primarily for citizens with cars. In cities and built-up areas pedestrian crossings are plentiful. It is best, however, to use a crossing controlled by lights – on an uncontrolled crossing the battle of wills with the average driver can be both trying and dangerous. It is an offence to jaywalk.

On-the-spot information

Public holidays

Most public holidays are taken nationwide, but there are state-by-state and local differences. For example, in Victoria only the Melbourne Metropolitan region has a public holiday for the Melbourne Cup horse race, on the first Tues in Nov.

The public holidays are: New Year's Day (Jan 1); Australia Day (Jan 26); Labour Day (first Mon in Mar in Western Australia and Tasmania, second Mon in Mar in Victoria); Canberra Day (ACT only – third Mon in Mar); Good Friday; Easter Saturday; Easter Monday; Easter Tuesday (Victoria and Tasmania only); Anzac Day (Apr 25); Labour Day (Queensland and Northern Territory only – first Mon in May); Adelaide Cup Day (South Australia only – third Mon in May); Foundation Day (Western Australia only – first Mon in June); Queen's Birthday (all states except Western Australia – second Mon in June); August Bank Holiday (NSW, ACT and Northern Territory only – first Mon in Aug); Melbourne Show Day (Melbourne Metropolitan area only – last Thurs in Sept); Labour Day (first Mon in Oct in NSW, ACT and Western Australia, second Mon in Oct in South Australia); Melbourne Cup Day (Melbourne Metropolitan area only – first Tues in Nov); Christmas Day; Boxing Day (Dec 26).

Time zones

Australia has three time zones: Eastern Standard Time (GMT plus 10hrs) covering Queensland, NSW (except Broken Hill), Victoria and Tasmania; Central Standard Time (GMT plus 9½hrs) covering South Australia, Broken Hill and the Northern Territory; and Western Time (GMT plus 8hrs) covering Western Australia. Daylight Saving (or Summer) Time operates in Victoria, NSW, South Australia and Tasmania but not in Queensland, the Northern Territory or Western Australia; in the eastern states the clocks go forward at the end of Oct and back at the end of March.

Banking hours

Banks are open Mon-Thurs 9.30am-4pm, Fri 9.30am-5pm. Most bureaux de change operate as part of large organizations such as

American Express and Thomas Cook and are open slightly longer hours than banks. There are exchange counters operated by the banks at the major international airports. Most larger hotels will gladly exchange travellers cheques and major currencies.

Shopping hours

Normal retail trading hours are 9am-5.30pm Mon-Fri and 9am-noon on Sat. Late-night shopping is either Thurs or Fri until 9pm – and many large department stores stay open late on both nights. Some supermarkets stay open until 9 or 10pm every night, and convenience stores, which are often franchized American operations such as 7 Eleven and Food Plus, may stay open 24hrs.

Public houses – called "hotels" in Australia – have slightly different opening hours from state to state, but as a rule open around 10am-10pm Mon-Sat; they also open for around 6hrs on Sun, though hours vary. Licensed restaurants can serve liquor with meals seven days a week.

Customs and etiquette

Australians pride themselves on the egalitarian nature of their society, most of them believing they are the equal of anyone. Consequently they immediately use Christian names, almost as if that demonstrates their equality. Men generally call one another "mate", and the greeting "G'day" is almost universal. Do *not* expect to be called "sir" or "madam" and you won't be disappointed, as Australians have an abiding dislike of anything that smacks of servility.

Many of Australia's social customs revolve around drinking. Buying a "shout" (round) in the pub is considered essential good manners. Similarly, when invited out to dinner at someone's house, it is polite to arrive with a small gift, usually a bottle of wine or perhaps a box of chocolates for the hostess.

Rush hours

Although they differ from city to city, the early-morning rush hour starts earlier the farther N one goes. Because of the heat in the tropics, Brisbane, for example, comes to life at least ½hr earlier than Melbourne. Generally the rush hour starts around 7am and lasts until 9am. In the evening the traffic starts to clog around 5.15-5.30pm and lasts until about 7pm. Friday nights in summer, when people go away for the weekend, tend to be worse than other peak periods.

Post and telephone services

Post offices, denoted by a sign carrying the legend *Australia Post* in red, are widespread. Each post office also has the post code (zip code) for its area prominently displayed together with the town's or suburb's name. They open Mon-Fri 9am-5pm. The central post office in each capital city has a counter open 24hrs a day and is usually still referred to as The GPO, although the postal system has been renamed Australia Post. Post boxes are painted red and are identical to those used in Great Britain. Many milk bars sell a range of the most commonly used stamps.

Public telephones, located at post offices and in the street, are subject to vandalism, as in other parts of the world. A local call costs 30 cents. Call boxes take 10, 20 and 50 cent coins.

Public lavatories

These are few and far between in most Australian cities, though there are one or two gems of Victorian cast-iron *vespasiennes* in the

Paris style in Melbourne and Sydney. Many people resort to the large department stores, which usually have generous facilities. Most railway stations have toilets for men and women, and public houses are often used in an emergency by non-drinking passers-by.

Electricity

Current is 240/250v, AC 50Hz. Australia uses 3-pin power outlets. Most hotels have special plugs for 110v shavers. Universal adaptors for overseas appliances are obtainable in most large department stores.

Laws and regulations

A law peculiar to Australia is the system of Total Fire Ban days in summer. Under this system it is an offence on designated days to light a fire in the open or allow one to remain burning. These days are usually announced 24hrs in advance but can be imposed on shorter notice, and are designated according to forecast weather conditions such as high winds and dry conditions accompanied by high temperatures. Penalties for ignoring a Total Fire Ban are severe and differ from state to state, but typically they can be a fine of A$5,000 or imprisonment for 2yrs, or even both. Southeastern Australia, particularly the states of Victoria and South Australia, is one of the most flammable regions in the world (think of the Ash Wednesday bushfires of 1983, which claimed more than 70 lives), so the concern with fire is understandable.

Penalties for importing drugs are severe. The laws governing trafficking and possession differ from state to state; those in Queensland are considered the toughest. Cigarette smoking is prohibited in public transport in most states. The transport of fruit and vines across most state borders is strictly forbidden.

Tipping

Tipping is not generally customary in Australia and no service charge is added by hotels or restaurants. It is customary to tip a waiter around 10 percent for good service, but cab drivers, barbers and porters do not expect it. Porters at rail terminals have set charges, but hotel porters do not and can be tipped at the discretion of the guest.

Disabled travellers

The law in most states requires all new buildings to provide for disabled people such facilities as ramps and special toilets. Many buildings erected in the past 5yrs have included them, and following the recent Year for the Disabled many local authorities have upgraded their provision for disabled people. Both the major internal airlines offer disabled travellers special assistance such as priority boarding and assistance with wheelchairs.

For booklets listing facilities in each state capital, write to the **Australian Council for Rehabilitation of the Disabled (ACROD)** (*P.O. Box 60, Curtin, ACT, 2605 ☎ (062) 82 4333*).

There is no national reference point for information for disabled people, but most state tourist authorities have information about the facilities available at leading tourist destinations. Other sources of information are the state departments of health, whose telephone numbers can be found in the front of each capital city's telephone book under the *State Government* listing. The Commonwealth Department of Youth, Sport and Recreation publishes a book, available from the department, listing facilities for the disabled at a number of tourist destinations around the country.

19

Useful addresses

Tourist information
Australian Tourist Commission   Head Office: 324 St Kilda Rd.,
Melbourne, Vic., 3004 ☎ (03) 690 3900; branch office:
5 Elizabeth St., Sydney, NSW, 2000 ☎ (02) 233 7233.
American Express   Head Office: 388 George St., Sydney, NSW,
2000 ☎ (02) 237 0777, is a valuable source of information for any
traveller in need of help, advice or emergency service. There are
American Express customer card service offices in all the capital
cities. Main addresses and telephone numbers: Sydney – American
Express Tower, Sydney, NSW, 2000 ☎ (02) 237 0777;
Melbourne – Elizabeth St., Melbourne, Vic., 3000 ☎ (03) 602
4044; Adelaide – Grenfell St., Adelaide, SA, 5000 ☎ (08) 212
7155; Perth – William St., Perth, WA, 6000 ☎ (09) 322 6797;
Brisbane – Queen St., Brisbane, Qld, 4000 ☎ (07) 221 7815;
Canberra City – Centrepoint, Canberra, ACT, 2600 ☎ (062) 47
7750. In addition there are a number of American Express Travel
Service offices around the country through which it is possible to
cash personal cheques in an emergency (see under individual state
capitals in the *A to Z*).
State Government Tourist Bureaux   See under individual state
capitals in the *A to Z*. In addition to the main offices most State
Government Tourist Bureaux have branches in other major capital
cities and are listed in telephone books.

Hotel reservations
Most of the state capitals operate hotel reservation services, and
information is usually available at airports, railway stations and
bus depots. Large motel chains such as **Flag Inns**, **Homestead**
and **TraveLodge** with free reservation services can book ahead.

Consulates
Most major countries have consular representation in the state
capitals. Their addresses are listed in the telephone book under
Consuls (in the alphabetical section).

Government departments
Federal and state government departments are listed together with
local councils at the front of all telephone books.

Conversion tables

	cm	0		5		10		15		20		25		30
Length	in	0	1 2 3 4 5 6 7 8 9 10 11 12											
	metres	0		0.5		1			1.5				2
	ft/yd	0		1ft	2ft		3ft(1yd)					2yd	

					(¼kg)		(½kg)		(¾kg)			(1kg)
Weight	grammes	0	100	200	300	400	500	600	700	800	900	1,000
	ounces	0	4 (¼lb)	8 (½lb)	12 (¾lb)	16 (1lb)	20	24 (1½lb)	28	32 (2lb)		

Fluid measures	litres	0	1	2	3	4	5	litres	0	5	10	20	30
	imp.pints	0 1 2 3 4 5 6 7 8						imp. gallons	0	1	2	3 4	5 6
	US pints	0 1 2 3 4 5 6 7 8						US gallons	0 1	2	3	4 5	6 7

Telephone interpreter service

The Telephone Interpreter Service's number, in the front section of the telephone book, has useful numbers, such as the Ministries of Immigration, Foreign Affairs and Ethnic Affairs, for non-English-speakers. This section is written in 12 languages.

State motoring organizations

See under individual state capitals in the *A to Z*.

Emergency information

Emergency services

Police
Ambulance ⎱ ☎ 000 and ask for the service required
Fire ⎰

Other medical emergencies

Doctors and dentists are listed in the *Yellow Pages* of the telephone directory. The doctors come under the heading *Physicians*, dentists under *Dentists*.

Late-night chemists

Late-night chemists are plentiful in the major cities, and most suburbs have at least one open until 9pm every night seven days a week. There are also some 24hr chemists in most cities. Chemists are listed under *Pharmacies* in the *Yellow Pages*.

Motorway accidents

— Do not admit liability
— Ask to see the other driver's licence and the name of his insurance company; exchange names and addresses.
— If someone has been injured, call the police and stay until they arrive.
— Ask any witnesses to remain, or ask them for their names and addresses.

Car breakdowns

Call the breakdown service number of the motoring organization listed for the state you are in (see under individual state capitals in the *A to Z*). A rental car could be registered in any state and will have membership in the motoring organization of its state of registry. However, state organizations offer full reciprocal services; when you contact the local service organization, simply state the name of the organization and your membership number. They will then either send a breakdown unit of their own or contact the nearest affiliated garage with a breakdown service. Try to be as specific as possible when giving your location to the emergency breakdown number.

Lost passports

Contact the state police and inform your consulate at once.

Lost travellers cheques

Inform the police immediately, then follow the instructions provided with your travellers cheques, or contact the issuing company's nearest office. Contact your consulate or American Express if you are stranded with no money.

Time chart

*c.*40000 BC	The first Aborigines are thought to have travelled across the land bridge from Asia.
*c.*1542	The Portuguese probably sighted Australia when exploring the East Indies.
1606	The Dutchman Wilhelm Janszoon, sailing from Java in the Dutch East India Company ship *Duyfken*, passed s of Papua New Guinea and sighted the w coast of Cape York Peninsula. He mapped part of the coast.
1642–43	Abel Tasman sighted the sw coast of Tasmania, which he named Van Diemen's Land.
1688	The pirate ship *Cygnet* sailed along the nw coast of Australia. On board was William Dampier, whose subsequent book published in England did much to excite interest in "New Holland".
1770	Captain James Cook in *Endeavour* sighted the e coast of the continent near what is now Cape Everard. He claimed the land for the Crown.
1788	The First Fleet arrived at Botany Bay with 1,044 people, including 568 male and 191 female convicts plus 13 children, under the command of Captain Arthur Phillip. A few weeks later the settlement was moved 14.5km (9 miles) to n to Port Jackson.
1790	The New South Wales Corps was formed in England to guard convicts.
1792	The colony came under the control of the officers of the NSW Corps, especially their leader John Macarthur. Macarthur adopted measures designed to benefit himself and his fellow officers. The Corps retained control until 1795 when a new governor arrived. The clique controlled the colony's economy largely through monopoly of the rum trade, which was *de facto* currency.
1806	William Bligh became governor and tried to break the power of the NSW Corps, but his stern measures led to a rum rebellion and his arrest. The military ruled the colony for 2yrs. London vindicated Bligh but removed him.
1824	The city of Brisbane was founded.
1825	Tasmania was detached from NSW and created as a separate colony.
1829	Britain formally claimed possession of the entire continent. Perth was founded. Newspaper compositors on *The Australian* staged Australia's first strike.
1834	A group of Tasmanians began colonization of what later (in 1851) became the colony of Victoria.
1835	The Tasmanians, under the leadership of John Batman, bought 240,000ha (600,000 acres), the land on which Melbourne now stands, from the local Aborigines.
1850	The British Parliament approved the Australian Colonies Government Act, extending a large measure of self-government to the colonies.
1851	Gold was discovered in NSW and Victoria, sparking a rush.
1854	The Eureka Stockade, an armed insurrection, at Ballarat, in which 30 died, led to some reforms of the colony's repressive legislation.
1856	South Australia introduced universal suffrage for men. The stonemasons' societies agreed with their employers on a 48hr week, working 8hrs a day – the first such

	agreement in the world and forerunner of much social experiment and enlightened legislation.
1859	Queensland separated from NSW and became a new colony.
1860–61	Robert O'Hara Burke and William John Wills travelled from Melbourne to the Gulf of Carpentaria, completing the first crossing of the continent from s to n.
1894	South Australia became the first colony to introduce votes for women and thus the first to introduce truly universal suffrage.
1899	A meeting of the colonial premiers in Melbourne resolved objections from NSW to the proposed federal constitution for a single nation.
1900	The draft constitution was approved by London and received the Royal Assent.
1901	The Commonwealth of Australia came into existence.
1908	Canberra was chosen as site for the national capital.
1910	The first federal Labour government under Andrew Fisher was elected.
1914	At the outbreak of World War I, Australia pledged its support for Britain "to the last shilling".
1916	The country was bitterly divided by a referendum on universal conscription, which was defeated.
1917	A second referendum was defeated. Australia retained a volunteer army.
1927	The Duke and Duchess of York (later King George VI and Queen Elizabeth) opened the new Federal Parliament in Canberra.
1930	Amy Johnson became the first woman to fly solo from England to Australia.
1932	Sydney Harbour Bridge was opened.
1939	World War II began. Again Australia supported the Allies.
1942	The Japanese bombed Darwin, killing 240 people.
1945	The war ended.
1946	Australia accepted United Nations trusteeship over the Territory of New Guinea.
1949	The Labour government was defeated by a coalition led by Robert Menzies (Liberal Party) and A. W. Fadden (Country Party).
1950	Australia, New Zealand and the USA signed the ANZUS pact for mutual defence in the Pacific. Menzies tried to outlaw the Communist Party, but a referendum was unsuccessful. Australia sent troops to the Korean War.
1954	Vladimir Petrov, a Soviet diplomat in Canberra, defected.
1956	The Olympic Games were held in Melbourne.
1965	Menzies committed Australian troops to Vietnam.
1966	Menzies announced his retirement and was succeeded by Harold Holt. Australia adopted decimal currency.
1967	Harold Holt drowned in a swimming accident.
1968	John Gorton took over as Prime Minister.
1971	Gorton was succeeded by William McMahon as Prime Minister.
1972	Gough Whitlam led Labour to power, breaking a 23yr monopoly by the Liberal-Country Party coalition.
1974	Cyclone Tracy devastated Darwin.
1975	Governor-General Sir John Kerr dismissed the Labour government, sparking the most serious political crisis in the country's history. Malcolm Fraser succeeded as

caretaker Prime Minister, a position he consolidated in elections held in Dec when he won a majority in both Houses of Parliament.

1978   Sir Robert Menzies died.

1983   The Labour Party under Bob Hawke defeated the Liberal-Country Party coalition after Fraser called an election 9mths early.

1984   An early election was called and Labour was re-elected with a reduced majority.

1987   Labour again won an early election, against a divided opposition.

Aborigines: the first Australians

Aboriginal Australians were the first on the subcontinent, inhabiting the Australian mainland and Tasmania for at least 40,000 years before the arrival of the Europeans some 200 years ago. The generic name given to cover their diverse tribes and cultures comes from the Latin *ab origine*, meaning "from the beginning".

There are several theories concerning the origins of the country's earliest descendants. Some believe that the Aborigines derived from Java Man; others that they come from three distinct groups. A third, more recent and popular theory is that the Aborigines are racially homogeneous – that they are members of the unique Australoid race. Their forefathers are said to have migrated s from Asia, moving from island to island, having set off from the N as early as 50,000 years ago.

Evidence of the way in which those early immigrants lived and died is scanty, though recent discoveries have begun to drop pieces into the historical jigsaw puzzle. The cremated skeleton of a woman found at Lake Mungo in western NSW has been carbon-dated at about 26,000 years old, and subsequent excavations have revealed stone tools dating back a further 10,000 years or more.

Archaeological evidence suggests that the earliest groups of Aborigines lived around the coastal areas and along the main river systems, where there was ample and easily acquired food, as semi-nomadic hunters and food gatherers, each tribe claiming certain specific rights over the territory they roamed. Their relationship with the land was, and is, extraordinarily complex.

These first Australians, who initially shared the land with now extinct animals like the giant marsupial diprotodon, the flightless genyormis and the giant kangaroo, rapidly adapted to their environment. They learned how to live with the land, the punishing climate and the flora and fauna around them; and the skills they learned were passed from generation to generation. In extended family groups they netted fish and collected seeds, berries, grubs, succulent honey ants, lizards and small marsupials. The men hunted emus and kangaroos, often using a harpoon-shaped spear attached by cord to a woomera (or spear-thrower). There were non-returning boomerangs also in their armoury, for use either as clubs or lethal missiles. In the coastal areas of the N, dugong and turtle were important sources of food for the family, and a feast of charred barramundi or goanna, served up on a bark plate, was a welcomed treat.

The Aborigines used the natural materials around them for their shelters and their weapons. They discovered the times of the year when certain fruits and plants could safely be eaten, where water might be found in times of drought, and how to thrive in conditions that would be considered deadly by most inhabitants of the planet. They learned how to read the Outback and developed an intimate knowledge of the landscape.

To incoming Europeans, the Aborigines' finely honed skills in gathering food and water, navigation and tracking, often seemed supernatural. Few would deny today that European colonization had a ruinous effect on Aboriginal society. From the beginning, huge tracts of land were "settled", fenced or insensitively developed by the Europeans; sacred Aboriginal sites were abused and destroyed; families were enslaved and murdered; and the traditional life of a people civilized in ways beyond the understanding of the colonizers was fractured beyond repair. No attempt was made to understand the Aboriginals' feeling of "responsibility" for the land. The Europeans took the view that the Aborigines had done nothing to "develop" Australia and thus had no visible rights to the land.

I think of land as the history of my nation. It tells me how we came into being, and what system we must live. My great ancestors, who lived in the time of history, planned everything that we practise now.

The law of history says that we must not take land, fight over land, or give land, and so on. My land is mine only because I came in spirit from that land, as did my ancestors. My land is my backbone. . . . My land is my foundation.
Aboriginal leader Galarrwuy Yunupingu

The Aborigines resisted the invasion and, in the battles that followed, some Europeans and many Aborigines died. There were shootings, spearings and a great deal of misery. In Tasmania, the Aborigines were eventually wiped out. In the Northern Territory groups of Aborigines were massacred or poisoned by Whites as recently as 1928. It is estimated that when Europeans first settled there were about 300,000 Aborigines throughout Australia; they comprised 500 tribes speaking about 200 different, distinct languages. Today, there are about 160,000 Aborigines, living mainly in rural areas.

In the early part of this century some steps were taken to provide assistance and protection for the Aborigines. Settlements and reserves were established and, with the best of intentions, government handouts to Aborigines were begun. Social welfare, religious do-gooding and government assimilation policies, however, quickly added to the troubles of a society linked closely with the land, tribal authority and self-sufficiency. Alcohol and a sense of rootlessness infected Aboriginal life. Not until the mid-1960s did most Australians really begin to understand, and show concern, that the Aboriginal people and their rich and ancient culture were in extreme danger. Today, clumsily but steadily, Blacks and Whites appear at last to be working together to counteract those bad times.

The Dreamtime

Aboriginal tribes, though not all holding the same religious beliefs, share several basic principles. Among them is the concept of The Dreamtime, or The Dreaming, a timeless continuum in which ancestral heroes first emerged from the night to create everything. The land existed without shape or life until these spirit-beings

25

produced oceans, springs, billabongs (waterholes), mountains, sky, sun, moon, stars and the laws that govern existence. There are parallels with the first chapter of Genesis in the Old Testament – and with the Christian idea of Heaven. The Aboriginal ancestor heroes also gave the people their own tracts of land, along with languages and social institutions. And the Aborigines believe the influence of these Dreamtime spirits remain with them today as a spiritual power in the land, in certain sites, and in some animals and plants.

The relationship between man and land is given special emphasis in the belief that for a child to be born, a spirit from one of these sites must first enter the mother's womb to give the child life. That site is the source of the person's life force and, consequently, he or she is inseparably connected with it, the spirit returning to the site at death.

Through ceremony, the land, animals, plants and the sacred sites, the spiritual power of the past is believed to flow into the living Aborigine. During many ceremonies, the Aborigine not only re-enacts the actions of his ancestor hero, but he *becomes* that ancestor hero.

To the Aborigine, then, the Dreamtime is far from imaginary. It is the very basis of his life.

Magic and mementoes

Bound up with the Dreamtime and their faith in ancestral powers is a strong Aboriginal belief in what outsiders would simply call "magic". This magic might be used to improve the food supply, nurse a sick person back to health, or punish someone who has defied tribal authority. Even today, magistrates and judges in Australian courts take into consideration the tribal judgments that those Aboriginals appearing before them will face. This might range from a spearing to banishment from tribal land.

The most feared form of magic known to Aborigines has been "pointing the bone". A medicine man would point a sharpened animal or human bone towards the victim and deliver a ritual chant. The victim, believing the bone was piercing his body, inevitably collapsed and died. Similarly *kurdaitcha* (medicine) men, wearing moccasins of marsupial fur, emu feathers and cord, would approach their victims with certain ritual movements, and have the same devastating effect. Awareness that a *kurdaitcha* man had been appointed to carry out a sentence was often enough to cause an Aborigine hundreds of kilometres away to collapse and die. The power of suggestion was apparently supreme.

In the past 20 years a greater appreciation and awareness of the complexities of Aboriginal life has grown, both in Australia and abroad. Aborigines have found that by making much of their traditional art and crafts available for sale they can supplement the economies of many Aboriginal communities and keep alive ancient traditions.

Among the more fascinating objects readily available to collectors visiting Australia are:

The didjeridu A difficult-to-play musical instrument made from eucalypt branches hollowed out by termites. Painted with distinctive designs, the didjeridu makes a low, fascinating, droning sound, familiar to those who know Aboriginal music. It ranges in size from 80-150cm (31-59ins) and, traditionally, is played only by men.

The boomerang Both a weapon and a clapping instrument used in the accompaniment of songs and dances. There are both returning and non-returning boomerangs. The non-returning kind has a shallow curve at one end and is a powerful hunting and fighting weapon. Returning boomerangs are occasionally used in hunting, but more often as an enjoyable form of competitive entertainment.

The coolamon A general-purpose dish, made from native soft wood. It can be about 85cm (33ins) long and generally has high sides. Aboriginal women use it for carrying water or food, as a bowl for food preparation, or as a bassinet or cradle for a baby.

Land rights

Since the late 1960s the question of Aboriginal landrights has emerged as a major political issue. The diverse requirements of farmers, miners and traditional "owners" of the land have created much friction. For in a European sense, the Aborigines do not own land: the land owns them. In Australia this has been a point of conflict and misunderstanding among city and rural Blacks and Whites right to the present time.

The Aboriginal Land Rights (Northern Territory) Act 1976 pioneered land rights legislation throughout the country. It provided a legal framework for Aboriginal groups to lay claim to unalienated Crown land on the grounds of traditional attachment. In South Australia, Victoria and NSW, titles to former reserves have been turned over to Aboriginal leaders. Perhaps the most dramatic "hand-over", however, took place on Nov 11 1983 when the Prime Minister announced the transfer of the title of the Uluru National Park (Ayers Rock-Mt. Olga) to the traditional owners. The agreement recognized that this area, one of Australia's most famous tourist spots, would continue to be run and protected as a national park.

Australia's formerly disenfranchized Aborigines are gaining a greater ability to determine and control their own destiny. Their red, yellow and black Aboriginal flag is seen more and more around the country today – the black in it symbolizing the people; the red, the colour of the earth; and the yellow, the warmth and optimism of the sun. The flag is an important mark of identity for a people who are beginning to show once again a pride in the accomplishments of their past.

The arts in Australia

Ever since the arrival of the First Fleet, the cultural life of Australia has explored and drawn upon the everyday interests of "ordinary", working Australians, focusing firmly on those local matters that interest most of the people. That is hardly to say that the world's finest arts and entertainment have swept by unappreciated Down Under: far from it. The intellectual treasures of Europe, America and Asia have always been devoured eagerly by a largely immigrant population anxious to stay in touch with its cultural roots, and have as well provided inspiration for generations of local artists, writers and performers. And a glance around the world's stages and galleries quickly lays to rest any suggestion that Australians have not marched enthusiastically and rewardingly to contribute to the great international artistic movements and traditions of the 20thC.

But with the ebb and flow of styles and attitudes, the truly Australian cultural inspirations have remained unfailingly the popular icons. In literature, poetry, theatre, painting, dance and cinema, it has been the bush, the race meeting, the beach, the Anzacs, the pub, the railways, the surfies, milk bars, the exotic fauna and, more recently, cityscapes that have produced, from the fresh palette this country offers, a picture that is distinctively Australian. Artists raised in the European tradition have had to learn both how to interpret a new landscape and to foster a new appreciation for it. Australians, too, caught in the often patronizing, inevitably smothering embrace of the old mother country, were slow to recognize their own gifts and their own gifted. The "colonial cringe", that apologetic deference to the critics of London and New York, has been a long time departing. And artistic activity in Australia was until recently bedevilled by the tendency of the local audience to believe that the product could only be inferior to that produced overseas. For many years talented Australians felt obliged to place themselves in artistic exile, daring to return home only when word of their triumphs abroad was received by the Australian press.

In the 1950s, the scene began to change dramatically. Australia produced artists who were not only well-known internationally, but who drew unequivocally upon their Australian background. But from 1970 onwards, this interest accelerated dramatically, and a vigorous new growth in arts activity became evident. Australians, wealthier and more travelled than in the past, came to realise that what they had on their own soil matched, if not surpassed, the quality of the imported product. With government and private-industry sponsorship, and the support of an increasingly hungry audience, the arts in Australia flourish as never before.

The writers

Australian literature began to achieve a national identity around the turn of the century, when a romantic patriotic sentiment was helping to encourage the birth of a new nation. In 1901, when the separate colonies united to form the Commonwealth, there were only 3.5 million Whites in the country, 95 percent of them British and xenophobic. The bush provided the most vivid contrast with what was normal for most of those fresh Australians, and it was to the bush ballads of A. B. "Banjo" Paterson (1864–1941) and the poems and short stories of Henry Lawson (1867–1922) that they turned for their nationalistic fuel. These writers, and others of the kind, found their audience through the likes of the Sydney-based *Bulletin*, a magazine that encouraged examination of Australian rather than European subjects. The *Bulletin*, founded in 1880, continues today as a weekly news magazine.

I come with strength of the living day,
And with half the world behind me;
I leave you alone in your cultured halls
To drivel and croak and cavil:
Till your voice goes farther than college walls
Keep out of the tracks we travel!

Henry Lawson, *To My Cultured Critics*

The short story remained a popular form long after Lawson: there have been fine examples from such Australian writers as Alan Marshall, Frank Moorhouse and, more recently, Peter Carey and Tim Winton. The bush ballads of Banjo Paterson (*The Man From Snowy River, Clancy Of The Overflow, The Man From Ironbark* and, of course, *Waltzing Matilda*) and others helped establish poetry as a popular form; but through such poets as Kenneth Slessor and, much later, Judith Wright both the techniques and subject matter changed considerably. Australian novelists who have attracted world attention with distinctively Australian themes include Henry Handel (Ethel Florence) Richardson, Xavier Herbert, Martin Boyd and Thomas Kenneally. The country's best-known writer, however, is Patrick White, whose non-naturalistic approach to his subject matter has disconcerted many local critics. White, the author of *The Tree Of Man*, *Voss*, *The Solid Mandala* and *The Twyborn Affair*, was awarded the Nobel Prize for Literature in 1973.

The stage

The theatre, which first drew its popular audiences during the gold rushes of the 1850s, has enjoyed mixed fortunes over the years. In the 1870s, impresario J. C. Williamson came to Australia, and the company's melodramas proved as popular then as its imported comedies and musicals would in the 1960s. But the cinema boom of the 1920s and then the Depression of the 1930s badly affected box office.

It was in the 1950s that "Australian theatre" received its first big boost, with the establishment of the government-assisted National Institute of Dramatic Art (NIDA). Ray Lawler's trilogy *The Summer Of The Seventeenth Doll* was produced in 1955, achieving critical success in Australia and then in New York and London. Alan Seymour's biting Anzac Day exploration *One Day Of The Year* followed.

By 1970 every state capital had a permanent professional drama company; and Australian actors, unlike their predecessors Peter Finch, Leo McKern, Judith Anderson and Diane Cilento, no longer found it necessary to go into exile to receive due acclaim. Today the plays of David Williamson (*The Removalists*, *Don's Party* and *The Perfectionist*), Dorothy Hewett, Jack Hibberd and Alexander Buzo, and the performances of Judy Davis, Robyn Nevin, Colin Friels, Peter Cummins and Freddie Parslow attract wide, sophisticated audiences at home.

Dance has a young and growing following in Australia although, with the exception of Edouard Borovansky's company in Melbourne, it was not until the early 1960s that local companies went beyond performance to creation in ballet. The Australian Ballet Company made its debut in 1962 and two years later helped establish the Australian Ballet School. In 1965, Sir Robert Helpmann and Dame Peggy Van Praagh, then the company's artistic directors, organized its first overseas tour. International acclaim and overseas awards have followed. In dance theatre, the Sydney Dance Company, under director Graeme Murphy, has played to packed houses with exhilarating original productions.

Music

Australia now has fully professional orchestras in all state capitals, as well as those that work with the Australian Opera and the Australian Ballet. There are also youth orchestras, the Australian Pops, chamber groups, and many popular ethnic groups. Standards vary considerably, and provide the critics with a fruitful source of argument. Musica Viva, which was founded in 1946 to encourage understanding of chamber music in the country, presents subscription concerts of overseas and distinguished Australian artists, which are particularly popular. And, with the proliferation of new and comfortable "arts centres" and concert halls, attendances have risen dramatically.

From the tradition of the country's best-known composers, Percy Grainger and Malcolm Williamson, have come Peter

Sculthorpe and Barry Conyngham, and, from the pop music/film world, Bruce Smeaton and Peter Best. Australian music of all kinds offers great variety. The country's rock bands have achieved fame in both Europe and North America, and jazz, from Don Burrows and exciting young players James Morrison and Allan Zavod, is currently going through one of its periodic revivals.

And opera?. It may be all that sunshine and clear air, but Australia has always enjoyed a world-famous reputation for its opera sopranos. From Dame Nellie Melba to Dame Joan Sutherland, these singers have surprised and delighted audiences everywhere. At home they have helped create a large following for opera. Today the productions of such companies as the Australia Opera and the Victorian State Opera are often sold out months ahead.

The visual arts

With the early European explorers and settlers of Australia came documentary artists – the equivalent of today's photojournalists – whose often bizarre interpretations of the continent's landscape and fauna may have been of dubious scientific value, but certainly created curiosity in Europe.

The Heidelberg School, founded in the 1880s by Tom Roberts and Frederick McCubbin, and named after the area of Victoria favoured by its members, was Australia's first distinct school of painting. Its artists painted in what they saw as an Impressionist style, striving to capture the lights and atmosphere of the Australian bush.

But the country's isolation from the European centres of art encouraged many artists to travel overseas for experience and, at the turn of the century, Roberts, Arthur Streeton and Rupert Bunny were among those who made the pilgrimage.

Post-Impressionist, or Modernist, art provided one of the great controversies in the Australian art world between the two World Wars, but gradually gained acceptance through the work of Russell Drysdale and William Dobell. A younger colleague of these artists, Sidney Nolan, became better known overseas, but to reach that wider audience he found it necessary to travel to London in 1953.

From Nolan, and his Ned Kelly and Gallipoli paintings, there followed, again in the late 1960s and 1970s, a period of rapid expansion in both painting and sculpture. Private galleries bloomed; dealers and collectors pounced on Australian paintings. Artists such as Brett Whiteley, Fred Williams and Jeffrey Smart attracted interest around the world. Sculptors like Tom Bass, Inge King and Stephen Walker, answering the home demand for art around public and commercial buildings, provided outstanding work.

The cinema

Cinema may seem the most recent of Australia's lively arts. In fact Australia was a pioneer of the world's film industry. The oldest surviving relic is a clip of the 1896 Melbourne Cup by French photographer Maurice Sestier. In 1900 Melbourne enjoyed the world premiere of *Soldiers of the Cross*, a Salvation Army film that, with the gusto of a C. B. De Mille epic, attracted an audience of 4,000 and had women in the first-night audience fainting in the aisles. *The Story Of The Kelly Gang* (1906) was Australia's first full-length feature. From the time of its premiere to 1960, Australian film-makers produced more than 330 movies. After World War II, however, the local film industry slumped, hit by

American imports and the arrival of TV in 1956.

In 1970 the government formed what has since become known as the Australian Film Commission, introducing tax incentives to film investors. Australian films began to attract worldwide interest, winning awards and critical acclaim, particularly for direction and cinematography. Films such as *Picnic at Hanging Rock*, *My Brilliant Career*, *The Getting of Wisdom*, *The Man from Snowy River*, *Mad Max: The Road Warrior*, *Careful He Might Hear You* and *Crocodile Dundee*; directors like Peter Weir, Fred Schepisi, Gillian Armstrong and Bruce Beresford; and actors and actresses such as Judy Davis, Mel Gibson, Jack Thompson, Ray Barrett, Bill Hunter and Paul Hogan have emerged as compelling attractions both at home and abroad.

Aboriginal art

The traditional arts of Australia – those of the Aboriginal people – have been the most underrated and least understood of all by the new arrivals. Only in the past few decades have the subtleties and skills, the passions and depths, and the beautiful mysteries of this non-European tradition received the attention they deserved. Aboriginal paintings, sculpture and carvings, which often tend to be related to the religious myths and beliefs of what the Aborigines know as "the Dreamtime", are now protected by law throughout the country. Aboriginal music consists mainly of singing and chanting and, perhaps accompanied by the sound of the *didjeridu* and clicking-sticks, may be heard at a *corroboree*, a song-and-dance performance that can include sacred as well as secular themes. Ceremonial and sacred sites in the Outback contain paintings and carvings, of which the earliest so far found is believed to be about 20,000 years old.

Today bark paintings and intricately designed totems, in natural ochre colours, are produced for sale. Different peoples specialize in different crafts. The Pitjantjatjara of the western desert, for example, are well known for their wood carvings. The government-funded Aboriginal Arts Board, among others, helps preserve and promote Aboriginal culture, arts and crafts.

Festivals

Most of Australia's major cities today hold large annual arts celebrations, as well as more general events like, in March, Melbourne's Mardi Gras-style Moomba Festival. The Adelaide Festival of the Arts, which began in 1960, is still the country's major arts festival, although the competition from Melbourne and Perth is growing fierce. Adelaide's festival takes place in three weeks over Feb-Mar, every second year. The Festival of Perth, which has been running since 1953, is held around the same time annually. The plush Victorian Arts Centre, the newest and possibly the most progressive major arts centre in Australia, has become the setting for both the Melbourne Summer Music Festival and, from 1986, the third base (with Spoleto, Italy, and Charleston, South Carolina) for Gian Carlo Menotti's Spoleto Festival. And Sydney, with the spectacular A\$102 million Sydney Opera House at its heart, enjoys its Festival of Sydney every year in sunny January.

These festivals and the opening of luxuriously appointed arts centres and theatres in the 1970s and 1980s have attracted new audiences and enthusiasm from the most in-demand international performers. Ultimately, new ideas and provocative alternatives will emerge from the current thriving arts activity. Today, Australians simply appear to be enjoying the show.

Architecture

The basic homes of the early convict parties were primitive hip-roofed box shelters, rectangular in plan, with the whole of the outer wooden face daubed with a heavy coat of mud to keep out wind and rain. The mud, applied with a trowel, was coated with pipe-clay, or whitewashed with lime made by burning oyster shells. Roofs were thatched with reeds from nearby swamps. Inside there was a fireplace of heavy mud and sandstone; the smoke rose through a chimney built from timber coated heavily with clay. A packed earth or clay floor lay below.

Coarse clay bricks began to be made a few months after the arrival of the First Fleet. The earliest construction with any real pretension to architectural quality, the Governor's official residence, was a two-storey design of brick set in lime and sheep "hair" mortar.

From Primitives to Colonials

But whether they were built of brick, wattle-and-daub or slabs, the early buildings were unstable monuments to European man. The mud of the mortar covering the wattles simply washed out in Sydney's torrential rain, and for years walls sagged and chimneys collapsed. Poor construction was to plague the colony for a decade or more after the First Fleet's arrival.

Australia's first town planner was Lieutenant William Dawes, one of whose first duties was to design Parramatta, near Sydney, a "plan of grace, balance, charm and utility."

Francis Greenway's Georgian St Matthew's Church at Windsor, NSW (*left*). The verandah (*below*) was a characteristic 19thC form.

Arthur Johnson's Como, in Melbourne's South Yarra suburb, reflected the tastes of the wealthy in mid-Victorian times.

In 1794 Captain John Macarthur, formerly an officer with the NSW Corps and a prosperous, hard-working landowner, moved into a farmhouse, Elizabeth Farm, on 250 acres (101ha) of land overlooking the Parramatta River. Elizabeth Farm, built of brick, with a hipped roof covered with swamp-oak shingles cut from local trees, was the primitive prototype of country farmhouses throughout NSW. Extended and altered, it still serves as a private home and is the oldest building in Australia.

When Lachlan Macquarie first took up his duties as the new Governor-in-Chief in 1810, he was appalled by the poor state of the buildings in the colony. His first act was to insist that Sydney's streets should be at least 66ft (20m) wide and that no building should be erected closer than 20ft (6m) to the street. Macquarie called for better construction throughout the colony, and stipulated the use of brick or stone, and that buildings should preferably be of two storeys wherever possible. In his travels through the state, he particularly encouraged the building of inns, well aware that such hotels would play a major role in the opening up of the countryside. The oldest hotel in Australia, the appropriately named Macquarie Arms in Windsor, NSW, was built in 1811 under the Governor's direction.

In Macquarie's plans for country towns, priority was also given to sites for churches, courthouses and, eventually, schools. Unfortunately, these building regulations were introduced on a local basis – and this pattern of local building control has bedevilled Australian architects and builders to this day.

In 1816 Francis Howard Greenway, that arrogant, malicious and vain man but imaginative, thorough and professional architect, was appointed Civil Architect and Engineer in NSW. He had been despatched there for life for the act of forgery. Within six years, he had singlehandedly created what was to be Australia's finest early architectural heritage. Greenway designed and supervised the completion of an enormous number of buildings, ranging from a lighthouse to a hospital, to a large school. He initiated plans for town sewers, a water supply, fortifications and bridges.

Greenway designed his buildings in the Georgian style favoured around Bristol at the time he left the West Country of England. He added his own highly personal touches, and his architecture was both stylish and forceful. Among the surviving examples of his work are the St Matthew's Church of England (built 1817–20) and rectory (1923–25) at Windsor, NSW, and the Hyde Park Barracks in Sydney (1819). They are straightforward, uncomplicated edifices, with simple, clever touches to add variety to the generally plain body of the buildings.

Temperature changes in the new land could be severe, prompting in some country homesteads the beginnings of a new indigenous architecture. The verandah, borrowed from the East, was used as both a means of access to rooms and a cool and shady place for the inhabitants. Together with an overhanging roof and supporting columns, it helped create a low-lying building in harmony with the climate and the landscape.

The years 1822–40 produced the riches of the Colonial period of architecture in Australia. The prevailing style continued to be Georgian, but eventually it was supplanted by the more elaborate Regency fashion, featuring walls of stone or plastered brick.

In Van Diemen's Land (Tasmania), however, there were other developments. Many fine buildings, utilitarian but attractive, were designed and erected by, among others, John Lee Archer, the Colonial Architect, a former colleague of Charles Beazley and John Rennie, with whom he had designed London's Waterloo and

Southwark bridges. Archer's most successful works were his elegant bridges and military buildings, but his excellence can also be seen in his design for several churches, the Treasury offices in Hobart, and hospitals, schools and lighthouses. Recent restoration work shows these buildings to great effect.

In 1837 Colonel William Light, the Surveyor General appointed by the South Australian Company, began laying out, around the Torrens River, what many feel is Australia's noblest town design. Light's plan for Adelaide involved a series of rectangular grids of broad streets wrapped in a swathe of natural parkland.

Meanwhile in Sydney an Australian high society was emerging that was determined to copy what was going on "at home". So Australian Regency, a simplified version of the imposing style popularized in Regency Britain by John Soane, was introduced. A good example is Elizabeth Bay House (1832–37), designed by John Verge, where the portico roof is an impressive balcony reached by French windows on the upper floor. On public buildings, however, just as in Britain, the Classical or Gothic style remained in favour. A strong proponent was Edmund Blacket, designer of the St Mark's Church of England, Darling Point, in 1848.

In the 1840s a NSW settler introduced a building practice destined eventually to spread around the world. He built double-layered stone walls and left out the normal rubble core. Brick veneer – a protecting sheath of brickwork placed around a

A mid-19thC **Queensland timber home** (*above*), built on a raised platform. **St Patrick's** bluestone Roman Catholic Cathedral in Melbourne (*right*), by William Wardell, was begun in 1850. Joseph Reed's massive Romanesque **Ripponlea** mansion (*below*) in Elsternwick, Melbourne, dates from 1868.

timber interior – was another Australian technique that emerged by the 1850s. The first brick veneer building in the world was erected near Swan Hill in 1850; it eventually developed into Tyntyndyer, one of the finest farming homesteads in Victoria.

Gold and the Victorians

The gold rush era of the 1850s changed the face of Australian architecture dramatically. As the harsher realities of the gold fields hit home, some discovered that there was an easier-found crock of gold in the building of hotels, homes, churches, warehouses and offices, all urgently required. In Melbourne, s of the Yarra at Emerald Hill, tens of thousands of people were living uncomfortably in a shanty town of tents.

Italianate terraces and mansions, with cast-iron lacework balconies, stained glass, columns, towers, turrets and plaster ornamentation, became the fashion among the wealthy, particularly in Melbourne. Fine examples of these lacework buildings are still found in the suburbs of Carlton, South Melbourne and Albert Park.

In the 1850s, a distinctive style of architecture began to develop in Queensland. Timber homes, with airy latticework exterior walls, were built on raised platforms, with high stumps or stilts. supporting them, providing coolness as well as protection against snakes and floods.

The most prominent architect in Sydney was Edmund Blacket, designer of the Great Hall at the University of Sydney, probably

Australia Square Tower in Sydney (*left*), circular in shape, is 48 floors high. It was designed by Harry Seidler, whose work inspired today's generation of Australian architects. One of them was Sir Roy Grounds, who designed the domed **Academy of Science Building** in Canberra (*below*), a copper-covered shell 45m (150ft) in diameter resting on arches.

The **Sydney Opera House**, Joern Utzon's unmistaka exterior sails are covered with white ceramic tiles.

the finest Gothic Revival building in Australia. But Blacket travelled farther afield. His buildings can be found from Brisbane and Geelong to St George's Cathedral in Perth.

Melbourne, then the younger city, attracted William Wardell, who had built at least 30 churches before he migrated to Australia. His first commission in Melbourne was for the huge St Patrick's (Roman Catholic) Cathedral, which became the largest and most impressive in the country. Wardell was appointed Government Architect for Victoria in 1859.

But it was another architect, Joseph Reed, who made the biggest impression on the appearance of Melbourne. Reed created the original Classical design for the Melbourne Public Library in 1854; the following year he designed the Town Hall for Geelong. His work includes one of Melbourne's best-known mansions, Ripponlea in Hotham St., in Elsternwick (one of his smaller commissions), more than 20 church buildings of all denominations, many of the University of Melbourne buildings, ten banks, the Town Hall, the Weather Bureau, the Trades Hall, the Exhibition Building and others.

Rising to the future

"Safe" passenger lifts arrived in Australia in the 1870s, enabling architects to design upwards and answer the demand for more rooms on less land. By the 1890s there were several buildings of ten or even 12 storeys. Though the new high-rise buildings had many critics, the main problems were overcome and, with developments in steel and reinforced concrete, the first authentic skyscrapers went up in the 1920s.

Following the depression years of the 1890s, a style known as "Queen Anne" predominated in domestic architecture. In this, the red brickwork of walls was openly displayed and Classical mouldings were carved, not in timber, but wholly in brick. Terra-cotta-tiled roofs topped it off in inner-suburban Melbourne and Sydney; elsewhere they used iron roofs painted red.

In 1912, a young American architect, Walter Burley Griffin, submitted the winning design in the Australian government's international competition for a national capital. Griffin's imaginative design for Canberra used natural features of the land, a geometric sweep of wide roads and the lake that now bears his name. A leader in the style known as Functionalism, he designed Newman College (1918) in the University of Melbourne, then went on to plan the NSW town of Griffith.

The arrival in 1947 of Harry Seidler – an Austrian-born, American-trained architect who studied under Walter Gropius – attracted much attention. He designed a highly sophisticated International style home for his parents at Turramurra, an outer suburb of Sydney. And it was Seidler's work, seen in all its glory in the soaring glass-and-concrete Australia Square Tower in Sydney, that inspired so many of today's Australian architects.

Among them was the late Sir Roy Grounds, who designed the Victorian Arts Centre in Melbourne and the domed Academy of Science Building in Canberra. Another disciple was Danish architect Joern Utzon, whose skills will be forever recognized in the graceful splendour of the magnificent exterior sails of the Sydney Opera House.

There have, it is true, been many acts of philistinism in Australian architecture. But as the country moves towards the 21stC, there are hopeful signs that Australians are more alert to what is wanted – signs that quality in design, conservation of the best, and a uniquely Australian approach to building are what young architects really do care about.

Calendar of events

Every year seems to bring new festivals and entertainments. The daily newspapers in Sydney, Melbourne and other capital cities have information-packed supplements on upcoming events, and there is a helpful booklet, *Australia: A Traveller's Guide*, published by the Australian Tourist Commission.

In this calendar, the seasons are merely a rough guide, generally meaning little in the subtropical N of Australia, where the year is more simply divided into the Big Wet and the Dry.

Winter: June, July, August

It's playtime in the N, with the festivities moving along from the Alice Springs camel races into the dubious delights of the Darwin Beer Can Regatta in June and, in Aug, Henley-on-Todd, a mock yacht race on the dusty dry bed of the Todd River at Alice Springs. The Townsville Pacific Festival offers a more traditional mix of art exhibitions, sports competition, fireworks and carnival at the end of Aug and beginning of Sept. The fit and energetic may feel like taking the 14km (9-mile) Sydney City-to-Surf fun run, a mini-marathon that takes thousands of amateur joggers and not a few professional runners rushing from the city heat to the beach in Aug.

Spring: September, October, November

This is the season for Australia's major sporting events. In Melbourne, the end of the football season is celebrated at the end of Sept with the VFL Grand Final, an Aussie Rules spectacular for which tickets are at a premium. The Australian Grand Prix, Adelaide's motor-racing carnival, follows (make hotel reservations well in advance), and then it's back to Melbourne for the horses and Victoria's Spring Racing Carnival in Nov. Do your best to get to the Melbourne Cup at Flemington, one of Australia's most colourful occasions. It takes place on the first Tues in Nov.

More cerebral pleasures can be enjoyed in Melbourne through the Spoleto "Festival of Three Worlds", a presentation of fine dance, theatre, opera, music and the visual arts. Meanwhile, in South Australia's Southern Vales, there is feasting and wine tasting in the annual McLaren Vale Bushing Festival, which in Oct welcomes the release of the new vintage wines.

Summer: December, January, February

Sydney Harbour never looks more colourful than on Boxing Day, with the start of the Sydney-to-Hobart Yacht Race. The competing yachts are surrounded by flotillas of spectator craft, and maritime chaos inevitably ensues. At the other end of the course the Tasmania Fiesta begins; the annual cultural and sporting festival is held in conjunction with the world-famous yacht race and runs from Dec through Jan.

This is arts festival time. At the end of Dec and well into Jan, the Festival of Sydney takes place. Melbourne's Summer Music Festival at the Victorian Arts Centre sounds sweetly around the end of the month (Jan 26 being Australia Day). The Festival of Perth, with concerts, art exhibitions, theatre, film and television, is held from mid-Feb, and (on even-numbered years) the Adelaide Festival of the Arts, Australia's most prominent cultural celebration, takes us into the first few weeks of March. This is also the heart of the cricket season and, whether it is a Test or World Series Cricket one-day match, tickets should be easily available for most games. And in Jan there is the annual Hahndorf Scheutzenfest in South Australia, a German-style beer, food and folk dancing festival, and, towards the end of Jan, the Australasian Country Music Awards Festival in Tamworth, NSW.

Autumn: March, April, May

In Melbourne it's Mardi Gras time, with the annual Moomba Festival getting into full swing at the beginning of Mar. Normally staid Melbournians let their hair down for the Moomba parade and days and nights of free entertainment, fairs, fireworks and surfing events alongside and on the Yarra River. A little farther N, in the old Victorian gold fields, the Ballarat Begonia Festival is a floral celebration in Mar, with arts and sports events.

In Apr, Australians all around the country commemorate Anzac Day, the annual day of remembrance for those who died in World War I, World War II, Korea and Vietnam. Servicemen march at dawn to memorials in towns and cities.

Orientation map

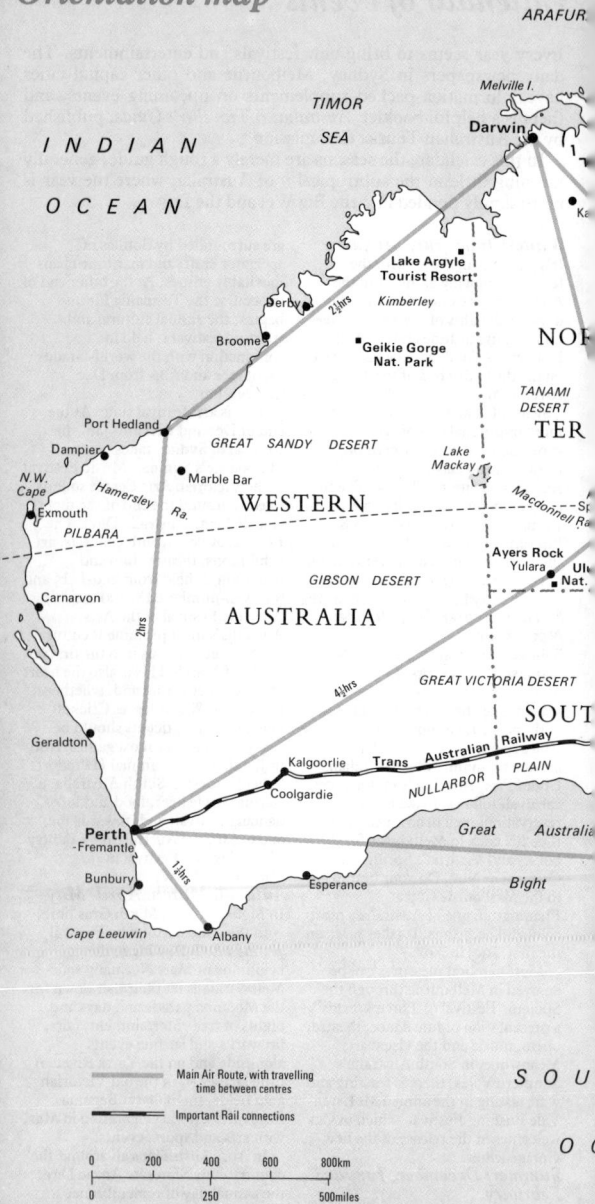

ARAFUR.

INDIAN
OCEAN

TIMOR
SEA

Melville I.

Darwin

Ka

Lake Argyle
Tourist Resort

Kimberley

Derby   2¼hrs

Broome

Geikie Gorge
Nat. Park

NO

TANAMI
DESERT

TER

Port Hedland

GREAT SANDY DESERT

Lake
Mackay

Dampier

Marble Bar

N.W.
Cape   Hamersley   Ra.

Exmouth

PILBARA

WESTERN

Macdonnell Ra

Sp

GIBSON DESERT

Ayers Rock
Yulara   Ul
Nat.

Carnarvon

AUSTRALIA

4¼hrs

GREAT VICTORIA DESERT

SOU

Geraldton

Kalgoorlie   Trans Australian Railway

Coolgardie   NULLARBOR   PLAIN

Perth

-Fremantle   1¾hrs

Great   Australia

Bunbury   Esperance   Bight

Cape Leeuwin   Albany

2hrs

SOU

O

Main Air Route, with travelling
time between centres

Important Rail connections

0	200	400	600	800km
0		250		500miles

38

N

Torres Strait

Cape York

PACIFIC

CAPE YORK
PENINSULA

*Gove
Peninsula*

Weipa

OCEAN

*Groote
Eylandt*

Gulf of
Carpentaria

Barkly
Tableland

1½hrs

Great

Cairns

CORAL
SEA

Barrier

1hr

*ils Marbles
Nat. Park*

1½hrs

Townsville

Reef

*Whitsunday
Group*
Mackay

Mt. Isa

1hr

GREAT

QUEENSLAND

1½hrs

Rockhampton

Tropic of
Capricorn

DIVIDING

2½hrs

Bundaberg

*SIMPSON
DESERT*

5hrs

Sunshine
Coast

RANGE

Brisbane

Lake Eyre

2hrs

Gold
Coast

AUSTRALIA

4½hrs

*Flinders
Ranges*

Darling

Coffs
Harbour

Port
Augusta

Broken
Hill

NEW SOUTH

1½hrs

RANGE

1hr

Whyalla

1½hrs

WALES

Newcastle

*Eyre
ninsula*

Mildura

1¾hrs

Wagga
Wagga

Sydney

DIVIDING

Adelaide

Murray

1hr

A.C.T.

1hr

CANBERRA

Kangaroo I.

VICTORIA

GREAT

Mt. Gambier

Bendigo

Ballarat

1hr

Portland

Geelong

Melbourne

TASMAN

1½hrs

SEA

Bass Strait

1hr

Launceston

HERN

Devonport

AN

TASMANIA

Hobart

When and where to go

Right now is the ideal time to visit Australia, for in such a large country clement weather can be found somewhere throughout the year. But there are times when some places are best avoided. For example, beach resorts can be extremely crowded during the school-holiday periods of Jan, Easter, the last week of June and first week of July, and the last week of Sept. Queensland's beaches are particularly busy at Easter and during Sept-Oct, when families from the southern states take advantage of the warmer weather in the N (Australia has recently adopted a 4-term school year). Yet though by Australian standards resorts are packed during the school holidays, to Europeans they must seem relatively uncluttered. Nothing in Australia compares with a crowded Spanish beach in Aug, or Blackpool on a British bank holiday.

While many people are taking their holidays in Jan, the cities tend to be far less crowded, rather like Paris during Aug. Many factories and businesses close down entirely for some or all of the month. The closures often start a day or so before Christmas, and commercial life does not return to normal unil the end of Jan or the beginning of Feb.

Generally Australia is dry and hot, becoming progressively hotter and drier the farther inland you go. There are vast areas of desert in the centre that see no rainfall for years – even decades – on end. Average rainfall is about 418mm (about 16ins), as against the world average of 660mm (26ins). Just how dry the continent is can be gauged from the total outflow of Australian rivers, which barely amount to that of just one major South American river.

Rainfall is unevenly distributed. Areas such as the desert centre receive less than 127mm (5ins) a year, and achieve that level only because of occasional torrential downpours every few years that increase the average. Conversely, areas of Tasmania and N Queensland receive more than 2,500mm (nearly 100ins) a year.

In the northern tropical area, summer and autumn are the wet seasons and little rain falls in winter and spring. The rain in the northeastern part of the country is produced by the NW monsoon, and in the NW by the cyclone season, which can be erratic and unpredictable. In the southern part the climate resembles that of the Mediterranean: rainfall is more evenly distributed, occurring mainly in winter and spring, and summer and early autumn tend to be dry.

Severe wintry cold spells are very unusual except in the mountains of the SE and in Tasmania. But even then temperatures drop only at nighttime a few degrees below freezing. Daytime sub-freezing temperatures are usually confined to the peaks and plateaux above 1,000m (3,280ft).

The southeastern coastal strip is generally more temperate than inland. Once N of the Great Dividing Range, which runs from Queensland to South Australia at varying distances roughly parallel to the coast, temperatures tend to be both higher and lower than the coastal cities. Hence it can freeze overnight in winter, but in daytime the temperature can possibly rise to 18°C (about 65°F). In summer the temperature can climb well above 40°C (about 105°F) on days when on the S coast it might be a hot 32°C (90°F).

Except in the SE and the extreme SW, summers range from hot to very hot, with maximum temperatures above 38°C (100°F) common inland from about Nov to mid- or late Mar. Jan and Feb are the hottest months in the southern states, when the state capitals usually experience a few days of above 38°C (100°F) temperatures. In the far N, Nov and Dec are hottest.

The northern third of the continent usually experiences a number of severe cyclones accompanied by torrential rain, which frequently causes flooding. Cyclone Tracy, which devasted Darwin in 1974, was an example of the most severe cyclone that can hit the area; but the vast majority cross the coast in uninhabited regions.

Predominantly a land of sunshine, Australia is less well known for its skiing. Few people outside the country realise that it has more skiable slopes than the Swiss Alps, though the Australian season is much shorter.

The major ski areas are concentrated in Victoria and NSW, and there are minor resorts also in Tasmania. Though the ski season is short – it opens in June, although often snow then has yet to fall, and lasts until early Sept, or in some years late Sept – it is intense. Facilities are generally first-class.

Area planners and tours

The main difficulty about planning a holiday in Australia is that there are so many choices. Broad decisions need to be made before you travel, and personal priorities need to be well defined. This book aims simply to present and help you select some of the options.

The sheer vastness and emptiness of the continent can sometimes be hard to grasp. At 7.68 million sq.km (nearly 3 million sq. miles), almost the size of the continental USA, 25 times larger than the British Isles and three-quarters the size of Europe, Australia is one of the most sparsely populated countries in the world, with about 1.84 people per sq.km. Two-fifths of the continent lies N of the Tropic of Capricorn.

The distances between population centres are also enormous. Two examples: Brisbane and Perth are separated by more than 3,600km (2,250 miles) by air, a distance greater than that between London and Moscow; Perth is virtually closer to Singapore than it is to Sydney, and is generally accepted as being the most isolated city of significant size anywhere in the world.

Because of the vast distances, a coast-to-coast motoring holiday is out of the question. However, Australia is very well geared to the fly-drive concept, which involves flying to a centre, collecting a rented car for the duration of your stay, then returning it and flying on to another centre. Both the main domestic airlines, Ansett and Australian Airlines, have their own car rental companies – Avis and Hertz respectively – and the other major international companies are all represented at most major airports.

Australia is a long way from almost anywhere else, and it takes a long time to get there even by jet. But given careful advance planning the rewards can be considerable. More than most countries, it would be quite pointless to arrive without planning where and what you want to visit and establishing a priority list of sights you don't mean to miss.

For touring purposes Australia divides up roughly into four regions. There is the "Top End", comprising the Northern Territory and the northern parts of Queensland and Western Australia; NSW and the southern part of Queensland; Victoria, the southern part of South Australia and Tasmania; and the rest of Western Australia. Obviously some of these areas overlap, so that any combination can make up a holiday itinerary.

A number of sights and places should be on everyone's list of priorities: Ayers Rock; the Great Barrier Reef and the Whitsunday

41

Islands; part of the Outback, preferably in the Northern Territory; Sydney, if only to see the Opera House; Tasmania, for a little bit of England in the southern hemisphere and some wonderful early colonial architecture; Ballarat and Bendigo, Victoria's golden cities; and Western Australia, for magnificent beaches and a sense of isolation possible to experience in few other places on earth.

The extended *A to Z* in this book, which covers all the important centres and touring regions in Australia, is conveniently arranged as a menu of options from which to select whatever most interests the visitor. Arranged alphabetically by state, each begins with a general introduction to the state and its capital city. Then follows a full description of the capital, arranged alphabetically by subject – what to see, where to stay, eat, drink and shop, and where the best recreation and entertainment can be found – and a selection of excursions by rented car (many of them also feasible by public transport) out of the city. Some of the excursions are short one-day or half-day trips. Others involve at least one overnight stop, and accommodation is then suggested. There are also concise pointers on how to arrange more ambitious expeditions, such as trips into the Outback.

Many readers, however, will find the routes suggested below and in the following *Planning* pages useful as a more focused planning foundation. They are based on some of the busier touring areas – Victoria, southern NSW, and South Australia E of Adelaide; Tasmania; the coast between Sydney and Brisbane; Western Australia S and E of Perth; and the W coast between Perth and Port Hedland. Outside the state capitals, many of the places mentioned in these routes are described in the excursions for the relevant state (in the *A to Z*).

Most visitors fly into either Sydney or Melbourne. Both cities are well worth a stay of several days. Subsequently, a drive N or S to the other city can form a good introduction to driving and touring in Australia.

Route 1: Sydney – Melbourne
Allow 2 days. Recommended stop: Merimbula or Eden.

Two major roads link Australia's largest cities. The Hume Hwy follows the direct inland route and offers a far less interesting though fast link between Sydney and Melbourne. Favoured by heavy trucks, it is much the busier road. It is largely dual carriageway in Victoria and is generally excellent until the NSW border; thereafter the quality deteriorates. (Because each state is responsible for the upkeep of its roads, quality can vary quite considerably from state to state.) A detour off the Hume Hwy can be made, S of Goulburn, to visit Canberra, the national capital.

The Princes Hwy, on which this suggested itinerary of 1,042km (651 miles) is based, takes the more picturesque and longer coastal route. It is designated Route 1, which circles nearly the entire continent. Leaving Sydney heading S, the highway skirts the Wollongong region, which, with Port Kembla and neighbouring communities, is one of the country's major steel- and coal-producing areas and also one of the largest urban areas in NSW outside of Sydney.

The highway then continues down the coast through the fishing and resort towns of Ulladulla and Batemans Bay before reaching Moruya, once a gateway to the Araluen gold fields and now a quiet resort. Narooma is a popular fishing resort, well known for its mud oysters. Merimbula, another popular holiday resort, is famous for its game fishing and oysters, which are cultivated under license in the river estuary. The coast running from Ulladulla to Merimbula

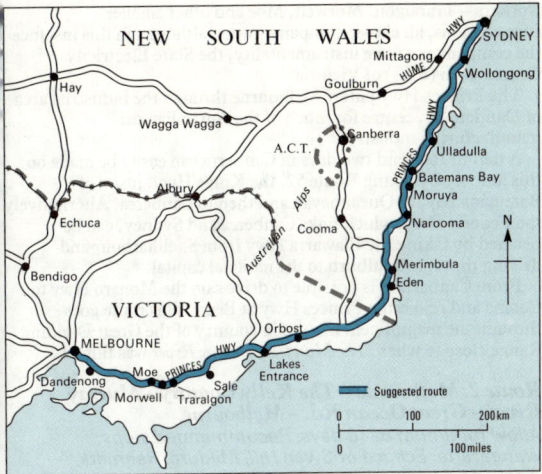

offers a wide variety of scenery with areas of bushland and forest that are the delight of bushwalkers, white surfing beaches, hills, lakes and inlets set against a backdrop of mountains. It is known as the Alpine Coast because of the proximity of the mountains of the Australian Alps, which form part of the Great Dividing Range.

Eden, the next town, is an important fishing centre, with one of the largest fleets in the country. In the 19thC it was a whaling centre, and the local museum has one of only two skeletons extant of a killer whale. Just 56km (35 miles) s of Eden is the Victorian border. From Eden the highway moves inland, the countryside changing quite dramatically as the road enters the heavily timbered and undulating region known as East Gippsland. From the NSW border to Orbost the road is forested on both sides. The area is home to the mountain ash, which is a variety of eucalyptus and the tallest hardwood tree in the world. Some examples have measured above 91m (300ft) – one in 1880 a massive 114.3m (375ft).

Care should be taken along this stretch of road, particularly at night, for animals, chiefly kangaroos and wombats – slow-moving marsupials about the size of a medium-sized dog – have a habit of slowly crossing the highway at night and being mesmerized by headlights. Harmless, gentle creatures, they can do a lot of damage to a car that hits them.

From Orbost to Sale the route is timbered on the northern side into the mountains of the Great Dividing Range. The highway next touches the coast at Lakes Entrance, which marks the beginning of a vast saltwater lake system, offering unrivalled waters for cruising and fishing. Cutting inland again to Sale, the countryside now becomes more rural, with numerous farms, mostly dairy, before the road enters LaTrobe Valley.

Here there is a mixture of industry and farming, town and country. Power stations, set as near as possible to their source of brown coal, rear up startlingly out of rural vistas. The valley is also a rich dairying region: it is not uncommon to see Jersey and Friesian cows grazing within a few hundred yards of a smoke-belching chimney, though the rural bliss is marred by higher-than-average pollution created by the burning of fossil fuels. The valley has several large towns that grew up mainly to house power station

43

workers – Traralgon, Morwell, Moe and other smaller conurbations, all classic company towns, although in this instance the company is a state instrumentality, the State Electricity Commission (SEC) of Victoria.

The Princes Hwy enters Melbourne through the industrial area of Dandenong, centre for much of the Australian car manufacturing industry.

A detour to spend two days in Canberra can easily be made on this journey by taking Route 52, the Kings Hwy, just N of Batemans Bay, to Queanbeyan and then to Canberra. Alternatively the Federal Hwy, which links Canberra and Sydney, can be reached by taking the Illawarra Hwy from Shellharbour and driving through Goulburn to the national capital.

From Canberra it is possible to drive S on the Monaro Hwy to Cooma and rejoin the Princes Hwy at Bega. This route goes through the magnificent mountain country of the Great Dividing Range close to where *The Man from Snowy River* was filmed.

Route 2: Melbourne – The Kelly Country – Murray River – Great Ocean Rd. – Melbourne
Allow minimum of 10 days. Recommended stops: Wangaratta, Echuca or Swan Hill, Mildura, Renmark, Adelaide, Mt. Gambier or Port Fairy or Warrnambool.
Victoria, Australia's smallest mainland state, is blessed with a network of generally well-maintained secondary roads that lead through rich rural country to places of scenic appeal or historical interest. And, for the Melbourne-based visitor, most are within a comfortable day's drive of "home". This circular tour takes in the countryside over which the bushranger Ned Kelly once roamed, as well as the mighty Murray River and spectacular Great Ocean Rd..

Drive the 235km (147 miles) N from Melbourne along the Hume Hwy to the prosperous agricultural and dairy centre of Wangaratta, a suitable first-night stopover. From here, the dual attractions of fine wines from nearby vineyards and the Kelly memorabilia are within easy reach. Local wineries, such as those of Brown Brothers at nearby Milawa and All Saints at Rutherglen, welcome visitors with a "taster" and the cellar-door opportunity to buy wines that compete favourably with the best from Europe and northern California.

Around here, too, it is impossible to forget that this was "Kelly country". In the 1870s, Ned Kelly and his gang waged their own private war on the authorities. Kelly was finally captured at Glenrowan, near Wangaratta, after a gun battle and was tried and hanged in Melbourne in 1880. The picturesque town of Beechworth, where the much romanticized Kelly was once imprisoned, is well worth a visit.

Travel on northwards to the NSW border and the towns of Wodonga and Albury. Then veer NW along the Murray Valley Hwy to Echuca, once a busy inland port packed with paddle steamers and barges laden with wool and wheat for the world. Echuca has restored its wharf area and from here visitors can enjoy a paddle-wheeler cruise up the Murray. Both Echuca and Swan Hill, another famous old paddle-steamer port farther up the Murray, offer a range of accommodation to suit most tastes. At Swan Hill, a paddle steamer has been converted into a riverside restaurant, offering such delights as kangaroo-tail soup, damper (unleavened bread) and (for the truly courageous) witchetty grubs.

The next stop is the city of Mildura at the heart of the Sunraysia district, a region of citrus groves, wines and dried fruit. The mild climate makes Mildura a favourite winter resort, with fishing and

water sports proving major attractions. Local delicacies worth sampling include the Murray cod, Murray perch, and "yabbies", or freshwater crayfish.

From Mildura it's a rather flat, fast trip across the South Australian border into Renmark. (Make sure the tank is full and that you have checked the water.) Like other Murray River towns, Renmark offers all the major facilities needed by visitors. Rental houseboats (with 4–6 berths) are available for those who want to explore the river more intimately. Nearby is the famous wine-growing district of the Barossa Valley.

From the elegant city of Adelaide, turn SE and take the Princes Hwy for the 455km (285 miles) to Mt. Gambier, a city well known for its crater lakes. One, the Blue Lake, changes colour to a vivid blue in springtime. Cross the Victorian border, heading for Warrnambool (Port Fairy, just before it, is one of actor Lee Marvin's shark-fishing haunts); then drive along the Great Ocean Rd. to enjoy magnificent seascapes, superb beaches and pleasant fishing villages. On the drive to Apollo Bay and Lorne, a major attraction is The Twelve Apostles, a formation of rocky islands.

Melbourne is an easy few hours away, with a freeway speeding up the journey on the other side of the industrial town of Geelong.

Route 3: Sydney – Melbourne – Adelaide – Broken Hill – Sydney
Allow at least 10 days if driving Sydney-Melbourne-Adelaide, otherwise 8 days. Recommended stops: Merimbula or Eden, Melbourne, Warrnambool or Port Fairy or Mt. Gambier, Adelaide, Broken Hill.

This four-centre tour offers a chance to see the two largest cities together with Adelaide and its surrounding wine-growing districts, the most extensive in Australia. It also offers a taste of the real Outback around Broken Hill, before a leisurely train journey back to Sydney.

Having driven from Sydney to Melbourne (see *Route 1*), there is a choice of either flying to Adelaide or continuing by road (following in reverse the final stages of *Route 2*) via the Princes Hwy, which goes inland until it reaches the port of Warrnambool

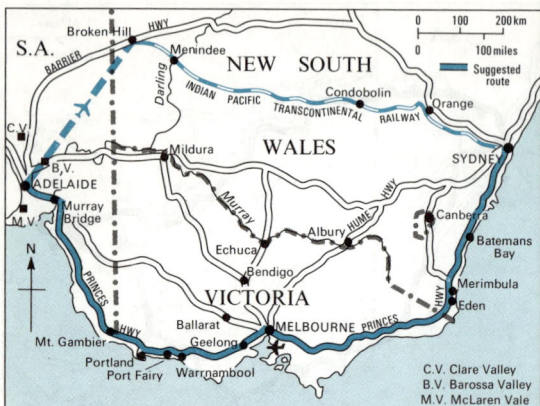

and then follows the coast to just N of Portland before again cutting inland to Mt. Gambier in South Australia. The road follows the coast again but slightly inland before coming into Adelaide via Tailem Bend and Murray Bridge.

From Adelaide, that most graceful city on Gulf St Vincent, tours can be made to the Barossa Valley, Clare Valley and McLaren Vale wine-growing districts. All these areas are within an easy day's or half-day's drive from Adelaide. South Australia – and the area around Adelaide particularly – produces some of Australia's finest wines, which increasingly are attracting world attention. Virtually all wineries have cellar-door sales and offer tastings to visitors, wine purchased at the winery usually entailing a saving on normal retail prices. A visit to the wineries for a tasting has become a great Australian tradition, and most of them are open seven days a week.

Adelaide and the surrounding wine districts having deserved perhaps three or four days, leave the rented car and fly to Broken Hill, only an hour distant but worlds away from the sedate setting of Adelaide. It is in NSW, but operates on Central Time, 1hr behind the rest of NSW.

Broken Hill sits on one of the world's largest lodes of silver, lead, zinc and other metals, and has been mined over a continuous length of 7km (about 4½ miles). It is still operating nearly 100yrs after it was first discovered. An oasis in the middle of a semi-desert region, Broken Hill has known no other existence but mining. Increasingly, however, it is attracting tourists. Here are just a few of the attractions: a fully working mine; a ghost town within a half-day's drive of the "Hill", used for many movies and TV series, including *Mad Max II* and *A Town Like Alice*; camels to ride; and the headquarters of the Royal Flying Doctor Service to visit.

From Broken Hill a connection can be made with the Indian Pacific transcontinental rail service to Sydney.

Route 4: Around Tasmania
Allow 2 nights for ferry crossing and minimum of 5 days in Tasmania. Recommended stops: Launceston, St Helens, Hobart, Strahan, Burnie.

Tasmania, a compact island packed with apple orchards, rugged hills and fast-flowing rivers, is often overlooked. Yet it is easy to get to and comfortable to get around. This tour needs careful planning, however, and for those really pressed for time, it may be easier to forget the ferry and fly in from Melbourne (or Sydney) to Launceston, pick up a rented car on arrival and adapt the tour.

But for something completely different, begin the journey in Melbourne with a 14hr overnight crossing on the Bass Strait passenger/vehicle ferry *Abel Tasman*. The ferry takes you into Devonport on the N coast of the island. To the E, 90mins' drive away, is Launceston, Tasmania's second-largest city, noted for its restored colonial buildings, its gardens and parks, and many nearby scenic attractions. Hotels and motels are good and, with the Launceston Country Club-Casino as an evening attraction, this may be the place for a first overnight stop. From Launceston the visitor can enjoy a trip on the chair lift over Cataract Gorge, the historic Franklin House and Entally House, or, with a little more effort, the trout-crammed lakes and peaks of the Central Plateau. This last is a joy for bushwalkers, fishermen and photographers.

From Launceston, travel 169km (105 miles) E along the Tasman Hwy to St Helens, a beach resort popular for its nearby bush walks, swimming and surf. Turning S, the road goes through Scamander, known for its good fishing, and Bicheno, an old whaling town that prides itself on the quality of its crayfish. To the S the clean white beach of Coles Bay is close by, with the imposing red granite peaks known as The Hazards towering from the sea. Just beyond, Freycinet National Park, a picturesque peninsula of bays, beaches and walking tracks, offers camping grounds, guesthouses and cottages.

Back on the highway, continue S to Hobart, Tasmania's charming capital, with its scattering of sandstone homes and freshly restored government buildings. There is more than enough to keep the most impatient traveller here a day or two: Constitution Dock, Battery Point, Mt. Wellington, Salamanca Place, Wrest Point Casino, the old Port Arthur penal settlement about 100km (63 miles) to the SE. . . .

From Hobart, take the NW route up the Lyell Hwy to the mining town of Queenstown and, 39km (24 miles) farther on, the fishing port of Strahan, which once bustled with international shipping. The rugged W coast here is untamed, raw and beautiful. Not far from Strahan is the white water of the Gordon and Franklin Rivers, the delight of skilled rafters.

The last leg is northwards along the Murchison Hwy and on to Burnie, a deep-water port that is Tasmania's fourth-largest centre. Note the Pioneer Village Museum, a re-creation of a commercial centre of a typical N Tasmanian town about the turn of the century. From Burnie, the Devonport ferry terminal is within easy reach.

Route 5: Sydney – Coffs Harbour – Tweed Heads – Coolangatta – Brisbane
Allow 2 days. Recommended stop: Port Macquarie or Coffs Harbour.

One of the most pleasing scenic drives for the traveller based in Sydney is the route N following the sun along the Pacific Hwy towards the Queensland border.

Escaping the Sydney suburbs may seem a little tiresome, but before too long picturesque Gosford is reached. Newcastle, busy and industrial though far from grim, is 175km (110 miles) N of Sydney, and then it's a road dotted with pleasant coastal resort towns. To the right are the long sandy beaches and spectacular headlands of the Myall Lakes National Park, which lies on the coastal side of the Pacific Hwy about 16km (10 miles) E and extends about 45km (28 miles) along the coast, occupying the region between the sea and Myall Lake. For those not in a hurry, the park offers camping sites, excellent fishing and swimming.

The sparkling Pacific Ocean surf gives way to year-round holiday playgrounds: Port Macquarie leads to Nambucca Heads, then Coffs Harbour, a favourite overnight stopping place surrounded by rich banana plantations. The warm, subtropical climate encourages the cultivation of tropical fruits and sugar cane. Together with the dramatic mountain peaks and unexpected valleys of the nearby Great Dividing Range, it makes for some delightful driving.

North of Coffs Harbour, there are the varying attractions of towns such as Grafton, Byron Bay and Tweed Heads to sample before crossing the NSW border and reaching the Queensland Gold Coast, one of Australia's busiest, most exuberant playgrounds. The 32km (20-mile) strip of white sandy beach is lined with resort hotels, luxury apartments, restaurants, clubs and shopping malls. Surfers Paradise is the major resort.

Just 65km (40 miles) N is Queensland's capital, Brisbane. Bustling and prosperous, it has recently begun to show increasing respect for its fine old colonial buildings. It is well served with modern hotels and fine restaurants (where you may be able to taste that most delicious fish, the barramundi).

Distance dictates everything in Australia. Brisbane is 1,031km

(644 miles) N of Sydney as the cockatoo flies; Cairns, a popular gateway to the Great Barrier Reef and an ideal touring base for the islands, the rainforest, and picturesque Port Douglas, is 1,710km (1,069 miles) farther N of Brisbane. The best advice is to leave the car in Brisbane and fly the rest of the way.

Route 6: Perth – Margaret River – Albany – Esperance – Kalgoorlie – Perth

Allow 2 weeks. Recommended stops: Mandurah, Busselton, Margaret River, Manjimup, Albany, Jerramungup, Esperance, Norseman, Kalgoorlie, Southern Cross or Northam.

Western Australia contains only 1.4 million people and yet is three times the size of Texas and bigger than any country in Europe. There may be few people between the barren plains of the Nullarbor desert and the Indian Ocean, but there is certainly a good deal to see. This tour takes in the most populous and fertile region of the state, the SW, offering comfortable drives through the wild-flower areas (Aug-Oct), leading on to the chance to strike gold around Kalgoorlie.

Drive to Fremantle and then S to Mandurah, a resort town where the pelicans nest and dolphins frolic. From the rural-industrial town of Bunbury, 175km (109 miles) S of Perth , it is a short distance to the resort town of Busselton on Geographe Bay.

Nearby, and well worth exploring, is the Margaret River wine-growing area, where some of the country's most surprisingly subtle prize-winning red and white table wines have been produced in recent years. Plan it well and you may be able to get to Leeuwin for the annual visit to a winery by an orchestra . . . their sort of Glyndebourne of the grape. This is held in Jan or Feb and, although the organizers cater for an audience of 12,000, the musical promise of such visitors as the Royal Philharmonic Orchestra, the Berlin Statskapelle or the Royal Danish Orchestra among the gumtrees and vines means that bookings must be made well in advance.

Return to the Bussell Hwy and, travelling S from Margaret River, detour inland along the Brockman Hwy to the small town of Nannup, nestled in tall pine forests beside the Blackwood Valley. Follow the scenic route eastwards to Bridgetown, which lays claim to having Australia's only public jigsaw puzzle gallery. Here also you can see Blechyden House, the old home of a pioneer farmer, or arrange a tour of local orchards where apples, nectarines, plums and peaches are grown.

From Bridgetown travel S along the South Western Hwy to Manjimup, sampling the unique scenery of the karri forests. Here, see the four Aces: four huge karri trees over 300yrs old growing in a line. Nearby, delicate, pastel-coloured wild flowers grow between giant trees that soar up to 80m (260ft) high. Karri trees, one of the world's finest hardwoods, provide a deep reddish-brown, strong timber. They blossom every 3yrs, and their nectar makes a delicately flavoured honey, much sought after.

If time is with you, take the 32km (20-mile) detour from the road S of Manjimup westwards to Pemberton. Here (if you're game!) you can climb the highest tree lookout in the world: the Gloucester Tree, 61m (195ft) above the ground.

Then return to the South Western Hwy, travelling SE to the small settlement of Walpole, where there are outstanding panoramic views, and then eastwards to Denmark, where the calm waters of the inlets and the protected beaches provide delights for both the fisherman and swimmer. Denmark offers another

surprise, for at Winniston Park is held one of the country's most outstanding collections of antiques.

Fifty-three kilometres (33 miles) farther E is the town of Albany, site of the first White settlement in Western Australia (in 1826). This former whaling port is located around an eye-catching, though now relatively underused, harbour, surrounded by lush green hills that reminded the early settlers of the English countryside. The traveller is well cared for in the historic town, where accommodation is clean, modern and economical. Allow ample time to explore Albany Whaleworld museum; see how the pioneers lived at Strawberry Hill Farm, the old Gaol, the Old Post Office and the Residency.

After this, the alternatives are to return to Perth by the direct route NW along the Albany Hwy – 408km (255 miles) of well-made road that most Australians would consider a comfortable day's drive – or, for hardier, more adventurous travellers, a journey that takes us farther E.

For the latter, the Hassell Hwy travels NE through rugged scenery into the Hassell National Park and on to Jerramungup. It is a solid, relatively unspectacular drive 110km (69 miles) onwards to Ravensthorpe, although invitingly to the S is the Fitzgerald River National Park, an oasis for fishermen, swimmers and golfers

Eventually, you arrive in the small coastal resort of Esperance, a rural town, with spectacular coastal scenery, that has proved popular with miners, artists and bushwalkers alike. The land surrounding Esperance is a rich farming area, producing beef, lamb, wool, wheat, oats and barley. The town itself was named by French explorer D'Entrecastaux in 1792 after his ship *L'Esperance*.

Travel N up the Esperance Hwy and then Route 94 and you move into the red dust and rich mining sites around Norseman and, eventually, Kalgoorlie – hard driving and hard country, with the occasional 'roo or emu. The attractions of this land remain with those who know it best.

Fascinating Kalgoorlie, which today has the feel of the old American frontier about it, in the 1900s dazzled the world with its gold. Most of the original buildings are retained and the main street is still known as the Golden Mile. And ghost towns abound nearby.

On the way out N to Broad Arrow, for example, once a bustling community, the gambling hall where the miners still play "two up" (a game in which participants bet on "heads" and "tails" for two thrown pennies) is one of the few signs of life.

More astonishing still is the ghost town of Coolgardie, to the SW, surrounded by the old mullock heaps (residues of gold mining, some still containing recoverable gold) of long-gone miners. Photographs in a museum there show the dramatic consequences when the gold runs out; even a town of 20,000 can disappear "overnight".

From Coolgardie, it's another long 188km (118-mile) and solid drive W along the Great Eastern Hwy to the gold town of Southern Cross. Gold was first discovered here in 1888, and buildings left in the town help it retain a turn-of-the-century atmosphere. A curiosity: all the streets in Southern Cross bear the names of either stars, planets or constellations.

West lies the heart of the wheat belt, the centre of which is the town of Merredin, 259km (162 miles) E of Perth. This old railway town is especially beautiful in Nov when hundreds of jacaranda trees burst into bloom. Travel onwards to reach the lush green paddocks of the Avon Valley. From Northam, the only inland town in the state with a continuously flowing river through its centre, there is a final, pleasant 100km (63 miles) before the circuit ends back in Perth.

Route 7: Perth – Geraldton – Carnarvon – Exmouth – Port Hedland

Allow 2 weeks. Recommended stops: Geraldton, Kalbarri, Denham, Carnarvon, Exmouth, Onslow, Port Hedland.
Another possibility for the more adventurous visitor based in Perth is the journey N across the Tropic of Capricorn to the rugged and immensely rich mining territory of Western Australia's Pilbara region. It is essential to seek local advice before embarking on this tour, since the journey takes you through remote regions prone to flash-flooding or other exceptional conditions. The Royal Automobile Club of Western Australia (RACWA) will recommend that you carry certain spare parts for your car and extra drinking water, and will provide you with information on the roads and climate.

Taking the route N through the lush wine-growing Swan Valley the first major point of interest is the city of Geraldton, 424km (265 miles) up the Brand Hwy from Perth. The countryside here, rich and green, reminds many British migrants of parts of Wales – albeit a sun-drenched Mediterranean Wales.

Geraldton, an attractive town that offers first-class motel and hotel accommodation, is a crayfish port as well as a popular resort among coastal sports fishermen. More than 400 boats fish for rock lobsters off the coast here, providing local fishermen with a major export to the USA. To the N, detouring from the North West Coastal Hwy, is the Kalbarri National Park, famous for its spring wild flowers. At Kalbarri, 167km (104 miles) from Geraldton overall, there is a campsite beside the ocean and, in the right spot, the fisherman can easily draw in a feast of delicious tailor fish and whiting.

The landscape N of Geraldton is harsh, often covered to the horizon in low purplish spinifex scrub. Snakes, foxes, hawks and eagles provide occasional distraction for the traveller. But from this seeming wilderness, you must detour for the spectacular. One such detour from the highway N leads to Monkey Mia, near Denham on Shark Bay; here "tame" dolphins come in to the beach to be fed by hand.

Back on the highway, continue N. *En route*, be a little careful if you see Old Man Emu up ahead investigating the road; he is not particularly bright. A blast on the horn may simply send him sprinting along the highway . . . in the same direction that you are travelling!

Surrounded by banana plantations, the sultry subtropical town of Carnarvon, 483km (302 miles) from Geraldton, offers motel accommodation and the opportunity to sample the sweet delights of the barramundi fish and ice-cold beer.

Move on N to experience unique wilderness landscapes; when alone on the highway here it's worth pulling over for a moment simply to experience "absolute silence", a memorable vacuum interrupted only by your heart beating or a cranky goanna sounding in the spinifex scrub.

Another detour, due N off the main highway, leads through the rust-red dust to Exmouth and the US naval communications base at North West Cape. Here, in the Cape Range National Park, are peaks and gorges, a small-scale Grand Canyon that literally takes the breath away.

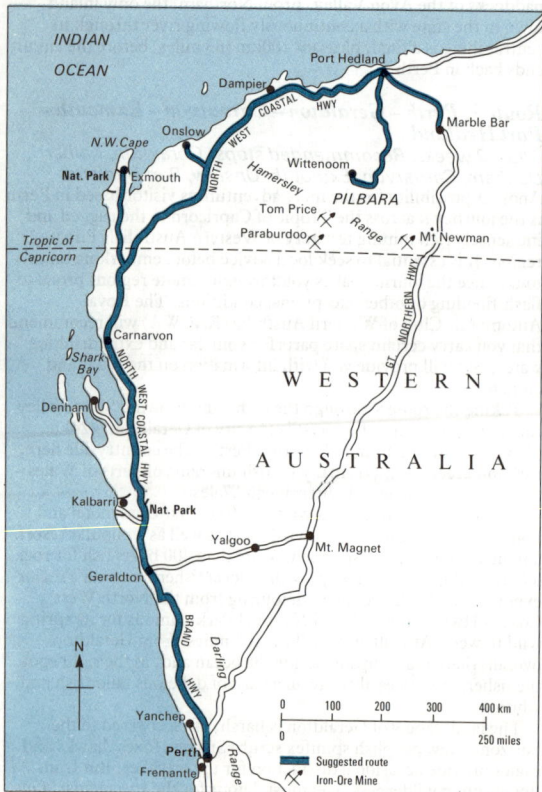

Crossing the Tropic of Capricorn, the road leads more and more into sparsely populated territory. This is land run by farmers and miners where huge iron-ore deposits are mined at Tom Price, Paraburdoo and Mt. Newman. The Pilbara, as this part of the country is known, is rich with iron ore and mineral deposits. It is pioneer country and still a land only for the more adventurous. To get to major centres often requires long drives that might be unthinkable in Europe.

From the North West Coastal Hwy another 82km (51-mile) detour w will take you to Onslow. It is a journey worth making. Onslow is a pleasant, tree-shaded coastal town that offers excellent fishing and safe swimming. The town was the farthest point s in Western Australia to be bombed by the Japanese in World War II. It was also the mainland base for Britain's nuclear tests in the Monte Bello islands.

From Onslow, rejoin the main highway to reach the sunny destination of Port Hedland, where bulk carriers line up to take Australia's mineral riches to Japan, South Korea and the world. E from Hedland, the visitor is within reach of the small town of Marble Bar, which has the reputation of being the hottest place in Australia and one of the hottest in the world. Another day excursion due s from Hedland might be Wittenoom, noted for its colourful gorges.

It is a rugged journey, but visitors who make it to Port Hedland go away knowing truly that they have been to Australia's wild west, a land still untapped of all its riches.

Getting into the Outback

And what, you may ask, about Alice Springs, Darwin, the Kimberleys and some of the more remote parts of the great subcontinent? How about a trip out to Ayers Rock or a drive through the territory made familiar by the film *Crocodile Dundee*?

Given time, visitors can indeed travel to many exotic and untouched locations in Australia. Given that time, however, they are more likely to follow the Australian pattern of using aircraft to get to the main centres (such as Alice, Darwin or Cairns) and then travel on by 4-wheel-drive, preferably escorted, into the bush.

For the adventurous there are safari tours in which a visitor can "rough it" in style. These involve 4-wheel-drive vehicles, camping out, with catering provided, and may venture off from civilization for a couple of weeks into the spectacular landscapes of the Kakadu National Park, Katherine Gorge and Ayers Rock.

Another way of coming to terms with the vastness of Australia is to take an air safari with a group of friends. A light aircraft, with a pilot-guide, can move you from city to Outback cattle station or tropical island all within a matter of hours. With a group booking, it need not be beyond the average tourist's pocket.

For those who prefer their vacation to be only slightly more civilized than that portrayed in the film *Deliverance*, there are now dozens of reputable companies that offer trips into the unknown. Ranging from 5-star service to help-yourself, these Outback safaris offer the whole gamut from riding white-water rafts to flirting with crocodiles, from bounding after wild pigs and buffalo in the Northern Territory to delighting in exotic orchids and rare birdlife, or from abseiling down gorges to inspecting rarely-seen Aboriginal art painted on rocks thousands of years ago. Those who do not mind roughing it might even go "walkabout" in the desert country to help find the relics of expeditions by the brave or merely foolhardy in the last century.

But be warned – such travelling is only for the most hardy.

53

Accommodation

Hotel accommodation in Australia ranges from international 5-star standard to a room in a country pub with a washbasin along the corridor. The most common style of accommodation is the motel; they are widespread and generally of a good standard.

The average motel unit has its own toilet and bathroom facilities, colour TV set, bedside clock and radio, refrigerator, and a table, a couple of chairs and an armchair. Most motels provide an electric kettle, tea, coffee and milk so that guests can make a hot drink. Breakfast can be served in the unit or, in larger, better-standard motels, in a dining room; more basic motels lack dining rooms, and breakfast is the only meal served.

Three large nationwide chains, Flag Inns, TraveLodge and Homestead, offer a universally reasonable standard, while having better motels within the chain. At the other end of the scale is, for example, Sydney's Regent Hotel, which ranks among the world's best; it overlooks Circular Quay and offers an unrivalled view across Sydney Harbour (with prices to match the view).

Recently a new trend in family accommodation has emerged in the form of self-catering, serviced apartments. Several have appeared in the capital cities and offer a one- or two-bedroom apartment within a hotel-style complex. A good example is Gordon Place in Melbourne, a magnificent Victorian building, completely modernized. It offers a range of apartments, all with superb modern kitchens, starting with studio apartments (along the lines of bed-sitting rooms) through to two-bedroom apartments with separate sitting rooms.

Food and drink

Australians, in the local argot, like their tucker. Restaurants abound in all the major cities, and Australians eat out far more frequently than their English cousins. Melbourne, for example, supports no fewer than 1,600 restaurants covering some 60 different cuisines.

But what of the homegrown product? Someone once remarked that the only truly Australian gift to the world was pavlova, a meringue topped with cream and banana, passion fruit or whatever one wishes. Once, the average Australian's idea of a "good feed" was roast lamb and two vegetables. Now, it is possible to eat as well in Melbourne or Sydney as in any major city in the world. Nor are other Australian cities in any sense lacking.

Melbourne and Sydney boast at least one restaurant for every major cuisine – and most minor ones – the world has fostered. There are good examples of Greek, Italian, Lebanese, Turkish, Afghan, French, German, all styles of Chinese, and even Nepalese. The predominant styles are Italian, Chinese and French. The latest arrival is Vietnamese cuisine, as some of the refugees start to open restaurants. This internationalization of the Australian diet is a direct consequence of the huge postwar influx of immigrants.

Most restaurants offer an à la carte menu; the fixed-price menu is still a rarity but gaining in popularity. Main courses usually include vegetables or salad in the price, although some, more expensive, restaurants list vegetables separately. (If they are not shown separately you can safely assume they are included.) It is customary to leave a tip: say, around 10-12 percent.

In most states there are two types of liquor licence available for restaurants: fully licensed and Bring Your Own licence (BYO). Victoria, and more particularly Melbourne, abounds in BYO establishments (see *Eating out in Melbourne* in *Victoria/ Melbourne restaurants*), but the system is not as widespread in other states. In this guide restaurants that have a *BYO* license or *no* license are indicated; if nothing is indicated the restaurant can be assumed to have a *full* license.

Fast food
Australians are fast-food addicts. McDonald's, Kentucky Fried Chicken and Pizza Hut grace many suburbs.

The indigenous snack food, though, is a meat pie eaten with liberal amounts of tomato sauce. This is the staple diet of football fans at matches in winter, and there is truly an art to eating a hot and often somewhat soggy pie while balancing tomato sauce on top. A local variation in South Australia – a pie floater, consisting of the above-mentioned pie in a bowl of pea soup – poses an even greater challenge.

Pub food
The other great traditional eating habit is the counter lunch (or dinner), otherwise known in Britain as a pub meal. The term "counter" is self-explanatory, although few pubs now expect their customers to eat sitting up at the counter; most provide tables.

Food in many pubs is increasingly upmarket. It is no longer rare to find venison, quail or lobster on the menu. But most pubs offer first-class, economical meals, seeking to make a profit out of bar sales and to cover only their costs on the food. More traditional pubs, particularly in inner-city areas and suburbs, often erect a blackboard on the footpath to advertise the day's offerings and prices. Mostly the fare is unambitious: sausages, chicken, lamb chops – but servings are usually generous and the food is wholesome if unimaginative.

Pub lunches generally run from noon-2.30pm. Dinner (or tea, as some Australians call any meal eaten after 4pm) is served from 5.30 or 6pm to 8 or 8.30pm.

See also *Australian wines* in *Special information*.

Shopping

Hours
In most Australian cities standard shopping hours are 9am-5.30pm Mon-Thurs, 9am-9pm Thurs or Fri (the late-shopping night varies from state to state), and Sat 9am-12.30 or 1pm. Certain categories of shops, such as garden nurseries, bookshops, milk bars and convenience stores (see *Shopping hours* in *Basic information*) open seven days a week; some convenience stores are even open 24hrs a day, and in certain tourist areas too shops stay open seven days a week. Some supermarkets remain open until 9pm every weekday. The federal system in Australia places responsibility for shopping hours with state governments, which leads to variations between states.

What to look for
Clothes The range of casual and leisure clothes available is remarkable. Traditional Australian bush gear – the clothes worn by shearers and station hands – is becoming highly fashionable.

Similarly the Akubra hat, the traditional Outback hat thrust into prominence by Australian golfer Greg Norman, has also hit the fashion high spots. The bush gear and hat are unique to Australia and in some cases can only be bought in the country.

Australian designer names to look out for include Trent Nathan, Prue Acton, Anthea Crawford and Maggie Tabberer. Designer Ken Done, whose internationally available work covers items as diverse as bed linen, towels, toilet bags and T-shirts, has a unique Australian style reflecting the relaxed nature of his country. His work is popular among teenagers and the early-20s, and is well regarded in the USA and Europe.

Souvenirs The standard of Australian souvenirs has risen markedly in recent years. Well-made, high-quality local souvenirs are available through outlets with aggressively Australian identities and names such as the Australiana General Store and Antipodes. Worth looking out for: items made in Australian woods (Huon pine fromTasmania, Queensland blackwood, myrtle, and others) such as serviette rings and bowls; sheepskin goods such as coats, boots, gloves, hats and rugs; and leatherwork such as handbags.

Antiques Australians have fallen in love with antiques almost on the same scale as Americans and Britons. Sadly there is a shortage of genuine Australian antiques, and much of the stock available in the many antique shops is either directly imported by the containerload from Great Britain and Europe or consists of local pieces no older than the early 20thC or the Art Deco or Art Nouveau periods. It is still possible to find genuine Australian antiques – but at a price. One local 19thC speciality was the mounting of emu eggs, often in silver. Some of these display excellent workmanship and are sought after by collectors, and consequently command a high price.

How to shop

Bargaining is not welcomed. Australians do not bargain and do not expect visitors to either. They do, however, shop around extensively, and visitors too will find wide variations in price.

There is no value-added or sale tax at the retail level, so the price marked on goods is what you can expect to pay. Most shops accept one or more of the major credit cards. "Lay by", a system of putting down a deposit on goods and paying for them interest-free over a period up to 3mths while they are held at the shop, is widespread. Anyone staying more than a few weeks may find the system useful.

For more details, see the *Shopping* section for each city.

Tour operators

Australia's four main internal airlines, **Ansett**, **Australian Airlines**, **East West** and **Kendell**, offer a range of package holidays and tours. So too do the major bus lines, **Ansett Pioneer**, **Greyhound**, **DeLuxe** and **AAT**. The state motoring organizations also operate travel departments and offer package tours (see under individual state capitals in the *A to Z*). Look too for specialist tour operators who concentrate on particular destinations such as the Northern Territory; contact the relevant state tourist office for a list.

For those seeking the unusual, **Australian Himalayan Expeditions** (*377 Sussex St., Sydney, NSW, 2000* ☎ *(02) 264 3366; Suite 602, Wellesley House, 126 Wellington Parade, East Melbourne, Vic., 3002* ☎ *(03) 419 2333; c/o Thor Adventure Travel, 40 Waymouth St.,*

Adelaide, SA, 5000 ☎ *(08) 212 7857)* has white-water rafting expeditions and hot-air ballooning, to name just two options. Another operator, **Wildtrek** (*also known as Peregrine Adventures, 343 Little Collins St., Melbourne, Vic., 3000* ☎ *(03) 602 3066)*, specializes in holidays-with-a-difference, such as cross-country skiing, bushwalking, rafting, canoeing or sailing.

Several smaller operators provide a personalized service and concentrate on one area. For example, **Bogong Jack** (*P.O. Box 209, Wangaratta, Vic., 3677* ☎ *(057) 212 564)*, a husband-and-wife team, can arrange weekend (or longer) cycling trips around the wineries of northeastern Victoria, staying at country pubs, or, in winter, snowshoe expeditions and cross-country ski camping trips above the snow line, spending nights camped in special tents.

The Australian Capital Territory

The ACT is an Australian oddity: a fragment chipped off the block of New South Wales; a lovely, pastoral plain on which was imposed a purpose-built capital charged with the task of establishing national unity. From here, in splendid isolation, the federal administration runs a country the size of the USA, but with one-twentieth the population.

To all intents and purposes, the ACT, with a total population of only 236,600, is Canberra. And Canberra itself is a potent symbol of regionalism in Australia, being the compromise solution to the intense rivalry between Sydney and Melbourne over which city would be the federal capital. In the end, the design owed nothing to either, being the work of Walter Burley Griffin, an American landscape architect who in 1912 won a city planning competition.

His concept has been meticulously executed. Canberra is a gracious and clean city. The tempo of life is unhurried, there are no slums, and the crime rate is low. It is spacious too, with a happy harmony between ambitious architecture and Burley Griffin's leafy, garden layout.

Still, oddities persist. This is Australia's capital, but it does not have an international airport. Nor, astonishingly, does it have, at the time of writing, a really top-class hotel. Few of the politicians and civil servants who live here for most of the year regard it as home. And despite its immaculate civic countenance and the pleasures of the climate (clean, crisp air at 2,000ft), it is rare that Canberra enchants the visitor. A young city, after 60yrs it has yet to find an identity.

For all that, it is not without interest and stimulus. Visit, for example, the Australian War Memorial. Looking around these sombre exhibits, the question raises itself naggingly: how was it that Australian (and New Zealand) soldiers paid the heaviest price of all combatant nations in a terrible war fought on the other side of the world, while remaining to the end a volunteer army?

Canberra

Maps 2–3 ☎ *STD code: 062. Airport* ☎ *43 5911 (domestic services only); Ansett* ☎ *45 6511; Australian* ☎ *68 3333. Railway station: Wentworth Ave., Kingston* ☎ *95 1555 (country services only). Car rental: Avis* ☎ *49 6088; Budget* ☎ *48 9788; Hertz* ☎ *49 6211. Australian Capital Territory Government Tourist Bureau: Jolimont Centre, Northbourne Ave., Canberra City, ACT, 2601* ☎ *459 6464. American*

Express Travel Service: Centre Point, P.O. Box 153, City Walk, Petrie Plaza, Canberra City, ACT, 2601 ☎ 47 2333. National Roads and Motorists Association (NRMA): 92 Northbourne Ave., Canberra City, ACT, 2601 ☎ 43 8800.

Orientation

Burley Griffin planned a city divided by a lake, with the commercial and residential areas to the N and the political/diplomatic centres to the s. The concept remains intact, although the population has boomed from the 25,000 he envisaged to almost ten times that number, and satellites have sprung up on all sides.

The Sydney/Melbourne feud over federal pre-eminence was resolved slightly in favour of the former. The ACT is enclosed entirely within NSW, and is 304km (190 miles) by road from Sydney, compared with 655km (409 miles) to Melbourne. Its total area is 6,200sq.km (2,400sq. miles).

Seeing the city

For a comparatively small city Canberra covers a great deal of territory. Public transport, however, is not good, and though taxis can be hailed in the city centre it is very advisable to phone-book (☎ 46 0444) from the political/diplomatic sector, across Lake Burley Griffin. To see the sights you could spend as much on taxi fares as on renting a car. Signposting is poor, and a street directory is essential. Main **tourist information centre:** Northbourne Ave., between London Circuit and Barry Drive (☎ 45 6464).

Two commercial operators run guided tours that include Black Mountain, the War Memorial and the old and new Parliament Houses: **Murrays** (☎ 95 3677) and **Ansett Pioneer** (☎ 45 6624).

Sights and places of interest

Australian War Memorial and Museum ★
Anzac Parade, Reid ☎ 43 4238. Map 3C5 ▣ & ✗ ▣ ➡ Open 9am-4.45pm.
This ugly but impressive and acutely poignant complex of buildings includes an extensive war museum. It should be remembered that in World War I, casualties from Australia and New Zealand were proportionally higher per capita than any of the combatant nations over whose territory the war was actually fought. The memorial and museum are a terrible reminder of that fact. Interestingly, more visitors come here annually than to any other site in Australia except for Sydney Opera House.

Black Mountain and Telecom Tower ★
Off Clunies Ross St., West Canberra ☎ 47 7371. Map 2B2 ▣ ➡ ▣ ➡ ◄ Open 9am-10pm.
Visible from all over Canberra, the Telecom Tower offers the best view of the city's layout on either side of Lake Burley Griffin. **Mt. Ainslie** in the NE also offers a grand panorama.

Black Mountain lies about 4km (2½ miles) w of the city centre at an altitude of 812m (2,664ft). The tower rises another 195m (640ft) above the summit. Its primary function is as a transmitting station, but there is ample provision for the public, with three viewing platforms and a revolving restaurant.

Blundell's Cottage
Wendouree Drive. Map 3C5 ➡ Open 2–4pm.
The visitor could be forgiven for wondering why this

undistinguished little dwelling figures in Canberra tours. The reason is that the capital is so patently of this century that any historical antecedents are, *ipso facto*, remarkable. The cottage was built in 1858 by Robert Campbell, a wealthy Scottish merchant, and the first settler in what is now the ACT, for his ploughman. Campbell's own fine residence, *Duntroon*, is 2km (1¼ miles) away. The cottage is furnished with period pieces.

Combine this with a visit to the *Carillon*. Access can be confusing and is via Constitution Ave., not Parkes Way.

Botanic Gardens
Clunies Ross St., West Canberra ☎ *67 1811. Map 2B2* 🄯 ⚷ ✗ *Sun 10am, 2pm* 🔲 ➴ *Open 9am-5pm.*
Situated on the eastern slopes of *Black Mountain*, this is the national collection of native flora. The 40ha (99-acre) site contains a rainforest and around 600 species of the ubiquitous eucalypt tree. There are set walks of up to 1.5km (1 mile), including an Aboriginal trail with plants labelled to explain how they were used by Aborigines.

Carillon ★
Wendouree Drive. Map 3D5 ➴ *45min recitals Sun 2.45pm, Wed 12.45pm.*
Built on Aspen Island in *Lake Burley Griffin*, the Carillon was a gift from Britain to mark Canberra's 1963 golden jubilee, though it was only opened by Queen Elizabeth II in 1970. In effect it is a gigantic musical instrument, with 53 bells (the smallest of which is about 7kg (15½lbs) and the largest 6 tonnes), which are sounded by a single player from a baton keyboard. Chimes like those of Westminster in London sound on the quarter-hour. The island is a picturesque spot, worth a visit for the view even if you miss the Wed and Sun recitals.

Duntroon Military College
Jubilee Ave., Duntroon ☎ *75 9111* 🄯 ➴ *Guided tours of college 2pm. Access to Duntroon House only on infrequent open days.*
Canberra's oldest property, built by a Scots merchant named Robert Campbell, is now incorporated in the Royal Military College. The residence was built in 1833 and added to in 1862. It was acquired by the government when Canberra was selected as the site for the federal capital, and has been a military college since 1911.

Lake Burley Griffin
Maps 2&3.
The central waterway that separates Canberra City from the political and diplomatic enclave is named after the American landscape architect who designed the new capital. The lake, with 35km (22 miles) of shoreline, has become a focus for picnicking and boating. Other features are the *Carillon* and the **Captain Cook Memorial**, which sends a jet of water to a height of 130m (426ft).

National Gallery ★
King Edward Terrace, Canberra South ☎ *71 2411. Map 3D4* 🄯 ⚷ ✗ 🔲 ➴ *Open 10am-5pm.*
The youngest of Australia's major art collections, this was only started in the 1960s. Nevertheless, generous government grants have enabled acquisition of significant and valuable works. A

particular feature is the collection of paintings by postwar Australian artists, including a rightly renowned series by Nolan known as the *Ned Kelly* paintings.

New Parliament House ★
Capital Hill, Canberra South ☎ 70 5237. Map 3E4 ➛ At time of writing, access limited to an Exhibition Centre on the new building, including models and audiovisual display, and overlooking site: open 9am-6pm.

Ambitious in concept, dramatic in scale and unprecedented in cost for an Australian public building, the New Parliament House is an affirmation of national pride and is due for opening during the bicentennial.

The only other architectural endeavour with which it bears comparison is the Sydney Opera House. The Parliament House too has had its critics, not just because of a huge budget blow-out (the final cost will exceed A$1,000m) but for the pace of construction, which has fallen well behind schedule. At the time of writing it appears unlikely that it will be in full use until the end of 1988.

Despite the problems the building bids fair to gain recognition as another grand Australian showpiece. Certainly its dimensions are remarkable, with an area of 40ha (99 acres), granite walls 460m (1,509ft) long, and a flagpole 81m (266ft) high. During construction an exhibition and public observation platform have been located overlooking the site.

Parliament House ★
King George Terrace, Canberra South ☎ 72 1211. Map 3D4 ▣ ✗ ➛ ◂ Open 9am-5pm.

Even when it was opened in 1927 this was intended as a provisional home for the federal legislature. The planned life of 50yrs has now exceeded 60, and required numerous extensions. Perhaps surprisingly under the circumstances, it is a quite handsome, low-slung building, with a striking view across *Lake Burley Griffin* up **Anzac Parade** to the *Australian War Memorial*. King's Hall, at the main entrance, has on exhibition one of just three surviving copies of the final and definitive version of the Magna Carta.

St John The Baptist Church
Anzac Park, Reid. Map 3C5 ➛ Open 9am-5pm.

A charming Anglican church, all the more pleasant for its antiquity in surroundings of relentless modernity. Building on the church started in 1841, and the grounds, once part of the estate of *Duntroon*, contain some interesting old graves. Although the interior is tiny, Queen Elizabeth II and Prince Philip attended divine service here in 1954.

Accommodation
Despite its status as the federal capital of Australia, Canberra offers a limited choice and distinctly moderate quality of accommodation. At the time of writing there is only one 5-star hotel, *Noah's Lakeside*, though another, a **Hyatt**, is due to open at the end of 1987.

The establishments listed below are in the northern/city-centre sector, rather than the inconvenient southern/diplomatic quarter. Many get fully booked during the week, but at weekends the city empties and some hotels offer special rates.

Canberra City TraveLodge

Corner of Northbourne Ave. and Cooyong St., Canberra City, ACT, 2601 ☎ 49 6911 ⅠⅮⅮ ☎ 62050. *Map 3B4* ⅠⅠ *72 rms* 🛏 🍴 🛄 AE 🔾 🔾 VISA

Location: Central, the city centre being a short walk down Northbourne Ave. Part of an established chain that usually maintains a good standard of food and accommodation, this can also be recommended for convenience of location.
�➡️☐ Y 🍴

Canberra International Motor Inn

242 Northbourne Ave., Dickson, ACT, 2602 ☎ 47 6966 ⅠⅮⅮ ☎ 62154 ⅠⅠ *153 rms* 🛏 🍴 🛄 AE 🔾 🔾 VISA

Location: On Northbourne Ave., the main road from the N, but 2km (1¼ miles) from the city. An inn with a spacious, airy feel to it because of the garden atrium, a pleasant spot to eat and drink. Rooms are comfortable but quite pricey.
🚹🚺➡️☐ Y 🍴 🛥 🛎

Noah's Lakeside

London Circuit, Canberra City, ACT, 2601 ☎ 47 6244 ⅠⅮⅮ ☎ 62374 ☎ 57 3071. *Map 3B4* ⅠⅠⅠ *216 rms* 🛏 🍴 🛄 AE 🔾 🔾 VISA

Location: The only Canberra hotel with views over Lake Burley Griffin; a few mins' walk from the commercial centre. The Lakeside does brisk business, and getting a room at short notice during the week is usually difficult.

It will probably benefit, however, from some 5-star competition when the new Hyatt opens. In the meantime it is Canberra's best. Attentive service.
🚹🚺➡️☐ Y 🍴 🛎

Olims Ainslie ♣

Limestone Ave. and Ainslie Ave., Braddon, ACT, 2601 ☎ 48 5511 ⅠⅮⅮ ☎ 62988 ☎ 95 1725. *Map 3B5* ⅠⅠ *120 rms* 🛏 🍴 🛄 AE 🔾 🔾 VISA

Location: To the NE of the centre, but within walking distance for those who enjoy some exercise. One of Canberra's oldest hotels, formerly the Ainslie Rex, but refurbished as one of a small Australian chain. The central feature is a courtyard garden surrounded by accommodation units, which include two-level suites and some self-contained rooms with cooking facilities.
🚹🚺➡️☐ Y 🛎

Parkroyal

102 Northbourne Ave., Braddon, ACT, 2601 ☎ 49 1411 ⅠⅮⅮ ☎ 61516. *Map 3A4* ⅠⅠ *77 rms* 🛏 🍴 🛄 AE 🔾 🔾 VISA

Location: On Canberra's hotel strip, the Northbourne Ave. main road, a brisk 10min walk from the centre. A fairly formal atmosphere by Australian standards in a hotel geared to the business visitor. Airport reception by a hostess. Some may find the blue decor heavy.
🚹➡️☐ Y 🍴 🛎

Eating out in Canberra

Fortunately, Canberra is better served for restaurants than it is for hotels. Indeed, there are some excellent eating spots, as might be expected in a major political and diplomatic centre. The choice below has been made with convenience of location in mind.

EJ's ♣

21 Kennedy St., Kingston ☎ 95 1949. *Map 3F5* ⅠⅠ 🍽 🛄 AE 🔾 🔾 VISA *Last orders 10pm. Closed Sun.*

Rather out of the way, but EJ's is a lunchtime institution with journalists and public servants. Courtyard and interior dining; the inventive menu changes daily.

Fringe Benefits

54 Marcus Clarke St. ☎ 47 4042. *Map 3B4* ⅠⅠ 🍽 🛄 AE 🔾 🔾 VISA *Last orders 11.30pm. Closed Sun.* Canberra generally closes down quite early and this late-night brasserie is worth bearing in mind. If the food is not exceptional, the coffee is, and the environment is pleasant.

Imperial Court

40 Northbourne Ave. ☎ 48 5547. *Map 3B4* ⅠⅠ 🍽 🛏 🛄 AE 🔾 🔾 VISA *Last orders 11.30pm.* A smart and comparatively pricey Chinese restaurant (although still reasonable by Canberra standards) but with some sumptuous food. Popular with the Orientals of the diplomatic community, and with the local press corps.

The Lobby

King George Terrace ☎ 73 1563. *Map 3D4* ⅠⅠ 🍽 🛄 AE 🔾 🔾 VISA *Last orders 10pm. Closed Sun, and when Parliament not sitting.* Situated within walking distance of the old *Parliament House* (see

Sights), and a favourite with its denizens when it comes to fairly formal dining. The food is ambitious, and usually enjoyable, but so it ought to be at these generous prices.

Rossini's ♥
Qantas House, London Circuit ☎ *48 0062. Map 3B4* ▮▮▯ ▭ ▬ AE ⊕ ⦿ VISA *Last orders 10pm. Closed Sat lunch, Sun.*

Italian, of course, and with a very good reputation among Canberra's serious eaters. The delicious antipasto might seem expensive for a starter, but is a meal in itself.

The risotto also comes recommended.

Seasons
Canberra Theatre Centre, London Circuit ☎ *49 7700. Map 3B4* ▮▮▯ ▭ ▬ AE ⊕ ⦿ VISA *Last orders 9.30pm. Closed Sat lunch, Sun lunch.*

A centrally located eatery offering a high standard of cuisine. The decor is attractive, with a welcome amount of space between tables, and a pianist provides unobtrusive music. The menu is sensibly limited, but there is enough variety for most palates. Vegetables are nicely prepared.

Nightlife and the arts

Canberra regulars have been making disparaging remarks about the nightlife for decades. In truth, it is not a city that welcomes outsiders. There are a number of clubs, most of which admit only members of affiliated bodies. The diplomatic, political and media communities tend to be clubs in their own right. All of which helps explain why the visitor who steps out into the city centre at night may wonder whether this is a ghost town.

Canberra Theatre Centre
Civic Square, London Circuit ☎ *57 1077. Map 3B4* ♀ ▬ AE ⦿ VISA *Box office open Mon-Fri 10am-5.30pm and from 7pm.*

Eclecticism is the keynote at the capital's only arts centre. Whether it is the Australian Opera or Elton John, Barry Humphries or Shakespeare, that Canberra is playing host to, the site will be the Theatre Centre. Check the *Canberra Times* or call the box office.

Juliana's
Noah's Lakeside Hotel, London Circuit ☎ *47 6244. Map 3B4* ♀

● ▬ ▦ AE ⦿ VISA *Open Tues-Thurs 5pm-midnight, Fri, Sat 5pm-3am.*

A discotheque at *Noah's Lakeside* (see *Hotels*) favoured by Canberra's young professionals. There are nice views too.

Yarralumla Woolshed
Cotter Rd. (behind Equestrian Centre) ☎ *68 8169* ♀

Traditional Australian bush dances are held here on the second and last Sat of each month. The Woolshed is an old farm building, now classified by the National Trust. The dances are organized by a local radio station and a folk-music society.

Shopping

Canberra is not a great shopping centre, and any intended purchases of Australiana or souvenirs would be better made in a bigger city, such as Sydney or Melbourne, which inevitably must be visited as Canberra lacks an international airport.

One thing Canberra is noted for is secondhand bookshops. (On the road down from Sydney, incidentally, is one of Australia's best, **Berkelouws**, about 4km (2½ miles) before the town of **Berrima**.) The following two establishments have rare and antiquarian books as well as collectable first editions: **Gilbert's Books** (*Cinema Centre Arcade, Bunda St.* ☎ *47 2032, map 3B4, open Mon-Fri 9.30am-5.30pm, Sat 9.30am-1.30pm*) and **Winchbooks** (*68 Wollongong St., Fyshwick* ☎ *80 5304, open Mon-Sat 9am-5pm*).

Excursion

You can drive from the northern to the southern extremities of the ACT in an hour, so there is no question of lengthy excursions. But

Canberra is well placed to visit parts of NSW, such as **Bateman's Bay** on the coast, about 150km (95 miles) by road, or the **Snowy Mountains**, just over 200km (125 miles) away.

The following easy drive is an introduction to the pleasant pastoral country around the capital, with wildlife and a little pioneer history thrown in.

South of Canberra
125km (80-mile) round trip. Allow a day, although can be done in half.

Leave the city travelling westbound on the main carriageway, Parkes Way. At Clunies Ross St. there are signposts to *Black Mountain* and the *Botanic Gardens* (see *Sights*).

The westbound carriageway becomes Lady Denman Drive. Turn off to the right at Tuggeranong Rd., then again at Cotter Rd., following signs for Cotter.

About 20km (12½ miles) from the city is **Cotter Reserve** recreation park, pleasant for river swimming and picnicking. From here the road turns s, passing through forestry range, and attractive sheep- and cattle-farming country. At **Tidbinbilla** the way is signposted to a large 5,000ha (12,300-acre) nature reserve for domestic wildlife, offering picnicking and walks (*open 9am-6pm*).

A few kilometers farther along the road, now signposted to **Tharwa**, is a turn-off for the **Gibralter Falls**, 7km (4½ miles) away. The falls themselves are unspectacular, but this is a lovely and quiet spot to stop for a picnic lunch if you have not already done so.

The historical focus of this excursion is the 19thC homestead of **Lanyon**, which lies just N of Tharwa on the road back to Canberra. Construction of this splendid old farm home began in 1859, some years after Europeans started settling on the well-watered plains. Nestling among trees, stables and other outbuildings, Lanyon looks now as it must have then, a handsome colonial homestead in rich pastoral countryside. The job of refurbishing the interior with period furniture only began in 1980 and still continues. Also at Lanyon is the **Nolan Gallery**, which houses a permanent collection of paintings by Sir Sidney Nolan (*homestead and gallery both open Tues-Sun 10am-4pm.*)

Returning to Canberra, from the s on the Monaro Hwy, it is possible to make a side trip to the **Canberra Wildlife Gardens**, a park with all the main Australian species of animals and a few others too. Turn off the highway at Mugga Lane, some 12km (7½ miles) s of Capital Hill; the wildlife gardens are about 5km (3 miles) up Mugga Lane on the right.

New South Wales

It can be hard today, when Sydney is accepted as one of the world's great cities, when her dazzling harbour and buoyant people seem to represent best the vigour and growth of the Pacific Rim region, to recall just how inauspicious were her origins. But for an understanding of this stylish, beautiful and brittle centre of the Australian dream, it is important to remember these origins.

The name New South Wales was the idea of Captain James Cook, who jotted it down in his journal after landing on the eastern edge of the great Southern Land in 1770. Eight years later a pathetic band of exiles landed a few hundred yards away from where the Opera House now stands, to establish a concentration camp for the detritus of Georgian Britain. The first New South Welshmen were 756 convicts, 450 civilian and military personnel, and 58 women and children.

There was always another Australia, of course: a unique indigenous culture, and a land mass whose sheer vastness had about it something both elemental and mystical. But until well into the last century, to the hardy early settlers eking out an existence around Sydney Cove, this was, effectively, the new Australia.

So far as Sydneysiders are concerned, that remains the case today. From the squalid, frequently brutal, sometimes famine-stricken settlement, a city gradually arose that, in many eyes, outshines for sheer beauty those other great harbour cities, Rio, San Francisco and Hong Kong. On a sunny afternoon, when a light breeze sends hundreds of sailing craft whipping across blue, glittering waters, and you can repair from the beach to an old sandstone pub by the harbour for refreshment, you have the essence of those qualities of life that make Australia, truly, the Lucky Country.

There are other reasons for the locals' not entirely unreasonable prejudice that this is the only part of Australia that matters. The population of NSW is a third of the national total, while more than a fifth of all Australians live in Sydney. The transformation in its ethnic makeup has been rapid and dramatic. Postwar immigration from Europe, and more recently from Asia, has made Sydney a more vivid and, perhaps surprisingly, a more tolerant place.

The majority have not forgotten their raffish past. There was a time when this heritage burdened Sydney folk. Pugnacious independence often masked a resentment towards the mother country, and its equivalent *in loco*, the more genteel Melbourne establishment. Even now there are occasional flashes of contempt for what is considered Victorian stuffiness and the world of old money. But although a strong sense of rivalry persists, Sydney is more secure these days, partly as a result of having been given the nod ahead of Melbourne by the international business community as the emergent financial centre of the Pacific.

Sydney people are witty and shrewd, with a devastating eye for pretension, and a flair for vivid imagery in language. They are confident, exuberant, and quick to extend the hand of friendship. Theirs is not, however, a particularly compassionate society. In a city where success is revered and celebrities adored, there is little pity for the casualties of life in the fast lane, and woe betide the public figure who falls on his face.

But if it can be a tough city, and if the Melburnian way of parrying a Sydney barb is to point to persistent reports of corruption in NSW public life as evidence that not much has changed in 200yrs in the former penal colony, the dominant features of the local temperament are still good humour and affability. Those, and old-fashioned pluck, the spirit of the little Aussie battler, are valuable and likeable qualities.

Nor is Sydney the cultural desert that it used to be characterized. It sustains the national opera company (an admirable one at that), three orchestras, 22 major theatres, an extraordinary variety and spectrum of artists, an occasionally inspired film industry, and enough rock and jazz musicians to keep feet tapping into 2001.

Primarily, however, Sydney's popularity has always come down to a simple outdoors formula. Here, after all, are the beaches of one's dreams, with all the trimmings – golden sands, bronzed bodies, endless sunsets and perfect waves: the Utopia of a hedonist or sun-worshipper.

It is common enough for visitors to be so seduced by Sydney harbour and the beaches of NSW that the interior is forgotten. That is a mistake. For huge though the distances in travel are, a great deal is easily accessible in a day or two's outing from Sydney. Indeed, the main attractions of the NSW countryside lie within a 200km (125-mile) radius of the city.

Once the outer limits are cleared, you are in the bush, the infinite Australian hinterland of sandstone and eucalyptus trees. The lovely Hunter Valley, the main wine-producing region, is between 2 and 3hrs' drive away. Even closer are the Blue Mountains, which used to be a sort of summer retreat, and still attract more visitors annually than anywhere else outside the city. Within an easy hour's drive, to the N and the S, are two magnificent national parks, Ku-ring-gai Chase and the Royal National Park. And even an afternoon's rowing on the Hacking River at the Royal National Park is enough to get a taste of the grandeur of the bush.

The state divides into four natural regions. There is, self-evidently, the coast, with beaches running virtually its full 1,500km (950-mile) extent. Behind that lies a mountainous tableland known as the Great Dividing Range, which follows the line of the coast; until it was crossed in 1813 it formed an impenetrable barrier to exploration of the interior. Then come the pastoral western slopes of the range, where sheep farming is concentrated. Finally, there are the barren western plains, which cover more than two-thirds of the state, and are known simply as the Outback.

Within this diversity there are enormous contrasts, from the country's only wintersport resort, the Snowy Mountains in the S, to subtropical Byron Bay in the N, which make it possible to go skiing and surfing in the same week. Probably, though, you will want to time a visit according to the weather in Sydney.

There is no categorically bad time to go to Sydney, where on average the sun shines 342 days a year. There is plenty of rain too, but it spreads itself around fairly obligingly. The winter months, May-Aug, are of course too cold for the beach, but the days are clear and this is a good time to be on an excursion to the Blue Mountains or the Southern Highlands, and spending the evening around a log fire in an old colonial hotel. The autumn months of Apr and May can be the nicest time of all if you don't insist on swimming. Logically, however, most visitors will be coming to Australia in the summer, from late Nov-Feb, when the temperature in Sydney averages 21.7°C (71°F); the midsummer average is 25°C (77°F).

But what, besides its sunshine and beaches, and its people, is it that makes Sydney remarkable? Not, clearly, a great history littered with architectural wonders, though the fifth, and greatest, governor of NSW, a high-minded egalitarian named Lachlan Macquarie, left a valuable legacy of buildings that still grace the city.

Macquarie, who turned a desperate penal institute into a land of opportunity, granted a pardon to one Francis Greenway, a convict architect. He made him a partner in public works that brought censure from London for the supposed extravagance of their ambitions, but earned them the gratitude of Sydney today. The fruits of this relationship can still be seen in the buildings around Queens Square, N of Hyde Park, and in the charming towns of Windsor and Richmond along the Hawkesbury River, which Macquarie intended to be NSW's breadbasket.

Nor is it the high rise buildings of glass, perspex and stainless steel, superimposed on Macquarie's Sydney, that draw locals and visitors back, though undoubtedly it is a pleasant environment to do business in. And it will remain the key regional finance centre, even if the notion that the Pacific Rim is leading the way into the 21stC turns out to be nothing more than a pipe dream.

In the end, Sydney is, quite simply, her harbour – all 240km (150 miles) of a shoreline of innumerable coves and bays, where tall-masted clippers and barques and great white P & O liners have been berthing for two centuries. The harbour is Sydney at her most elegant, and her most flagrantly materialistic. Yachting marinas like Rushcutters Bay and Rose Bay are so full of sleek, gleaming craft that it seems everyone here must own a boat. Indeed, the ratio of Sydney residents to boat owners is reputed to be the highest in the world.

Property prices for houses along these eastern suburban shores fall into a similar category, the convenient million-dollar tag being a starting point. The older, leafy eastern suburbs of Paddington and Woollahra are less inclined to flaunt their wealth, and are generally more distinguished architecturally.

But Sydney's real structural wonders are found on the harbour, and are distinctively of this age. The 1950s design by a Danish architect for an opera house at the water's edge, dismissed variously as preposterous or just impractical, has become one of the landmark structures of the century, though the production process was so difficult that Joern Utzon has never returned to see the completed building.

An earlier landmark, the 1932 Harbour Bridge was, at 503m (1,650ft), the world's largest single-span bridge for almost 50yrs. The task of repainting it is such that workmen have no sooner finished at one end than they have to go back and start again at the other. Now that the bridge can no longer cope with the flow of traffic across to the new business district of North Sydney, plans are in hand to build a tunnel under the harbour, at twenty times the cost.

The redevelopment of Darling Harbour is another ambitious project, which the planners maintain will transform this dilapidated dockland into a dazzling new symbol of Aussie enterprise, in time for the climax of the bicentenary festivities. Along the way, however, it has stirred up scarcely less civic controversy than did the Opera House.

The bicentenary, centred on Sydney, was conceived as a rousing, and fully justified, celebration of Australia's diversity and prosperity. For NSW has a lot to be proud of. What its third century holds in store is anyone's guess, although certainly it will be different. The easy wealth that lay in the state's pastures and pits, and made this one of the richest of 20thC nations – "living off the sheep's back," they called it – are gone. NSW, like the rest of Australia, is going to have to discover a new formula for prosperity.

Sydneysiders have little doubt that they will. Optimism and tenacity are part of their credo, and if the mines and the farm are played out . . . well, something will come up. It always has before.

This, after all, is where the Lucky Country was born.

Sydney

Maps 4–7 ☎ *STD code: 02. Airport: Kingsford Smith (Mascot); Ansett* ☎ *268 1111; Australian* ☎ *693 3333. Main railway station: Central, between Broadway and Elizabeth St.; contact NSW Rail Authority for inquiries about country and suburban services* ☎ *20942 (24hrs). Car rental: Avis* ☎ *516 2877; Budget* ☎ *339 8888; Hertz* ☎ *669 0066. New*

South Wales Government Travel Centre: 16 Spring St.,
Sydney, NSW, 2000 ☎ 231 4444. American Express Travel
Service: American Express Tower, 388 George St., Sydney,
NSW, 2000 ☎ 239 0666. National Roads and Motorists
Association (NRMA): 151 Clarence St., Sydney, NSW, 2000
☎ 260 9222.

Orientation

Shorn of the descriptive prose that it inspires, Sydney is a riverside
city of 3½ million people, sheltered from the Pacific Ocean by two
massive bluffs. It is the most remote of the world's great cities,
being more than 24hrs flying time from London, 19 from New
York, 13 from Los Angeles and 10 from Tokyo.

Distances to other Australian state capitals are scarcely less
tyrannical. Melbourne is 893km (558 miles) away by road,
Brisbane 1,027km (642 miles) and Adelaide 1,431km (894 miles).
Perth and Darwin are slightly absurd at 3,988km (2,492 miles) and
4,060km (2,537 miles) respectively.

Sydney is laid out along the northern and southern banks of the
Parramatta River, the magnificent natural harbour of Port Jackson
that gives the city its unique character. The harbour is Sydney's
pulse, as well as its greatest vanity, and though expansion
continues to the N, S and W, it remains the immutable centre.

The southern sector has traditionally been the main residential
area, stretching from the Pacific's edge at Bondi, through the
leafy, affluent suburbs of Woollahra and Paddington to the
western suburbs of Balmain, Leichardt, Strathfield and
Parramatta.

N of the harbour, however, lie some of Sydney's prettiest
residential areas, which have become even more sought-after since
the development of the North Sydney business district.

Seeing the city

The nucleus of Sydney's public transport system is Circular Quay.
From this point, where the First Fleet landed in 1788, ferries
depart across the harbour for North Sydney, and buses and trains
fan out across the city.

Taxi charges are reasonable, and given that many of Sydney's
sights are within a 2km (1¼-mile) radius, most visitors are inclined
to take a cab rather than the bus.

An essential telephone number of general use, for information
on anything to do with staying in Sydney, from accommodation to
guided tours, and from shopping to how to register a complaint, is
the **Tourist Information Service** (☎ *669 5111, 8am-6pm*).

Buses

Perhaps the best way to get acquainted with the city is through the
Sydney Explorer Bus (*inquiries* ☎ *231 4444*). This bus service,
operated by the state transport authority, offers a one-day circuit
of the 20 top tourist spots. The Explorer runs every 15mins or so
from 9.30am-5pm daily, and for a modest fare you can travel the
circuit at leisure, staying at any of the destinations for as long or as
short as you like before reboarding. The 18km (11-mile) route
starts from Circular Quay. Among its stops are the Opera House,
the Royal Botanic Gardens, Hyde Park Barracks, Kings Cross, the
Australian Museum, Elizabeth Bay House, Chinatown and The
Rocks.

The transport authority also offers a Day Rover ticket that
entitles the holder to unlimited travel by bus, train or ferry within
Sydney. (*For details and information about other city bus services*
☎ *20543*).

The harbour is Sydney's greatest sight of all, and a trip out on the water is virtually obligatory. Transport authority ferries leave Circular Quay regularly, crossing the harbour to Manly and Taronga Park Zoo. The authority also offers full harbour cruises, with commentary, lasting more than 2hrs. (*Departure 1.30pm from Jetty No. 5; inquiries ☎ 29 2622*).

Captain Cook Cruises, a private operator, offers a more expensive but also more pampered service, with refreshments (*departures 10am, 2pm*). This operator has also taken a leaf from the transport authority's book, and offers a **Harbour Explorer**, a cheaper five-stop ticket that you can use at your own pace: stops are the Opera House, The Rocks, Watsons Bay, Taronga Park Zoo and Pier One. (*All Captain Cook departures from Jetty No. 6 ☎ 27 1879*).

From the air
There is a more hair-raising way of seeing Sydney, and that is from the air. The **Red Baron** (☎ 709 5943) is a Sydney pilot who has painted his Tiger Moth scarlet in the manner of the World War I flying ace. Choose from a 40mins' birds-eye view of the Harbour Bridge or 1hr flights.

On foot
Ultimately, walking is the best way of all to see some parts of Sydney, and again the harbourside is a convenient launching pad. For three suggested routes in the central city area, look at the *Circular Quay* and *The Rocks* entries in *Sights*.

Car rental
For excursions outside the city, you really need a car. In addition to the usual rental companies – such as **Avis**, **Budget** or **Hertz** (*see details on page 66*) – there are a number of organizations renting no-longer-immaculate but adequate vehicles at reduced rates. One such is **Half Price Rent-A-Car** (☎ 357 1191), which has cars for a flat daily fee, with unlimited city mileage.

Sights and places of interest

Art Gallery of New South Wales
Art Gallery Rd., The Domain ☎ 225 1700. Map 7D4 ▣ Ӿ ▣
Open Mon-Sat 10am-5pm, Sun noon-5pm. Explorer Bus.
Sydney takes art seriously but not earnestly, as this excellent gallery shows. The original building, opened in 1885, is something of an architectural oddity, but has been imaginatively extended and offers a superb harbour view.

The fine collection of Australian art on show here includes early colonial paintings, significant works by the so-called Heidelberg School, including Tom Roberts and Arthur Streeton, and a few genuine masterpieces by Sir William Dobbell – Australia's greatest portraitist – and Sir Russell Drysdale. There is also a section of Aboriginal and New Guinea art. Exhibitions of new Australian works change regularly.

Australian Museum
William St./College St. ☎ 339 8111. Map 6D3 ▣ ▣ ✱ Open Mon noon-5pm, Tues-Sun 10am-5pm. Explorer Bus.
This museum examines the unique anthropology and natural history of the Australian continent, with lucid exhibits on the tragic history of the Aborigines, and on marsupial fauna; the birdlife display is another strong feature. Its focus extends to the Pacific, and the Melanesian cultures in particular, with a re-created New Guinea village (Australia had responsibility for Papua

New Guinea until independence in 1975). Although the museum is of a high standard, it leaves some with the impression that with such a heritage, it should be even better.

Beaches

Sydney's beaches are as good as you will find in any city, and are the very embodiment of the Australian concept of hedonism. Harbour beaches are sheltered from currents and surf, and consequently are favoured by families and inexpert swimmers, although lifeguards always patrol the main beaches. City beaches are always crowded at weekends, and parking can be a problem. Don't concern yourself unduly about sharks, Sydney's last fatal attack was more than 20yrs ago, but make sure you take suntan lotion, and repellant for the ubiquitous and relentless Antipodean fly. Topless sunbathing goes unremarked at most beaches.

Some of the best beaches are well out of Sydney and it is practical only to consider visiting them by car. See entries in *Environs* for *Palm Beach*, in the N, and *Royal National Park*, in the S.

Harbour beaches

Camp Cove This short, pretty stretch of beach near Watsons Bay can reasonably claim to be among Sydney's most picturesque and popular swimming spots. It is also a historically important location, as Captain Arthur Phillip and the First Fleet landed here to establish the penal colony of New South Wales in 1788.
Nielsen Park This safe, pleasant beach at Vaucluse is set in a nature reserve. Walks among rock pools and a large, shady park make it popular for picnics. Particularly recommended for families.
Balmoral Beach A long, sandy beach set in an attractive part of Sydney, near Mosman. It has grassy verges, and, at the western end, known as **Edwards Beach**, there is a shallow, rock swimming pool. (Ferry from Circular Quay to Taronga Park Zoo, then bus.)
Reef Beach This officially designated nudist beach on the N side of Sydney Harbour National Park, near Manly, has been made inaccessible enough to discourage the voyeur, or even the merely curious. (Ferry from Circular Quay to Manly, then bus, then a hike.)
Manly This popular northern suburb is a pleasant ferry ride away from *Circular Quay*, and is well worth the effort involved in visiting it. Next to the harbour beach (whose calm waters are ideal for toddlers) is the **Marineland** (see *Manly*), which has performing seals and a shark-viewing aquarium. Manly also has an ocean beach, just a stroll across the peninsula.

Ocean beaches

Surfing is as Australian as iced beer and kangaroos, and does not necessarily require enormous expertise in all its forms. Riding a wave on your body can be as exhilarating as doing it on a surfboard, but be warned that the currents off the ocean beaches can be treacherous. You should only swim within the flagged areas, which are kept under observation by lifeguard crews, but in difficulty, wave an arm to attract attention.
Bondi Australia's most famous beach (pronounced Bon-dye) is by no means the best. This rather ugly suburb in Sydney's E boomed after World War II, and on summer weekends is tightly packed with local residents. The best time to enjoy the surf and discover what made it popular is on a quiet weekday.
Coogee Another popular beach in the SE, which has been memorably captured on canvas by Australian Impressionist painters. It is much busier these days, but the current is generally

milder than at other Sydney ocean beaches. Recommended.

Tamarama This beach, in an attractive setting, is for the young and body-proud. Sun-worship tends to be more important here than the mundane business of swimming, partly because the currents can be dangerous.

Long Reef Favoured by adventurous swimmers – windsurfing, surfing and skin-diving are popular here, but beware of the current. The lagoon provides safer swimming.

Centennial Park
Oxford St., Paddington. Map 5C5 ⊡ ✴ ⬲ *Open sunrise-sunset.*

Founded in 1888 to celebrate the centenary of the arrival of the first settlers, this is Sydney's equivalent of London's Regents Park or New York's Central Park. There are acres of space in which to stroll, feed the ducks or have a snooze. You can also rent horses (☎ *332 2770*), bicycles or tandems.

A visit to Centennial Park would not be complete without a stroll around the leafy eastern suburb of **Paddington**. Built during the Victorian period, this treelined residential area had, by the end of World War II, become a virtual slum. But the trend for restoring terrace homes with their characteristic wrought-iron balconies has made this one of Sydney's most fashionable suburbs. *Paddington Village Church Bazaar* (see *Shopping*), off Oxford St., is a picturesque Saturday menagerie.

For lovers of Victorian architecture, the neighbouring suburb of **Woollahra** has some even grander residences than Paddington.

Centrepoint (Sydney Tower) ★
Pitt St. ☎ *231 6222. Map 6D3* ⚏ ⟞ *Open Mon-Sat 9.30am-9.30pm, Sun 10.30am-6.30pm. Explorer Bus.*

Although no more attractive than any city tower, this one has the redeeming feature of a view, which helps to fix in the mind's eye the complexities of the city layout. From the observation deck you can look westwards up the Parramatta River, with its innumerable bays and coves, across the harbour to the suburbs of *North Sydney*, and eastwards up the harbour to the Heads, at the entrance of this magnificent natural harbour; so be sure to go on a clear day. There is a restaurant (☎ *233 3722*) for which reservations are essential.

Chinatown
sw Sydney. Map 6E2. Explorer Bus.

Less intriguing, perhaps, than its equivalents in San Francisco and London, it is nonetheless an interesting district to wander in – and the best spot for an Oriental blow-out. There are dozens of restaurants, including the *Marigold* (see *Restaurants*) and the **Tai Yuen Palace** (*Sussex St.* ☎ *211 0845*). There are also a few specialist supermarkets, and a food-stall centre in Dixon St., which offers a passable imitation of similar establishments found in Singapore.

Circular Quay ★
Map 6B3 ⚏ *Explorer Bus.*

If Sydney has a transport nerve-centre, this is it. Once, tall-masted barques and schooners arrived here from the mother country; now, ferry services depart across the harbour for the northern suburbs of *Manly* and Mosman, and numerous bus services terminate here (☎ *29 2622 for bus and ferry inquiries*). The Sydney Explorer Bus and the Harbour Explorer both start here, and the city centre is only a 15min walk away.

For all these reasons Circular Quay is an excellent place to begin your investigation of the city. It is also a good starting point for a number of central walks. Here are two suggested routes.

Walk A

Total distance about 5km (3 miles), broken up by lunch along the way.

Follow **Circular Quay East** to **Bennelong Point**, site of the *Opera House*. Continue walking eastwards along the harbourside cove, through the *Royal Botanic Gardens* to **Mrs Macquarie's Chair**. A road, which also bears the name of this early governor's wife, then runs for approximately 1km (½ mile) s past the Charlton swimming pool to the *Art Gallery of New South Wales*, which has a good cafeteria for lunch. Even if you don't go in, pause to enjoy the Henry Moore sculpture of a reclining female figure, on the lawn. Return to the quay by striking back across the Botanic Gardens, or continue along Art Gallery Rd. until you emerge at *Hyde Park*.

Walk B

Total distance about 2km (1 mile). Can also be combined with a visit to the Opera House, or undertaken separately.

On emerging from Circular Quay turn left and continue until you reach the bottom end of Macquarie St. It is a stiffish uphill walk to the top, but contains much Sydney history. (The less fit and energetic may prefer to take a taxi or a train – the nearest station is St James – to the top of Macquarie St. and walk downhill to Circular Quay.)

Starting from the bottom of the hill the first important building you come to, on the left, is the *Conservatorium of Music*. Farther along, on the right, are two elegant early town terraces, preserved as **History House** and the **Royal College of Physicians**. On the left is the *Library of New South Wales*. In the next section of Macquarie St. are the *Parliament House*, the *Mint Museum* and, finally, *Hyde Park Barracks*. On the opposite side of the road to the barracks is *St James Church*, dating from 1819.

Circular Quay is also a good starting point for visiting *The Rocks*, one of the best walking areas of Sydney.

Conservatorium of Music

Macquarie St. ☎ *230 1222. Map 6C3* 🖭 *Open 8.30am-5pm. Closed Sat, Sun. Explorer Bus.*

The original design for this distinctive building was created in 1821 by Francis Greenway (a former convict, and Australia's first recognized architect) as stables for Governor Macquarie. "The Con", as it is known, was established in 1916. During the school year it is open to the public, and is a place for weekly lunchtime recitals and concerts (☎ *or check the press for details* 🖭).

Darling Harbour

sw Sydney. Map 6C1–2.

This major redevelopment of the rundown docks area, to mark the bicentenary, has attracted brickbats as well as bouquets. It is an ambitious project, which its supporters maintain will one day be regarded as another Sydney landmark, no less distinctive than the Opera House, which also had its critics prior to completion. The components include a casino, museum complex, aquarium, exhibition centre, hotels and a monorail link to the city (which provoked spirited public opposition when it was announced as part of the package). The first phase of Darling Harbour is due for completion at the beginning of 1988.

Elizabeth Bay House ★
7 Onslow Ave., Elizabeth Bay ☎ *358 2344. Map 7D5* 🚇 🚃
Open 10am-4.30pm. Closed Mon. Explorer Bus.

This splendid example of a colonial mansion has been maintained
with an eye for authenticity, setting the standard by which other
historic homes in Australia are judged.

"The finest house in the colony" (according to a contemporary
record) is handsomely sited in what is still an elegant part of central
Sydney. It was built in 1835 for Colonial Secretary Alexander
Macleay, and was originally set in 22ha (54 acres) of gardens,
which ran down to the water's edge of what is now a yachting
harbour.

Principal features are the eliptical reception salon, with its grand
sweeping cantilevered stone staircase, the panelled dome ceiling,
which is naturally lit, and magnificent cedar doors. There are
interesting exhibitions on aspects of colonial life, which are
changed regularly.

Fort Denison ★
Map 7A5 🚇 *✗ compulsory* ⇜ *Maritime Services Board
(*☎ *240 2111, ext. 2036) organizes ferry tours from Circular
Quay, departing 10.15am, 12.15pm, 2pm.*

This fortified island in the middle of Sydney Harbour is a poignant
reminder that in the 19thC it was feared that Australia faced
invasion – first by the USA, then by the USSR.

Allow 1½ hrs for a round trip of this island, 0.2ha (½ acre) in
area and less than 100m (328ft) long, which was the first detention
place in the new penal colony, being used to hold convicts
temporarily while a prison was being built on the mainland. In this
time it acquired its other name, "Pinchgut". The unheralded
arrival in the harbour of American sloops around 1840 stimulated
the concept of fortifying the rock, which gained momentum
during the Crimean War. Fort Denison, named after the governor
of the day, was completed in 1857.

The martello tower, barracks, battery and underground
magazines are all accessible for viewing. Needless to say, the
cannons were never fired in anger.

George Street ★
Map 6C-F3. Explorer Bus.

This is one of Sydney's earliest thoroughfares, which in a short
section around Town Sq. contains three handsome historic
buildings: *St Andrew's Cathedral*, the **Town Hall** (built in
Renaissance style and completed in 1874) and the **Queen Victoria
Building**.

The history of the Queen Victoria Building is a cautionary tale in
town planning, and it has taken Sydney nearly 90yrs to appreciate
the grandeur of this huge, Romanesque-style market complex.
Completed in 1898, the sandstone building fell into neglect, and
suffered major civic vandalism between World War I and II, and
by the 1950s there was a concerted move to have it demolished. In
1983 the huge task of restoration began, and was completed 3yrs
later at a cost of A$82 million. This splendid arcade of shops,
boutiques and restaurants (see *Shopping*) is now a major Sydney
sight.

This is also a convenient starting point for a city shopping
expedition. The major stores *David Jones* and *Grace Brothers*,
and the *Strand Arcade*, another complex of fashionable shops,
are within easy walking distance of Town Sq. (see all these in
Shopping).

Harbour Bridge ★
Map 6A3 🚇 ⬅ *se pylon and museum display open Fri-Sun 10am-5pm, closed Mon-Thurs. Explorer Bus.*

Until the construction of the *Opera House*, the "Old Coathanger" was Sydney's most instantly recognizable symbol. The spectacular N-S harbour link was completed in 1932 at a cost of a mere A$20 million. Now that it is no longer capable of handling the traffic flow, there is a plan to build a tunnel under the harbour, for around A$400 million.

Pedestrians can reach the bridge by stairs from *The Rocks*, and although it is possible to walk across, the best view is from the top of the SE pylon.

Pier One, at the southern end of the bridge, has some attractions for children, such as a merry-go-round, and live entertainments, but Sydney's main amusement centre, **Luna Park**, is at the N bridge end.

Hyde Park
Elizabeth St. Map 6D3 🅿 *Open sunrise-sunset. Explorer Bus.*

Its central location makes this park popular with city workers at lunchtime, also with the ubiquitous drunks, and during the school holidays in Jan it becomes an amusement centre. The Art Deco-style **Archibald Fountain**, designed by French sculptor François Sicard, caused a furore when it was unveiled in 1927 in memory of Australia's association with France in World War I. The **Anzac Memorial** is a moving reminder that Australia and New Zealand suffered a higher proportion of casualties in that conflict than any other combatant nation. The annual Anzac Day parade, commemorating the Gallipoli landing on Apr 25 1915, culminates here.

Opposite the park, in Elizabeth St., is the **Great Synagogue**, a 19thC sandstone structure with fine detail.

Hyde Park Barracks Museum ★
Queens Sq., Macquarie St. ☎ *217 0111. Map 6E3* 🅿 *Open Wed-Mon 10am-5pm, Tues noon-5pm. Explorer Bus.*

This is the first product of what became a fertile partnership between Governor Lachlan Macquarie and Francis Greenway, the great convict architect of colonial Australia. This handsome 3-storey structure, designed as an accommodation for convicts, was completed in 1819, and so pleased the governor that he pardoned Greenway. The building has been converted into Sydney's main museum of colonial history, and displays illustrate the Macquarie era and convict life.

Excellent-value lunches and teas are served at the **Barracks Square Cafe**.

King's Cross
About 2km (1 mile) from city centre. Map 7D5. Explorer Bus.

Sydney's sin centre has benefited from a recent clean-up campaign to get narcotic abuse off the streets. The main thoroughfare, Darlinghurst Rd., can still be an ill-tempered, somewhat desperate spot late at night, but "the Cross" has some good eating places, such as the *Bourbon & Beefsteak* (see *Nightlife*), and in addition to the strip joints and porn establishments, there is plenty of activity here. It contains many small hotels and guesthouses, which have made the area a centre for young budget travellers. At the top end of Darlinghurst Rd. is the **El-Alamein Fountain**, an intriguing dandelionlike design. The **King's Cross Waxworks** is at

73

the Village Centre (*Springfield Ave.* ☎ *358 5638* 💳 *open Sun-Thurs 10am-11pm, Fri, Sat 10am-1am*).

Library of New South Wales
Shakespeare Place ☎ *230 1414. Map 6C3* 🔲 *Open Mon-Sat 9am-9pm, Sun 2pm-6pm. Explorer Bus.*
Sydney's main reference library overlooks the *Royal Botanic Gardens* and contains a general reference section, as well as a major collection of historical documents and illustrative material. Principally of interest to students of Australiana.

Manly ★
N of the city. Map 5B5. Ferry across the harbour from Circular Quay: departures on the ¹/₂hr.
This residential suburb of N Sydney is also a popular resort and is worth visiting just for the ferry trip. Manly's harbour beach, known as **South Steyne**, is particularly calm, but the ocean beach across the peninsula, **North Steyne**, can be dangerous, though the surf is good.

At the **Marineland** (*West Esplanade* ☎ *949 2319* 💳 *open 10am-5pm*) there are seal performances (*noon and 2pm*) and a large tank with sharks, turtles and rays. You can take lunch at the *Manly Pacific International* (see *Hotels*).

Maritime Museum
Birkenhead Point, Drummoyne ☎ *81 4374. Map 5C4* 💳 ✴ ⚓
Open Tues-Sun 10am-5pm, Mon 1.30pm-5pm. Ferry from Circular Quay (or bus).
Australia, discovered and settled by sea, has a fascinating maritime history. This is a private museum, and as such it has not obtained the public funding that it deserves, but nevertheless the displays do it credit. Standard features include an historic film of the rounding of Cape Horn by a sailing vessel, and an exhibition based on the extraordinary seafaring feat accomplished by Captain William Bligh when set adrift in a lifeboat by his mutinous crew on HMS *Bounty*. (Bligh, incidentally, was no more successful when he was governor of NSW from 1806-8, provoking a near-civil war in which he was again deposed by rebellious junior officers.)

There are four old **sailing vessels** moored by the museum, which the public can visit (*only open at weekends*).

Mint Museum ★
Macquarie St. ☎ *217 0111. Map 6D3* 🔲 *Open Thurs-Tues 10am-5pm, Wed noon-5pm. Explorer Bus.*
This is actually a museum of colonial history, from the perspective of the decorative arts. Fine furniture, made of indigenous red cedar, and silverware are among the most collectable Australian objects, and there are excellent examples here, as well as stamps, coins, earthenware and glass. The Mint building is part of what was once known as the Rum Hospital, which, like so many old NSW structures, was built during the governorship of Lachlan Macquarie, in a deal that involved granting the two citizens who funded the hospital a trade monopoly in the colony's favourite tipple.

North Sydney
Map 5C4.
The commuter strain imposed on the *Harbour Bridge* and other city transport resources have been mainsprings for the decentralization of Sydney. Over the past decade the area

immediately N of the bridge, known as North Sydney, has grown rapidly as a commercial district. The **Luna Park** amusement centre is at the harbour's edge, with ferry services running frequently to *Circular Quay*. The suburbs around here – **Kirribilli**, **Neutral Bay**, **Cremorne** and **Mosman** – are among the most pleasant of the city's residential areas.

Opera House ★
Bennelong Point ☎ 20525 (bookings), 250 7111 (inquiries). Map 6B3 ⊡ ✗ at regular intervals from 9am-4pm ⏴ Explorer Bus.

It is as well to remember today, when this marvellous building is accepted as embodying modern Sydney style, that during a difficult gestation period it was often dismissed as the most pallid of all pachyderms. When Joern Utzon's sketches won a design competition in 1957, it was generally estimated that the sails-on-the-harbour design (alternatively nuns-in-a-scrum) would cost around A\$8 million and take no more than 5yrs to build. In the event, it cost well over A\$100 million, and took more than a decade.

All but the dourest Sydneysiders would agree today that it was worth waiting for. The city has gained a symbol even more distinctive than the *Harbour Bridge*, as well as a splendid arts centre. In addition to the opera theatre there is a concert hall, drama theatre and cinema.

The *Australian Opera* company (see *Nightlife*) generally offers vigorous and well-sung productions, and, despite one Wagnerian fiasco, has staged some exhilarating triumphs in recent years; ticket prices are reasonable (*for programme details consult the press, or contact the box office*). The **Bennelong** restaurant offers the same splendid setting, and reasonable value (☎ 250 7578/250 7548).

Parliament House
Macquarie St. ☎ 230 2111. Map 6C3 ⊡ ✗ by arrangement. Open 9.30am-4pm. Closed Sat, Sun. To inspect the interior or attend debates ☎ the Sergeant-at-Arms' office. Explorer Bus.

The state legislature is contained in this, Australia's oldest parliamentary building. With its large verandahs, it resembles a classically colonial administrative block, but in fact used to be part of what was called the Rum Hospital. The other wing is now the *Mint Museum*. The hospital was an inspired innovation by that indefatigable builder, Governor Macquarie, who, finding the public coffers empty, granted two wealthy citizens control of the rum trade in return for constructing a hospital.

Power House Museum
Mary Ann St., Ultimo ☎ 217 0222. Map 6E2 ⊡ ⛁ ✼ Open 10am-5pm.

Part of a Museum of Applied Arts and Sciences, which is due to move to *Darling Harbour* when the new site has been developed. At present the collection reflects technological change since the Industrial Revolution, and contains participant displays for children.

The Rocks ★
Map 6B3 ✗ Explorer Bus.

This is where it all began: Old Sydney, where the settlement founded by Captain Arthur Phillip after landing at Sydney Cove grew and developed. It was a rude society. Dimly lit streets were

75

the haunts of grog traders, whores and sailors, and press gangs lurked among the alleys of the harbour. An outbreak of bubonic plague here in 1900 killed more than 100 people. All this is hard to imagine today, among these charming sandstone cottages and old pubs, and nowadays The Rocks offers one of the best walks in Sydney. Organized walking tours lasting 1hr leave from **Argyle Centre** (*Argyle St.* ☎ *27 4972, at hourly intervals every morning*). If walking on your own, the **Rocks Visitors' Centre** (*104 George St.* ☎ *27 4972*) will provide maps.

Your first stop should be **Cadman's Cottage** (*110 George St.* ☎ *27 7971*), overlooking the harbour, which would be unremarkable but for the fact that it is Sydney's earliest surviving dwelling. Follow George St. N to the 19thC terraced houses known as **Sergeant Majors Row**, then turn left into Playfair St. for the shops of Argyle Terrace. At Argyle St. turn right and walk through the **Cut**, a tunnel carved out of cliff, to the **Holy Trinity Anglican Church** (the garrison church), which was built from the quarried rock, and consecrated in 1843. Along Argyle Pl. and Lower Fort St. are a range of handsome terraces from the Georgian and Victorian eras; also the **Colonial House Museum** (*53 Lower Fort St.* ☎ *27 6008*).

Back at Argyle Pl. is **Observatory Park**, on the far side of which is the handsome building of the **National Trust Centre**.

Refreshment, after thirsty work, is obtainable at two of Australia's oldest licensed establishments, the **Lord Nelson** (*19 Kent St.*), which has a pleasant upstairs restaurant, and the **Hero of Waterloo** (*81 Lower Fort St.*). There are a great number of shops in The Rocks – too many, in fact, particularly aimed at tourists.

Royal Botanic Gardens ★
The Domain ☎ *231 8111. Map **7C4** ⬚ ✗ Wed-Fri 10am* 🖼 ◛ *◀ Open sunrise-sunset. Explorer Bus.*
This pleasant harbourside walk can be combined with a visit to the *Opera House*. Other sights within walking distance are the *Art Gallery of New South Wales*, the *Conservatorium of Music* and the *Library of New South Wales*.

The first colonists cultivated vegetables here, but from 1816 the 69ha (170-acre) site became established as a garden. Today it supports a fine tree collection and tropical plants. It is an excellent spot for a nap on the lawn after a long walk, and has a prime view of the Opera House. **Mrs Macquarie's Chair**, named after the wife of Governor Lachlan Macquarie, greatest of the early colonial administrators, is a rocky vantage point projecting into the harbour.

The **Domain** is another park, adjacent to the gardens. The main interest for visitors is the Sun afternoon soapbox oratory – a local blood sport.

St Andrews Cathedral
Town Hall Sq., George St. ☎ *265 1555. Map **6D3** ⬚ ✗ after last two services and after 1.15pm Wed service. Open Mon-Fri 7.30am-6pm, Sat 9am-4pm, Sun 8am-8pm. Organ recitals Thurs 10.30am, 7pm. Explorer Bus.*
The design of this Gothic Anglican cathedral, built in sandstone and consecrated in 1868, was based on two structures in Oxford, England. The nave and aisle were modelled on those at St Mary's Church, and the steeple on the tower at Magdalen College. Music is an important feature of worship here: the organ is a unique two-in-one combination, with sets of pipes both from the 19thC

and 20thC; and the cathedral has one of the finest male-voice choirs in the country.

St James Church ★

King St., Queens Sq. ☎ *232 3952. Map* **6D3** ◻ *Open 8am-4pm. Sun services 8am, 9am, 11am. Explorer Bus.*

A finely proportioned Anglican church by Francis Greenway, the convict-architect who designed many of Sydney's most notable buildings. Greenway and his patron, Governor Lachlan Macquarie, had already started building a courthouse on this site when a commissioner, sent out from London to restrain their civic ambitions, forced readjustments to projects already in hand. St James Church took the place of the courthouse. It opened in 1822.

St Mary's Cathedral

College St. ☎ *232 3788. Map* **6D3** ◻ ✗ *first Sun in month 2pm. Open 6.30am-7.30pm. Sun services 9am, 10.30am, 6.30pm. Explorer Bus.*

Catholicism is the faith of the NSW polital establishment, and this imposing structure, built on a fine site overlooking the **Domain** (see *Royal Botanic Gardens*), is the headquarters of the faith in Australia. The cathedral has had a chequered history. The foundation stone of the first Catholic chapel was laid by Governor Macquarie in 1831, but was destroyed by fire in 1865. 3yrs later a new foundation stone was blessed, and building commenced on the ruin of the old structure; but St Mary's was not opened until 1928, and is still incomplete, the twin towers having no spires.

Taronga Park Zoo ★

Bradleys Head Rd., Mosman ☎ *969 2777. Map* **5C5** ⊠ ▣ ✻ ⇚ *Open 9am-5pm.*

Situated in *North Sydney*, overlooking the harbour, and a short ferry ride from *Circular Quay*, Taronga Park is as attractive a setting as you could find for a zoo, and during the week a good spot for picnics. It also contains the finest collection of Australia's unique fauna. Some of the animal accommodations are less impressive, but these are being upgraded. Special features of Taronga include an entertaining **seal show** (◻ *1.15pm and 3.15pm, additional show Sun 11.15am*), an **aquarium**, and the **chimpanzee park**.

Vaucluse House

Olola Ave., Vaucluse ☎ *337 1957. Map* **5C5** ⊠ ▣ *Open 10am-4.30pm. Closed Mon.*

This historic home was once the residence of W. C. Wentworth, architect of the Australian constitution, and an explorer who was involved in the first successful crossing of the Blue Mountains.

The house, begun in 1803, is built in Gothic style, with turrets and castellations, and has been furnished with period pieces. The grounds, covering more than 8ha (20 acres), are among the main attractions, with period outbuildings and fine gardens. There is a small beach at the bottom of the grounds, and **Nielsen Park** beach (see *Beaches*) is an easy stroll away.

Victoria Barracks

Oxford St., Paddington ☎ *339 0455. Map* **5C5** ◻ ✗ *by reservation on Tues after changing of the guard Tues 11am-noon. Closed Wed-Mon.*

Unlike *Hyde Park Barracks*, which was built to accommodate convicts, this was a true military barracks, and was the headquarters of British colonial troops until 1871, when an Australian defence force was raised. The barracks is a handsome Georgian structure 225m (738ft) in length, consisting of twin 2-storey wings, and it remains a military headquarters and administrative centre. Access to the public is confined to the weekly changing of the guard on Tues, which is followed by a free guided tour of the barracks and museum (booking essential).

Accommodation

The most common complaint about Sydney's best hotels is that there are too few of them. Certainly the demand for international 4- and 5-star-standard accommodation is growing, outstripping Sydney's ability to respond. There is a sorry lack of time-proven top-class establishments, and few can offer an atmosphere to compare with the grand old hotels of Europe or the USA.

Most of the hotels described below are within easy reach of the sea – the distance from the city to the harbour beaches, for example, or to the eastern ocean beaches, such as Bondi, is less than 10km (6 miles) – though only one on the following list is situated right on the beach. All the others are conveniently located for central sightseeing. For good accommodation, which by Australian standards is expensive, it is advisable to book ahead.

Sydney has no shortage of the standard, clean – if basic – motel unit, which can be found all over Australia. Motels and motor inns, however, tend to be located out of the centre, making car rental a near-necessity. Such accommodation can be found around the eastern beaches such as **Bondi**, **Coogee** and **Maroubra**, and in the N at **Manly** and **Dee Why**.

In addition to hotels and guesthouses, Sydney offers a range of self-catering, serviced accommodation: establishments that provide simple, clean rooms with all basic amenities, such as TV and laundry (and often swimming pools and sauna), with the independence of private kitchens, crockery and cutlery. Examples below, chosen mainly for their convenience, are *Hyde Park Plaza*, *Park Apartments* and *Zebra Hyde Park Motel*.

Central Plaza
Corner of George St. and Quay St., Sydney, NSW, 2000 ☎ *212 2544* ⅢⅮⅮ ● *74862. Map 6F2* ▮▮
116 rms ➞ ▱ AE ● ●● VISA
Location: Opposite Central Station.
The convenient location of this modern hotel in the SW of the city, a short walk from Chinatown and the Entertainment Centre, compensates for the uninspiring locale. Most of the rooms contain spa baths, and some suites have their own patio garden. There is a large private terrace with barbecue area and bar for guests and a 24hr coffee shop.
➞ ▣ ▼ ➤ ⚓ ⛷

Florida Motor Inn ♣
1 McDonald St., Potts Point, NSW, 2011 ☎ *358 6811* ⅢⅮⅮ ●
21128. Map 7C5 ▮▮ *121 rms* ➞
▱ AE ● ●● VISA
Location: Between Kings Cross and Potts Point, 5 mins' taxi ride from the city. Well-equipped apartments,

conveniently located in a pleasant residential area.
➞ ▣ ➤

Gazebo Ramada
2 Elizabeth Bay Rd., Elizabeth Bay, NSW, 2011 ☎ *358 1999* ⅢⅮⅮ
● *21569. Map 7D6* ▮▮ *400 rms* ➞
▱ ▱ AE ● ●● VISA
Location: In the heart of Kings Cross, overlooking Fitzroy Gardens and Elizabeth Bay. Taking a dip in the pool here can leave you breathless, not from exertion but at the panorama across the bay; for the glass-enclosed pool is on the 17th floor, at the top of a circular tower, an unmistakable landmark in downtown Kings Cross. Upper-level rooms also have fine views of the harbour and city. Back on *terra firma*, the view from the ground-floor **Pavilion** restaurant is more strange than stunning, as guests look out on an artificial downpour.
♿ ➞ ▣ ▼ ➤ ⚲ ⛷

Hilton International

259 Pitt St., Sydney, NSW, 2000
☎ 266 0610 ⅠⅠⅮ ☎ 25208 ⓧ 265
6065. Map **6D3** ⅠⅠⅠⅠ *605 rms* ⊶ ⇌
 AE ⊕ ⓒⓄ VISA

Location: In the heart of the city centre,
opposite the impressive Queen Victoria
Building. This Hilton is surprisingly
anonymous, buried within a
shopping complex, but this does not
detract from its elegant and
comfortable interior. The chefs of
the **San Francisco Grill Room** have
won a number of awards; the hotel
also has an Art Deco-style nightclub,
and the magnificent **Marble Bar**,
which, dating from the turn of the
century, was a feature of the George
Adam hotel originally on this site.
There are two executive floors with
extensive business services.
♿ ⇌ 🖃 ☗ ⬳ ⬳ ⚓ ⚑

Hilton International Sydney Airport

20 Levey St., Arncliffe, NSW,
2205 ☎ 597 0122 ⅠⅠⅮ ☎ 70795
ⓧ 597 6381. Map **5D4** ⅠⅠⅠⅠ *270 rms*
⊶ ⇌ 🖾 AE ⊕ ⓒⓄ VISA

Location: Opposite the international air
terminal, about 20mins from the city.
Obviously not the surroundings for a
holiday, this is the businessmen's
domain, useful for quick stopovers or
conferences and providing the usual
Hilton standards of efficiency and
courtesy. For more relaxed
moments, there are squash and
tennis courts – or take the
opportunity of using the nearby
18-hole Kogarah Golf Course (in a
suburb that calls contemporary wit
and writer Clive James one of her
sons). A shuttle service operates
every ½hr to and from the airport
and every 2hrs to and from the city
centre.
♿ ⇌ 🖃 ☗ ⚘ ⚐ ⚑ ⚓

Holiday Inn Menzies

14 Carrington St., Sydney, NSW,
2000 ☎ 20232 ⅠⅠⅮ ☎ 20443 ⓧ 290
3819. Map **6C2** ⅠⅠⅠⅠ *441 rms* ⊶ ⇌
🖾 AE ⊕ ⓒⓄ VISA

Location: In the city centre, 5 mins'
walk from Circular Quay. The
Holiday Inn chain spent A$15
million on refurbishing the Menzies,
which had become something of a
Sydney institution. The lobby now
consists of gleaming black granite,
oak panelling and mirrors; the lobby
bar and stylish **Park Lounge**, where
high tea is served from a silver
service, look out over Wynard Park.
There are five restaurants, including
the Japanese **Keisan**, a non-smoking
floor, and 24hr medical service.
♿ ⇌ 🖃 ☗ ⬳ ⚐ ⚓ ⚑

Hyatt Kingsgate ♥

William St., Sydney, NSW, 2011
☎ 357 2233 ⅠⅠⅮ ☎ 23114 ⓧ 356
4150. Map **7D4** ⅠⅠⅠⅠ *389 rms* ⊶ ⇌
AE ⊕ ⓒⓄ VISA

Location: Towering over the Kings
Cross district, offering spectacular
views of the harbour and city, which are
less than 10mins away. This might not
be Sydney's most salubrious district,
but the luxurious interiors of this
fine, recently refurbished hotel, and
its attentive staff, are a world away
from the *risqué* street life. The new
Craigend restaurant suggests the
style of a splendid old Italian villa,
and the chefs are hoping to give the
trendy neighbouring restaurant *Chez*
Oz (see *Restaurants*) some
competition. With an eye to another
successful eating place, the *Suntory*
(see *Restaurants*), they have also
opened a Japanese restaurant with a
sushi bar. The hotel is proud of
patronage by sporting personalities,
mainly golfers and cricketers.
⇌ 🖃 ☗ ⚐ ⚑

Hyde Park Plaza ♥

38 College St., Sydney, NSW,
2010 ☎ 331 6933 ⅠⅠⅮ ☎ 22450
ⓧ 331 6022. Map **6E3** ⅠⅠⅠⅠ *180 rms*
⊶ ⇌ 🖾 AE ⊕ ⓒⓄ VISA

Location: Overlooking Hyde Park on
the corner of Oxford St., gateway to the
eastern suburbs. Comfortable and
pleasantly refurbished, these
apartments are served by a restaurant
and cocktail bar.
⇌ 🖃 ☗ ⚘ ⚓ ⚑

Inter-Continental

117 Macquarie St., Sydney, NSW,
2000 ☎ 230 0200 ⅠⅠⅮ ☎ 176890
ⓧ 251 2342. Map **6C3** ⅠⅠⅠⅠ *531 rms*
⊶ ⇌ 🖾 AE ⊕ ⓒⓄ VISA

Location: Near the central business
district, close to the Botanic Gardens
and the Opera House. Sydney's most
stylish new hotel, the Inter-
Continental was designed around the
19thC sandstone Treasury Building,
and is a welcome addition to the
city's quality hostelries. The concept
used here makes sensitive use of the
features of the historic building to
create an atmosphere combining the
best of tradition and modernity. The
palazzo-like central courtyard,
surrounded by vaulted arcades of
sandstone, is the focal point.
Bedrooms on the upper floors have
outstanding harbour views. Banquets
and conferences can be
accommodated in a selection of
rooms, from the **Grand Ballroom** to
the faithfully restored 19thC
boardrooms.
♿ ⇌ 🖃 ☗ ⬳ ⚐ ⚓ ⚑

Jackson ♧
94 Victoria St., Potts Point, NSW, 2011 ☎ *358 5144* IDD *Map 7D5* ▯ *17 rms* 🚗 🖵 AE ⊕ ⓒ VISA
Location: On a pretty treelined street in Potts Point, close to Kings Cross, and a few kilometres from the city. A carefully restored Victorian terrace house, classified by the National Trust, this small establishment offers comfortable but economical guesthouse-style accommodation of a sort common in Europe but all too rare in Australia. Its attractive wrought-iron balconies, high, ornate ceilings and gleaming brass and cedar all add to the charm. The inclusive continental breakfast is served in a sunny conservatory.

Koala Motor Inn Oxford Square ♧
Corner of Oxford St. and Pelican St., Oxford Sq., Sydney, NSW, 2010 ☎ *269 0645* IDD ☎ *121868* ⊕ *261 2148. Map 7E4* ▥ *350 rms* 🚗 🖵 🖵 AE ⊕ ⓒ VISA
Location: On the edge of the city, above the Ansett air-and-coach terminal in Oxford Sq. A good-value hotel conveniently close to the city – a rare thing in Sydney. The decor might not be to everyone's taste, particularly the rather garish **Red Room** and restaurant, but the staff is friendly and the clientele certainly lively.
≋ ▣ Ψ ⌂ ✓ 🍴

Macquarie Private Hotel
Corner of Hughes St. and Tusculum St., Kings Cross, NSW, 2011 ☎ *358 4415. Map 7D5* ▯ *25 rms* 🖵
Location: In Kings Cross, less than 2km (1 mile) from the city. Kings Cross is the cheap-rate hotel district of Sydney, popular with young travellers. If you enjoy the raffish, and are not too fussy about frills, there is excellent value to be had here.

Manly Pacific International ♧
55 North Steyne, Manly, NSW, 2095 ☎ *977 7822* IDD ☎ *73097* ⊕ *977 7822. Map 5B5* ▥ *170 rms* 🚗 🖵 AE ⊕ ⓒ VISA
Location: Overlooking one of Australia's most famous surfing beaches. This is the only luxury hotel in *North Sydney* (see *Sights*), situated in one of the city's most attractive suburbs. It offers the best of both worlds – sand and surf on the doorstep, and easy accessibility to the centre of Sydney, just 15mins away by hydrofoil.
≋ 🐾 ▣ Ψ ☂ 🍴 ⚓ 🍴

Metro Gateway Motor Inn ♧
Corner of Abercrombie St. and Meagher St., Chippendale, Sydney, NSW, 2008 ☎ *699 4133* ⊕ *26474. Map 5C4* ▯ *34 rms* 🚗 ⁼ 🖵 AE ⊕ ⓒ VISA
Location: Just outside the city in a light-industrial and residential district. There is nothing very distinguished about this or other Metro Motor Inns, which are characteristic of the ubiquitous Australian motel, but they generally offer value for money in clean and comfortable surroundings. The group maintains several establishments reasonably close to the city, but this one is particularly convenient, and close to Sydney University.
▣

Metropole
305 Military Rd., Cremorne, NSW, 2090 ☎ *909 8888* IDD ☎ *25931. Map 5B4* ▥ *84 rms* 🚗 ⁼ 🖵 AE ⊕ ⓒ VISA
Location: Right in the hub of Sydney's Lower North Shore at Cremorne, close to the North Sydney business district and popular Balmoral Beach and Taronga Park Zoo. Pleasantly refurbished, and situated in a fashionable residential area, the Metropole is a good alternative to staying in the centre of Sydney, while still gaining fine views of the city and harbour. As well as the hotel's brasserie, there are numerous restaurants along Military Rd.
♿ ≋ ▣ Ψ 🍴 🍴

North Sydney TraveLodge
17 Blue St., North Sydney, NSW, 2060 ☎ *92 0499* IDD ☎ *26644* ⊕ *922 3689. Map 5C4* ▥ *215 rms* 🚗 ⁼ 🖵 AE ⊕ ⓒ VISA
Location: In the centre of North Sydney's business district. The **Farthings** restaurant offers good views of the harbour from an unusual perspective; if you prefer *al fresco* dining, there are umbrellas and tables by the pool. The hotel is within walking distance of the best view of the Opera House, from Pelican Point, and not far from Balmoral Beach, probably the best on the lower N shore. There are two non-smoking floors.
♿ ≋ ▣ Ψ 🍴 🍴

Old Sydney Parkroyal
55 George St., Sydney, NSW, 2000 ☎ *20524* IDD ☎ *72279* ⊕ *251 2093. Map 6C3* ▥ *174 rms* 🚗 ⁼ AE ⊕ ⓒ VISA
Location: In the heart of the historic Rocks area, site of the first European settlement, and within easy walking

distance of the city. As *The Rocks* area (see *Sights*) is poorly served for hotel accommodation, this modern hotel's main attraction is its location. It was converted a few years ago from a 1920s building, and its amphitheatrelike interior gives a feeling of spaciousness. The ground-floor **Cove Cafe** looks out onto the pedestrian parade of The Rocks. Good breakfasts.
ᦕ ⇌ ▣ ⵙ ☞ ⚓ ♨

Olims
26 Macleay St., Sydney, NSW, 2000 ☎ *358 2777* IDD ☎ *23752. Map 7C5* ⫴ *118 rms* ⚗ ⫤ ⚗
AE ⬦ ⬤ VISA
Location: Potts Point, about 2km (1 mile) from the city, close to Kings Cross. Harbour views at a reasonable price make this hotel an attractive proposition. Most of the rooms have a harbour or city view, and the swimming pool is situated on a terrace overlooking the harbour. Only the suites have full baths, the rest of the rooms having half-baths and showers. An informal brasserie overlooks busy Macleay St.
⇌ ▣ ⵙ ♨

Park Apartments ♣
16–32 Oxford St., Sydney, NSW, 2010 ☎ *331 7728* IDD ☎ *74824. Map 7E4* ⫼ *133 rms* ⚗ ⫤ ⚗
AE ⬦ ⬤ VISA
Location: On the edge of the city, opposite the Ansett terminal in Oxford Sq. Modern, light and airy single- and two-bedroom apartments, in pleasant surroundings. Each one has a fully-equipped kitchen, including dishwasher, and the additional feature of 24hr room service.
⇌ ▣ ⵙ ☞ ⚓ ♨

Regent
199 George St., Sydney, NSW, 2000 ☎ *238 0000* IDD ☎ *73023* ℗ *251 2851. Map 6B3* ⫼ *620 rms* ⚗ ⫤ ⚗ AE ⬦ ⬤ VISA
Location: Ideally situated – a stroll away from the Opera House, the historic Rocks area and the central business district. Thought by many to be Sydney's finest hotel, the Regent has been ranked among the world's top dozen hotels. Service for business executives, including a business reference library, is unmatched in Sydney. Other features are the pricey **Cable's** restaurant, probably Sydney's best hotel restaurant; the *Don Burrows Supper Club* (see *Nightlife*), where you can hear some of the best jazz in Sydney; and executive suites offering a personal butler. Despite these facilities, some

visitors might find the cool efficiency lacking in charm, and it is hardly the place for a honeymoon.
ᦕ ⇌ ▣ ⵙ ♨

Rushcutter TraveLodge
110 Bayswater Rd., Rushcutters Bay, NSW, 2011 ☎ *331 2171* IDD ☎ *71524. Map 7E6* ⫼ *113 rms* ⚗ ⫤ ⚗ ⬦ ⬤ AE VISA
Location: In a quiet cul-de-sac overlooking picturesque Rushcutters Bay, within 3km (2 miles) of the city centre. The main attractions here are being close to fashionable Double Bay, with its expensive boutiques and café life, and the beaches of the eastern suburbs. The TraveLodge stable has established a generally high reputation in the Pacific region for good value, and this is no exception. The hotel's **Jonc's** restaurant has a fine view.
⇌ ⵚ ▣ ⵙ ♨ ♨ ♨

Russell ♣
143A George St., Circular Quay, Sydney, NSW, 2000 ☎ *241 3543* IDD ☎ *10101. Map 6B3* ⫴ *18 rms* AE ⬦ ⬤ VISA
Location: The Rocks. Despite having none of the facilities required by businessmen, the Russell can confidently be recommended to anyone who appreciates the special pleasures that only a small establishment can offer. It was built in 1887 and is furnished in keeping with the period, but with a modern touch of great care and charm. Each room is different, offering a refreshing change from the conformity of large hotel chains. Besides the inclusive continental breakfast, light lunches and snacks are available during the day in the Victorian-style tearoom. Two drawbacks: it is unlicensed, and some rooms lack private bathrooms.

Sebel Town House
23 Elizabeth Bay Rd., Sydney, NSW, 2011 ☎ *358 3244* IDD ☎ *20067* ℗ *357 1926. Map 7D6* ⫼ *165 rms* ⚗ ⫤ ⚗ AE ⬦ ⬤ VISA
Location: On a quiet street in Elizabeth Bay, a few kilometres from the city and a stone's throw from Kings Cross. This hotel has fine views of the yachting basin, and is appreciated by celebrity visitors for its discretion and polished efficiency. The rooms are decorated with taste, and the suites, one of which was designed by Hardy Amies, are the height of simple elegance. The **Encore** restaurant claims to be able to prepare whatever a guest desires.
ᦕ ⇌ ▣ ⵙ ☞ ⵚ ♨

Sheraton Potts Point ⚘
*40 Macleay St., Potts Point, NSW,
2011* ☎ *358 1955* ⊙ *21174. Map
7D5* ▐▌▌ *60 rms* ⚊ ⚌ AE ⊕ ⊚
VISA

*Location: In a leafy, pleasant part of
Kings Cross, towards Elizabeth Bay,
within 2km (1 mile) of the city.* There
are one or two eccentric features
about this small hotel with views of
the bay. One is a computer-
controlled robot entertainer named
Jo Jo (evidently modelled after Ray
Charles), who plays the piano, talks
and sings in the bar of the Cajun-
Creole restaurant. Perhaps
Australia's increasing number of
Japanese visitors is the reason why
the hotel's **Brass Monkey Club** is
run along the lines of a Tokyo club,
where patrons sing as well as dance.
▣ ☿

Sheraton Wentworth
*61–101 Phillip St., Sydney, NSW,
2000* ☎ *230 0700* ▐▌▌ ⊙ *21227*
⊗ *227 9133. Map 6C3* ▐▌▌ *443 rms*
⚌ ⚌ AE ⊕ ⊚ VISA

*Location: In the heart of the central
business district.* Another of Sydney's
old-established hotels, taken over by
an international chain. It obviously
has the business clientele in mind,
with its facilities for large
conferences. The rooms have been
given the full Sheraton treatment,
while still retaining the Wentworth's
unusual Art Deco curved bathrooms
with marble floors. The main
Garden Court restaurant overlooks
an attractive willow tree garden, and
seafood is its speciality.
♿ ⇌ ▣ ☿ ⚘

Southern Cross
*Corner of Elizabeth St. and
Goulburn St., Sydney, NSW, 2000*
☎ *20987* ▐▌▌ ⊙ *26324* ⊗ *211
1806. Map 6E3* ▐▌▌ *176 rms* ⚊ ⚌
⚏ AE ⊕ ⊚ VISA

*Location: In the city centre, close to
Chinatown and the Entertainment
Centre.* Opened in 1983, having been
tastefully converted from an old city
office block, the Southern Cross has
gained a reputation for fine service.
An unusual feature is the **Cartoon
Bar** where the pick of Australian
satirical humour is displayed.
♿ ⇌ ▣ ☿ ⚊ ⚘

Sydney Boulevard
*90 William St., Sydney, NSW,
2011* ☎ *357 2277* ▐▌▌ ⊙ *24350*
⊗ *356 3786. Map 7D4* ▐▌▌ *300 rms*
⚊ ⚌ ⚏ AE ⊕ ⊚ VISA

*Location: Between the city and Kings
Cross.* The Australian flagship of the
Southern Pacific Hotel group, this is
one of Sydney's best hotels, with a
young and courteous staff. It is hard
to imagine that anyone would want to
leave the *à la carte* restaurant on the
25th floor, as the outlook is
genuinely breathtaking, giving an
uninterrupted bird's-eye-view of
Hyde Park and the harbour; the food
is highly regarded too, having won
local awards. The **Williams** supper
club offers *à la carte* dining as well as
a disco.
⇌ ▣ ☿ ⚊ ⚊ ⚘

Wynyard TraveLodge
7–9 York St., Sydney, NSW, 2000
☎ *20254* ▐▌▌ ⊙ *26690* ⊗ *290
9888. Map 6C2* ▐▌ *205 rms* ⚊ ⚌
⚏ AE ⊕ ⊚ VISA

*Location: In the heart of the city, close
to the main shops, and a few mins' walk
from the historic Rocks area and
Circular Quay.* An informal, cheerful
atmosphere, if sometimes a bit
flurried because of its popularity
with group tours. Features include a
club lounge, exclusive to guests and
friends; the **Kache** international
restaurant on the 22nd floor
overlooking the city and harbour;
and the more informal **Cafe on York**,
good for observing Sydney folk.
▣ ☿ ⚘

Zebra Hyde Park Motel ⚘
*271 Elizabeth St., Sydney, NSW,
2000* ☎ *264 6001* ▐▌▌ ⊙ *25304.
Map 6E3* ▐▌ *86 rms* ⚊ ⚌ AE ⊕
⊚ VISA

*Location: Opposite Hyde Park, close to
Sydney's shopping and business centre.*
Owned by the Return Services
League, an association of former
members of the armed forces, this
hotel offers reductions to ex-
servicemen. Nearly every room,
prettily furnished in soft pastel
shades, has a balcony overlooking the
park. Bathrooms are only fitted with
showers, but the kitchens are fully
equipped.
▣

Eating out in Sydney
Given that little more than a decade ago this was considered one of
the world's great culinary deserts, Sydney now has an astonishing
choice of restaurants. Indeed, food has been one of the city's major
growth industries, stimulated by immigrant arrivals since World
War II, bringing with them the cuisines of not only France, Italy

and Greece, but those too of Lebanon, Vietnam, Malaysia and Thailand. The Australian palate has in the process been greatly educated.

Prices are mostly extremely reasonable, particularly by comparison with other service industries, and the overall standard is highly respectable – as it should be, given the quality of the available ingredients. The bounty of the sea, for example, is one of NSW's blessings.

Visitors from Melbourne tend to be a bit sniffy about Sydney food. Local gourmets concede that Victoria might have more top-class restaurants, but then, they say chauvinistically, Melbourne has precious little else to cheer about, and the quality here is still high enough to be remarked upon by most international visitors. Sydney oysters are not famous for nothing.

The "ethnic" restaurants – Vietnamese and Thai, for example – often offer the best value. Many of these places are BYO licensed establishments to which you are invited to take your own liquor.

Balkan II ♣
215 Oxford St., Darlinghurst
☎ *331 7670. Map 7F5* ■ □ AE
⊕ ⊕ ▥ *Last orders 11pm.*
Closed Mon. BYO license.
A lively, crowded, fun place which, although a bit noisy, is nevertheless one of the best-value eateries in town. A large variety of charcoal grills is served, with fish being a particular favourite (try the grilled calamari with thick garlic sauce). A couple of doors down is the original **Balkan**, which only differs in not serving fish dishes.

Bangkok
234 Crown St., Darlinghurst
☎ *33 4804. Map 7E4* ■ □ AE
⊕ ⊕ ▥ *Last orders 9.30pm.*
Closed Sun, Mon, dinner Wed-Fri.
Thai food, sometimes subtle and aromatic, sometimes fiery and robust, is at last being given the recognition it is due. Many Thai restaurants in Australia follow a routine yet successful formula, and this is one of the best – certainly in Sydney.

Barrenjoey House
1108 Barrenjoey Rd., Palm Beach
☎ *919 4001* ■ □ ■ ≠ AE ⊕
▥ *Last orders 9.30pm. Closed lunch Dec-Feb Mon-Fri, Mar-Nov Mon-Thurs.*
What could be more pleasant than a leisurely drive along the N coast of Sydney, stopping off for a dip along the way, and ending up at a first-class restaurant for a splendid *al fresco* lunch? This is what makes the French-influenced Barrenjoey so popular. The food is highly recommended, and a booking is essential if you want to join the weekend clientele.

Bayswater Brasserie ♣
32 Bayswater Rd., Kings Cross
☎ *357 2749. Map 7D5* ■ □ ■
⊕ ⊕ ▥ *Last orders 11.15pm.*
This is one of Sydney's smartest eating places, and though fashions change so rapidly among the local socialites that it might be out of date next year, the food here is good enough to ensure that it will continue to satisfy its patrons. Careful attention to detail and a real concern for food are its strongest virtues. The decor, aimed at reproducing a French atmosphere, might strike some as too studied, but you can be assured of a good night out.

Berowra Waters Inn
Berowra Waters, 35km (21 miles)
N ☎ *456 1027* ■■■ ■■ ≠ ∈ AE
⊕ ⊕ ▥ *Closed Mon-Thurs.*
A ferry-ride across the Berowra Creek, an inlet of the Hawkesbury River N of Sydney, will bring you to what a number of Sydney folk swear is the finest restaurant in Australia. This may or may not be too grand a claim, but it is by common consent the best around Sydney. The Berowra serves French cuisine and changes its set menu every day. The price is intimidating by Sydney standards, as is the distance of the drive home afterwards, but there is never a shortage of eager patrons, and booking in advance is necessary.

Chez Oz
23 Craigend St., Darlinghurst
☎ *332 4866. Map 7E5* ■ □ AE
⊕ ⊕ ▥ *Last orders 9.45pm.*
Closed Sat lunch, Sun.
Sydney's most successful new restaurant is bound to spawn a host of imitators, but at the time of writing it has no rival for originality. This unashamedly Antipodean

establishment was actually started by a family from Melbourne, who in the process may have made a point about restaurant standards in the two cities. The decor and exuberantly modern style of the place are distinctive, and, of course, the food – innovative local – is good too.

Claude's
10 Oxford St., Woollahra ☎ *331 2325. Map 5C5* ▥▥ ■▬ ▬▬ *Last orders 8.30pm. Closed Sun, Mon.*
For a gastronomic treat you can't do better in Sydney. The monthly Festival de la Fine Bouche draws out gourmets who have otherwise given up on eating out, and the milk-fed goat sent the competition back to the cutting-board – not for the first time. Don't bother unless you have booked.

Desaru
28 Falcon St., Crows Nest, North Sydney ☎ *438 4331. Map 5C4* ▯▯ ▭▭ ■ ▾ ▣ ⊕ ⊛ ▨ *Last orders 10pm. Closed Sat lunch, Sun.*
The food here is a satisfying blend of Southeast Asian styles – Nonya, Indonesian, Thai, Malaysian and South Indian. Should you have any difficulty in choosing, the friendly and good-humoured staff will lead you in the right direction.

Doyle's On the Beach
11 Marine Parade, Watsons Bay ☎ *337 2007. Map 5C5* ▥▥ ▭▭ ▾ ▬ ◁ ⊛ ▨ *Last orders 9.15pm.*
A Sydney institution, Doyle's enormous popularity might leave some visitors a bit perplexed. But oysters and very fresh fish and chips are a firm favourite with Australians, and the Doyle family were frying fish long before anyone else here. Although there may now be more restaurants of this kind, few can match the location.

Harpoon Harry's
Macquarie Hotel, 42 Wentworth Ave. ☎ *264 9089. Map 6E3* ▥▥ ▭▭ ▬ ▾ ▣ ⊕ ⊛ ▨ *Last orders 10pm. Closed Sat lunch, Sun.*
A worthy antidote to those who think that *Doyle's* is the only restaurant in town that serves fish fresh and simply prepared fish dishes. In thoroughly civilized surroundings, despite the unprepossessing exterior, the staff quietly gets on with the business of satisfying a small but loyal clientele of diners. You can expect to find starched, white tablecloths, gleaming cutlery and friendly and efficient service.

Imperial Peking Harbourside
15 Circular Quay, West, The Rocks ☎ *27 7073. Map 6B3* ▥▥ ▭▭ ▬■ ◁ ▣ ⊕ ⊛ ▨ *Last orders 10.15pm.*
Set in an old restored warehouse in the historic Rocks area, the Imperial Peking not only boasts fine views of the harbour but some very superior, and expensive, food, and is, by general consent, Sydney's best Chinese restaurant. It specializes in seafood dishes of perfect freshness, in the admirable Chinese tradition, and has dinner "on the fin" in tanks waiting for a customer. This is one of four Imperial Peking restaurants in Sydney, and there's another in Manly.

Kim Van
147 Glebe Point Rd., Glebe ☎ *660 5252. Map 5C4* ▯▯ ▭▭ *Closed lunch, Tues.*
Since Sydney's top restaurant critic nominated this unpretentious, basic, out-of-the-way little restaurant as the best Vietnamese in town, the demand for a table has increased dramatically. But the food is still good and cheap.

Marigold ✿
299–305 Sussex St. ☎ *264 6744. Map 6E2* ▯▯ ▭▭ ▬■ ▾ ▣ ⊕ ⊛ ▨ *Last orders 11pm.*
Chinese diners are much in evidence here, particularly at lunchtime when the speciality of the house is *yum cha*, a meal consisting of a dazzling variety of savoury oddments – dough and pastry with delicious fillings, which come in a seemingly endless procession of little bamboo baskets. The rest of the menu is also of a high standard.

Mayur
MLC Centre, 19 Martin Pl. ☎ *235 2361. Map 6D3* ▥▥ ▭▭ ▣ ⊕ ⊛ ▨ *Last orders 9.30pm. Closed Sat lunch, Sun.*
Considering how Sydney diners have taken to exotic fare, it is perhaps surprising that there are not more Indian restaurants in the city. However, there are new signs that they are on the increase, and the Mayur is a distinguished representative of what may be the taste of things to come.

Mixing Pot ✿
178 St Johns Rd., Glebe ☎ *660 7449. Map 5C4* ▥▥ ▭▭ ▣ ⊕ ⊛ ▨ *Last orders 8.30pm. Closed Sat lunch, Sun, hols. BYO license.*
Outdoor dining adds to the informal atmosphere of this old Italian

favourite situated in the Glebe area (which has a remarkable number of restaurants). There are daily specials.

Puligny's ♥
240 Parramatta Rd., Neutral Bay, North Sydney ☎ *908 2552. Map 5C4* ▥ ◻ ◉ ᵛᴵˢᴬ *Last orders 9pm. Closed Sat lunch, Sun, Mon, Tues-Thurs lunch.*
There are few more elegant establishments than this on the lower N shore. As the name suggests, the cuisine is French, and this is an excellent place to taste refined food, choose from a well-selected wine list and enjoy efficient service.

La Rustica ♥
435 Parramatta Rd., Leichardt ☎ *569 5824. Map 5C4* ◻ ◻ ᴬᴱ ◉ ◉ ᵛᴵˢᴬ *Last orders 10pm. Closed Sun.*
This Italian restaurant is situated a little out of town, in the heart of the Italian community. The food is simple, hearty fare, and as the restaurant is well patronized, seating can be tight when things get busy, as they often do – so book ahead.

Suntory
529 Kent St. ☎ *267 2900. Map 6E2* ▥ ◻ ▬ ▬ ⩑ ▬ ⇇ ᴬᴱ ◉ ◉ ᵛᴵˢᴬ *Last orders 10pm. Closed Sun, hols.*
This is the best Japanese restaurant in Sydney, and also among the most expensive of any type. It is full of

businessmen clinching big deals – and Japanese, to whom it may actually seem cheap.

Taylor's ♥
203–205 Albion St., Surry Hills ☎ *33 5100. Map 7F4* ▥ ◻ ▬ ᴬᴱ ◉ ◉ ᵛᴵˢᴬ *Last orders 9.45pm. Closed Sun, Mon, Fri dinner.*
What sounds like a Devonshire tearoom is actually a superb North Italian restaurant. It gets top marks for the setting, as well as the food.

Villani's
143 Devonshire St., Surry Hills ☎ *698 9681. Map 5C4* ◻ ◻ ᴬᴱ ◉ *Closed Sat lunch, Sun, Mon.*
A good place to eat in an unexciting part of town. There isn't much to keep the average tourist around Central station, but if you find yourself in the area and looking for lunch you could do a lot worse than treat yourself to the international menu here. Lunch specials are available daily.

The Wharf ♥
Pier 4, Hickson Rd., Walsh Bay ☎ *250 1761. Map 6B2* ◻ ◻ ⵆ ⇇ ◉ ᵛᴵˢᴬ *Last orders 11pm. Closed Sun.*
It is difficult to imagine any better value in Sydney than lunch at The Wharf. It is a bit out-of-the-way, but quite accessible for those who have been walking in The Rocks in the morning.

Nightlife and the arts
There is no need ever to be bored in Sydney. If by day it is the sheer beauty of the place that holds the attention, at night the energy and determination with which her inhabitants set about letting off steam are both remarkable and infectious.

The best spot-guide to what is happening in the entertainment world is the *Sydney Morning Herald* newspaper. There is a comprehensive guide every day, and the Fri edition has a pull-out section called *Metro* outlining weekend attractions. The *Herald* also has a sharp nose for which nightclub is the current hot spot. Local clubbers are as fickle as their fellows anywhere, and the favourites at the time of writing, the *Hip Hop Club* and *Kinselas*, may have been buried by the time this appears.

Wit and humour go down best, and there are enough club and pub cabarets featuring stand-up comics for a city twice the size. The standard tends to be high too, because the bad or mediocre get massacred.

Opera and theatre both have strong followings. The *Australian Opera* is a touring company, but spends most of the time at its incomparable local headquarters. While theatre is variable as well as varied, *Sydney Theatre Company* productions can be relied upon. But for a city of well over 3 million people, with a conservatorium of its own, it is surprising that there is not more, and better, classical music.

Biggest crowd-puller of all is the pub rock scene, which has almost 100 bands (mainly part-timers) working the local circuit. The band names are frequently more inventive than the music, but everyone seems to have fun.

Australian Opera

Opera House, Bennelong Point.
☎ *information 250 7111,*
bookings 20525. Map 6B3 ♈ Ⓐ
Ⓐ Ⓥ

The national company is in residence at the Opera House twice a year, the summer season generally running from Jan-Feb and the winter season from June-Oct. Opera and Australia go together like oysters and lemon, and the country has a tradition of producing great sopranos, from Melba to Sutherland. Dame Joan still makes the occasional appearance here, though you are more likely to see performances featuring robust, young singers giving it their all. Despite administrative problems, the company has had a splendid run of successes in recent seasons.

The Basement

29 Reiby Pl., Circular Quay ☎ *27 9727. Map 6B3* ♈ Ⓙ ⇌ Ⓐ Ⓔ
Ⓒ Ⓥ *Open Mon-Sat 7pm-3am.*

A long-established jazz club, where the music is good and the atmosphere informal.

Bourbon & Beefsteak

24 Darlinghurst Rd., Kings Cross
☎ *358 1144. Map 7D5* ♈ ⇌ Ⓐ
Ⓒ Ⓒ Ⓥ *Open 24hrs.*

A bar-cum-eatery renowned among Sydney's insomniacs and bitter-enders, who crowd here into the wee small hours. This is the place to come when the party has gone on until dawn and you are looking for somewhere to have a last bottle of wine with a huge cooked breakfast.

Don Burrows Supper Club

Regent Hotel, 199 George St.
☎ *238 0000. Map 6B3* ♈ Ⓙ
≣ Ⓐ Ⓒ Ⓒ Ⓥ *Open Mon-Fri 6pm-1.30am, Sat, Sun 9pm-2.30am.*

A smart spot for the best in jazz. The club is part of the *Regent* (see *Hotels*), generally regarded as the city's finest hotel, and is somewhere to enjoy a big night out. Light meals are also available.

Hip Hop Club

11 Oxford St., Paddington ☎ *332 2568. Map 6E3* ♈ Ⓒ Ⓙ ≣ Ⓐ
Ⓒ Ⓒ Ⓥ *Open 7pm-3.30am.*

This lively, fun club has comedy acts as well as live music, ranging from Tamla to rock.

Jamison Street

Jamison St. ☎ *251 1480. Map 6C2* ♈ Ⓒ Ⓙ ⇌ ≣ Ⓐ Ⓒ Ⓒ Ⓥ
Open Tues-Sat 9pm-3am.

This disco-and-nightclub is part of the same establishment as the **Comedy Store**, the established stand-up comic club. Prices for dinner and a show tend toward the expensive.

Juliana's

Hilton Hotel, 259 Pitt St. ☎ *266 0610. Map 6D3* ♈ Ⓒ Ⓙ ⇌
Ⓒ Ⓒ Ⓥ *Open Tues-Sat 9pm-2.45pm.*

Another club-within-a-hotel offering a stylish night out. Top entertainment, including international names, perform at the dinner show, followed by a late disco. Inevitably bookings are essential.

Kinselas

383 Bourke St., Darlinghurst
☎ *331 3100. Map 7E4* Ⓒ Ⓙ ⇌
≣ Ⓐ Ⓒ Ⓒ Ⓥ *Open 6pm-midnight.*

Perhaps it is the idea of being entertained in what used to be a funeral parlour that makes Kinselas so fashionable. Sydney's most far-in nightspot is where you can watch the city at play, and the cabaret is usually good too.

Kirribilli Pub Theatre

Broughton St., Milson's Point
☎ *560 5093. Map 5C4* ♈ *Open Thurs-Sat from 8pm.*

Comedy spot where the acts stand up and take on the house. Anarchic and offbeat humour.

Selina's

Coogee Bay Hotel, 253 Coogee Bay Rd. ☎ *665 0000. Map 5D5* ♈
Open Fri, Sat 8pm-2am.

One of the liveliest and steamiest pub-rock spots.

Sydney Dance Company

Pier Four, Walsh Bay ☎ *221 4811. Map 6A2.*

This innovative and dynamic young ensemble, who perform both in the modern and classical style, have changed the face of dance in Australia, and have also made an impact abroad. When the company is not touring, its main theatre is at the Opera House.

Sydney Theatre Company
Wharf Theatre, Hickson Rd.,
Millers Point ☎ *250 1777.* Map
6B2 🍸 🚃 💳 💳
The premier drama company divides
its times between two theatres. The
Opera House theatre is used for the
big productions with popular appeal,
and the Wharf (the STC's residential

base) is used for staging new or
experimental work. It is an eclectic
outfit, and in recent seasons has
mounted highly creditable
productions ranging from
Restoration comedy and Russian
classics, to Stoppard and "nouveau
Australian". The **Wharf** restaurant is
also highly recommended.

Shopping
If money is no object, there isn't much that can't be bought in
Sydney, where only food is particularly cheap. But there are
bargains to be had at duty-free stores that operate in the city and
are a great bonus for tourists.

For quality goods there are the big stores and shopping arcades
in an area roughly bordered by Hunter St., Park St., George St.
and Phillip St. Just out of the centre are the specialist shops and
boutiques of Paddington and Double Bay, as well as those farther
N along Military Rd. on the Lower North Shore. However, the
shops mentioned below are mainly located in the city centre.

Normal shopping hours are Mon-Fri 9am-5pm (with late
opening on Thurs until 9pm) and Sat 9am-noon (department
stores until 4pm).

Aboriginal art
Aboriginal artifacts must be the most original items available to the
shopper in Australia, and if your purchase is old and has a sacred
relevance it is best to get the vendor to inquire about an export
permit.

Aboriginal Art Centre Dreamtime Gallery
Argyle Arts Centre, 18 Argyle St.,
The Rocks ☎ *27 1380.* Map *6B2*
💳 💳 💳 💳
Bark paintings, modern acrylic dot
paintings, baskets and numerous
other items are on sale here, ranging
dramatically in price. There is
another branch (7 *Walker Lane,*

Paddington) that concentrates on
older artifacts.

Aboriginal Artists Gallery
Civic House, 477 Kent St. ☎ *261*
2929. Map *6D2* 💳 💳 💳 💳
This knowledgeable gallery has
interesting exhibitions, from fabric
designs to modern paintings, as well
as various artifacts and bark paintings.

Antiques
The largest concentration of antique shops in Sydney is along
Queen St., Woollahra, just off Oxford St. But there are a number
of large antique centres around the city. These are the two largest.

Sydney Antique Centre
531 South Dowling St., Surry
Hills ☎ *33 3244* 💳 💳 💳 💳 💳
There are about 50 stalls in this large
converted warehouse and basement,
covering a wide range of mainly
Victorian furniture, and objects
ranging from large, cedar tables to
silver sauceboats. A coffee shop
serves light refreshments.

Woollahra Galleries
160 Oxford St., Woollahra ☎ *32*
9947. Map *5C5* 💳 💳 💳 💳
These galleries extend over three
floors, with a small restaurant in the
basement. As with other Australian
antique markets, most stalls are
unattended: prospective buyers
inquire at a central desk near the
entrance.

Australiana
Most department stores and shopping centres have the usual
koalas and T-shirts and frightfully tacky cheap bits and pieces, but

the *Australian Museum Gift Shop* has a more novel selection. There are also many craft centres, like the **Argyle Arts Centre** and others in The Rocks, that offer something different.

Australian Museum Gift Shop
Corner of William St. and College St. Map 6D3 ⟨⟩ ▉ AE CO VISA
Finger- and glove-puppets of Australian birds and animals; unusual, locally-made jewellery; pieces of Australian rock; and lots of books on Australian fauna and flora.

Coo-ee
98 Oxford St., Paddington ☎ 332 1544. Map 7F5 AE CO VISA
An emporium of interesting Australian crafts, including fabrics made by the Tiwi Aboriginal group from islands off the coast, near Darwin.

Department stores
The department store is a great Australian tradition – which produced some striking 1920s-30s architecture, such as the *Grace Brothers* store in The Broadway. The city branch of *David Jones* claims to be the finest department store in the world.

David Jones
Corner of Market St. and Elizabeth St., and corner of Market St. and Castlereagh St. ☎ 266 5544. Map 6D3 ⟨⟩ ▉ AE CO VISA
Australia's answer to Harrods (or any other of the world's great stores), the lavishly decorated, recently renovated Elizabeth St. store specializes in female fashions. Its less

glamorous Castlereagh store next door sells men's attire.

Grace Brothers
436 George St. ☎ 238 9111. Map 6D3 ▉ CO VISA
The staff in Grace Bros. stores is what helps to make it a success – they are always cheerful, friendly and most obliging. As you would expect, this is the chain's showpiece.

Duty-free shops
An opportunity to do your duty-free shopping while looking around for the best deal. Anyone with an air ticket out of the country can purchase at the dozens of such establishments, specializing in electronic and photographic equipment. **Downtown Duty Free** (*84 Pitt St.* ☎ 232 2566, map 6C3 AE CO CO VISA) is recommended for camera equipment, and at **Sterling Nicholas Duty Free** (*105 Pitt St.* ☎ 33 3251, map 6C3 AE CO CO VISA) they promise to match the price of any other duty-free store.

Markets
Sydney's markets are hardly in the same league as its department stores, but they are pleasant enough places to while away a sunny afternoon.

Balmain Market
Corner of Darling St. and Curtis Rd., Balmain. Map 5C4 ▉
An untidy mixture of secondhand junk and the odd real antique, but it can be good fun. Open Sat only.

Paddington Village Church Bazaar
Village Church, Oxford St., Paddington. Map 5C4.
In fashionable Paddington (and near

too to Woollahra): a colourful, lively collection of the innovative creations of young designers, together with secondhand clothes. Open on Sat only.

Paddy's Market
Hay Street, Haymarket. Map 6E3.
There is a fruit and vegetable section as well as large number of stalls selling cheap clothes, shoes, toys and other items. Open Sat, Sun.

Shopping arcades
There are numerous centres crammed with expensive boutiques. A selection of the better ones is listed below.

Birkenhead Point
Cary St., Drummoyne ☎ 81 3922.
Map 5C4 🚹 💻 ✱
This complex is situated on a
peninsula overlooking the harbour,
just a short drive out of the city, and
is home for what is thought to be the
largest permanent exhibition of Lego
outside Denmark.

Centrepoint
Corner of Market St. and Pitt St.
☎ 231 6222. *Map 6D3* 🚹 💻
Close to both the *Grace Brothers*
and *David Jones* department stores,
this centre has four levels of nearly
200 shops, with the accent on
modernity.

MLC Centre
*Corner of King St. and Castlereagh
St.* ☎ 231 6411. *Map 6D3* 🚹 💻
The centre sells lots of imported
wares, and also houses one of
Sydney's finest Indian restaurants,
the *Mayur* (see *Restaurants*).

Queen Victoria Building
455 George St. ☎ 29 1172. *Map
6D3* 🚹 💻 AE CB VISA
Erected to celebrate the jubilee of
Queen Victoria in 1893, this truly
glorious Victorian edifice was
actually threatened with demolition
in the 1950s. Now restored, it houses
over 200 shops, from the stylish
Bunda Fine Antiques to the
colourful clothes of Australian
designer Jenny Kee. Fast food
available 24hrs.

Strand Arcade
*George St., between King St. and
Market St.* *Map 6D3* 💻
Until the restoration of the *Queen
Victoria Building*, this arcade was
considered to be the city's most
elegant. Carefully reconstructed after
a fire some years ago, it now
accommodates some of Sydney's top
clothes designers, and a delightful
little shop that specializes in
buttons.

Sydney environs
A number of Sydney's most striking attractions are outside the city
proper. The following is a selection of places that, generally
speaking, are close enough to Sydney to be quite easily
encompassed inside a day. Combinations are possible. In a day w
of the city you could see both *Parramatta* and *Windsor*. A tour of
the *Hawkesbury River* could be turned into a full-blown
excursion. In all cases, frankly, a car is necessary.

Captain Cook's Landing Place Park
*Captain Cook Drive, Kurnell, about 45km (28 miles) s of
Sydney* ☎ 668 9923. *Map 5E5* 🚗 ➤ *Open 7.30am-7pm,
museum 10.30am-4.30pm. Getting there: best by car; or
slowly, by train to Cronulla, then bus to Kurnell.*
This historical site at Kurnell in Botany Bay tends to be
overlooked, by locals as well as foreigners, possibly because it is a
bit out of the way. This should not deter you, for despite industrial
development, which blemishes the bay, the Landing Place Park is
a pleasant and well-kept spot. It is within a ½hr's drive of the city,
but allow longer if travelling by public transport. Wood is
provided for barbecuing, and you can picnic and swim within sight
of the spot where Cook first set foot on the Great South Land in
1770.
    The small **museum** is a bonus attraction, illuminating the
voyage of the *Endeavour*, and the lives of Cook and others who
accompanied him in his discoveries.

Gosford
*85km (52 miles) N of Sydney. Getting there: by car, via
Route 1.*
Scenic and historic interest are the basis for this full-day excursion
to the Brisbane Water region. Gosford itself has little to draw the
visitor, but is a convenient centre for the tour.
    After crossing the *Harbour Bridge* (see *Sights*) northbound,
follow signs to the Pacific Highway and Hornsby. Join the
Sydney-Newcastle tollway, which offers panoramic views of the

Australian bush *en route* to Gosford.

Old Sydney Town (*Pacific Hwy, Somersby* ☎ *(043) 40 1104* ▨ *open Wed-Sun 10am-5pm*), which is signposted from the first Gosford turn-off, is a living-theatre reconstruction of the early days of the penal colony, featuring Redcoats and convicts, floggings and duels, and tall-masted ships in the harbour. There are picnic facilities and a restaurant.

Just N of Gosford on Route 83 is **Eric Worrell's Reptile Park** (☎ *(043) 28 4311* ▨ *open 10am-6pm*), which has platypuses as well as deadly taipans, pythons and crocodiles. (Check times of daily "milking" of venomous snakes.)

Back in Gosford (and before heading for the beach) you might call in at **Henry Kendall Cottage** (*off Brisbane Water Drive* ☎ *(043) 25 2270* ▨ *open Wed and weekends 10am-4pm*), a museum dedicated to a 19thC Australian poet. Beaches within easy reach of Gosford include **Forresters** (*about 20km (12 miles)* N), **Terrigal** and **Avoca** (*about 16km (10 miles)* W).

Within 5km (3 miles) of Gosford, off Route 83 back to Sydney, **Brisbane Waters National Park** (☎ *(043) 24 4911* ▨ *open sunrise-sunset*) offers views, walking and picnicking.

▭ On the way back to the city, you can visit one of Australia's best restaurants, the **Berowra Waters Inn** (see *Restaurants*).

Hawkesbury River

50km (31 miles) N of Sydney. Getting there: by car, via Route 1.

The first tentative steps of exploration in NSW were up the Hawkesbury River, and some of the earliest settlements were established along its banks. The river remains a scenic and historic highway to the interior, which can be seen by car, or at greater leisure by renting a cabin cruiser.

The following is a suggested one-day excursion around the mouth of the river. An itinerary for a tour of the historic towns on the upper reaches will be found under *Windsor*.

Ku-ring-gai Chase National Park, on the banks of the Hawkesbury, is a convenient starting point. Cross the *Harbour Bridge* (see *Sights*) northbound, following Route 1 (the Pacific Hwy) to Hornsby and Mt. Colah, the entrance to the park. Ku-ring-gai has numerous walking trails, along with good picnic and barbecue sites. Recommended: **Cottage Point**, which is situated on the river; more information is available from the National Parks office (☎ *457 9853*) at the entrance.

Palm Beach is easily reachable from Ku-ring-gai Chase. To get there, follow the main road in the park, McCarr's Creek Rd., eastwards until it joins the Barrenjoey Rd. Turn left (N) for Palm Beach, a fine stretch of beach with excellent surfing. Nude bathing is permitted at the northern end.

Palm Beach lies at the edge of the Hawkesbury. From here ferries ply around the coves and inlets at the river mouth. An hourly service, starting at 9am, runs around one of the largest of these coves, the **Pittwater**, from the Public Wharf at **Pittwater Park** (☎ *918 2747*). It calls at a number of pleasantly sheltered beaches that are actually in the Ku-ring-gai park, including the **Basin** (camping available) and **Great Mackerel Beach**, which is especially suitable for families. Ferries depart from the same wharf for **Patonga**, on the northern bank of the Hawkesbury, at 9am, 11am and 3.45pm.

More extensive river trips can be made by renting cabin cruisers and houseboats. This is an option well worth considering, as the

Hawkesbury is not only a great river passing through some majestic scenery, but the most historic of Australia's waterways. The first governor, Arthur Phillip, explored it in 1789. 20yrs later, Governor Lachlan Macquarie compared the Hawkesbury with the Thames, and saw it as a civilizing highway into the interior.

No sailing licence is required for renting a boat. Three days is quite enough for a leisurely trip as far as *Windsor*, about 140kms (88 miles) upstream. Standard equipment on cabin cruisers includes cooker, refrigerator, cutlery, crockery, 2-way radio and depth sounder. Details from **Halvorsen Boats** (☎ 457 9011). Houseboats are slightly cheaper, from **Able Hawkesbury River Houseboats** (☎ (045) 66 4299).

Captain Cook Cruises (☎ 27 4548 ☻ 72316) has 4-night trips up the river on the cruise vessel *Lady Hawkesbury*. One-day cruises run downstream from Windsor daily: contact **Windsor River Cruises** (☎ 621 4154).

Koala Park
84 Castle Hill Rd., West Penant Hills, 26km (16 miles) w of Sydney ☎ 84 3141. Map 4A2 🚉 💺 ✱ ☛ *Open 9am-5pm. Getting there: by bus, Ansett Pioneer run full-day tours including the Blue Mountains* ☎ 268 1881.
The continent's most cuddly inhabitants are a favourite with visitors. There are about 30 of them in 4ha (10 acres) or so of wildlife park, and feedings, with commentary by a member of staff, are held four times daily. The park also has other indigenous animals – kangaroos, wallabies, wombats and dingoes – and children can wander among the animals and feed them. *Waratah Park Animal Reserve* is a similar and in some respects better establishment, but the koala section here offers closer contact. But neither of these parks is close to the city or easily accessible by public transport.

Ku-ring-gai Chase National Park ★
Ku-ring-gai Chase Rd., Mt. Colah, 40km (24 miles) n of Sydney ☎ 457 9853. Map 4A3 🚉 ☛ ✖ *Open sunrise-sunset. Getting there: by car, follow Route 1 across the Harbour Bridge to Hornsby and Mt. Colah.*
This tract of splendid NSW bush, strung out along the banks and inlets of the *Hawkesbury River*, is the ideal place to take a picnic or barbecue food, and combine with a visit to *Waratah Park Animal Reserve*.

There are numerous animals in Ku-ring-gai too, including goanna lizards (an Aboriginal delicacy), koalas and possums. **Cottage Point** is an attactive spot for a picnic, and for launching off on a bush walk, either up the granite hills or following one of the creeks that flow into the river. More information on walks can be obtained from the National Parks office at the entrance, and they can give directions to Aboriginal rock engravings.

Palm Beach ★
50km (31 miles) n of Sydney ☛ ✖ *Getting there: by car, take the Harbour Bridge n, then follow Route 14 for Mosman, Manly, Dee Why, Narrabeen and Palm Beach.*
This splendid stretch of sand, situated outside the city, makes an enjoyable and comfortable day excursion, and there are other good beaches to stop at along the way.

The main attractions of Palm Beach are its comparative quiet and the quality of its surf. There is nude bathing at the northern end, but newcomers are urged to swim only between the patrol

flags, as the rip tides here are treacherous. A ferry-ride away you
will find the safe, pleasant beaches of the **Basin** and **Great
Mackerel Beach** in *Ku-ring-gai Chase National Park* (*departures
hourly 9am-4pm from the Public Wharf, Pittwater Park* ☎ *918
2747*).

▭ Another good reason to visit Palm Beach is **Reflections** (*1075 Barrenjoey
Rd.* ☎ *919 5893* ▌▌▌▌ *open Sun lunch only*), one of NSW's best restaurants,
serving French cuisine. Booking is essential.

Parramatta
*22km (13 miles) w of Sydney. Map 4B2. Getting there: by
car, via Route 32; by train, from Central station.*
This busy extension of Sydney, having today a population of
130,900, was founded in 1790 and is the second oldest European
settlement in Australia. It has more than enough of interest to
compensate for the drive to get there, along what is arguably the
ugliest stretch of road in Australia.

It can be a confusing place to find your way around, and it is
worth stopping first at the **Tourist Bureau** (*corner of Prince Alfred
Park and Market St.* ☎ *630 3703*) for a map.

Parramatta was founded because the soil at Sydney Cove was
unsuitable for growing vegetables, and the Experiment Farm was
set up in 1798, literally to test the ground. Successful cultivation
here by an ex-convict named James Ruse established that
agriculture in the colony was viable. The **Experiment Farm
Cottage**, built in the early 19thC (*9 Ruse St.* ☎ *635 5655* ▨ *open
Tues-Thurs, Sun 10am-4pm*), is also worth a visit.

If you visit only one historic building in NSW it should be **Old
Government House** (*Parramatta Park* ☎ *635 8149* ▨ *opening
hours as Experiment Farm Cottage – see above*). It took some years to
build, spanning the rule of three governors, and was completed in
1816 by Macquarie and his able aide, Francis Greenway. It was
used as a boardinghouse and a school, before restoration started in
1909, and again in 1968. That work has now been tastefully
accomplished, and the interiors are superb, with the colonial cedar
furniture being a particular feature.

The **Elizabeth Farm House** (*Alice St.* ☎ *635 9488* ▨ *open
Tues-Sat 10.30am-4pm*) is another early colonial building, lovingly
restored.

The twin towers of **St Johns Church** have been a distinctive
feature of Parramatta since the 19thC, but the original 1804
structure has been added to.

▭ **Barnaby's** (*66 Phillip St.* ☎ *633 3777* ▌▌▐) is recommended for lunch.

Royal National Park ★
Princes Hwy, Sutherland, 36km (22 miles) s of Sydney
☎ *521 2230* ▨ ▣ ✳ ⬟ ⬳ *Open sunrise-sunset. Getting
there: by car, via Route 1, the Princes Hwy.*
An excellent spot in which to sample the pleasures of the
Australian outdoors from the comforts of Sydney not far away.
The park has one or two magnificent beaches set amid tracts of
bush. A car is necessary, and you would do well to consult the
parks official on entry, as there are numerous corners to explore.

For reasons of space, just two suggestions follow. You could
take a picnic hamper out on a weekday and follow the signs to
Wattamolla, a lovely beach sheltered by cliff surrounds.
Alternatively, stop at **Audley** on the Hacking River and rent a
rowing boat. Galahs, cockatoos and kingfishers inhabit the trees

along the banks there, and a kilometre or so upstream you should get the feeling that you are in unexplored territory; you can picnic anywhere along the bank. This is one of the most pleasant ways to spend a sunny afternoon around Sydney.

Waratah Park Animal Reserve
Namba Rd., Terrey Hills, N of Sydney ☎ *450 2377* 📷 🖥 ♿ ⚓ *Open 10am-5pm. Getting there: by car, via Route 1, N to Terrey Hills.*

Australian animals are visible at close quarters here, you can wander in enclosures and feed kangaroos and emus, and there is also a koala enclosure, which makes it a good place for the obligatory Australian holiday snap. The park is a particular favourite with local youngsters, as it is the home of a wallaby named Skippy, a sort of Down Under television version of Lassie.

Windsor
56km (35 miles) NW of Sydney. Getting there: by car, via Route 32 to Eastern Creek, then Route 61.

Windsor and its historic sister town of **Richmond** on the *Hawkesbury River* were among the first White settlements established after the founding of Sydney. Governor Macquarie clearly had the towns of England's River Thames in mind when he named them. As well as this easy one-day excursion by car, they can also be reached by river in a rented cabin cruiser (see *Hawkesbury River*). You can stop at the **Tourist Information Centre** (*Thompson Sq., Windsor* ☎ *(045) 77 2310, open 10am-4pm*) for a map. Thompson Sq. itself has some interesting Georgian buildings, such as the **Doctor's House**.

Other important buildings in Windsor include two designed by Francis Greenway, the **Court House** (*open Mon-Wed 10am-noon, weekends 11am-4pm*) and **St Matthews Church**, dating from 1817, the oldest Anglican church in Australia. The nearby graveyard is worth a visit to let the old headstones tell their tales of pioneer life. At Richmond, the cemetery at **St Peters Church** is interesting.

🍴 The **Richmond** (*315 Windsor St.* ☎ *(045) 78 3914* 💳 *open Sun lunch only*) is recommended.

New South Wales excursions

Handsome a city as Sydney is, it gives no idea of the grandeur of the Australian countryside. Because the dimensions of internal travel are so vast, a great many Australians have never travelled outside their own home state, and the visitor can find himself intimidated into confining his stay to one locale. The following excursions are designed to show that much of beauty is accessible by car within a day or two of the city. With more time, various permutations indicated in the text become possible; for greater detail these should be discussed with the appropriate Visitor Centre. It is as well to remember that though food and accommodation are in some cases as good as in Sydney, the general standard of service industries in the countryside is less exacting.

The Hunter Valley
430km (270-mile) round trip. Allow 2 days. Recommended stop: Pokolbin.

This excursion, to Australia's main wine-producing region, is

popular at weekends, so aim for midweek and book
accommodation in advance.

Cross the Harbour Bridge northbound and follow the Pacific
Hwy, Route 1. Take the Sydney-Newcastle tollway, carved out of
mountainside and offering magnificent views over *Ku-ring-gai
Chase National Park* and the *Hawkesbury River*; turn off the
tollway for *Gosford* (see *Environs* for possible side-trips to all
three), perhaps stopping at **Old Sydney Town** and following the
signs to Peats Ridge. This is the start of the scenic route N to
Cessnock, main town of the Lower Hunter Valley.

The road, formerly the convict-built Great North Rd. dating
from 1830, passes through settlements with characteristic
Aboriginal names: Kulnura, Bucketty and Yalambie. To the w lies
the McPherson State Forest, and a panorama of hills and
bushland.

Wollombi, 30km (19 miles) sw of Cessnock, is a historic village
much cherished by the National Trust. **St Michaels Church**, a
sandstone structure, was built in 1843, and **St Johns** dates from
1846. Almost every building in the village is from the last century,
including the **courthouse** (1866), now a museum, and a **post
office** (1850). It is a convenient as well as a picturesque spot for
lunch.

The lovely, pastoral country here is set against a backdrop of the
Watagan Mountains. It was once bushranger territory and also a
ceremonial meeting place of local Aboriginal tribes. Wollombi is
an Aboriginal word meaning "meeting of the waters".

Cessnock is an industrial town of little historic or architectural
interest, but stop at the **Visitor Information Centre** (*Wollombi Rd.*
☎ *(049) 90–4477*) for information (including a map) on nearby
Pokolbin (NW of Cessnock) and the vineyards of the Hunter Valley.
Besides the scenery, the local wine is what makes the region worth
visiting.

The Hunter Valley is Australia's oldest commercial wine-
producing region: the **Wyndham** estate was established as long ago
as 1828. What was once the hobby of a few gentleman growers has
become an important industry, ever since Australians and
foreigners started becoming alert, little more than a decade ago, to
the quality of the local produce. There are those who believe that
Australian wine is a fad, but consumption of the grape in NSW
itself – which in colonial times used to drown itself in rum, then
went over to beer before discovering the fruit of the vine – suggests
that it is not. At any rate, a visit to the Hunter is the way to make
up your own mind, and the process is certainly pleasant enough.

The custom here is to arm yourself with a map of the Pokolbin
region showing the location of the 30 or so wineries, and to stop at
a number of chosen establishments, where you are invited to taste
and discuss wine with informed staff. You then make your way,
carefully, back to your accommodation for a nap before dinner.
Food and drink are among the pleasures of Pokolbin, and several
recommendations are given at the end of this excursion.

The Lower Hunter has some of the country's biggest producers,
and a few small establishments that turn out wines – good whites in
particular – not available from retail outlets. The larger vineyards
include **Tyrrells Vineyard** (*Broke Rd.* ☎ *(049) 98 7509, open
Mon-Sat 8am-5pm*) and **McWilliams** (*Mt. Pleasant, Marrowbone
Rd.* ☎ *(049) 98 7505, open daily*). And among small producers
offering a limited range of excellent wines and friendly, personal
advice are **Petersons Vineyard** (*Mt. View Rd.* ☎ *(049) 90 1704,
open daily*) and **Allanmere** (*Lovedale Rd.* ☎ *(049) 30 7387, also
open daily*).

For a tour of the valley, the remainder of the day after arriving in the area from Sydney and the following morning are usually sufficient. It is pleasant countryside to see by bicycle. These can be rented at the **Trading Post** (*Broke Rd.*), though the distances would make a serious bicycle tour of the wineries a hard slog. For horse riding, inquire at the Visitor Information Centre at Cessnock.

What you do when leaving Pokolbin is a matter of choice. The following are a few options.

The Upper Hunter, centred on **Singleton** and **Muswellbrook**, is the gateway to New England, in the N of the state, which, with its green pastures, trout streams and the university town of **Armidale**, is indeed akin to the mother country. E of Armidale is some lovely, rugged country, riven by gorges, where good rainbow trout are to be caught in rivers with names like the **Styx** and the **Guy Fawkes**. Bear in mind the distances, however. Armidale is 560km (350 miles) N of Sydney, and **Tenterfield**, at the top end of the New England region, is 750km (469 miles) away. If you are coming this far, telephone the **Tourist Information Centre** at Armidale (☎ *(067) 72 8666*) for information on accommodation, fishing and any other details.

There are two other ways of making your way back from the Lower Hunter to Sydney. From Cessnock head E on Route 82 via **Kearsley**, then S to **Cooranbong**. Farther E is **Lake Macquarie**, a resort area particularly popular for windsurfing and sailing. Back on the Pacific Hwy, Route 1, Sydney is only an hour or two away and you can make a detour to beaches like **Shelley** or **Forresters**.

Another route is from Singleton, which lies on the Hunter River, S on the road through **Howes Valley** to the historical 19thC *Hawkesbury* district (see *Environs*) and the towns of **Ebenezer** (which has the oldest church in Australia, dating from 1807), *Windsor* (see *Environs*) and **Richmond**.

Peppers Guest House (*Ekerts Rd.* ☎ *(049) 98 7596* ▮▯) is a pleasant colonial-style guesthouse, tastefully kept, with good views and thoughtfully prepared food: recommended, though at weekends heavily booked. The **Brokenback Motor Lodge** (*Hermitage Rd.* ☎ *(049) 98 7777* ▮▯) has modern facilities and is both comfortable and popular. The **Pokolbin Wine Village Inn** (*Broke Rd.* ☎ *(049) 98 7600* ▮▯) is a resort suitable for families.

Clos de Corne (*Hermitage Rd.* ☎ *(049) 98 7635* ▮▮▮), recommended for French cuisine; **Casuarina** (*Hermitage Rd.* ☎ *(049) 98 7562* ▮▯); **Blaxlands** (*Broke Rd.* ☎ *(049) 98 7550* ▮▯).

The Southern Highlands
370km (230-mile) round trip. Allow 2 days. Recommended stop: at entrance to Southern Highlands. Take a bathing suit.

Leave the city driving W on the hideous Parramatta Rd. as far as Ashfield, then turn left onto the Hume Hwy. At Liverpool the industrial concentration starts to thin out, and you join the South Western Freeway, Route 31. In normal circumstances you should be in Mittagong, gateway to the Southern Highlands, in 2hrs or so.

Mittagong has numerous craft shops, but your main purpose here should be to visit the regional **Tourist Information Centre** (*Winifred West Park* ☎ *(048) 71 2888*), which can provide current advice, detailed information, and licences to fish for trout in the highlands.

Bowral, just S and adjacent to Mittagong, is a garden township of great charm. Founded in 1860, it has some attractive colonial homes but no building of major architectural distinction. For lovers of cricket, the town's most distinguished building is at **28 Glebe St.**, the home of the young Donald Bradman. This remains a private residence, and plans to build a museum to perhaps Australia's most famous son, at the **Bradman Oval** cricket ground opposite the house, have not yet born fruit. Bowral's busiest time is the annual Oct Tulip Festival.

Just 11km (7 miles) w of Bowral is the historic village of **Berrima**. This important National Trust site is the best-preserved example of an early NSW settlement, though some visitors might find its quaintness somewhat contrived. The pretty location on the banks of the Wingecarribee River was surveyed in 1830, when Berrima was envisaged as an inland city.

The major buildings are within easy walking distance of Market Place, where you can park. They include the **Courthouse** (1838), containing a surprisingly tawdry trial tableau, and two genuinely lovely country churches, **St Francis Xavier** (Catholic, 1851), built in sandstone in Gothic-revival style, and **Holy Trinity** (Anglican, 1849), which has stained-glass windows of great antiquity brought here from a church in Cornwall, England.

Other structures worth inspecting are the entrance to old **Berrima Gaol**, in which were incarcerated German prisoners of World War I, and which is still used as a training centre for young offenders, and **Bellevue House**, a home in Georgian style. Sadly, the old **Anglican rectory** is not open to the public. There is no shortage of eating places and watering holes back in the centre of town.

From Berrima drive w the 10km (6 miles) to **Moss Vale**. Here Route 48, the Illawarra Hwy, starts for the Southern Highlands proper, and it is around here that you will be looking to spend the night.

The tour now enters terrain where the interest is scenic rather than historic, for the Southern Highlands is an agglomeration of mountains, swirling mists, lakes, rivers and waterfalls. From Moss Vale take the road sw to **Exeter**, a charming village, and **Bundanoon**, an area so evocative of Scotland that the clans come here for their annual Apr gathering to toss cabers, hurl haggis and dance to the pipes.

Bundanoon is also the entrance to the **Morton National Park**, 130,000ha (320,000 acres) of startling mountain landscapes. There is a camping ground near the entrance, leading to a number of lookout points: **Echo Point** is to be recommended.

From Bundanoon, head back towards Moss Vale but turn off before the town and follow Route 79 se to the **Fitzroy Falls**, a plunge of more than 100m (330ft) in three stages over sandstone cliffs. A license obtained at the Mittagong Visitor Centre entitles the holder to fish for trout at the Fitzroy Falls reservoir.

Two options now present themselves. You can get back to Sydney by turning N for Robertson and the Illawarra Hwy (though you should try to stop at the lovely **Belmore Falls**) and thence E on Route 48 to **Wollongong** and the coast. This takes you back to Sydney in between 2 and 3hrs by a different and scenic drive.

The second option is preferable if you can spare an extra half-day and fancy a side trip to the sea. Continue from the Fitzroy Falls on Route 79 to **Kangaroo Valley**, across the picturesque 19thC **Hampden Bridge**. The **Pioneer Farm**, a reconstructed dairy farm opposite the bridge, offers interesting insights into 19thC Australian rural life.

About 10km (6 miles) farther se along Route 79, it is worth making the short detour to the lookout point of **Cambewarra** (an

Aboriginal word meaning "Smoke coming out of mountain"), which on a clear day offers a spectacular view from the edge of the highlands, an altitude of 678m (2,224ft), out to sea.

A few kilometres on join the Princes Hwy, Route 1, and turn s for **Nowra**, an undistinguished port town, and **Jervis Bay**. The bay, a Royal Australian Navy base, has a number of excellent beaches, including **Huskisson**, where you can also get a good pub lunch. After a leisurely swim here, Sydney is 190km (119 miles) N and easily reachable by dinner.

Farther s along the coast are some of arguably the best beaches in Australia, and in season you might do well to think of extending your excursion. **Ulladulla** is only 225km (140 miles) s of Sydney, and ever-popular **Bateman's Bay** is about 280km (175 miles) s. Nor are swimming and skin-diving the only attractions. In the 1930s, the American novelist Zane Grey visited the fishing centre of **Bermagui**, 380km (238 miles) s of Sydney, and his subsequent accounts of heroic tussles with giant marlin remain classics of fishing literature.

The **Milton Park Country House** (*Hordens Rd., Bowral* ☎ *(048) 61 1862* ▮▮▮) offers gracious country-estate accommodation in pastoral surroundings, though children aren't welcomed. The **Solar Springs Country Club** (*96 Osborne Ave., Bundanoon* ☎ *(048) 83 6027* ▮▮), a health retreat, provides natural foods and optional fitness activities. **Ranelagh House** (*Illawarra Hwy, Robertson* ☎ *(048) 85 1253* ▮) is a rambling, eccentric guesthouse whose shabbiness is offset by its grand highland setting; unlicensed. Or try the **Braemar Lodge** (*Hume Hwy, North Mittagong* ☎ *(048) 71 2483* ▮).

All handy for lunch in the centre of Berrima: the **Surveyor General Inn** (which, for students of trivia, is Australia's oldest continuously licensed hotel), the **Victoria Inn** and the **White Horse Inn**.

For dinner: **The Colonial Inn** (*Hume Hwy, Berrima* ☎ *(048) 77 1389* ▮▮); **Hume House** (*Hume Hwy, Mittagong* ☎ *(048) 71 1871* ▮▮).

The Blue Mountains
270km (170-mile) round trip. A long one-day excursion, or, if extended to Jenolan Caves or Windsor, recommended stop at Blackheath or nearby.

These mountains, part of the Great Dividing Range, once posed so formidable a barrier to the interior that early explorations from Sydney were by sea rather than land. In 1791 a group of convicts took to the interior believing that thither lay China, and freedom. It was not until 1813 that the range was crossed. Since then, the Blue Mountains have been a favourite Sydney escape.

Head w on Route 32 via *Parramatta* (see *Environs*) and Penrith. At **Springwood**, 74km (46 miles) w of Sydney, is the handsome **country home** of Norman Lindsay, an artist whose bacchanalian fantasies once outraged his compatriots (*open Fri-Sun 11am-5pm* ☎ *(047) 51 1067*). Today it is the house and gardens rather than the pictures that make the detour worthwhile – and there is a very pleasant tearoom here.

Your main destination is the town of **Katoomba**, 105km (66 miles) w of Sydney. Katoomba and, to the E, the neighbouring centres of **Leura** and **Wentworth Falls** are strung out over about 10km (6 miles) at the edge of the **Jamison Valley**, with spectacular views over the **Blue Mountains National Park**, the second-largest such park in the state.

In Katoomba there is a **Tourist Information Centre** (*Echo Point* ☎ *(047) 82 1833, open 9am-5pm*), which is useful for a map of the area and advice on bushwalks. This is also a good vantage point for the region's most enduring symbol, a rock formation called the **Three Sisters**.

A kilometer or so to the w is the **Scenic Skyway**, a cable car across a gorge with panoramic views, among them another formation, **Orphan Rock**. Also along the valley's edge and clearly signposted are **Sublime Point** and **Inspiration Point**, both with commanding views. (Incidentally, it is the dispersal of oil from eucalyptus forests into the atmosphere, intensifying the effect of light refraction, that makes these mountains appear so blue.)

Worth seeing are two waterfalls, the **Wentworth Falls** and **Leura Cascades**, Also at Wentworth Falls, **Yester Grange** (*Yester Rd.* ☎ *(047) 57 1110, open Fri-Sun 10am-5pm*) is a restored Victorian house of characteristic Australian design. In Leura, the landscaped gardens of **Everglades** (*Denison St.* ☎ *(047) 84 1236, open 10am-4pm*) are well kept.

If you are returning to Sydney the same day, the excursion will probably end in Katoomba. But don't leave before tea and cake at the **Paragon** (*Katoomba St.* ☎ *(047) 82 2928*), a genuine 1930s Art Deco refreshment parlour and a Blue Mountains institution. If you are staying on, however, two establishments in **Blackheath**, 10km (6 miles) NW of Katoomba, are recommended (see the end of this excursion) for truly excellent food and accommodation, if you can get a booking.

From the Blue Mountains, you could motor on the next day to the **Jenolan Caves**, by road about 75km (47 miles) SW of Katoomba. Tours of these spectacular underground limestone caves are conducted from 9.30am-5pm (☎ *(063) 59 3304*).

Even if, after returning to Route 32, you strike N 10km (6 miles) or so, instead of turning directly E for Sydney, and return to the city on Route 40 via *Windsor* (see *Environs*) and, just before it, **Richmond**, stopping in these historic Hawkesbury towns, you should still be back comfortably by the end of the second day.

☞ ⇌ Both highly recommended, for comfort and excellent French cuisine: the **Cleopatra Guest House** (*4 Cleopatra St., Blackheath* ☎ *(047) 87 8456* ▐▐▐▐), which has only five rooms, and the **Glenella Guest House** (*Govetts Leap Rd., Blackheath* ☎ *(047) 87 8352* ▐▐▐).

Alternatively, try the following: the **Carrington** (*Katoomba St., Katoomba* ☎ *(047) 82 1111* ▐▐▐), the region's most popular hotel since the turn of the century; the **Hydro Majestic** (*Great Western Hwy, Medlow Bath* ☎ *(047) 88 1002* ▐▐▐), another grand old establishment; the **Victoria & Albert Guest House** (*Station St., Mt. Victoria* ☎ *(047) 87 1241* ▐▐▐).

Specialized accommodation for disabled people is provided by the **Santa Maria Holiday Centre for Handicapped People** (*253 Great Western Hwy, Lawson* ☎ *(047) 59 1116*).

The Snowy Mountains

It can come as a surprise to discover that NSW has a winter sports region within 200km (125 miles) of surf-swept beaches. The "Snowies", as the region is known here, is unlikely ever to spark an exodus from the European Alps, but it is unique in Australia, and by common consent has certainly one resort of international standard.

The Snowy Mountains are no hop, skip and jump from Sydney. By road it is a round trip of more than 1,000km (600 miles) to Thredbo, the best resort, and when time is pressing it has, really, to be reached by air. Thus, although the **Kosciusko National Park** contains some glorious scenery (**Mt. Kosciusko**, at 2,173m (7,129ft), is Australia's highest peak), we will concentrate here on brief advice on how to go about taking a winter holiday in NSW.

Cooma (*Visitor Information Centre* ☎ *(0648) 21177*) is the main centre of the Snowy region, and has the only airport. Neither of the two major domestic airlines flies to Cooma, the only service being one daily flight (two in mid-season) by **Air New South Wales** (*bookings* ☎ *268 1242*).

During the season, which lasts from June-Oct, **Ansett Pioneer** runs bus services the 80-90km (50-55 miles) from the airport to the main resorts, **Thredbo**, **Perisher Valley**, **Smiggin Holes** and **Charlotte Pass**. The trip takes about 90mins. **Avis** (☎ *(0648) 31216*), **Hertz** (☎ *(0648) 23500*) and **Budget** (☎ *(0648) 22036*) have local offices.

Thredbo has the only genuine giant slalom course in Australia and generally has the most advanced runs, although conditions are less predictable here early in the season. Perisher Valley offers settled conditions and is recommended for cross-country skiing. All resorts have skis for hire, instructors, ski-tows and chairlifts, and a range of hotels and motels.

Skiing is becoming increasingly popular. To get a booking at the height of the season can be awkward unless you go midweek or are able take up a vacancy at short notice. For this reason a specialist winter holiday agency such as **Sydney Snow Centre** (*Level 4, 74 Pitt St., Sydney, NSW, 2000* ☎ *231 1222* ☎ *10717687*), who will endeavour to arrange a package to your needs, can be useful.

Farther afield

The *Excursions* section has given suggestions on seeing parts of NSW that are distant from Sydney – the Snowy Mountains and the s coast, for example. To these can be added **Broken Hill**, the western Outback town where the first of the great mineral finds that transformed Australia from a pastoral nation was discovered.

Since the 1880s and the mining rush to Broken Hill innumerable other deposits have been found – indeed Australia sometimes seems just one vast quarry – but this remains the richest streak of silver, lead and zinc in the world. At the same time it is Outback, the true rugged heartland of Australia.

Broken Hill is actually closer to Adelaide, 508km (318 miles) away, than Sydney, 1,157km (723 miles). It is reachable by air daily from Adelaide with **Kendell Airlines**, and from Sydney with **Air New South Wales** on Sun, Mon, Wed and Fri.

Leisurely travellers might be more inclined to go by rail. One of the world's great trains, the **Indian Pacific** (*bookings* ☎ *217 8812*), leaves Sydney for Perth at 3.15pm on Sun, Thurs and Sat, arriving at Broken Hill at 9am the next day. This is a very comfortable train with sleeping cars, lounge and dining cars, and the flavour of an epic rail journey. Broken Hill also connects with Adelaide.

The Northern Territory

The Northern Territory is still, in parts, frontier country – the real Outback of Australia, still remote, still rough 'n' ready. But this magnificent part of Australia has flora, fauna, landforms and people unmatched anywhere else on the continent. It has been aptly named "the land of God's eighth day" (after six days of making the world and one of rest He decided He could do better – so He made the Northern Territory).

The whole character of the NT, all 134 million hectares (331 million acres) of it, is as contrasting as the skins of its people. It ranges from true desert in the SE (the notorious Simpson Desert), through semi-desert in the sw (the Gibson) and w (the Tanami), to the humid, tropical N with its majestic rivers, waterfalls, billa-bongs, lagoons and pounding surf beaches.

Flora and fauna also differ according to the terrain. In the Red Centre, around Alice Springs, grow the stark-white eucalypts called ghost gums, and the unique salmon gum, its trunk and limbs a delicate pink salmon hue. These and other semi-desert flora are not to be found in the N of the Territory.

The fauna of the dry Centre – timid desert rats, lizards, dingoes and small marsupials – give way to large kangaroos, crocodiles, buffalo, jabiru, brolga and big sea eagles in the so-called Top End (the Territorians' way of distinguishing the water country of the northern third of the NT from the Centre).

Parts of the NT are still remote enough not to have felt the tread of the white man nor, indeed, in some of the more remote parts of the Arnhem Land Aboriginal Reserve, the Aboriginal.

The Territory (so-named by the locals, who call everywhere else in Australia "down south") is home to some of the world's most primitive people. These are the Aborigines of the desert to the far w of Alice Springs, the *Pintupi* and *Wailbri*, who still live their traditional lives, hunting lizards and other small game, as they move from one waterhole to another in the spinifex and sandhills of the Gibson and Great Sandy deserts.

The first seafarers discovered Port Darwin in 1839 (in Charles Darwin's ship, the *Beagle*; hence the city's name), and there are now 130,000 of these "European invaders" in the NT, as against about 20,000 Aborigines. Settlers made four unsuccessful attempts to establish a base on the N coast before John McDouall Stuart, the third-ever white man successfully to lead an expedition s to N across the continent, reached the coast in July 1862. A settlement was finally established at Port Darwin in 1869.

The Top End was gradually settled by people such as gold miners, cattlemen and traders moving here from the coast. Alice Springs was established as a relay station and telegraph office on the Overland Telegraph line that was pushed through from Adelaide to Darwin in 1872, with the first electric telegraph message being transmitted from London to Adelaide and other Australian colonial cities in Aug that year.

The NT was originally "the Northern Territory of South Australia". From 1911 it was taken over by the federal government. In 1922 an MP was instated, but without the right to vote. He was eventually given that right, though only on matters affecting the NT, and not on any financial bills. Full enfranchisement was only granted in 1968. There has been limited self-government since 1978, though the federal government retains control of uranium mining, Aboriginal matters, national parks and other areas considered to be of more than local significance. Full statehood, however, cannot now be far off.

The Aborigines, the original inhabitants of this Land of God's Eighth Day, have a complex society and culture. Their music (with didjeridu and tapsticks) is compelling and haunting; their art (in the sand, on rock or bark) is painstaking and diverse in form and meaning; and their myths and legends of the Dreamtime are as inventive and allegorical as any philosopher's attempts to explain humanity's existence. If you take time to get to know these people, listen to their music, examine their art and read their legends, you will be richly rewarded.

The "new" Territorians – those who have lived here since 1869 – are a multiracial mixture. Origins represented in the NT include Indonesian, Malaysian, Filipino, Chinese, Timorese, Greek,

Italian, Yugoslav, German, Cypriot, Sri Lankan, Indian, Fijian and, of course, British and American. They mix well, both at work and socially, and their children grow up and go to school together. The possibility of racial disharmony does not seem to exist here, and their attitude towards life is still one best described by the Australianism, "She'll be right, mate."

There seems to be a fierce sense of equality, or pride, both here and in the rest of the country; a municipal ditch-digger will consider himself the equal of the mayor, though this attitude of "you're no better than me" and mañana can sometimes alienate visitors. "Sir" and "madam" are seldom-used courtesies, and the slightest impatience from a visitor can sometimes result in even slower service. But the Territory's flourishing tourist industry is forcing a gradual reappraisal of such ingrown attitudes.

This is Australia's real Outback, which richly repays the effort entailed in visiting it. The NT's many attractions are scattered over vast distances of difficult terrain, to which this guide aims to provide only a series of pointers. Specific advice useful when planning your trip completes this introduction and is followed by two condensed city guides, to the Territory capital, *Darwin*, and the southern centre, *Alice Springs*. Using the cities as a base, many places in the Top End and the Red Centre can be visited. Some representative examples are suggested here.

Getting there

Darwin and Alice Springs are the two bases most visitors use for excursions to the NT. Both are served daily by major internal airlines from other state capitals, and some international airlines.

The "Ghan" passenger train (named after the Afghan camel drivers who in the 19thC transported passengers through the Outback) provides a comfortable and interesting journey from Adelaide to Alice Springs, with facilities for passengers to take their vehicles with them.

Those who wish to drive at least have the advantage of using the Stuart Hwy, stretching all the way from Adelaide to Darwin. The disadvantage is that the amount of time taken to drive some 3,000km (1,850 miles) would leave less time to explore places "off the beaten track". There are also regular long-distance bus lines serving the N, but the same problems of time and distance arise as with private vehicle travel.

Getting around

The airport bus will take you to your hotel or motel, but after this the easiest way of getting around Darwin and Alice Springs is to use their taxi firms. There are government-run buses too, but these are basically suburban commuter services.

The major car rental companies, **Avis**, **Budget** and **Hertz**, and several smaller companies, provide a good service in both cities. The rates are slightly higher than elsewhere, and it is advisable to book a car before arrival, especially in the high season (Apr-Oct).

Tour operators run bus and minibus trips for city sightseeing, day tours to places of interest out of town, and longer camping or bush-lodge "safari" trips to such attractions as Ayers Rock and Kakadu National Park. Car rental and bus tours can be arranged at hotel reception desks, travel agents and at NT Tourist Bureaux.

Climate

The NT has two distinct climatic zones: the arid (or continental) in the Centre, and the monsoonal at the Top End.

The best time of year to visit both the Centre and the Top End is during the dry season (known as the Dry). This is the Australian winter (Apr-Sept), when, in the Centre, the nights are cold, falling as low as 0°C (32°F), and the days are cool-to-warm, with maximum temperatures from 25–30°C (77–86°F). In the Oct-Mar wet season (or the Wet) – something of a misnomer in the semi-arid heart of Australia – the nights are still cool, but the days are fiercely hot.

In the N, dry-season days are perfect, with temperatures falling to about 20°C (68°F) at night and rising to about 30°C (86°F) during the day. The months that build up to the Wet (Oct-Dec) are hot and very steamy, as are the "let-down" months of Mar and Apr, and torrential rain (150cm – about 60ins – a year) falls in Dec, Jan and Feb. The early months of the year are also the cyclone season, although there have been only three completely destructive cyclones in the past 100yrs, in 1897, 1937 and 1974 (Cyclone Tracy).

There are certain disadvantages in visiting the Top End in the Wet. Swimming in the sea, for example, is highly dangerous, as the monsoon brings with it lethal sea wasps and other stingers. And the remarkable wetlands, with such attractions as Kakadu National Park, are so extended by the heavy rain that the wildlife disperses over a wide area. In the Dry the waterholes contract and wildlife is concentrated in this area.

Clothing
Territorians dress sensibly. Men wear cotton slacks and short-sleeve, open-neck shirts during the Dry, and in the Wet, shorts and knee-length socks. Ties are generally worn only at official functions, and suits are worn only by visiting politicians or businessmen who don't know the procedure. In the Wet, women wear sundresses or cotton blouses with slacks or a skirt. You might need a sweater on mornings in the dry season (even some Top Enders resort to woollens when their temperatures "plunge" to 20°C (68°F) in the early morning).

Warnings
In parts of the Territory, especially in the bush, flies are a menace, so it is essential to carry insect repellant at all times. Also, observe signs that warn against swimming in the wet season and against swimming where there might be crocodiles.

If travelling extensively out of the towns, find out where the Aboriginal Reserves are and make sure you don't enter them without the permission of the relevant Aboriginal council. There is, in fact, only one main "adventure" route that goes through a reserve, from Alice Springs to Halls Creek in Western Australia, through the Tanami Desert – a 4-wheel-drive-and-camping trip. In this case permission is not necessary, as long as the traveller does no more than buy petrol, and perhaps an artifact or two from the store at Yuendumu, an Aboriginal town on the route, and keeps moving: few would be tempted to stay in Yuendumu, even with permission.

Darwin
☎ *STD code: 089. Air: daily flights by Australian Airlines and Ansett. Bus: regular services by national companies; Ansett Pioneer, DeLuxe and Greyhound offer unlimited-mileage 14-, 15-, 30- and 60-day passes, allowing flexible travel to and around the NT. Car rental: Avis ☎ 81 9922; Budget ☎ 84 4388; Hertz ☎ 81 6686. NT Government Tourist Bureau: 31 Smith St., Darwin, NT, 5790 ☎ 81 6611. American Express Travel Service: c/o Travellers World Pty Ltd, 18 Knuckey St., Darwin, NT, 5790 ☎ 81 4699. Automobile Association of the Northern Territory (AANT): 79-81 Smith St., Darwin, NT, 5790 ☎ 81 3837.*

Darwin is the capital of the Northern Territory, set on a beautiful harbour, larger than Sydney's. It has a population of 70,000, and its growth rate is higher than any other Australian city, apart from the national capital, Canberra. This is a city of contrasts – going against the Australian norm, Darwinians play football in summer (their wet season) and cricket in winter (their dry season). The racial mix is as varied and harmonious here as in the rest of the NT. You will find Darwinians of Chinese, Filipino, and particularly Greek and Italian descent, with Aborigines also forming an integral part of the community.

The city has been destroyed three times by tropical cyclones – in 1897, 1937, and on Christmas Day, 1974 by Cyclone Tracy. Each time, Darwin has risen, phoenix-like, and today it ranks among the world's most pleasant, small, tropical cities, with a variety of good shops, restaurants and beaches, and some interesting sights. And because Darwin is the NT's "front door" for visitors from Britain and Asia, and the base for those wishing to tour such Top End delights as *Kakadu National Park* (see *Excursion*), hundreds of millions of dollars have recently gone into new hotel and motel development.

Points of interest include the **Museum of Arts and Sciences** (*Bullocky Point, Fannie Bay*). This fine, air-conditioned building, at the city end of Fannie Bay, houses the most extensive collection of Aboriginal and non-Aboriginal art, natural history and social history in N Australia; it also has a good licensed restaurant, *Beagle* (see *Restaurants*), favoured by locals for sunny lunches and relaxed dinners. Also of interest are the **East Point War Museum** (*East Point, Fannie Bay*); **Howard Springs** (*30km (18 miles) s on the Stuart Hwy*), a big, natural spring and swimming complex; and for a day trip, take the ferry across the harbour to **Mandorah**, on the Cox peninsula, where you can have lunch and see displays of Aboriginal dancing and singing.

Accommodation

The choice of hotels is limited compared to other major cities. Most of the older establishments seem not to have survived the cyclone. And for motels and cheaper accommodation you will need to look well away from the city centre.

Beaufort
The Esplanade, Darwin, NT, 5790
☎ 82 9911 🔟 ☎ 85818 ⓟ 81 5332 ▥ 235 rms ⚊ ⚊ 🆎 💿 💿 💳

Location: *Central, with fine views over Darwin Harbour.* Despite its appearance – like a series of pink and blue boxes – this hotel complex comes up to the best international standards. Its many facilities include a health studio and a business centre. 24hr room service.
♿ ⇔ ☎ ▤ 🍽 ⚓ 🅿 ⚓ 🎿

Darwin TraveLodge
122 The Esplanade, Darwin, NT, 5790 ☎ 81 5388 🔟 ☎ 85273 ▥ 183 rms ⚊ ⚊ 🆎 💿 💿 💳

Location: *Just 10mins' walk from city centre.* Built in 1972, this conveniently located hotel is now one of Darwin's oldest new hotels. Similar in character to other TraveLodges in the chain, it has a good restaurant, bistro, swimming pool, and you can get the best views in the city from its top floor.
⇔ ⚓ ▤ 🍽 🎿

Diamond Beach Hotel Casino
Gilruth Ave., Mindil Beach, Darwin, NT, 5790 ☎ 81 7755 🔟 ☎ 85214 ▥ 96 rms ⚊ ⚊ 🆎 💿 💿 💳

Location: *1.6km (1 mile) from Darwin's centre.* A pleasant casino-hotel, set on the beachfront.
♿ ⇔ ⚓ ▤ 🍽 ⚓ 🅿 ⚓ 🎿

Four Seasons Darwin
Dashwood Crescent, Darwin, NT, 5790 ☎ 81 5333 🔟 ☎ 85309 ▥ 89 rms ⚊ ⚊ 🆎 💿 💿 💳

Location: *2km (1 mile) from city centre.* Originally known as the Territorian, this 1960s hotel nestles in green parkland, across the road from the **Botanic Gardens**, and just a 5min walk from the beautiful, white-sand **Mindil Beach**.
⇔ ▤ 🍽 🎿

Hotel Darwin
10 Herbert St., Darwin, NT, 5794
☎ 81 9211 ☎ 85194 ▮▮▮ 70 rms
⬅ ⬜ AE ⊕ ⊚ VISA
Location: In the heart of the city. A
grand old hotel in the tropical/
colonial style, with magnificent views
across Darwin Harbour. 24hr room
service.
⇌ ⬛ ☗ ☗

Sheraton Darwin
32 Mitchell St., Darwin, NT, 5790
☎ 82 0000 ▮▮▮ ☎ 85991 ⊛ 81
1765 ▮▮▮ 233 rms ⬅ ⬜ AE ⊕
VISA
Location: City centre. Opened in
1986, this modern hotel is a
convenient 1min walk from the main
shopping thoroughfare, Smith Mall.
& ⇌ ⬛ ☗ ☗ ☗

Restaurants

The fast-changing restaurant scene in this fastest growing part of
Australia makes it hard to pick examples with real staying power.
Good prospects, all licensed, include **Seaview** (*Seaview Motor Inn,
60 East Point Rd., Fannie Bay* ☎ 81 8809 ▮▮▮ AE ⊕ ⊚ VISA), a true
gourmet restaurant with magnificent views over Fannie Bay;
Beagle (*Museum of Arts and Sciences, Conacher St., Fannie Bay*
☎ 81 7791 ▮▮▮ AE ⊕ ⊚ VISA), situated virtually on the beach
overlooking Fannie Bay, with a colonial theme and waitresses in
19thC costume; and **Lee Dynasty** (*21 Cavenagh St., Darwin* ☎ 81
7808/81 2700 ▮▮▮ AE ⊕ ⊚ VISA), an elegant Cantonese restaurant
serving leisurely dinners.

Nightlife

In the vanguard of nightspots is the **Diamond Beach Hotel
Casino** (*Gilruth Ave.* ☎ 81 7755). Within the casino complex is
Crystals, a spacious disco with regular cabaret entertainment.

But for something different, try **Fannies** (*3 Edmunds St.* ☎ 81
9761), an all-night disco where entertainment includes live variety
acts that intersperse music with comedy, magic and fire-eating. In
the same complex and offering an alternative to discos is **Squires**,
an intimate tavern-style meeting place for an evening drink in
relaxing, colonial surroundings, serving delectable steaks and
grills, and with late-night live bands Wed-Sun.

Shopping

The city-centre **Smith Street Mall** is a picturesque paved
thoroughfare, lined with bougainvillea and palms. Numerous
smaller arcades lead off it. On Sat it's filled with the fragrance of
satays and other Asian delicacies from open-air food stalls, and in
the Dry there's live entertainment.

Casuarina Square, in the northern suburbs, is vast: more than
160 speciality shops plus four major stores. Adjacent is **Casuarina
Village**, Darwin's newest one-stop shopping centre.

Excursion

Kakadu National Park ★

150km (93 miles) E of Darwin ▣ ✗ ⇜ *Open all year; some
roads in the park closed in wet season. Getting there: by
car, via Stuart Hwy S for 35km (21 miles), then left on
Arnhem Hwy; by bus, contact tour operators in Darwin.*
Kakadu is a fascinating and mysterious place of Aboriginal rock
art, towering escarpments, grasslands and wetlands, crocodiles,
buffalo, birdlife in great variety, and unique flora. Previously
unreachable by conventional vehicles in the Wet season and an
arduous journey even in the Dry, Kakadu is now a mere 3hrs'
drive from the Territory capital.

Darwin tour operators run day trips to the park, which

unfortunately tend to be tiring and inadequate because of the distances needing to be covered; but they can also arrange longer visits. Independent travellers either camp out in the areas designated by the National Parks and Wildlife Service or stay at the *Cooinda Motel* (see below), near the town of Jabiru (an incongruous support town for the big uranium mine in an area excised from the park), or at the *South Alligator Motor Inn* (see below), just outside the park boundary.

The **Cooinda Motel** (*near Jabiru* ☎ *(089) 79 2545* 🔲 🖭 ⊙ 🖭 🖾), small and basic, stands on the fabled Yellow Waters lagoon, where boat cruises can be arranged. The **South Alligator Motor Inn** (*Arnhem Hwy, Kakadu* ☎ *(089) 79 0166* 🔲 🖭 ⊙ 🖭 🖾), on the edge of the National Park, can arrange cruises on the South Alligator River.

Alice Springs

☎ *STD code: 089. 1,529km (950 miles) s of Darwin on Stuart Hwy. Air and bus: daily services from southern capitals. Rail: the "Ghan" service takes 24hrs from Adelaide, the "Alice" service 48hrs from Sydney. Car rental: Avis ☎ 52 4366; Budget ☎ 52 4133; Hertz ☎ 52 2644. Northern Territory Government Tourist Bureau: 51 Todd St., Alice Springs, NT, 5750 ☎ 52 1299*

Alice Springs is a thriving, fast-growing city with a population of 20,000 people. It is the starting point for most visitors on their way to the fabled *Ayers Rock* and the *Olgas* (see *Excursions*) and the base for those interested in the lesser-known (but equally interesting) chasms, gorges and gaps in the Macdonnell Ranges surrounding the city. *Standley Chasm* (see *Excursions*) is an easy day trip from "the Alice" (as the city is called locally).

Although John McDouall Stuart crossed the Macdonnell Ranges six times in his journeys to the N coast in 1860, 1861 and 1862, he saw neither the Todd River nor the plain on which Alice Springs stands. Those discoveries were made by surveyors plotting the Overland Telegraph route in 1870. The isolated town, consisting of a few shacks, a store and hotel, was originally known as Stuart, but the telegraph station and post office were situated at a waterhole 3km (2 miles) away called Alice Springs. When the post office was transferred to the township the name moved too.

Alice Springs has come a long way since those shantytown days. Today it has reasonable accommodation, good leisure facilities and a broad range of shops. Points of interest include the old **telegraph station** (*3km (2 miles) N, off the Stuart Hwy*) and **Pitchi Richi** (*Aranda Terrace* ☎ *52 1931* 🖾 🖛 *open 9am-sunset*), central Australia's largest outdoor museum, a bird-and-flower sanctuary that also features remarkable sculptures of Aborigines by William Ricketts. Events in the Alice include camel races in May and in late Aug the Henley-on-Todd regatta on the bed of the Todd River, which runs through the town and is nearly always dry.

Accommodation

Alice Springs is quite well provided for in its range of places to stay, from expensive (by NT standards) to budget accommodation. Surprisingly, motels are generally not cheap.

Lasseters Casino

Barrett Drive, Alice Springs, NT, 5750 ☎ *52 5066* 🔟🔟 ⊙ *81126* 🎬 *75 rms* 🖛 ═ 🖭 ⊙ 🖭 🖾

Location: *s of town centre.* Alice Springs' only casino-hotel complex has excellent views of the beautiful Macdonnell Ranges. See *Nightlife.*
 🚹 ≋ ▣ 🍷 ⁀ 👪

Oasis Motel ♣
*10 Gap Rd., Alice Springs, NT,
5750* ☎ *52 1444* |100| ☺ *81245* |◉|
102 rms 🛏 ⚖ |AE| |◉| |VISA|
Location: Just S of town centre. This
motel, set in several acres of lawns
and aviaries, offers the best-value
accommodation to be found in Alice
Springs.
& ⚖ |◉| ♈ ♉ 🎿

Sheraton Alice Springs
*Barrett Drive, Alice Springs, NT,
5750* ☎ *52 8000* |100| ☺ *81091* |◉|
238 rms 🛏 ⚖ |AE| |◉| |◉| |VISA|
Location: On SE edge of town. This
brand new hotel complex blends in
well with its surroundings. It is
spread out over several acres of
lawns, with an 18-hole golf course.
& ⚖ |◉| ♈ ♂ ⚓ 🎿

Restaurants

The **Outback Winery** (*Petrick Rd.* ☎ *21 5771* |◉| |AE| |◉| |◉| |VISA|) is a
thoroughly Australian-style restaurant, operated by Dennis and
Miranda Hornsby at their winery, Chateau Hornsby. The setting
is open-air with a cover to protect patrons from rain or hot sun,
and a small amphitheatre features nightly Australian
entertainment. It's all relaxed and friendly in the true Outback
tradition.

Nightlife

There are few true late-night spots in the Alice. But **Bojangles**
(*80 Todd St.* ☎ *52 2873*) is hugely popular (get in early!), yet
surprisingly intimate. And at **Lasseter's Casino** (*Barrett Drive*
☎ *52 5066*), there is a disco featuring stunning lighting; strict
dress regulations demand neat, clean casual clothes.

Shopping

The **Todd Street Mall** is a pleasantly landscaped pedestrians-only
thoroughfare spanning two blocks and containing some 80 shops
plus offices and banks; other arcades lead off, with one, **Ford
Plaza**, providing late-night shopping until 9pm.

Excursions

Ayers Rock ★

450km (280 miles) by road sw of Alice Springs |◉| ✗ 🛏 ◁≡
*Open all year. Getting there: by air, from Alice Springs and
Perth; by bus, from Alice Springs and Adelaide.*
Ayers Rock was named by the South Australian explorer W. C.
Gosse in 1873. He wrote, "What was my astonishment when, two
miles distant, to find it was an immense pebble rising abruptly
from the plain . . . it is certainly the most wonderful natural
feature I have ever seen." Ayers Rock is not, however, the biggest
monolith known; that honour goes to the far less eye-catching Mt.
Augustus in Western Australia.

Measuring 9km (5½ miles) in circumference and 348m (1,142ft)
in height, the Rock famously changes colour through darkening
shades of glowing red at sunset, reversing this spectacle at dawn;
its colour is affected too by the quality of the light and the mood of
the weather. The stiff climb is rewarded by astonishing views of
the endless red plain, sometimes covered, after a thunderstorm, by
flowers. Walking trails around the base take in caves containing
Aboriginal rock paintings, and **Maggie Springs**, where wildlife
thrives.

The Rock is unquestionably the most impressive living symbol
of Aboriginal ritual and myth. The tribespeople believe that within
Ayers Rock their mythological heroes, who came into the country
at the dawn of time, are resting, awaiting the moment to
re-emerge. They believe each part of the mountain is a creative

symbol kept alive by a sacred rock python (*Wanambi*) living at a waterhole in *Uluru*, the Aboriginal name of the Rock.

☙ Four Seasons Ayers Rock (*Yulara Drive, Yulara* ☎ *(089) 56 2100* ▮▮▮ AE ⊕ ⊙ VISA), a handy 20km (12 miles) from the Rock, with courtesy bus service from Yulara Airport.

Devil's Marbles ★
400km (249 miles) N of Alice Springs ☙ ≼ *Open all year. Getting there: by car, via Stuart Hwy.*
These two granite boulders cover several sq.km and weigh thousands of tonnes. They range in shape from almost perfectly rounded boulders, stacked in precarious tiers, to rocks sliced clean in half by nature's knives.

The Olgas ★
25km (15 miles) w of Ayers Rock 🚐 ✗ ☙ ≼ *Open all year. Getting there: see Ayers Rock.*
Ernest Giles was the first explorer to see the Olgas, and it was he who named them for the Queen of Spain. He wrote, "Mt. Olga displayed to our astonished eyes rounded minarets, giant cupolas, and monstrous domes. There they have stood as huge memorials of the ancient times of earth, for ages, countless aeons of ages, since its creation first had birth. The rocks are smoothed with the attrition of the alchemy of years, [but] Time, the old and dim magician, has laboured ineffectually here . . . Mt. Olga has remained as it was born."

Unlike the single dome of *Ayers Rock*, the Olgas have more than a dozen separate heads, divided by deep clefts and water-filled gorges teeming with wildlife; the tallest peak, **Lotherio**, rises to a height of 546m (1,791ft). The Aborigines know the Olgas, home of many myths, as *Katajuta* (many heads).

Standley Chasm ★
50km (31 miles) w of Alice Springs 🚐 ☙ ≼ *Open 8.30am-4.30pm. Getting there: by car, via Larapinta Drive.*
This sheer cleft is a delightful subject for photographers, when the sun stands directly overhead and illuminates its red walls. The phenomenon lasts for only a few minutes in the middle of the day; but this vertical slice is only one of many spectacular gorges in the **Macdonnell Ranges**, a number of which have rocky waterholes and support much wildlife – and even wild flowers in spring.

Queensland

The Sunshine State they call it, and with good reason. Queensland is the centre of Australia's holiday industry, having experienced the sort of growth in international tourism since the mid-1970s that is as pleasing to governments as it is alarming to environmentalists. Images of beaches so perfect they could only exist in a rum commercial, of a dazzling, silent world of coral reefs, of epic struggles with giant fish – all these have established Queensland firmly in the international register of desirable destinations. And fairly so, for the Sunshine State in nearly every way measures up to its reputation.

The omens for European settlement were even less auspicious than elsewhere in Australia. Although the Queensland coast had been charted by Captain Cook in 1770, the first step towards establishing a colonial administration was taken only in 1824, more than three decades after the founding of Sydney, the purpose being to set up a last-resort colony for incorrigible offenders from NSW. By all accounts Brisbane's early years were ugly and brutal, and the commandant of the penal settlement, Captain Patrick Logan, has come down in Australian folklore as one of the most notorious of the many villains produced by the mother country.

Queensland's progress towards prosperity was founded on the land. A great pastoral industry evolved out of free settlement, as did agriculture. Sugar cane plantations larger than European principalities drew an immigrant labour force of Pacific Islanders, still a prominent section of the state's population. Minerals sustained the growth.

Today the source of much of the state's wealth is the sea, the lure for a tourist industry contributing 12 percent to gross state product. And vast though the land area is – more than 1.7 million sq.km, second in size only to Western Australia – the sea and the coast are what we are concerned with here.

On the question of when to go, it is advisable to avoid the period from Dec-Mar if possible. Most visitors will find the climate, in the tropical N in particular, uncomfortably hot when it is not pouring with rain. There is danger too, on the beaches N of Gladstone, from the box jellyfish, which appears near the coast at this time and has a sting that was proved fatal as recently as Jan 1987.

Queensland is not an easy place to see. Its attractions do not present themselves conveniently close to the urban centres. The Great Barrier Reef, which is the one reason above all others to visit Queensland, sprawls over a length of more than 2,000km (1,250 miles), and in places is well over 100km (60 miles) offshore. The islands so successfully promoted by the state authority, in an era when the idea of tourism seems geared to getting away from absolutely everything, are in most cases by no means easily, or cheaply, accessible.

Queensland, it should be emphasized, is expensive for travellers who insist on the highest standard of accommodation and want to fly everywhere in order to save time. There is more than a whiff of the old Australian disease, protectionism, about the Queensland tourism industry. Even package visits to offshore destinations like Heron Island, an exquisite coral cay with magnificent skindiving on the reef, are expensive enough for Queenslanders to save money by taking their holidays in Bali and Thailand.

But it is possible to travel independently, and with a flexible itinerary, and not spend a fortune, provided the visitor plans carefully, uses motels (many of which are no less comfortable for being in the moderate-to-inexpensive price range) and shops around for stand-by rates on island accommodation.

Be assured that the rewards that Queensland offers are well worth any effort entailed. To provide practical advice to this end, this section of the guide has been devised in a slightly different form. The state capital, Brisbane, is presented under the usual convenient A to Z headings, but a second part concentrates on information about getting to see the Great Barrier Reef, and visiting the islands.

A word about your hosts: Queenslanders have a reputation among other Australians for a certain eccentricity, an image fostered by the long-enduring and archly conservative Bjelke-Petersen state administration, which in 1986 passed legislation forbidding the serving of alcohol to "drug-dealers, perverts and child molesters."

At the same time, perhaps because they are only like simple and kind country people anywhere else, Queenslanders present a genuinely warm welcome to visitors. A great deal of spurious nonsense is written about "traditional Aussie hospitality". But in Queensland it really is true.

Brisbane

Map 16 ☎ STD code: 07. Airport: ☎ 268 9511; Ansett ☎ 226 1111; Australian ☎ 223 3333. Railway station: Roma Street ☎ 225 0211. Car rental: Avis ☎ 52 7111; Budget ☎ 52 0151; Hertz ☎ 229 9533. Queensland Government Travel Centre: Corner of Adelaide St. and Edward St., Brisbane, Qld, 4000 ☎ 31 2211. American Express Travel Service: 68 Queen St., Brisbane, Qld, 4000 ☎ 229 0222. Royal Automobile Club of Queensland (RACQ): 300 St Pauls Terrace, Brisbane, Qld, 4000 ☎ 253 2444.

Orientation

Brisbane, along with the rest of Queensland, is sometimes imagined by outsiders as being located beside a great white beach on the Pacific where the sun shines perpetually and the surf is always up.

It is a misleading impression. Like most early settlements in Australia, Brisbane was established and developed on the banks of a river, and the modern city is in fact more than 20km (12½ miles) inland from where the muddy waters of the Brisbane River empty into Moreton Bay. From the mountains of the D'Aguilar range, some 35km (22 miles) to the w, you can look out to the bay, and the islands of Moreton and Stradbroke, which shelter it from the Pacific. The dazzling beaches of Surfers Paradise and the Gold Coast are about 70km (44 miles) to the s, and the Sunshine Coast, another holiday resort area, is about 110km (69 miles) N.

Brisbanites pride themselves on the rural identity of their state, and regard Southerners with a certain wariness. Geographically, however, they are closer to NSW and Canberra than to the northern areas of Queensland. The state border is a bare 100km (63 miles) away, the merest hop in Australian terms, and Cairns, the main city of the N, is almost twice as far away as Sydney, so that Brisbane folk themselves tend to be tagged Southerners in their own state.

Brisbane presents most of its attractions in a central, convenient location, and can be comfortably seen in 2-3 days. The city centre is easily encompassed on foot, and, as the streets named after kings run parallel roughly N-to-s, and those for the queens run w-to-e, it is hard to get lost.

Seeing the city

The place for information of every kind, on Brisbane and the rest of Queensland, is the **Queensland Government Travel Centre** (*196 Adelaide St. ☎ 226 5337*).

The local transport authority runs a sightseeing tour called **City Lookabout** (*departs 9.30am Mon-Fri; inquiries ☎ 225 4444*), a 3hr guided excursion stopping at Mt. Coot-tha, Queensland University and Newstead House. **Boomerang Tours** (*☎ 221 9922*) runs visits to Lone Pine Koala Sanctuary and other destinations.

A cruise on the Brisbane River offers another view of the city. Operators include **Miramar** (*☎ 221 6149*), **Koala Cruises** (*☎ 229 7055*), taking in Lone Pine Koala Sanctuary; and the **Kookaburra Queen** (*☎ 52 3797*), a replica paddle steamer, which has no set route but cruises in the city environs.

Ballooning offers a spectacular perspective of Brisbane and its environs (*inquiries* ☎ *844 6671.*)

Sights and places of interest

Albert Street Uniting Church ★
Corner of Albert St. and Ann St. ☎ 221 6788. Map 16D2 ⊡ K (ask at office). Open 7am-6pm.

This 19thC gem of church architecture was formerly the Wesley Central Mission, now attached to the Uniting Church in Australia. Situated in the heart of the city, it once dominated the position overlooking *City Hall*, but due to civic carelessness towards historic buildings (only too common in Brisbane) it is now reduced in the landscape by surrounding high-rise structures.

The red-brick and white-sandstone exterior was completed in 1889 and is harmoniously proportioned. The interior, lined from ceiling to pews with highly polished timber, is intimate and welcoming. The communion and gallery rails are in cedar. There are some fine stained-glass windows.

Art Gallery of Queensland
Queensland Cultural Centre, South Bank, South Brisbane ☎ 240 7303. Map 16E2 ⊡ K ▣ ⬟ Open Thurs-Tues 10am-5pm, Wed 10am-8pm.

It may come as a surprise to find this excellent collection of pictures in what is, after all, a small city. Located in the modern surroundings of the *Queensland Cultural Centre* on the s bank of the Brisbane River, the state collection has been compiled over almost a century with discrimination and taste. It contains works by Renoir, Degas, Toulouse-Lautrec and Picasso (all acquired in a 1959 windfall through a local benefactor). But the real meat here is the important and comprehensive record of Australian art, including major works by Frederick McCubbin and William Dobell.

Botanic Gardens
George St. Map 16E3 ⊡ Open sunrise-sunset.

Situated at a pleasant and secluded end of George St. in the city, the gardens face two fine 19thC buildings, *Parliament House* and *The Mansions*. Here the havoc wrought upon Brisbane's heritage in recent years can almost be forgotten. Palms in a subtropical setting, which extends down to the banks of the Brisbane River, make this an exotic spot to relax after a stroll through the city. Handsome though the gardens are, they have been overshadowed as a botanic exhibition by the more specialized displays lately established at *Mt. Coot-tha*, though that is less conveniently located about 5km (3 miles) from the city.

City Hall
Adelaide St. ☎ 225 4048. Map 16D2 ⊡ K (☎ 225 4360). Open 10am-noon, 2–4pm. Closed Sat, Sun.

This characteristic Late Empire hybrid of architectural styles, situated in the heart of the city, has been long regarded as its showpiece. Building started in 1920 and took 10yrs. The **clock tower**, at 92m (302ft) once Brisbane's highest point, has an observation platform that features in the conducted tour. Also contained within the Neoclassical framework are the rather grand foyer at the King George Sq. entrance and a civic art gallery and museum.

Early Street Village
75 McIlwraith Ave., Norman Park ☎ *398 6866* 🚗 💻 � *Open 10am-5pm.*

A private enterprise that appeals to Australians' fascination with heritage, this fails to live up to its promise. The so-called village is a collection of early Queensland structures, including a cottage, a general store and a pioneer hut. It also features the remains of **Auchenflower House**, a fine old mansion in which three state premiers lived, but which nevertheless was being demolished in the 1960s when two rooms were salvaged and brought here. The one structure of real significance on the site is **Eulalia**, but as this colonial home is a private residence it is not open to visitors. For what is on show, the entry fee is steep, and a visit to *Newstead House* might give a more rewarding insight into colonial life.

Expo 88
South Bank, South Brisbane. Map **16E2**.

No site better illustrates the transformation of Brisbane since the mid-1970s from a placid, overgrown town to a modern city of the Pacific Rim. A bid to host the 1992 Olympic Games was lost, but Expo 88, scheduled to open in Apr of the bicentenary, is similarly calculated to attract international attention. A 40ha (99-acre) tract, s of the river and beside the *Queensland Cultural Centre*, has undergone major development to host an exhibition titled *Leisure in the Age of Technology*.

Lone Pine Koala Sanctuary
Jesmond Rd., Fig Tree Pocket ☎ *378 1366* 💻 ✳ 🚌 *Open 9.30am-5pm.*

The biggest sanctuary in Australia for this delightful but vulnerable marsupial (the koala is not a bear at all) can be reached by ferry departing from North Quay at lunchtime daily (*inquiries* ☎ *378 1366*). Lone Pine also has kangaroos and emus, which visitors may hand-feed, and offers a rare opportunity to see at close quarters the extraordinary egg-laying mammal of Australia, the duck-billed platypus.

The Mansions ★
40 George St. Map **16E3** 💻 *Shopping arcade open in trading hours.*

This stately old terrace building near the *Botanic Gardens* and *Parliament House* was completed around 1890 and has been refurbished, like so many historic structures in Australia, as an arcade of shops. Yet this and the old **Salvation Army headquarters** in Ann St. (adapted for office accommodation) are the grandest remaining buildings of their type in Brisbane.

Mount Coot-tha and Botanic Gardens
Mt. Coot-tha Rd., Toowong ☎ *377 8898* 🅿 💻 🚌 ◄€ *Open 9am-5pm.*

About 5km (3 miles) w of the city is this large site, worth the drive as much for its fine views and picnic spots as for the gardens. From the summit of **Mt. Coot-tha**, overlooking Brisbane, you get a good idea of the layout of the city along the river banks, and a panorama of the hinterland stretching away to the distant **D'Aguilar Mountains**. The summit restaurant serves lunches, teas and dinner.

   The new botanic gardens are at the foot of the mountain and include an enclosed tropical display. Also on the site is the **Sir Thomas Brisbane planetarium** (*two showings daily* ☎ *377 8896 for* *times*). The surrounding natural parkland is a popular local picnic spot, although quiet on weekdays. From the car park just beyond the turn-off for the summit there are signposted walks to the **J. C. Slaughter Falls**.

Newstead House ★
Breakfast Creek Rd., Newstead ☎ *52 7373. Map **16**B3* 🚗 🚆 🚤 🍴 *Open Mon-Thurs 11am-3pm, Sun 2-5pm. Closed Fri, Sat.*

This lovely old residence is the oldest house in Brisbane. The meticulous care given by a local heritage group, combined with its stately position overlooking the river, place it among the country's finest historic houses. Built in 1846 for a pioneer Queensland farmer, a Scot named Patrick Leslie, the original shell was extended and embellished over the decades. More recent residents were US servicemen during World War II, and, following his visit here in 1967, an area behind the house is named Lyndon B. Johnson Place as a memorial to them. Restoration has been rounded off with period furniture and objects, many of them treasures in their own right.

The Old Windmill
*Wickham Terrace. Map **16**C2. Not open to the public.*

There is actually not a great deal to be seen of the oldest surviving building in Brisbane, but its history is interesting enough to warrant a visit. Built in 1829 by convicts under the supervision of Captain Patrick Logan, much-hated commander of the penal settlement established here for incorrigible offenders, it was designed as a windmill, and is sometimes called the Observatory. In fact it was not used as either, although it has functioned as a grain mill, a fire lookout, a signal station and, in 1840, as a gallows when two Aborigines were hanged from the windmill arm for murdering a government land surveyor.

Parliament House
George St. ☎ *226 7111. Map **16**E3* 🔲 ✗ *compulsory: six tours daily, from 10.30am.*

This is an enduring symbol of the independence won by Queensland from NSW in 1854, when a design competition was launched for a state legislative chamber. The winning design, for a building in the grand French style and said to have been modelled on the Louvre, has been in use as a parliament since 1868 and is an altogether more splendid affair than its equivalent in NSW. The imposing stone façade and blackened copper domes are in picturesque contrast to the subtropical setting of palm trees and the adjacent *Botanic Gardens*.

Queensland Cultural Centre
South Bank, South Brisbane ☎ *inquiries 240 7229, bookings 844 0201. Map **16**E2* 🔲 ✗ *hourly* 🚆 🚤 *Open Thurs-Tues 10am-5pm, Wed 10am-8pm.*

An ambitious concept modelled along the lines of London's South Bank, although arguably it has more architectural appeal. Like the South Bank, the Cultural Centre consists of a series of arts venues built on the banks of a major river. It includes a performing arts complex containing three auditoriums, now Brisbane's main venue for concerts, ballet, opera and drama, and new homes for the *Art Gallery of Queensland*, the *Queensland Museum* and the state library. Among the acres of space are a number of restaurants, bistros and plazas.

Queensland Museum
Queensland Cultural Centre, South Bank, South Brisbane
☎ *240 7555. Map* **16E2** 🔲 💻 ✳ 🚗 *Open Thurs-Tues
9am-5pm, Wed 9am-8pm.*
Recently moved to the *Queensland Cultural Centre*, the
museum is next to the *Art Gallery of Queensland* with which it
can be combined in a half-day visit. Main themes are
anthropological and natural history, but many of the other exhibits
are no less intriguing, such as the section on early Australian
aviators like Charles Kingsford Smith. (The *Southern Cross*, the
aircraft in which "Smithy" made his crossing of the Pacific, is on
show at Brisbane airport.) The museum also houses a display,
including a film, on the continuing underwater excavation of the
18thC wreck of HMS *Pandora*. This British frigate was on its way
home from Tahiti carrying captured mutineers from the *Bounty*
affair when it sank off the Queensland coast.

St Johns Cathedral
417 Ann St., Fortitude Valley ☎ *355 4569. Map* **16C3** 🔲 ✗
10am Wed, Fri 🚗 *Open 9am-5pm.*
Building of the headquarters of the Anglican Church in
Queensland started in 1901 and is still far from complete. What
appears at present to be a modern façade imposed on the old
stonework is in fact the first stage of a western extension, to
include a bell tower, although funds are short and completion is
unlikely before the 21stC. The interior is spacious and grand.

Treasury Building ★
Corner of Queen St. and George St. ☎ *224 2111. Map* **16D2**.
This most imposing of Brisbane's old buildings was designed by
John Clarke, the Colonial Architect, who also created the Treasury
in Melbourne and whose liking for the Italian style is evident in the
high arcades. Work started in 1885 but because of technical
problems took more than 40yrs to complete.

Accommodation
Brisbane's accommodation standards, once dire, have been
transformed in recent years with the opening of the *Hilton*, the
Sheraton and two other international-quality hotels, the
Brisbane City TraveLodge and *Gazebo Ramada*. This growth
has been stimulated by the city's emergence as a Pacific business
centre, but at the weekend it empties for the surrounding coastal
resorts, and many hotels cannot maintain an adequate occupancy
rate. The happy consequence for the visitor is that even the
five-star chains offer weekend packages that are well worth
investigating, as they can save you between 20 and 30 percent of
the normal cost. Your excursion to, say, the Sunshine Coast can
then be taken during the week, when it will be less crowded anyway.
   The city also has its share of motels, some quite centrally located
and good value; but it is comparatively short of self-catering
accommodation. Examples of both types feature below.

Brisbane City TraveLodge ♣
Roma St., Brisbane, Qld, 4000
☎ *238 2222* ● *41778* ℗ *238
2288. Map* **16D2** 🔢 *191 rms* 🚗
🔲 🏠 AE 💲 ⓒⓓ VISA
*Location: Above the new interstate rail
and bus terminal; though not in the very
centre still close enough to be an easy*

walk. A recent addition to the
TraveLodge stable, which is tackling
the big international chains in the
Pacific by offering broadly
comparable facilities and services at
reduced rates. The **Drawing Room**
restaurant is recommended.
🔲 ♈ 🍽 🍷 ♦ ♣

Camelot Inn ♣
*40 Astor Terrace, Brisbane, Qld,
4000* ☎ *832 5115* ✆ *45347. Map
16C2* 🛏 *70 rms* 🚗 🖼 AE ⊕ ◉
VISA

*Location: On a quiet street, but close
enough to the centre to be walkable.*
Recommended for budget travellers.
An unpretentious establishment
offering all the benefits of a town
apartment. Decor is the usual motel
drab, but with well-equipped
kitchenettes, a pool and laundry, it is
hard value to beat.
⇌ 🖃 🛎

Gazebo Ramada ♣
*345 Wickham Terrace, Brisbane,
Qld, 4000* ☎ *831 6177* ✆ *41050.
Map 16C2* 🛏 *180 rms* 🚗 ⇌ 🖼
AE ⊕ ◉ VISA

*Location: A commanding position
overlooking the city, a brisk 10mins
away.* The decor of this 4-star
establishment emphasizes cane and
rattan to complement the subtropical
setting. Given the ungainly
pyramidlike structure, the interiors
are surprisingly spacious.
⇌ 🖃 ▼ 🛎

Hilton International Brisbane
*190 Elizabeth St., GPO Box 1394,
Brisbane, Qld, 4000* ☎ *224 9740*
✆ *43476* ® *224 9899. Map 16D2*
🏨 *323 rms* 🚗 ⇌ 🖼 AE ⊕ ◉
VISA

*Location: Central, between Queen St.
shopping mall and Elizabeth St.* An
impressive addition to Brisbane's
quality hotels. The most distinctive
feature is the open-plan 25-floor
interior, a futuristic-looking atrium
with balconies at each floor looking
down on the lobby. The so-called
Wintergarden, a shopping arcade,
covers three floors. Business centre
and three executive floors.
♿ ⇌ 🖃 ▼ 🛥 ✈ 🛎 ⛵ 🛎

Lennons
66 Queen St., Brisbane, Qld, 4000
☎ *222 3222* ✆ *40252* ® *229
9389. Map 16D2* 🏨 *150 rms* 🚗
⇌ 🖼 AE ⊕ ◉ VISA

*Location: Central, next to the Queen
St. shopping mall.* Old Queensland
hotels that have stood the test of time
are an endangered species. This is a
hotel name that goes back more than
a century, though sadly the original
building in George St. has, like many
another historic address in Brisbane,
been demolished. Visitors to
Australia longing for a hotel that
combines comfortably aged leather
and a certain style seek in vain.
Lennon's, however, is doing a
manful job of competing with the big

chains by offering old-fashioned
service.
🖃 ▼ 🛎

Mayfair Crest ♣
*King George Sq., Brisbane, Qld,
4000* ☎ *229 9111* ✆ *41320* ® *229
9618. Map 16D2* 🏨 *403 rms* 🚗
⇌ 🖼 AE ⊕ ◉ VISA

Location: Central, opposite City Hall.
The terrace café is a popular spot
with a Continental feel, overlooking
the throng of King George Sq. A
youthful, lively clientele is drawn to
the facilities, which include a
nightclub, six bars and four
restaurants. 24hr TV news service.
♿ ⇌ 🖃 ▼ 🛥 🛎 🛎

Parkroyal
*Corner of Alice St. and Albert St.,
Brisbane, Qld, 4000* ☎ *221 3411*
✆ *40186* ® *229 9817. Map 16D3*
🏨 *165 rms* 🚗 ⇌ 🖼 AE ⊕ ◉
VISA

*Location: A prime situation, within
easy walking of the city centre and
Parliament, and having attractive
views over the Botanic Gardens.* The
Parkroyal's location is its biggest
draw. The terraced dining area
overlooks the *Botanic Gardens* (see
Sights). As at the *Sheraton* and
Hilton, the facilities are very much
geared to businessmen's needs.
♿ ⇌ 🖃 ▼ 🛥 ✂ 🛎 🛎

Sheraton Brisbane and Towers
*249 Turbot St., Brisbane, Qld,
4000* ☎ *835 3535* ✆ *44944* ® *835
4960. Map 16C2* 🏨 *503 rms* 🚗
⇌ 🖼 AE ⊕ ◉ VISA

*Location: Above the old Central
railway station in the downtown
shopping and business district.* This is a
truly luxurious and elegant Sheraton.
The trend towards two-class
accommodation is represented by the
Towers section, located in the three
top storeys, which offers clublike
seclusion with its own check-in desk
and lounge, and other additional
luxuries. To be thus cocooned from
the hoi poloi costs around 40 percent
more than the standard rate. Top-of-
the-world dining at **Denisons**
restaurant on the 30th floor.
♿ ⇌ 🖃 ▼ 🛥 🛎 🛎

Tower Mill Motor Inn
*239 Wickham Terrace, Brisbane,
Qld, 4000* ☎ *832 1421* ✆ *40382.
Map 16C2* 🛏 *70 rms* 🚗 ⇌ 🖼
AE ⊕ ◉ VISA

Location: Overlooking city centre. A
quality motel-style inn with rooftop
restaurant, bar and a few self-
catering units.
🖃 ▼ 🛎

Eating out in Brisbane

Restaurant standards have not kept pace with the great strides made in improving Brisbane's accommodation in recent years. Given the quality of local ingredients, seafood, beef and tropical produce, there is little excuse for this. Visitors staying at one of the better hotels may find the in-house restaurant offers better dining than many city eateries. The following, however, can be recommended.

Barrier Reef Seafood Restaurant ✿
138 Albert St. ☎ *221 9366. Map 16D2* ▮▮ ▭ ▭ ▭ ᴁ ⊕ ⊙ 𝖵𝖨𝖲𝖠 *Closed Sat lunch, Sun.*

The unpretentious surroundings will not be favoured by diners seeking stylish presentation, but fresh seafood, simply and well prepared, and quite reasonable prices add up to good value. Try the barramundi, a meaty Queensland game fish, which, if fresh, is a genuine treat.

David's
157 Elizabeth St. (upstairs) ☎ *229 9033. Map 16D2* ▮▮ ▭ ᴪ ᴁ ⊕ ⊙ 𝖵𝖨𝖲𝖠 *Last orders 11pm.*

Most of Brisbane's restaurants seem to be named after men. (As well as David's and Michael's, there are Aldo's and Jann's.) The cuisine here is actually Chinese-based (Cantonese) but with international variations.

The Drawing Room ✿
Brisbane City TraveLodge, Roma St. ☎ *238 2288. Map 16D2* ▮▮ ▭ ▭ ᴪ ᴁ ⊕ ⊙ 𝖵𝖨𝖲𝖠

Surprisingly good dining is offered in the restaurant of the *Brisbane City TraveLodge* (see *Hotels*). Unambitious though it may be, it is nevertheless satisfying: a sensible menu, carefully prepared, simple cuisine, and pleasing surroundings and service.

Michael's on the Mall
1st floor, 164 Queen St. Mall ☎ *229 4911. Map 16D2* ▮▮ ▭ ▭ ᴪ ᴁ ⊕ ⊙ 𝖵𝖨𝖲𝖠 *Closed Sun.*

One of Brisbane's most popular restaurants, this can be erratic. The interior is pleasant, and there's a cocktail bar. Local specialities include coral (sea) trout and the Moreton Bay bug, a flavoursome crustacean.

Nightlife and the arts

Like Queensland politics, Brisbane is conservative in its nightlife. The main focus is the performing arts complex at the *Queensland Cultural Centre* (see *Sights*, and below) for theatre, opera and concerts, which has gone some way towards silencing the innumerable Sydney and Melbourne jokes about culture in Queensland.

Flashy discos and urban chic have never been Brisbane's style, but there are a few spots that bop until late. Visiting international artists now include Brisbane on their itinerary, which in the past was not always the case. Check current productions and shows in *This Week in Brisbane*, a giveaway guide available at most hotels, and the daily *Courier Mail*.

Queensland Cultural Centre
South Bank, South Brisbane ☎ *information 240 7229, bookings 844 0201. Map 16E2* ᴪ ᴁ ⊕ ⊙ 𝖵𝖨𝖲𝖠

The performing arts complex has transformed the cultural life of the city, bringing under one roof the **Lyric Theatre**, which has become the principal venue for stage shows, and the **Concert Hall**. It can cost less to see a visiting artist here than in, say, Sydney. Otherwise, for drama productions, the **Brisbane Arts Theatre** (*210 Petrie Terrace* ☎ *369 2344*) remains an important venue.

Sibyl's Nightclub
383 Adelaide St. ☎ *839 2355. Map 16C3* ᴪ ⊙ ⬤ ▭ ▭ ᴁ ⊕ ⊙ 𝖵𝖨𝖲𝖠 *Open Wed-Sat 7pm-3am, Sun 7pm-midnight. Casual dining until 11.30pm.*

This disco-cum-nightclub is Brisbane's most popular young spot. The two-floor establishment includes a casual dining area, open until 11.30pm. The promotion says Sibyl's is open until 3am, but there are actually times when not enough young Brisbanites bop on to warrant staying open very much beyond midnight.

Shopping

Brisbane might not offer the variety of Sydney or Melbourne, but shopping here can be less hectic, with the odd chance, in antiques particularly, of a good buy. Like other centres with international airports, Brisbane's duty-free shops can produce real bargains.

Late-night shopping in the city is on Fri until 9pm, but on Sat shops are open only until noon. The main concentration of shops, including the modern Queen St. Mall, is roughly between George St. and Edward St., and Ann St. and Elizabeth St.

Aboriginal art

Considering that more Aborigines live in Queensland than any other state, one might have expected a good selection of Aboriginal artifacts. Unfortunately this is not the case.

Queensland Aboriginal Creations

135 George St. ☎ 224 5730. Map **16D2** & AE ⊕ ⊚ VISA
This is the curio section of the Department of Aboriginal and Islanders Advancement, and is worth visiting. Boomerangs, T-shirts and bark paintings for the tourists – but also work with more soul. Open Mon-Fri.

Antiques

There is no single hub of the antique trade – rather a few centres with many small stalls under one roof.

Cordelia Street Antique Centre

Corner of Cordelia St. and Glenelg St., South Brisbane
☎ 44 8514. Map **16E2** AE ⊕ ⊚ VISA
Housed in an old church, this centre specializes in quality pieces rather than bric-a-brac. Open Wed-Sun 10am-5pm.

Paddington Antique Centre

167 Latrobe Terrace, Paddington ☎ 369 8458 AE ⊕ ⊚ VISA
Collectors of objects from the 1940s and 1950s will delight in this centre, open seven days from 10am-5pm. Another attraction hereabouts is the **Paddington Circle**, a specialist shopping area in the old suburb to the w of the city on the way to *Mt. Coot-tha* (see *Sights*). The shops are in restored Queensland bungalows in Given Terrace and Latrobe Terrace.

Arcades and department stores

There are a number of modern shopping arcades, including the large **Wintergarden** on the Queen St. Mall, and the **City Plaza** next to the City Hall. But if it is style and old-world charm you seek, *Rowes Arcade* is the first choice. There are the usual department stores, including **Myer** and **David Jones**.

Rowes Arcade

*235 Edward St. Map **16D2*** ▣ AE ⊚ VISA
Restoration skills have transformed a rather nondescript 1950s shopping arcade, in a late-19thC building, into what it might have been: a grand Victorian structure with vaulted ceilings and Australian red-cedar columns. About 20 boutiques. Glassed-in terrace area for lunches.

Brisbane environs and excursions to the coast

There are a number of things to be done with a spare day in the environs of Brisbane. Drive w, for example, to **Mt. Nebo**, 35km (22 miles) into the **Brisbane Forest Park**, which has many pleasant picnic spots, and fine views from the **D'Aguilar Range**. Or take the road N a similar distance to **Redcliffe**, now a rather run-down resort, but actually the first European settlement in Queensland, which had to be abandoned because of fierce opposition from local Aborigines.

Unfortunately, the beaches in the vicinity of Brisbane are not up to Queensland's high standards, and for good swimming you must travel farther afield. The excursions described below offer the same basic features: vast stretches of white beach, superb surf and almost continuous sunshine. Choice of destination will be dictated by what sort of environment you prefer. The distinction, it should be stressed, is an important one. As always in Australia, the distances make it preferable to set aside at least 2 days, and a car is essential.

The Gold Coast
Round trip of 210km (131 miles) to Coolangatta, southern limit of the coast, but allow for an overnight stop.

This is, by a long way, Australia's most popular resort area, and offers very much what you might expect of a local version of the Costa del Sol or Miami, with similar advantages and drawbacks. The beachfront is a solid 30km (19 miles) of high-rises, neon, motels, fast-food outlets and nightspots. At its worst, the Gold Coast is tawdry and overcrowded. On the credit side, there is a great deal to do, particularly for families and younger holidaymakers, and keen competition has given local services, and prices, the sort of edge it would be good to find elsewhere in Australia. The beach everywhere is splendid.

Leave Brisbane via Ann St., following the signs to the South East Freeway, which becomes Route 1, the Pacific Hwy. The turn-off for Southport – the start of the Gold Coast – is 62km (39 miles) s of the city.

From here the resorts run one into the other: **Main Beach**, **Surfers Paradise**, **Broadbeach**, **Mermaid Beach**, **Burleigh Heads**, **Palm Beach**, **Currumbin**, **Tugun**, **Bilinga** and **Coolangatta**. Most populous of all these is Surfers Paradise, where the skyscraper jungle blots out the sun from the beach in the late afternoon. Generally speaking, the farther s you go, the less crowded the resorts become.

There are several off-beach attractions along the way. **Dreamworld** (*open 10am-5pm* ☎ *(075) 53 1133*), a Disneyland imitation on the Pacific Hwy 4km (2½ miles) before the Southport turn-off, is recommended for children young and old, but is pricey. **Sea World** (*open 10am-5pm* ☎ *(075) 32 5131*), a marine showland at Main Beach, features dolphins and sea lions and has an amusement park; as at Dreamworld, a hefty entrance fee gets you admission to all shows and rides. The **Great White Shark Expo** (*open 9am-5.30pm* ☎ *(075) 32 7230*) is also at Main Beach. And **Magic Mountain** (*open 9am-5pm* ☎ *(075) 52 2333*), another fantasyland with illusion shows, is located beyond Mermaid Beach.

☙ The range of accommodation on the Gold Coast is so vast – literally hundreds of motels, hotels and self-catering apartments – that to offer more than a few pointers is impossible. At the height of the season you may be lucky to find a bed at short notice at all; at other times you can take your pick, and even negotiate a rate. Bear in mind that catering standards are variable: self-contained units can mean you eat better, as well as save money.

The **Conrad International Hotel and Jupiters Casino** (*Southport* ☎ *(075) 92 1133* ▥ *to* ▥) offers Hilton-style accommodation and the chance 24hrs a day to lose your shirt. The **Ramada** (*Surfers Paradise* ☎ *(075) 59 3400* ▥) is another 5-star establishment. The **Greenmount Inn** (*Coolangatta* ☎ *(075) 36 1222* ▥) is comfortable and located in a comparatively quiet resort.

The Sunshine Coast
Caloundra, nearest point on the Sunshine Coast to Brisbane, is a round trip of 220km (138 miles). Noosa Heads, the farthest, is 320km (200 miles).

Another sun-drenched stretch of perfect beach, roughly the same distance N of Brisbane as the Gold Coast is S, the Sunshine Coast is, however, much less a resort. The beaches are splendid, the weather just as good, the environment less gaudy, but there are not the distractions of, say, Surfers Paradise. Most travellers are apt to prefer this less commercial development. If your idea of heaven is basking with a good book, and swimming (the surf is good here too), this could be your favourite spot in Australia.

To get there, take Turbot St. going N out of Brisbane and follow signs for Route 1, the Bruce Hwy. The Caloundra turn-off is about 10km (6 miles) beyond Landsborough. From Caloundra the road runs N along the coast for 60km (38 miles) or so to the attractive development of **Noosa Heads** before swinging back inland to the Bruce Hwy. Resorts along the Sunshine Coast include **Maroochydore**, **Marcoola Beach**, **Coolum Beach** and **Peregian Beach**. These are all pleasant spots with excellent surf and swimming, and preferences are a matter for the individual. However, Coolum can be particularly recommended for its beach, placid pace and comfortable accommodation at reasonable rates; Noosa offers plenty of diversion and some fine accommodation.

But the Sunshine Coast has a few attractions besides the beach. At Caloundra there is a two-thirds-scale replica of **Cook's ship**, HMS *Endeavour* (*open 9am-4.45pm* ☎ *(071) 92 1278*). The headland overlooking the Pacific at Noosa is a national park where this splendid coastline is preserved, and offers 10km (6 miles) of walking tracks around the headland, with fine views and good picnicking.

☛ There is no shortage of hotels and motels along the Sunshine Coast, as well as numerous self-catering apartments (although these are usually for a minimum of 2 days). Agencies such as **Accom Noosa** (*Hastings St., Noosa Heads, Qld, 4567* ☎ *(071) 47 3444* ● *43494*) will make bookings and give advice.

The following all have self-catering facilities as well as restaurants: the **Noosa International** (*Noosa Heads* ☎ *(071) 47 4822* ▥▥ *to* ▥▥▥), a luxurious resort with 65 units; the **Terrace Village Inn** (*Noosa Heads* ☎ *(071) 47 3077* ▥▥), centrally located, with studio units and suites; and the **Stewarts Allamanda** (*Coolum Beach* ☎ *(071) 46 1899* ▥), an excellent-value, comfortable motel.

The Great Barrier Reef and islands

When all is said and done, Queensland has one unique natural resource that transcends all others. The beaches in NSW may be almost as good. Tasmania is probably prettier. Victoria is undoubtedly more stimulating. What finally makes Queensland worth visiting is the Great Barrier Reef.

So what, in fact, is the Great Barrier Reef? Quite simply, it is the world's largest complex of coral reefs – more than 2,600 in all – which follow, roughly, the coast for about 2,000km (1,250 miles), incorporate some 300 islands, and – as any self-respecting Queenslander will tell you, with a fondness for dimension that is a local characteristic – also constitute the largest creation of living creatures in the world.

More to the point, the reef is the infrastructure for a quite marvellous marine fauna. Here, at depths in some cases of no more than a couple of feet, are literally hundreds of coral forms in different colours, thousands of shellfish varieties, and, most dazzling of all, the many fish species: vivid parrot fish, angelfish, rays and sharks, which glide through these turquoise waters almost like visions of a fantasy underwater world glimpsed by most people only on film.

You need not be an experienced underwater diver either with scuba or snorkel to enter this world. The wonders of the Great Barrier Reef can be seen as readily from a glass-bottom boat, although skindiving offers profounder pleasure, and can be accomplished by ordinary swimmers.

There are other reasons for visiting the islands. They offer splendid isolation in the sort of Pacific setting represented by exotic advertising campaigns. It is all quite genuine: this is an idyllic, tropical Australia of coconut palms and astonishingly blue seas.

Getting there

One myth has to be dispelled, and that is the idea that having arrived in Queensland, you will find coral reefs lying off the beach. This is not the Red Sea, where you step straight into a brilliantly coloured subaqueous world. The Great Barrier Reef does not start until you are around 450km (280 miles) N of Brisbane, and the southern section is more than 100km (60 miles) out to sea. Generally speaking, the farther N you go, the closer the reef comes to the mainland, but there is no one point at which they meet.

To get to the reef, therefore, involves cruising from the islands as well as the mainland. Some tour operators unfortunately tend to perpetuate the common misconception that the islands are located on coral reefs. In fact, of the 20 or so islands that have been commercially developed as resorts, only three – Green Island, Heron Island and Lady Elliott Island – are genuine coral cays. Others may have fringing reef close by, but to see the Great Barrier Reef in its full splendour you will still need to join a cruise ship or one of the high-speed catamarans operating along the coast.

A word of warning, however. Most of the islands have just one, often extravagantly expensive, resort, and if you have booked an extended stay and find you dislike it, there is little to be done. Quite a number of guests come away from an island with a feeling that what the system needs is an injection of old-fashioned competition. When all fares, accommodation and extras are paid, an excursion to the islands and reef is not going to be cheap, so find out as much as you can in advance. (It is worth asking about stand-by offers available at most island resorts out-of-season, which provide cut-rate accommodation at short notice.)

Cautionary advice should not be regarded as a deterrent. The reef is arguably Australia's greatest natural wonder, with its hundreds of varieties of coral encrusting the seabed, from large mushroom formations to delicate fan shapes. It should leave a memory to cherish.

But, at the risk of labouring a point, avoidable disappointments do occur. You may, for example, go out for a day's sailing on one of the numerous charter yachts in the Whitsundays, a cluster of islands off the coast near Mackay. You will be told that the vessel will be calling at a number of islands, and that during the day you will be able to dive at the reef. Now the chance to island-hop on a graceful 40ft yacht is another of Queensland's attractions. These cruises can be great fun, and they do indeed offer an opportunity to do some snorkeling. But they are decidedly not specialized reef visits, and often what you get to see gives no idea of the wonders of the coral world. Broadly speaking, the visitor who has a week or so to explore the Queensland coast should keep skindiving and sailing apart. That way, neither is likely to be a disappointment.

It is for these reasons that this section has been divided into two main parts. The reef is closest to the mainland and thus most accessible in the far N of the state, and much of the section under the heading *Cairns to Townsville* deals with ways of visiting the reef from here. The central coast, on the other hand, is the cruise capital of Queensland, and the emphasis is in the section *Mackay and the Whitsundays* is on sailing and island resorts.

For further information, contact the **Great Barrier Reef Marine Park Authority** (*P.O. Box 1379, Townsville, Qld, 4810* ☎ *(077) 71 2191*), which has produced an excellent series of pamphlets on corals and marine life.

Cairns to Townsville

This section, which covers the Far North, is presented in the form of an extended excursion. The distance involved, around 650km (400 miles) with side trips, is not great in Australian terms, but 4 days is a minimum time-framework; the region is full of variety, and even a week would not be too long.

Both Cairns and Townsville have international airports, which makes it possible to start, or end, your Australian visit here. Most travellers will want to see *Cairns*, the main centre for visiting the reef. The point of the 370km (231-mile) drive s along the coastal road is that it affords access to a number of islands off the usual track, and ends in *Townsville*, which is one of Queensland's few unheralded pleasures. Cars rented in Cairns can be returned in Townsville, which connects by air with Brisbane and Sydney, as well as other centres. If you were departing Australia from Cairns, the excursion could be done in reverse, starting at Townsville. Either way, much of what is best in Queensland can be found in this relatively small section of the Far North.

Cairns
1,840km (1,150 miles) NW *of Brisbane* ☎ *STD code: 070. Airport* ☎ *50 5222; Ansett* ☎ *51 3366; Australian* ☎ *50 3777. Railway station: McLeod St.* ☎ *51 1111. Car rental: Avis* ☎ *51 5911; Budget* ☎ *51 9222; Hertz* ☎ *51 6399.*
Despite the enormous commercial development that has overtaken Cairns in the past decade, it retains a flavour of the tropics that makes it not quite Australian, rather of the South Pacific. The **wharf**, once called the Barbary Coast, the old **Hides Hotel**, the palm trees, the ethnic blend, which includes Torres Strait islanders: all these seem to belong more in the pages of William Somerset Maugham than Banjo Patterson.

Still, the impact on the town flowing from the tourism boom of the past decade has been immense. Cairns has become a major game-fishing centre, the black marlin being the lure for big-spending sportsmen. The other main attraction, of course, is the Great Barrier Reef. Because of the reef's proximity to Cairns and the little town of **Port Douglas**, about 60km (38 miles) N, these are the best points on the Queensland coast from which to explore the reef.

For the visitor, this is Cairns' main significance. The town has little of intrinsic interest, being more a launching pad for the environs, which include not only the reef, but the splendid tropical

Daintree rainforest, and, to the w, the **Atherton Tablelands**.

Just what you can accomplish will depend on how much time you have. The advised minimum for a stay in the Cairns area would be 2 days, this allowing a day for a visit to the reef and a day for a side trip to the rainforest. An additional day could be spent on a side trip to the Atherton Tablelands, or on the beach.

Odd though it may sound, it is worth considering whether you actually need to stay in Cairns at all. There is no beach to speak of in town, and if you want to spend your 2-3 days here alongside a fine palm-fringed beach it is necessary to drive N. From **Holloway Beach**, about 12km (7½ miles) from Cairns, there are a string of splendid beaches with good accommodation. Some of these are mentioned below under the heading *North to Port Douglas and Daintree*.

What follows is a series of options that could be fitted into a stay in the Cairns region. Additional information from the centrally located **Visitor Information Centre** (*41 Shield St.* ☎ *51 7366, open 8am-6pm*).

☛ The **Pacific International** (☎ *51 0210* ☎ *510210* ▮▮), on the esplanade, is the best hotel at the time of writing; the **Four Seasons** (☎ *51 2311* ☎ *48415* ▮▮), also on the seafront, is comfortable and good value; the old **Hides** (☎ *51 1266* ☎ *48081* ▯), with its stylish facade, is a sentimental favourite, now being refurbished. A **Hilton** is scheduled for completion at the end of 1987.

Seeing the reef

There are two main commercial cruise operators to tne reef, **Hayles** of Cairns (☎ *(070) 51 5644*) and **Quicksilver and Low Isles Cruises** of Port Douglas (☎ *(070) 98 5373*). Both offer a range of cruises to the nearby islands and to the outer reef.

Green Island
Hayles serves this popular resort off Cairns. The *cognoscenti* tend to be contemptuous of Green Island, which hosts a stream of day-trippers and which, far from being a secluded Pacific hideaway, can on a busy day seem more like England's Brighton. It remains, however, a genuine coral cay, and is the easiest and cheapest way of seeing the reef. There are fast and slow (and cheaper) services daily from the Hayles wharf, which include lunch and a spin round the reef in a glass-bottom boat. The coral here suffered quite severely from the voracious crown-of-thorns starfish, but has regenerated to some extent.

The Low Isles
The Low Isles are also coral cays, but without a resort – indeed, the isles are uninhabited except for a lighthouse keeper. They are served by the highly professional Quicksilver and Low Isles Cruises from Port Douglas, with bus connections possible from Cairns and points in-between. A day's outing, departing 10.30am and returning 4.30pm, includes a good lunch, instruction on and use of snorkeling gear, a diving platform, and glass-bottom-boat viewing. The reef here has more varied coral than Green Island, and this excursion arguably offers better value.

The outer reef
The same operators also run cruises to the outer reef. What, it may be asked, does the outer reef offer that is not found elsewhere? The short answer is visibility. Sediment from the seabed is stirred far less than on the inner reef, so that the clarity and colours of coral life and fish are greatly enhanced. The cost of the outer-reef one-day excursion is high but well worth considering as a once-in-a-lifetime experience. If you are only ever going to make

121

one trip out to the Great Barrier Reef, this should be it.

The high-speed catamaran *Quicksilver* moors at a diving platform off Agincourt Reef. Snorkeling equipment, glass-bottom boat viewing and lunch are included. Optional extras are guided snorkeling with a marine biologist and, for those with recognized certificates, two 40mins' dives.

Hayles also cruises to the outer reef, from Cairns, with a stop at Green Island to pick up guests at the resort; but less time is spent

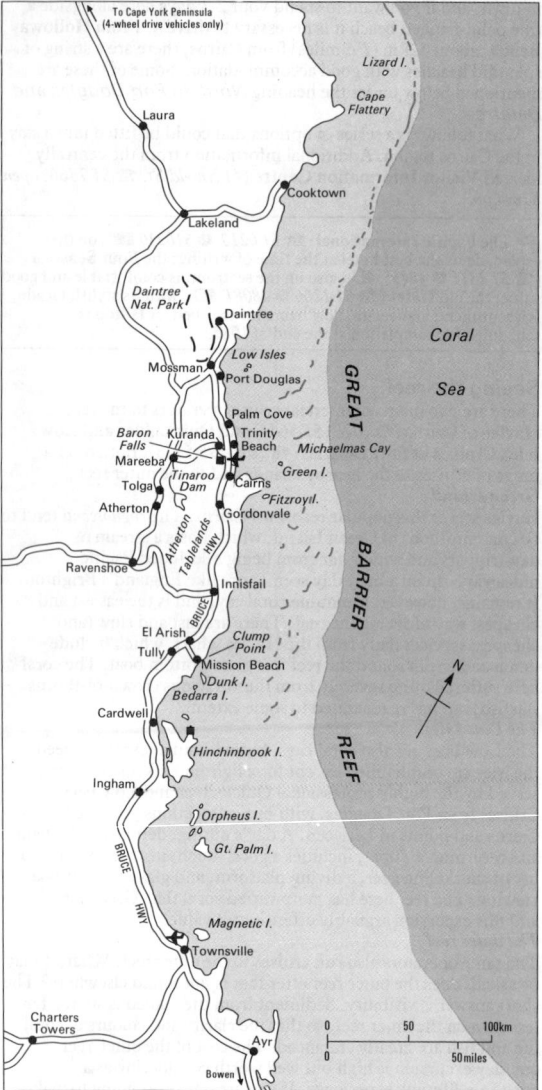

To Cape York Peninsula
(4-wheel drive vehicles only)

Lizard I.

Cape Flattery

Laura

Lakeland

Cooktown

Daintree Nat. Park

Daintree

Coral

Low Isles

Mossman

Port Douglas

Sea

Palm Cove

Baron Falls

Kuranda

Trinity Beach

Mareeba

Michaelmas Cay

Tolga

Tinaroo Dam

Cairns

Green I.

Atherton

Fitzroyl.

Gordonvale

GREAT

Ravenshoe

Innisfail

El Arish

Clump Point

Tully

Mission Beach

Dunk I.

Bedarra I.

BARRIER

Cardwell

Hinchinbrook I.

N

Ingham

Orpheus I.

Gt. Palm I.

REEF

Magnetic I.

Townsville

Charters Towers

Ayr

Bowen

Atherton Tablelands HWY

BRUCE HWY

0   50   100km

0   50 miles

at the outer reef. Another Hayles service, also calling at Green Island, runs to Michaelmas Cay, a protected breeding ground for seabirds.

Other options

Cairns offers access to two other island resorts on the reef. One is **Lizard Island**, possibly Australia's most exclusive getaway, apparently favoured by celebrities and with prices to match. Lizard is reachable only by air, from Cairns.

Fitzroy Island is a happy medium between Green and Lizard islands. This is an attractive spot with good beaches, some walking and a fast catamaran service to the outer reef.

Other pointers for seeing the reef from Cairns: the **Deep Sea Divers Den** (☎ *(070) 51 2223*) offers scuba-diving instruction; **Down Under Aquatics** (☎ *(070) 51 6360*) runs extended diving trips for certified scuba users; and **Sundancer Cruises** (☎ *(070) 51 0444*) has a fast service up the coast to Port Douglas and **Cooktown**, last frontier town of the Far North.

☞ Green Island accommodation: 27 bungalow units (*inquiries and bookings* ☎ *(070) 51 4644* ■□). Fitzroy Island accommodation: in lodges (*inquiries and bookings* ☎ *(070) 51 9588* ■□).

North to Port Douglas and Daintree

Over a distance of only 80km (50 miles) or so, the road N of Cairns runs by some of the loveliest, most unspoiled beaches in Australia, passing the delightful settlement of Port Douglas and the rainforests of Daintree. If at all possible, it really ought not to be missed.

Follow Route 1, the Cook Hwy, N of Cairns. There are turn-offs to beach resorts until at Palm Cove the road joins the coast, and from here to Mossman is a glorious drive. There is accommodation at **Holloways Beach**, 12km (7½ miles) from Cairns, **Trinity Beach**, 24km (15 miles) and **Clifton Beach**, 26km (16 miles). At **Palm Cove**, 30km (19 miles) N of Cairns, is the **Ramada Reef Resort**, a most attractive and comfortable development (see below). Also at Palm Cove is **Wild World** (☎ *(070) 55 3669 for feeding times*), which has a few specimens of the estuarine saltwater crocodile found in these parts; it is not generally appreciated that this is the world's largest and most fearsome reptile.

Port Douglas, although 60km (38 miles) N of Cairns, could serve just as well as your base for N Queensland. This charming little fishing port has as its main attraction the magnificent **Four Mile Beach**, and is the centre of operations for Quicksilver and Low Isles Cruises. Local folk are starting to regret, however, that their sleepy hollow is becoming an exclusive international destination. The **Quintex Sheraton**, a 5-star resort with 300 rooms, golf course and a swimming pool covering 1.6ha (4 acres), is due to open late in 1987, and the impact on a community of just a few hundred is already proving enormous.

The **Daintree National Park**, one of Australia's great, but diminishing, tropical rainforests, stretches almost 57,000ha (140,000 acres), but its southern end is within 20km (12½ miles) of Port Douglas. To get there, continue N on the Cook Hwy to **Mossman**, a small farming town, and follow the turn-off on the left to **Mossman River Gorge**, a lovely unspoiled wilderness where you can picnic and enjoy swimming in a large freshwater pool at the bottom of some rapids (no danger of crocodiles). Platypuses, rarely seen in the wild, can sometimes be spotted surfacing on quiet stretches of the river, and there is grand walking in the rainforest.

There is no shortage of attractions N of Cairns, and if you have only a day to spare after seeing the reef you could spend it well here. **Quandong Quest Rainforest Tours** (☎ *(070) 51 4055*) runs one-day tours of the Daintree in 4-wheel-drive vehicles.

☙ Two alternatives to staying in Cairns are the **Clifton Sands** (*right on Clifton Beach* ☎ *(070) 55 3355* ◼), a secluded spot with self-catering units, and the **Ramada Reef Resort** (*Palm Cove* ☎ *(070) 55 3999* ✆ *48342* ◼◼◼◼ *to* ◼◼◼◼).

Perhaps the best accommodation value in Port Douglas is the **Island Point Motel** (☎ *(070) 98 5126* ◼): superb sea views, and a short walk to the beach. Also comfortable is the **Rusty Pelican Inn**, (☎ *(070) 98 5266* ◼).

Accommodation overlooking Mossman River Gorge is available at the **Silky Oaks Colonial Lodge** (☎ *(070) 98 1666* ◼◼).

🍽 Recommended for dinner in Port Douglas is **Danny's** (☎ *(070) 98 5187* ◼◼), at the waterside, a restaurant of unusual quality in N Queensland. Good bouillabaisse.

Atherton Tablelands

These highlands, at an altitude of 700m (2,300ft), are a popular weekend trip among Cairns residents looking to escape the coastal humidity. A round trip taking in all points along the way is about 185km (115 miles), but although the attractive scenery includes waterfalls, lakes and rainforests, the foreign visitor pressed for time will not miss a great deal by doing only part of the circuit.

An off-beat excursion of obvious interest to rail buffs is offered by Queensland Railways. The **Cairns-Kuranda line**, opened in 1891 and an engineering wonder in its time, is still in service: tourist specials depart from Cairns station twice daily (*8.30am, 9am* ☎ *(070) 51 0531 for bookings*). It stops at the **Barron Falls**, a spectacular sight when in spate, and terminates at the picturesque old station of **Kuranda**.

For motorists, the route to the Atherton Tablelands is clearly signposted from Cairns. Kuranda is 27km (17 miles) by road, and the Barron Falls are passed *en route*. The road continues through **Mareeba**, but a turn-off at Tolga for **Tinaroo Dam** cuts out the town of Atherton, which is of no particular interest. At **Kairi** on Tinaroo Dam it is worth taking the dirt road that rounds the dam to the N and passes through tropical rainforest, where there is a giant old tree known as the **Cathedral Fig**. The road rejoins a tarmac road to **Gordonvale** and Cairns. A short detour, back towards Atherton, leads to **Lake Barrine**, an extinct volcano.

Other trips from Cairns

Cape York Peninsula, the great prong of northern Queensland jutting out into the Coral Sea, is a truly awesome wilderness with access limited strictly to 4-wheel-drive vehicles. Such trips are more in the nature of expeditions of 2wks and more, and are confined to the dry season, June-Dec. Queensland Government Travel Centres can help with information.

Air Queensland (☎ *(070) 50 4333* ✆ *48448*) flies to its own Wilderness Lodge at the tip of Cape York. One Cairns operator, **Going Places** (☎ *(070) 51 4055* ✆ *48338*), runs 5-day camping trips that offer an introduction to the peninsula.

The road to Townsville

The road S, around 370km (230 miles), some distance from the coast, is unremarkable scenically. But it takes in lovely **Mission Beach**, and is the stepping-off point to three islands, Dunk,

Bedarra and Hinchinbrook.

Leave Cairns heading s by Route 1, the Bruce Hwy. Innisfail, 88km (55 miles) away, is an unremarkable commercial centre, but at El Arish, about 40km (25 miles) farther, there is a turn-off to Mission Beach. A few kilometers away is **Clump Point**, the starting point for trips out to **Dunk Island** and the reef.

There are three operators to Dunk, and fares are consequently competitive. The *Quick Cat*, a high-speed catamaran, is one of these, and cruises on from Dunk Island to the Great Barrier Reef; the reef fare includes lunch, snorkeling equipment and glass-bottom-boat viewing.

Dunk Island is lush and unspoiled, but the tariff puts the sole resort, owned by Australian Airlines, in the luxury category (*air transfers from Cairns or Townsville ☎ (070) 68 8199 for inquiries and bookings*). **Bedarra Island** nearby is reachable from Dunk, and is being refurbished to turn it into another exclusive resort. Small wonder that Queensland's islands are quickly becoming inaccessible to all but wealthy travellers.

From Mission Beach the road is signposted to **Tully**, where you rejoin the Bruce Hwy. **Cardwell**, about 50km (30 miles) farther s, is the terminus for ferries to **Hinchinbrook Island**. Having an area of 642sq.km (248sq. miles), this is the largest of the islands, and it has one of the smallest and most luxurious resorts. But it is also possible to camp on Hinchinbrook, with permission from the National Parks office in Cardwell.

The remaining distance to Townsville is about 160km (100 miles).

At Mission Beach a new resort, **Castaways** (☎ *(070) 68 7444* ☻ *48861* ▮▮), is secluded and tasteful and, compared with the adjacent islands, not expensive. For Dunk Island, contact Australian Airlines (☎ *(070) 68 8199* ▮▮▮). Hinchinbrook Island's luxurious resort (☎ *(070) 66 8585* ☻ *148971* ▮▮▮) accommodates just 30 people in great luxury.

Townsville

1,470km (919 miles) NW *of Brisbane ☎ STD code: 077.*
Airport ☎ 81 1211; Ansett ☎ 81 6666; Australian
☎ 50 3777. Railway station: 502 Flinders St. ☎ 72 8211. Car
rental: Avis ☎ 75 2888; Budget ☎ 72 2755; Hertz
☎ 71 6033.

There are few more pleasant urban centres in Queensland than this place of 86,000 souls. It is described as a city – indeed, the second largest in the state – but in most terms it is a charming, leafy town nestling at the foot of a 290m (951ft) peak, **Castle Hill**, overlooking the Pacific. Civic heads have been far more circumspect in allowing new development than their fellows elsewhere in the state, and apart from a new Sheraton hotel-casino down at the port, high-rise building has been confined to the small city-centre. The suburb of **North Ward**, below Castle Hill, consists largely of stylish old colonial homes with wide verandahs.

The city's sights can be easily fitted into a half-day. The lookout at the top of Castle Hill offer a great panorama on either side: out to the Pacific, and back to the hinterland. Down on the park-lined waterfront of **The Strand** are two superb 19thC colonial buildings, the **Customs House** and **NQ Television Centre**, formerly the Queens Hotel. Neither is open for public inspection, but the exteriors alone are worth going to see. At the eastern end of The Strand is the wharf on Ross Creek where the ferries leave for Magnetic Island, and where the **Great Barrier Reef Wonderland**, an attractive concept combining scientific research and entertainment, is scheduled to open in 1987.

The **Information Centre** (*Flinders Mall* ☎ 71 2724) is central.

☞ Townsville has only gained quality hotels quite recently. The **Sheraton Breakwater Casino-Hotel** (☎ 72 4066 ☎ 47999 ▮▮▮▮) is a new high-rise. There is also the **TraveLodge** (*The Strand* ☎ 72 4255 ▮▮▮). The budget-conscious should consider the **Townsville Reef International** (*The Strand* ☎ 21 1777 ☎ 47811 ▮▮▮), good value and on the waterfront.

☞ Recommended for eating out: **Monty's** (*Flinders St. East* ☎ 71 3111 ▮▮▮), for imaginative cuisine, an open-air setting, weekday lunches and dinner Mon-Sat.

Islands and the reef

Two islands are served by transport from Townsville: **Magnetic Island** and **Orpheus Island**. The latter is one of the most expensive of the luxury off-coast Queensland resorts – with astronomic rates per night and similar developments proliferating, it may be wondered where all the guests are coming from.

Magnetic Island, 35mins' ferry ride away (Hayles departs from the wharf roughly on the hour) is far from exclusive. It has a resident population, five resorts and more than a dozen sets of holiday units. But because it is one of the largest islands, being more than 10km (6 miles) across, it still has quiet beaches and coves: Arcadia, for example, is a quieter spot than Picnic Bay. Island transport is by bus or rented Moke.

One of the new generation of fast catamarans, the *Reef Link*, runs from the Townsville wharf, via Picnic Bay on Magnetic Island, to a diving platform on the Great Barrier Reef. The fare covers lunch and snorkeling at the reef (☎ (077) 72 5733 *for bookings*). It should be mentioned, however, that the coral around Townsville was ravaged by the crown-of-thorns starfish, and if possible it is better to take one of the reef cruises that start in Port Douglas or Cairns.

If you end this excursion in Townsville, you can fly s to *Mackay and the Whitsundays*, to Brisbane, Sydney or Melbourne, or internationally.

☞ For details of self-catering accommodation on Magnetic Island contact the information centre at Picnic Bay (☎ 78 5117).

Mackay and the Whitsundays

This region, virtually unknown outside Queensland a decade ago, is now the fastest growing in terms of tourism. The attraction is the island group known as the **Whitsundays**, so named in 1770 by Captain James Cook on his epic *Endeavour* voyage. Of the 74 islands, eight have been developed as resorts, a concentration that offers the widest choice of island accommodation along the Queensland coast. Moreover, the shelter provided by the island chain makes the **Whitsunday Passage** a favourite all-year sailing ground, with opportunities for even the inexperienced and relatively impecunious to get the feel of a wooden deck under canvas.

Once again, the object of this section is to offer a few options to the visitor who has limited time but intends to make full use of it. The approach is necessarily a subjective one, because of the great choice of resorts and cruises. Allowing for transfers, 3 days would be the minimum necessary for anyone wanting to stay on an island and do some sailing. The more specialized sailing packages are generally for 5-7 days.

Those wanting more detailed information before setting out should write to the **Whitsunday Tourism Association** (*P.O. Box 83, Airlie Beach, Qld, 4802* ☎ *(079) 46 6673* ☻ *46493*) for their unusually helpful guides.

Where to start

Begin at **Mackay**, capital of the sugar-growing region, a pleasant and unhurried town roughly halfway up the Queensland coast. It can be reached by air from Sydney, Melbourne or Brisbane. Or extend the previous excursion from *Townsville*, about 5hrs away by road – or do it in reverse, flying one-way to Mackay, renting a car, then driving N to Townsville and Cairns, a total distance of about 740km (460 miles).

In this part of the country a car comes in even more handy than usual, because the logistics of getting to the Whitsundays are complicated. Mackay is the main regional centre, but it is still more than 150km (94 miles) s of **Shute Harbour**, centre for island departures (and the busiest yachting marina outside Sydney). Island guests usually take another flight for the short hop to **Proserpine**, but the independent traveller is better off renting a car in Mackay, where it is unnecessary to linger, and heading N on Route 1, the Bruce Hwy.

Proserpine is about 120km (75 miles) from Mackay. Just to the N of the town is the exit to **Airlie Beach** and Shute Harbour, another 35km (22 miles) away. Airlie Beach is the principal mainland resort of the Whitsundays, and as accommodation at Shute Harbour is extremely limited most visitors use this as their base. Much of the accommodation is undistinguished, but in season it gets crammed: bookings are necessary.

At Airlie Beach you can make your plans for cruising and visiting the islands. The resorts have a bewildering array of brochures on cruising and other entertainment. The **Whitsunday Tourism Association** (☎ *(079) 46 6673*) is good for advice. Island accommodation is bookable in town.

☙ Recommended at Airlie Beach: the **Whitsunday Village Resort** (☎ *(079) 46 6266* ☻ *48529* ▭) has attractive Polynesian-style huts; just out of town, the **Reef Oceania Village** (☎ *(079) 46 6137* ☻ *46021* ▭) is good value for a mainly young clientele.

Sailing in the Whitsundays

The readiest way to get a taste of sailing is on a one-day trip from Airlie or Shute. A number of vessels cruise daily and offer a similar package: a cruise, usually with up to 30 passengers, taking in two or three islands and stopping for snorkeling, windsurfing and lunch (all included in the package price).

Two recommended examples are the *Gretel*, a 67ft sloop that challenged for the America's Cup, and the *Tri Tingira*, a spacious 45ft trimaran more suitable for families, and good value. For snorkeling most vessels cruise to a reef known as **Langford**, but though it is still pleasant to dive here, it should not be imagined that this is the Great Barrier Reef at anything like its best. The first of the large coral reefs, **Hook Reef**, is another 40km (25 miles) or so farther out.

More serious sailing is also more expensive. There are two options for longer cruises: crewed charters, in which you are a guest on board, with all meals and services provided; or what are known as bareboat charters, where you rent a yacht and sail it yourself. Obviously the latter requires some competence, but courses can be arranged at short notice, for which inexperience is not necessarily a disqualification.

Crewed charter options include *Cygnus*, a 55ft ketch, which takes 18 passengers on a one-week cruise, anchoring each evening to camp on an island, and the *Golden Plover*, a square-rigged brigantine, which makes one-week cruises with 30 passengers on a similar basis. Details from **Coral Sea Line** (*P.O. Box 497, Airlie Beach, Qld, 4802* ☎ *(079) 46 6049*).

Bareboat charter operators include **Queensland Yacht Charters** (*P.O. Box 293, Airlie Beach, Qld, 4802* ☎ *(079) 46 9784*) and **Whitsunday Rent-a-Yacht** (*PNB 25, Mackay, Qld, 4741* ☎ *(079) 46 9232*).

The islands

The trend on the islands is increasingly towards exclusive, high-tariff resorts for a pampered few. Of the eight commercial islands in the Whitsundays, for example, two – **Lindeman** and **Hayman** – are undergoing major refurbishment, with a consequent price hike. Another, **Hamilton Island**, is being developed with a budget of the order of A$200m to take around 1,000 guests, with flights from state capitals.

Rates of less than A$100 per person per day are exceptional, but remember that stand-by rates apply when the resort has vacancies, and these can involve big savings. For example, at **Whitsunday 100**, one of the more reasonably priced resorts, on **Long Island**, the daily rate is reduced by 35 percent on stand-by. Some choices:
Daydream Island A tiny island that is just about all resort. Windsurfing, waterskiing, canoeing, tennis, and access by launch to the reef for snorkeling and scuba diving (☎ *(079) 46 9200* ☏ *48519*).
South Molle Island A resort for the young – plenty of nighttime activity. Usual watersports, launch to reef, tennis, golf; 400ha (990 acres) of national park walks (☎ *(079) 46 9433* ☏ *48132*).
Long Island In addition to the **Whitsunday 100** resort mentioned above (☎ *(079) 46 9400*), Long Island has a remarkably cheap resort, **Palm Bay**, with self-catering cabins (☎ *(079) 46 9233*).
Hook Island This large island of unspoiled beauty does not have a resort. What it does have to make the 90mins' launch-ride out from Shute Harbour worthwhile is an underwater observatory, a viewing platform 9m (30ft) below the surface that is an obvious attraction for the elderly, for children, and for anyone unable to view the reef as a swimmer.

Other islands

For the overseas visitor there are two other islands that are remote and do not fit into a convenient excursion-type framework, but nevertheless have specific attractions. One of the islands, **Heron**, is a true coral cay – in other words, it is actually part of the reef, with coral growing up to the beach. The other is **Great Keppel Island**, where the emphasis is on entertainment and a fairly hectic nightlife. Both are at the bottom end of the Great Barrier Reef, between Rockhampton and Gladstone. In general terms, the cost of getting there is such that it is only worthwhile if you intend staying some time, and it would be advisable to think in terms of a package, which includes air transfers.

Great Keppel Island

The island is directly off the coast from **Rockhampton**, capital of
the Queensland cattle-farming region and a town of some interest
to students of colonial architecture. If only more hotels were like
the 19thC **Criterion** (*Quay St, Rockhampton* ☎ *(079) 22 1225* ☐):

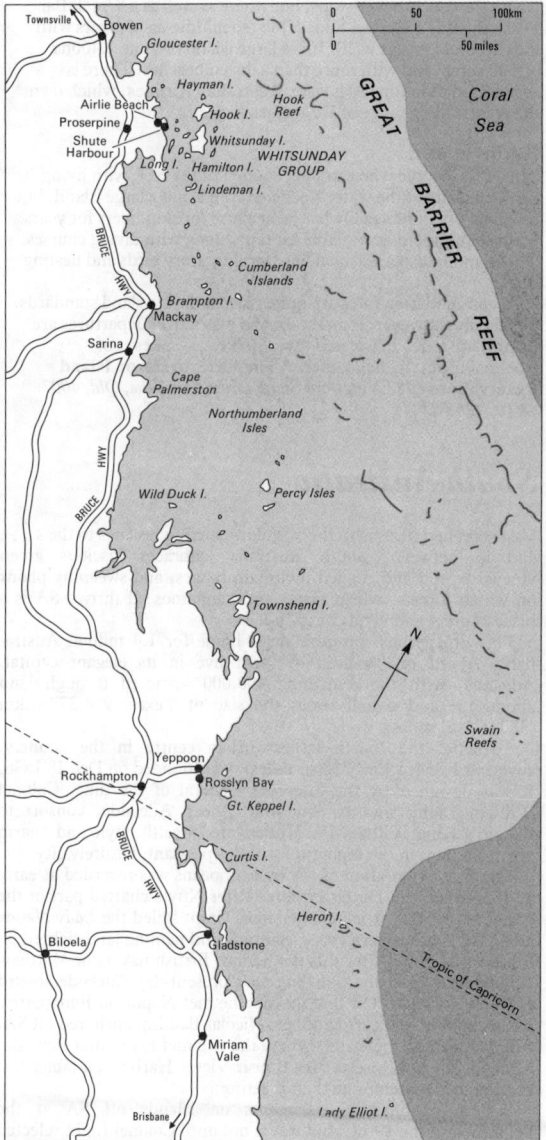

not only splendid to look at, but quite acceptable accommodation at exceptional value.

For those not on a fly-in package, Great Keppel is accessible by launch from **Rosslyn Bay**, a rather seedy little port that is itself a 40km (25-mile) bus ride from Rockhampton.

Great Keppel is billed as being all about up-tempo fun: a resort where the music never stops, but where as well as a Wreck Bar Disco there is a Keppel Kids Klub (so middle-aged ravers with kids are welcome as well). It is a large island of some 1,400ha (3,500 acres) and with more than a dozen beaches. There is accommodation for 320 guests. **Australian Airlines**, which owns the resort, has a range of Keppel packages.

Heron Island

This is for people who can't get enough of the reef, with living coral virtually at the water's edge. Heron is not a large island, but the diversity of its sea life has been a lure for skindivers for years. Scuba equipment is available for rent, along with diving courses. The island is also a seasonal base for migratory birds and nesting turtles.

Accommodation rates are quite reasonable by island standards. Transport, however, is awkward and expensive: departures are from Gladstone, an isolated town 107km (67 miles) s of Rockhampton, by helicopter. All inquiries to **Heron Island Reservations** (*482 Kingsford Smith Drive, Brisbane, Qld, 4007* ☎ *(07) 268 8224*).

South Australia

Vast scorched deserts to the N, golden surfing beaches to the s . . . and in between, South Australia embraces luscious green vineyards, red and rugged mountain ranges, and sweeping plains on which forests, wheat farms and kangaroos all thrive. SA is a place of great and vivid contrasts.

This prosperous, proud state is home for 1.4 million Australians. About one million of them live in its elegant capital, Adelaide, with the remaining 400,000 scattered through land about one and a half times the size of Texas: 984,377sq.km (380,071sq. miles).

Adelaide, the fourth largest urban centre in the country, covering 1,854sq.km (716sq. miles), was founded on Dec 28 1836. It was designed by the Surveyor General of the time, Colonel William Light, and named after Queen Adelaide, consort to Britain's King William IV. Understated wealth, style and charm are prominent in the topography of this pleasant, leisurely city.

The first exploration of SA by Europeans was recorded as early as 1627 when the Dutch explorer Peter Nuyts charted part of the coastline. In 1801 Lieutenant James Grant sailed the *Lady Nelson* along the southeastern coast, claiming and naming land sighted on his journey. Soon after this the famous British navigator Matthew Flinders explored the coastline near present-day Adelaide aboard HMS *Investigator*. On that journey he met Napoleon Bonaparte's naval explorer and cartographer, Nicolas Baudin, anchored off SA. Flinders named the waters where the two met Encounter Bay (and a 100yrs later at Rosetta Head, near Victor Harbour, a tablet was erected to commemorate their meeting).

Sealers established settlements on islands off SA at the beginning of the 19thC, but it was not until Colonel Light selected his site for Adelaide, on the banks of the Torrens River, that the first settlers put down their roots in the new land. No convicts were transported to SA; it is the only state that was settled entirely by free settlers. Perhaps as a result, SA has bred a distinct elite: families that cling onto their ancestral and social connections in a way that is seen nowhere else in the country.

The lack of cheap convict labour did little to help those struggling to establish themselves. But then the discovery of copper in 1842 helped solve their problems, raising finance and attracting hopeful and skilled newcomers to what was by now a crown colony. Adelaide swiftly developed into an agricultural centre, processing and transporting wheat, wool and fruit. From Europe came Lutheran refugees. They brought with them the wine-making talents of their native land and settled in the Barossa Valley, establishing what was to become the foundations for the Australian wine industry.

In 1856 a legislative assembly was elected and the colony attained self-government. (From 1863 until 1911 its administrators were also responsible for the Northern Territory.) Then in 1901 SA became a State of the Commonwealth of Australia.

Most of SA is less than 300m (1,000ft) above sea level, although there is a series of "hills" in the NW that rise to 1,440m (4,725ft). But that is remote and inhospitable country. More accessible is the Flinders Ranges, 430km (270 miles) NE of Adelaide, a ribbon of majestic peaks and gorges that abounds in scenic delights and wildlife. Wedge-tailed eagles, frilly-necked lizards, cockatoos, emus and wallabies . . . they, along with artists, photographers and other visitors, all lay claim to territory in this dramatically beautiful national park.

The Outback can be as astonishing as it is unique. This really is the land of the last frontier. Unforgettable for those who venture into the desert country is Andamooka and the lunar landscape of the underground city of Coober Pedy. From these two comes 75 percent of the world's opal, gouged from the yellow earth by fortune-seeking miners from all over the world. Coober Pedy is like no other place; the diggers have carved intricate dug-outs from the rock, creating surprisingly elegant underground homes that enjoy "natural air conditioning" in the desert heat.

SA, of course, is the centre of the Australian wine industry, producing between 60 and 75 percent of all wine, making the finest of the best-known Australian wine styles, and winning the majority of the country's wine show awards. Many of the vineyards are close to Adelaide. The state's major wine areas are the Adelaide Hills, Adelaide Plains, Barossa Valley, Clare Valley, Coonawarra, Padthaway-Keppoch, Langhorne Creek, McLaren Vale and Riverland.

The most fertile area is in the SE where the mighty Murray River makes its way from Renmark through to the Southern Ocean at Lake Alexandrina. The Murray itself, which flows through three states, offers visitors to SA hundreds of kilometres of picturesque, navigable waters to chug along. There are luxury cruisers, with every conceivable fitting for the would-be pampered, as well as paddle-wheel houseboats that allow independent boatsmen or women to explore the great river. Some of these self-drive rental-boats have two-way radios to allow their crews to call for "room service" from base; a speedy courtesy boat delivers whatever is required when the fish are not biting.

And the state has 3,700km (2,300 miles) of coastline, from long, secluded, sandy beaches to 100m (330ft) sheer-drop cliffs that are battered by huge seas, the haunting cries of the albatross and, in winter, chilling Antarctic winds. The more hospitable parts of this coast, however, are there to delight swimmers, sailors and fishermen, or those who simply crave a place to walk in solitude.

There are more than 100 islands off SA. The biggest, Kangaroo Island, 145km by 50km (90 by 31 miles), is easily reached by plane or ferry from Adelaide. American sealers established a base here as far back as 1803. Kangaroo Island, which provides some of the most rewarding fishing in Australia, is unspoiled and fascinating. Teeming in accessible wildlife, it is a favourite attraction for visitors. Seals play on its beaches, and a tour through its national park will quickly reveal why it was given its name.

The boot-shaped Yorke Peninsula, to the w of Adelaide, has become known as "Little Cornwall". For when copper was discovered there, it attracted Cornishmen from halfway round the world, and though the copper is now exhausted, the Cornish heritage lives on in towns like Moonta.

Still farther to the w is the Eyre Peninsula, enjoying some of the state's most rugged coastal scenery. Its main centre, Port Lincoln, is the focal point for the tuna- and lobster-fishing industries. A popular coastal resort, it was once considered as the possible capital for SA.

To the SE of Adelaide, stretching towards the Victorian border, is the flat, almost mysterious Coorong, the lagoon country protected from the open sea by the Younghusband Peninsula. This land of islands, inlets and lakes is the nesting place for thousands upon thousands of pelicans. The Australian film *Storm Boy*, about a youngster who befriends a pelican, was shot here.

SA has large deposits of iron ore and natural gas. There are important engineering plants, and chemical processing and oil refining take place in and around Adelaide. The state has also been a centre for the automobile industry in Australia. From the 1950s, it has attracted to its assembly lines many immigrants, a big percentage of them British car workers, who, riding waves of hope and recession, have made their mark on Adelaide and its satellite city, Elizabeth.

To the NW of Adelaide is Whyalla, which, with a population of 30,000, is the second largest city in the state. It holds the third biggest steelworks in Australia. The country's largest shipbuilding plant was also here until recession brought closure in 1978.

Adelaide, a city nestling calm and distinguished between the Mount Lofty Ranges and the waters of St Vincent Gulf, was designed for those who want to live well without living dangerously. The air is clean, the pace relaxed; the streets and the parkland are inviting to walkers, the driving free of choking traffic jams. Thanks to the foresight of its planner, Colonel William Light, the city is wrapped in an unbroken, winding green belt of parks and recreation areas.

But Adelaide is a lively city. The Australian Grand Prix, a magnet for the country's enthusiastic band of motor-racing followers, is run here, enhanced by a week of frantic state, civic and private celebrations. Certainly, Adelaide enjoys its partying; nightlife – discos, piano bars, cabarets, rock and jazz clubs – thrives here. A focal point for the city's entertainment is the new Adelaide Casino, conveniently housed in a splendidly restored old Adelaide railway station building on North Terrace.

Above all, though, Adelaide is *the* festival city. The first biennial Festival of Arts was staged in 1960 and has grown to become Australia's premier occasion for the performing and visual arts. The Adelaide Festival is held mainly in and around the Festival Centre complex on the bank of the Torrens.

This is a place of fine architecture: "the city of churches", it has been called. From central Victoria Sq., you can walk in any direction and appreciate eye-catching examples of colonial building at its finest. There are the impressive spires of St Peter's Cathedral, the elaborate face of Edmund Wright House on King William St., Ayers House, the lacework verandahs of old hotels, mansions, and carefully restored bluestone villas and cottages.

Adelaide's grid-system of streets and squares encourages the pedestrian, making the city particularly easy to get around. One stroll that is a must for the shopper is along Rundle Mall, Australia's most concentrated shopping precinct. Department stores, boutiques, arcades, fast-food shops, fruit and flower stalls, and buskers . . . they elbow one another for space in this street cut off from the traffic. But if that becomes too crowded, then Adelaide's tranquil green belt is only a stroll away.

It can be deceptive to the first-time tourist. The beat appears to be a touch slower than most of Australia's major cities, yet there is always something going on, always something to see. It is a beautiful, charming and generally relaxing place to visit.

Adelaide enjoys a warm, temperate "Mediterranean-style" climate: a short, generally mild winter and a long, dry summer. Summer (Dec-Feb) is warm to hot, with an average maximum of 29°C (87°F); winter (June-Aug) has an average maximum of 17°C (62°F). For other parts of SA, the climate varies greatly.

The city throws itself into a celebratory frenzy for two big events: the annual Australian Grand Prix (Formula One motorracing) and the biennial Adelaide Arts Festival. When these take place there is no shortage of things to see and do; but even when Adelaide life is a lot quieter there is much to discover and explore. Be warned: the broad, long streets encourage you to stroll farther than you would in lesser cities.

Adelaide

Maps 12–13 ☎ *STD code: 08. Airport:* ☎ *352 9211; Ansett* ☎ *212 1111; Australian* ☎ *217 3333. Railway stations: for country and interstate services, Passenger Rail Terminal, Keswick* ☎ *217 4111/217 4444; for suburban services, Adelaide railway station, North Terrace* ☎ *210 1000. Car rental: Avis* ☎ *354 0444; Budget* ☎ *223 1400; Hertz* ☎ *51 2856. South Australian Government Travel Centre: 18 King William St., Adelaide, SA, 5000* ☎ *212 1644. American Express Travel Service: 13 Grenfell St., Adelaide, SA, 5000* ☎ *212 7099. Royal Automobile Association of South Australia (RAA): 41 Hindmarsh Sq., Adelaide, SA, 5000* ☎ *223 4555.*

Orientation

Adelaide holds a central position on Australia's southern coast. The city lies on a coastal plain, between the Mount Lofty Ranges in the E and 32km (20 miles) of the beaches of Gulf St Vincent to the W. Although there has been some growth in the N and the S, most people still live within 15km (10 miles) of the city centre.

The city's central business district, in keeping with Colonel Light's original plans, is 1sq. mile. A grid pattern of streets, with five squares transposed upon it, makes it easy to explore. Framing this pattern of streets are North, East, South and West terraces. Treelined North Terrace is considered one of the city's most elegant avenues; on it stands Parliament House, the Holy Trinity Church, the State Library, the South Australian Museum, the Art Gallery, Government House and the University of Adelaide.

A kilometre or so N along King William Rd., separated from the main part of the city by the Torrens River and the ubiquitous parklands, are the bluestone cottages, old mansions and quaint hotels of splendidly restored North Adelaide.

Adelaide airport is about 6km (4 miles) w of the city. Port Adelaide, 10km (6 miles) NW, has a container terminal and modern international cruise ships terminal. Railways link Adelaide with Sydney, Melbourne, Perth and Alice Springs.

Seeing the city

Do make sure you have a comfortable pair of walking shoes when you visit Adelaide, since there is no better way to explore the city than on foot. Its main streets are broad and lined with a blend of impressive 19thC and modern architecture, with many sights of interest close at hand. In the fierce heat of Feb, of course, walking can be something to restrict to early morning or late evening, though the shade of trees and the relief offered by cool shopping arcades or hotels is never too far away.

The hub of the city, its central point, is Victoria Sq. There is much to see whatever direction you travel. A stroll N along King William St., however, will take you beyond the insurance offices and banks, across North Terrace, and down to the Adelaide Festival Centre, where you can wander along the grassy banks of the Torrens River. It is a perfect place for a picnic. On the river itself are the small paddle boats and motor cruisers of the so-called "Popeye fleet", all of which can be rented.

The Zoo is a little to the E along the river; and the really energetic may care to continue , past Adelaide Oval, where Test cricket is played, into North Adelaide. Boutiques, art galleries and restaurants are among the many extra attractions in this area.

For those who have walked too far, Adelaide's public transport system is there to offer relief. It brings most places of interest within easy reach, and is generally inexpensive. For the disabled there is a free information service, the **Disability Information and Resource Centre** (*215 Hutt St.* ☎ *233 7522*).

Buses

Adelaide and its suburbs are well catered for by clean and efficiently run State Transport Authority (STA) buses. There are various designated departure points within the city, while elsewhere the pick-up and set-down points are clearly signposted. The buses run 6am-11.30pm from Mon-Sat and 9am-10.30pm on Sun. A route map and timetables are available at the **STA Centre** (*79 King William St.* ☎ *210 1000*). The centre will also provide information on the **Circle Line** bus. This operates around Adelaide every 15mins, linking outbound bus, train and tram services. It runs 7am-6pm from Mon-Fri, and 8am-noon on Sat.

Adelaide also has its free bus services. The **Beeline** and **City Loop** buses circle the main shopping area 8am-6pm from Mon-Fri, and 8am-noon on Sat.

The Adelaide Explorer

This tourist bus, somewhat eccentrically decorated as an old Adelaide tram, takes visitors around some of the city's major attractions – Adelaide Casino, HMS *Buffalo*, the Old Parliament House and Adelaide Zoo among them. Passengers may board or alight as many times as they wish. The Adelaide Explorer starts its circular journeys at the **South Australia Government Travel Centre** (*18 King William St.*) Further information: **Briscoes Coach Holidays** (*101 Franklin St.* ☎ *212 7344*).

Trams

Adelaide's only electric tram route runs between Victoria Sq. in the city's centre to the seaside suburb of Glenelg, where the first colonists landed. The trams operate 6am-11.30pm from Mon-Sat, and 9am-10.30pm on Sun. The journey takes about 25mins. Further information: **STA Centre** (☎ *210 1000*).

Railways

Suburban trains operate from Adelaide railway station on North Terrace to Bridgewater, Noarlunga, Outer Harbour, Grange and Gawler from 6am-11.30pm weekdays, with reduced services at weekends and public holidays. Tickets may be bought at the major stations or on trains, and can be used, within a 2hr time limit, on the STA tram and buses as well. Further information: **STA Centre** (☎ *210 1000*).

Taxis

As in other Australian state capitals, meter-operated taxis are to be found at hotels, transport terminals and taxi ranks around the city. Or you can simply hail them in the street. Vacant cabs have an illuminated sign on the roof. Where multiple hiring occurs (and the first customer makes the decision on this) only 75 percent of the metered fare is payable. The main taxi companies include **Amalgamated** (☎ *223 3333*), **Suburban** (☎ *211 8888*) and **United Yellow** (☎ *223 3111*).

Bus tours

Adelaide has an excellent selection of half-day and full-day sightseeing bus tours covering the sights in and around the city. For details, contact the **South Australian Government Travel Centre**.

Sights and places of interest

Adelaide Festival Centre

King William Rd. ☎ *216 8713/211 8999. Map 12C3* & *✗* ▣
☜ Open for guided tours (🚌) on the hour Mon-Fri
10am-4pm, Sat at 10.30am, 11.30am, 1pm, 2pm (check day
before ☎ *213 4788).*

The Adelaide Festival Centre's peaceful location on the bank of the Torrens River, overlooking parkland, tends to remind English visitors of Stratford-on-Avon. It both welcomes and relaxes those who wish to stroll, rest or think within its gaze.

The architecture may be somewhat overly geometrical to inspire great passion, but it is neither too grand nor intimidating. Adelaide's performing arts complex suggests an easy intimacy. It is very egalitarian, very much a place for all the people, certainly not elitist.

This popular centre, which was built within 3yrs and completed in 1973, contains a main 2,000-seat auditorium, a remarkably versatile drama theatre (612 seats), and an experimental theatre (360 seats). Outside there is an open-air amphitheatre, framed by vine-covered fences and a backdrop of trees and shrubs.

Adelaide has its own symphony orchestra, chamber music group, theatre, opera and dance companies, and the theatres are kept well lit throughout the year. There are restaurants, bars and 1.2ha (3 acres) of open plaza and terrace that make the complex one of the city's favourite meeting places.

Art Gallery of South Australia

North Terrace ☎ *223 7200. Map 13C4* ▣ & *✗* ▣ *Open*
10am-5pm. Closed Christmas Day, Good Friday.

The focal point for South Australian art-lovers, this has impressive collections of Australian, English and European paintings, intriguing historical material from the early days of SA, and a comprehensive display of prints. Among the gallery's most prized exhibits are its Thai, Annamese and Chinese ceramics.

For the gallery's guide service, contact its education section (☎ *223 7200*). There is a bookshop in the foyer, and meals and refreshments are available in the coffee shop, located on the gallery's basement level.

Ayers House

288 North Terrace ☎ 223 1196. Map 13D4 ⚏ *✗ by appointment (☎ 223 1655). Open Tues-Fri 10am-4pm, Sat, Sun 2-4pm.*

An elegant bluestone mansion, once the home of a former state premier, Sir Henry Ayers, and today the headquarters of the South Australian National Trust. Ayers House was designed by Sir George Kingston and took almost 30yrs to build. Its central one-storied section was completed in 1846; Sir Henry later added to it the bow window dining and drawing rooms. Now completely restored, the present building contains two restaurants. It is a favoured choice of students of early colonial architecture. (See *Henry Ayers Room* in *Restaurants*.)

Botanic Gardens ★

North Terrace ☎ 228 2311. Map 13C4 ⚏ ⚙ *✗ Fri 10am from the kiosk* ⚐ *Open Mon-Fri 7am-sunset, Sat, Sun, hols 9am-sunset.*

Choose a cool, sunny morning or a fine late afternoon, a few hours before sunset. Dress comfortably, casually . . . and walk quietly through the verdant arch of the Botanic Gardens. Then feast your eyes on 16ha (40 acres) of Australian and exotic trees, shrubs and flowers, among them fine displays of lilies and lotuses, cacti and succulents. The greenhouses and hothouses also contain many spectacular and rare plants. The glass **Palm House** was made in Germany in 1871.

HMS Buffalo ★

Patawalonga Boat Haven, Adelphi Terrace, Glenelg North ☎ 294 7000 ⚏ ⚙ ✴ ⚐ *Open Mon-Fri 9am-5pm, Sat, Sun, hols 10am-5pm.*

Forget your qualms. This full-scale replica of the *Buffalo*, the ship that brought Governor Hindmarsh and the state's first colonists to Glenelg in 1836, is far from maritime kitsch for the tourists. It contains old seafaring artifacts, fascinating extracts from the captain's log, and personal diaries of the original immigrants. These, together with illustrations and photographs, recall the voyage from Portsmouth, England, in July 1836 to Holdfast Bay on Dec 28 1836. The ship, constructed from the original 1813 Admiralty plans at a cost of A$1.5 million in 1980, also holds a restaurant and bar and a small aquarium.

Constitutional Museum (Old Parliament House) ★

North Terrace ☎ 212 6066. Map 12D3 ⚏ *for audiovisual show. Open Mon-Fri 10am-5pm (and Wed 6-9.30pm), Sat, Sun 1.30-5pm. Closed Christmas Day, Good Friday.*

One of Adelaide's more unlikely star attractions, the Old Parliament House, built in 1855 as SA's original Legislative Council Chamber, is now Australia's only museum of political history. As well as the curios and recollections of the pioneers, there is a well-produced audiovisual show, *Bound For South Australia*, which depicts the story of the state from its Aboriginal beginnings to the present day.

Light's Vision
Corner of Pennington Terrace and Montefiore Rd., North Adelaide. Map 12B2 ⊡ ✱ ➤ ⟪

At the peak of Montefiore Hill, this is an appropriate tribute to Colonel William Light, the man who planned the layout of the city that lies below. The lookout provides excellent views across parklands and the Torrens River, over the city of Adelaide and onto a backdrop of the Adelaide Hills.

Col. Light is also commemorated once a year with a toast in South Australian wine by the Mayor at Adelaide Town Hall. A silver bowl was presented to the city by some of the colony's original founders for just this purpose.

St Peter's Cathedral
Pennington Terrace, North Adelaide. Map 12B3 ⊡ ✗ *3pm second Sun of each month.*

The building of St Peter's, the Anglican pride of the City of Churches, began in 1869 and was completed in 1876. Its towers and spires were built and consecrated in 1902. The cathedral has the heaviest and finest bells in the southern hemisphere.

South Australian Museum
North Terrace ☎ *223 8911/223 8863. Map 12C3* ⟐ ✗ *Sun from 2-3pm: check first. Open Mon, Tues, Thurs-Sat 10am-5pm, Wed 1-5pm, Sun 2-5pm. Closed Christmas Day, Good Friday.*

This museum holds the largest and most carefully researched collection of Aboriginal artifacts in the world. It also boasts a comprehensive Melanesian collection and a fine display of New Guinea amphibia. The **Natural History Museum** contains the world's largest collection of Australites.

Zoological Gardens
Frome Rd. ☎ *267 3255. Map 13B4* ▨ ⟐ ▣ ✱ ➤ *Open 9.30am-5pm. Closed Christmas Day.*

The Zoo, like so many of the appealing tourist spots in Adelaide, is close to the city. This and its attractive parklike setting rightly puts it at the top of most sightseeing lists.

The Zoo enjoys a particularly high reputation in Australia and abroad both for its collection of Australian birds and its skills in breeding rare species of animals in captivity. Among its treasured exhibits are sloths, ring-tailed lemurs, agoutis, coatis, giant anteaters, squirrel and spider monkeys, and polar bears. There is also a special "children's zoo" in which youngsters are encouraged to meet tame animals at close range.

Accommodation

Adelaide provides the full range of accommodation, from first-class international hotels to small motels, private hotels and self-catering apartments. Generally, prices are a little cheaper than in Sydney, Melbourne and Perth, although there are signs that this is changing. Extras in larger hotels, as in other cities, range from courtesy buses to valet parking, from a daily bowl of fresh fruit or flowers in the room to in-house video movies, or from free drinks to tickets for a disco.

As well as the hotels listed below, there are homestay and farm holidays available for visitors to SA. These can be organized through the **South Australian Government Travel Centre** (*18 King William St., Adelaide, SA, 5000* ☎ *212 1644*).

Adelaide Parkroyal
226 South Terrace, Adelaide, SA,
5000 ☎ *223 4355* IDD ☺ *82156*
☺ *232 0769. Map 12E3* ▥ *95 rms*
🛏 🚗 🍴 AE ☺ ☺ VISA
Location: At southern end of city. This
peaceful hotel provides superb views
of the Adelaide Hills as well as access
to a jogger's paradise in the nearby
parks. The management have
obviously gone out of their way to
attract visiting business executives,
with secretarial services, and a
lounge-cum-private bar for guests
only. There is 24hr room service and,
for insomniacs, in-house movies.
The **Christies** restaurant offers an
"international" *à la carte* menu.
🛏 ▣ 🍴 🍸 🎿

Earl of Zetland
44 Flinders St., Adelaide, SA,
5000 ☎ *223 5500* IDD ☺ *88765.*
Map 13D5 ▥ *30 rms* AE ☺ ☺
VISA
Location: Corner of Gawler Pl., in the
heart of Adelaide's busy shopping
district. A modest but comfortable
Victorian-style hotel. Its rooms are
clean and brightly decorated, with
the facilities you might expect from a
pricier hotel. Friendly atmosphere in
the bars below.
▣ 🍴

Gateway
147 North Terrace, Adelaide, SA,
5000 ☎ *217 7552* IDD ☺ *88325*
☺ *216 5131. Map 12D2* ▥ *226*
rms 🚗 🍴 AE ☺ ☺ VISA
Location: Close to Festival Theatre,
opposite the Casino. This favourite
choice of the interstate arts festival
crowd is within a glance of the most
important buildings in the city. The
smartly efficient Gateway, a sister to
the Ansett International in Perth,
contains one of the more
distinguished of the city's hotel-
restaurants, the **Chelsea**, whose
French/international cuisine appeals
to discerning locals as well as the
hotel's regular guests. The piano
cocktail lounge is a popular meeting
place for young players.
🎿 🛏 ▣ 🍴 🍸 🎿 🎿

Grosvenor ♣
125 North Terrace, Adelaide, SA,
5000 ☎ *51 2961* IDD ☺ *82634*
☺ *231 0765. Map 12D3* ▥ *289*
rms 🚗 🍴 AE ☺ ☺ VISA
Location: Directly opposite Adelaide
Railway Station. A comfortable
Edwardian establishment with an
admirable two-tiered system of
accommodation: budget rates are
available for those prepared to accept
rooms a little less luxurious than the
standard fare. Within the hotel is a
gift shop, hairdresser and
gymnasium. Four large rooms are
reserved for conventions.
▣ 🍴 🐂 🍸 🎿

Hilton International Adelaide ♣
233 Victoria Sq., Adelaide, SA,
5000 ☎ *217 0711* IDD ☺ *87173*
☺ *231 0158. Map 12E3* ▥ *387*
rms 🚗 🍴 AE ☺ ☺ VISA
Location: Centrally placed in the city's
leafy and graceful Victoria Sq. First
class! Since its opening in 1982, the
Hilton has maintained a position as
Adelaide's most distinguished luxury
hotel. Among its attractions is **The
Grange**, arguably the city's finest
restaurant. Both it and **Herbig's
Gum Tree**, a more comfortably
priced family restaurant, are
decorated with specially
commissioned artworks. One of
several special features of this
unusually good hotel is a "non-
smokers floor"; another is a floor of
19 rooms specially equipped for
handicapped guests. The Hilton also
offers comprehensive secretarial
services for international
businessmen.
🔱 🎿 ▣ 🍴 🍸 🎿 🏊 🍸 🎿 🎿

Hotel Adelaide
62 Brougham Pl., North Adelaide,
SA, 5006 ☎ *267 3444* IDD
☺ *82174* ☺ *239 0189. Map 12B3*
▥ *146 rms* 🚗 🍴 AE ☺ ☺ VISA
Location: Overlooks central Adelaide
from one of the oldest parts of the city.
Recently redecorated North Adelaide
hotel with panoramic views over the
main business and shopping district.
Management is smart and helpful.
Two main restaurants offer
international meals. Try to insure
you get a room overlooking the
parklands and the Adelaide Festival
Theatre.
🔱 🎿 ▣ 🍴

Old Adelaide Inn
Corner of O'Connell St. and
Gover St., North Adelaide, SA,
5006 ☎ *267 5066* ☺ *89271* ☺ *267*
2946. Map 12B2 ▥ *63 rms* 🚗 🍴
AE ☺ ☺ VISA
Location: Right in the bluestone heart
of swanky North Adelaide. A hotel
that prides itself on its "old-world
charm". Built in the early 1980s, it is
a perfect base for exploring the
mansions of North Adelaide.
🔱 🎿 ▣ 🍴 🍸 🎿 🏊 🍸

Patawalonga Motor Inn
13 Adelphi Terrace, Glenelg
North, SA, 5045 ☎ *294 2122* IDD
☺ *82824* ☺ *295 7331* ▥ *56 rms*

🛥 ⬌ AE ⬦ ⬥ VISA
Location: Close to the sea, within walking distance of the popular Glenelg beach. Ideal for families with children, this clean, well-run, unpretentious motel-style establishment faces a yacht-filled boat haven. It incorporates a pleasant, reliable restaurant, the **Adelphi**, whose menu often betrays the Hong Kong origins of its chef.
♿ ⬌ 🐟 ⬦ ▼ ⬩ ⬩ ⬩

Richmond
128 Rundle Mall, Adelaide, SA, 5000 ☎ *223 4044* 🔟 ⬦ *86330. Map 12D3* ⬜ *31 rms* 🛥 ⬌ AE
⬦ ⬥ VISA
Location: A unique position within Adelaide's pedestrians-only shopping mall. A small, sensible, older-style city hotel, modernized a few years ago, with three restaurants. Valet parking.
♿ ⬌ ▼

Eating out in Adelaide

Adelaide may have neither the number nor the variety of restaurants found in Sydney or Melbourne, but there are establishments here that can delight the tastebuds as well as, if not better than, any of their kind around the world.

Not surprisingly, with the sea lapping at the door, seafood tends to be among the local specialities. Lobsters, prawns and (in particular) King George whiting are among the local delights well worth sampling. And the wines of SA are not to be missed.

Licensing laws are more liberal in SA and Adelaide does not have the BYO restaurants found elsewhere. The advantage is that wine is readily available at most restaurants; the disadvantage is that they do not sell them at "bottle shop" prices.

Adelaide caters to all tastes. Indian and Pakistani restaurants are more prevalent in this part of Australia, and there are also Chinese, Lebanese, Italian and German restaurants.

A fast-food speciality that is not to all tastes, but is peculiarly South Australian, is the "pie floater". This delicacy, served from one of the pie carts outside Adelaide's railway station or post office late at night, comprises a hearty meat pie floating in a thick soup of peas. You will never be offered that at Maxim's!

Bangkok ♣
1st floor, 217 Rundle St. ☎ *223 5406. Map 13D4* ⬜ ⬜ ⬌ AE ⬦
⬥ VISA *Last orders 9.30pm. Closed Sat lunch, Sun.*
Busy and unpretentious, this centrally located Thai restaurant has flourished under the careful eye of Peter Thanissorn. Its three Asian chefs specialize in *satays*, noodles and curries. The green curry (spiced with green chilis) is excellent, but if you want to taste something sensational try the *tom yum* soup.

HMS Buffalo Restaurant
Patawalonga Boat Haven, Adelphi Terrace, Glenelg North ☎ *294 7000* ⬛ ⬜ ⬌ ▼ 🛥 ⬇
AE ⬦ ⬥ VISA *Last orders 8.30pm. Closed Sat lunch, Christmas Day, Good Friday.*
Distinctly G & S rather than Royal Navy, but the rich, warm, natural timbers and relaxing views across the boat haven make the *Buffalo* easy sailing for the fussiest of landlubbers. Seafood, of course, is the speciality of the galley, and "authentic" pewter dishes are used. (See *Sights*.)

Chief Charley's
12 Grenfell St. ☎ *51 4432. Map 12D3* ⬜ ⬜ AE ⬦ ⬥ VISA *Last orders 8pm Mon-Thurs, 9.30pm Fri-Sun, hols.*
A small and cheerful, low-budget basement restaurant that attracts Adelaide showgoers with its fast service and friendly atmosphere. The menu is based around fresh fish, with some imaginative variations on the norm. Try the seafood *shashlik*.

The Feathers
516 Glynburn Rd., Burnside ☎ *332 6133* ⬛ ⬜ ⬌ ▼ 🛥
AE ⬦ ⬥ VISA *Last orders 11.30pm. Closed Sat lunch, Sun dinner.*
Modelled on the hotel of the same name in Shropshire, England: the decor of the three rooms – the Doulton, Alfresco and Georgian – is aggressively Olde English, but the food, wines and service are warmly Australian. The menu is straightforwardly "European", with a smorgasbord-carvery on Sun. Desserts include superb freshly-cooked donuts.

The Grange ✿

Hilton International, 233 Victoria Sq. ☎ 217 0711. Map 12D3 ▮▮▮▮ ◻ ☰ ❤ 🍴 🅰🅴 ⊕ 🆎 🆅🆂🅰 *Last orders 11.15pm. Closed lunch, Sun.*

This is arguably Adelaide's grandest restaurant, with food, wine and service of the highest quality. Named after SA's renowned Grange Hermitage wine, it features a walk-in cellar where, on polished brass racks, are displayed limited-release wines. The Grange stocks more than 400 Australian labels and a remarkable selection of overseas wine. Under the guidance of its young Singaporean executive chef, Gerard Taye, The Grange has gained a reputation for innovative "Australian" variations to a European-styled menu. Among the specialities are delicious preparations of buffalo and kangaroo. The fresh poached salmon is also worth sampling when available. (See *Hilton International* in *Hotels*.)

Henry Ayers Room

Ayers House, 288 North Terrace ☎ 224 0666. *Map 13D4* ▮▮▮▮ ◻ ☰ ❤ 🅰🅴 ⊕ 🆎 🆅🆂🅰 *Last orders 10pm. Closed lunch, Sun.*

Elegant formal dining in a 19thC atmosphere. This fine, centrally located restaurant, within historic *Ayers House* (see *Sights*) – note the home's original marble fireplace – offers attentive service and outstanding food. The menu is "French-international". Among its extraordinary delights are marinaded goat in Indian spices with yogurt.

Jarmer's Restaurant ✿

297 Kensington Rd., Kensington Park ☎ 332 2080. *Map 13E5* ▮▮ ◻ ☰ ❤ 🅰🅴 ⊕ 🆎 🆅🆂🅰 *Last orders 2.30am. Closed lunch, Sun.*

A fashionable favourite, the restaurant, just 5-10mins away from the city by taxi, is located in an elegant old villa, with the main dining room overlooking a pleasant courtyard and fountain. Peter and Kathy Jarmer describe their menu as "creative French"; it includes venison, buffalo, veal, pork and seafood dishes (the Morton Bay bugs are notoriously delicious). There is a large range of predominantly South Australian wines in the cellar. Peter Jarmer, a member of the international *Les Disciples d'Auguste Escoffier*, holds a set-price gourmet night at the restaurant on the first Mon of each month. There are seven courses (typical choices might be

beluga caviar, goose livers from France, and smoked buffalo) and three fine wines from the Clare Valley.

Magic Flute

109 Melbourne St., North Adelaide ☎ 267 3172. *Map 13B4* ▮▮▮ ◻ ☰ ❤ 🅰🅴 ⊕ 🆎 🆅🆂🅰 *Last orders 10pm. Closed Sat lunch, Sun.*

This charming, popular North Adelaide restaurant serves imaginative "international" food in a relaxing garden setting. On a sunny, early autumn day, there could be few better choices for lunch than here. The wine list is exclusively Australian.

Petaluma Restaurant

Bridgewater Mill, Mt. Barker Rd., Bridgewater ☎ 339 4227 ▮▮ ◻ ☰ ❤ ❤ ⊱ 🅰🅴 ⊕ 🆎 🆅🆂🅰 *Last orders 9pm. Closed Mon, Tues lunch, Sun dinner.*

Well worth the drive into the Adelaide Hills, this fine restaurant, located within the old Bridgewater Mill, combines stylishness with friendliness. Chef Cath Kerry's creative menus may include such tasty dishes as kangaroo in *pesto* butter with parsnip chips, roast wild boar with persimmons in batter with a kumquat glaze, spatchcock, and tripe *lyonnaise*. For dessert try poached cherries with an almond jelly, or kirsch-soaked yeast sponge with winter fruit and King Island cream. On summer nights there is outside dining on a balcony adjacent to the mill's revolving water wheel. Wine-tasting and casual lunches are available in the **Granary** next to the restaurant. (see *Adelaide Hills* in *Excursions*.)

Pheasant Farm ✿

Samuel Rd., near Nuriootpa ☎ (085) 62 1286 ▮▮ ◻ ☰ ❤ ⊱ 🆎 🆅🆂🅰 *Last orders 9pm. Closed Mon, Tues, Wed-Fri dinner, Sun dinner.*

Colin and Maggie Beer's Barossa Valley restaurant was once the ill-kept secret of local gourmets with a taste for game. Now early reservations are essential. The Pheasant Farm, with its timberlined walls and warm furnishings, is on the edge of a trout-filled dam and in the middle of a vineyard. The views are magnificent. Chef Maggie Beer's specialities include warm salad of quail, roast breast of pheasant, guinea fowl and rainbow trout. The wine list is exclusively Barossa Valley.

Nightlife and the arts

Adelaide was once the most staid of Australian cities, conservative and "wowser-ish", a place where the nightlife went little further than evensong on Sundays, or putting out the cat. In the past 25yrs that has all changed dramatically.

Today, largely because of the immense cultural impact of the **Adelaide Arts Festival**, a forward-thinking state government, the clamour of a new generation, and the influence of immigrants, it is a progressive city of people who enjoy going out to be entertained. SA produces some of the world's finest wines, and Adelaide has no qualms about celebrating that proud fact.

For music, opera, ballet and drama, the A\$20 million *Adelaide Festival Centre* (see *Sights*) is the venue that the visitor should investigate first. The top international and local concert, jazz and popular music performers appear here, as well as all the major Australian companies.

The theatre also has a major presence in central Adelaide: **The Arts Theatre** and **The Royalty Theatre** in Angas St., **The State Opera Theatre** in Grote St., **Union Hall** and the **Little Theatre** in the University of Adelaide, and **The John Edmund Theatre** in Halifax St. Bookings through the relevant box offices or the **Bass Bookings Agencies** (☎ *information 213 4788, bookings 213 4777*).

Adelaide's hotels offer a great deal of entertainment, ranging from rough 'n' ready rock bands to comedy and sophisticated modern jazz. Performances are advertised daily in the local newspapers.

Discos are studded around the city – **Mr Bojangles** (*Newmarket Hotel, 1 North Terrace* ☎ *211 8533*), **Jules's** (*94 Hindley St.* ☎ *51 3023*), and **Regines** (*69 Light Sq.* ☎ *212 6044*) – and there are cinemas and adults-only clubs, mixed with good restaurants and cafés, around Hindley St.

For the past few years a company called **Ace Promotions** has been operating a reasonably priced Mystery Disco Bus Tour on Fri and Sat nights, taking visitors and locals around the city's major discos by bus (American Express Cards accepted), and including a complimentary drink on board the bus. The tours set off from the Newmarket Hotel on the corner of North and West terraces (*bookings and further information* ☎ *337 3399*).

Adelaide Casino
North Terrace ☎ *212 2811. Map 12C3* ☘ ⇒ *Open Mon-Thurs 10am-4am, continuous Fri 10am-Mon 4am. Closed Christmas Day, Good Friday.*

The vast Adelaide Casino, which occupies the northern half of the old Adelaide railway station, uses the Gothic grandeur of that building (there are 1,000sq.m of pink and green marble in the Great Hall) to re-create the elegant opulence of Europe's finer gaming palaces. In looks, at least, it is Monte Carlo-plus, and has an astonishing 2.5 million visitors annually. For weekend players, there are few better places in Adelaide for Sunday brunch than the casino's superb 300-seat **Pullman** restaurant (AE ⊕ ⊕ VISA); it serves up its winners at 11.30am.

Adelaide Greyhound Racing Club
Days Rd., Angle Park ☎ *45 8574/268 1923* ☘ ⇒ *Open Mon and Thurs nights.*

On a fine evening Adelaide likes nothing better than going to the dogs. To capture a different flavour of the city, look up the race times in the local newspapers and set off to lose a few dollars at the Angle Park dog track. Increasingly popular too are Australian Rules football (Apr-Sept) and cricket (Oct-Mar) under the floodlights at **Adelaide Oval** (*King William Rd.*) There is also often late-night international tennis at **Memorial Drive Tennis Club** (*corner of War Memorial Drive and Montefiore Rd.*). Check the newspaper sports pages for details.

141

Bogart's
151 Melbourne St., North Adelaide ☎ *267 3018. Map 13B4* ⚲ ● ♫
⇥ *Open about 6pm-2pm or later.*

This North Adelaide wine bar/restaurant/disco has become a magnet for the
yuppies and trendies of the city without losing its original good-natured
atmosphere. Bar prices are cheap, the music is loud, the dancing is near
impossible, the food is actually edible . . . sheer blissful torture!

Tivoli Hotel
261 Pirie St. ☎ *223 2388. Map 13D4* ⚲ ⇥ *Open till late; rock
evenings Tues-Thurs 8pm-3am.*

The Tiv offers rock bands from Tues-Thurs and comedy on Fri and Sat
nights, with an obligatory meal (▭).

Shopping

The busiest shopping area in SA is Adelaide's **Rundle Mall**, a
tightly packed, brick-paved, pedestrians-only street that contains
the city's leading department stores (**David Jones**, **Myer** and **John
Martins**), boutiques, cafés, restaurants and intriguing arcades.
The Mall, with its fruit and flower stalls, newspaper stands and
open-air cafés, provides the shopper with the greatest temptation
in the most pleasant of surroundings.

But for bargains, for the rare or unusual, and for surprises, it
pays, of course, to wander. Browse around the southern suburb of
Unley, and through **Melbourne St**. in North Adelaide. The city's
well-known best-buys include locally mined opals, wine, leather
goods, jewellery, pottery, paintings and sports goods.

Normal shopping hours are Mon-Fri 9am-5.30pm, Sat 9am-
midday. City shops are open late on Fri night up to 9pm; in the
suburbs late-night shopping is on Thurs night.

Aboriginal art
Most state capitals have reputable outlets for Aboriginal artifacts,
but *Adella Gallery* stands out.

Adella Gallery
28 Currie St. ☎ *212 2171. Map 12D3* 🄰🄴 ●

Authentic Aboriginal art and traditional and modern artifacts can be bought
here. There is a fine collection of didjeridus, boomerangs, bark paintings,
emu-egg carvings, and basketry.

Australiana
It is worth searching for the authentic local product.

Elmswood Fine Crafts
189 Unley Rd., Unley ☎ *272 3198* 🄰🄴 ● ● 🆅🅸🅂🄰

Six rooms packed with Australian-made crafts. They include silver and gold
jewellery, pottery (decorative and functional), hand-blown glass, and clothing.

Books
Adelaide has won a reputation as one of the country's most literary
cities, and there are many fine bookstores to be found here.

Europa Bookshop
16 Pulteney St. ☎ *223 2289. Map 12D3* 🄰🄴 ● ● 🆅🅸🅂🄰

The Europa specializes in foreign-language texts. As well as novels,
non-fiction works, newspapers and magazines from around the world, it has
a wide selection of dictionaries, phrase books, maps, and language courses on
record and cassette.

Fables Bookstore
65 Gawler Pl. ☎ *212 7449. Map 12D3* ● 🆅🅸🅂🄰

A good selection of unusual Australian and art books.

Fashion

In keeping with Adelaide's culturally progressive image, its clothes stores have become increasingly sophisticated.

The Kilt Shop
1st level, 112 Gays Arcade, off Adelaide Arcade ☎ *224 0676. Map 12D3* AE ⊙ ⊙ VISA

The shop for homesick, or would-be, Scots. This fascinating establishment, which imports all its stock from Scotland, carries kilts, clan jewellery, scarves and ties. Maps, books and accessories; friendly service and advice.

Shouz
144 King William Rd., Hyde Park ☎ *272 1270* AE ⊙ ⊙ VISA

A high-fashion shoe boutique for women. There is a large selection of imported and local shoes, from casual to dressy. Shouz also stocks handbags.

Toffs Fashion House
167–171 King William Rd., Hyde Park ☎ *271 3711/274 1030* AE ⊙ ⊙ VISA

This stylish shop carries an extensive range of designer labels and accessories from Australia and overseas. Among the women's fashions are the works of Harry Who and George Gross.

Jewellery

Locally mined and cut opals are a South Australian speciality.

Adelaide Gem Trading Co.
26 Currie St. ☎ *212 3600. Map 12D3* AE ⊙ ⊙ VISA

Opals – black, boulder, solids, triplets and rough opals – are the gems this company trades in. They mine them, cut them and sell them. Free courtesy car service for visitors, and for serious buyers after-hours appointments can be arranged.

Cowell Jade Pty Ltd
153 Unley Rd., Unley ☎ *272 6814* AE ⊙ ⊙ VISA

Cowell jade, mined in SA, comes in beautiful shades of green through to black. This rare black jade is recognized by experts for its high

quality. The Nephrite jade deposits were discovered by a local farmer in 1965 and are among the largest in the world. Jade from the mine has been fashioned into jewellery and carvings.

Opal Field Gems
Ground and 3rd floors, 29 King William St. ☎ *212 5300. Map 12D3* AE ⊙ ⊙ VISA

This is the largest opal-cutting factory in Australia: 100,000 carats of solid opal and 750,000 triplet opals a year. Visitors can see the gems being cut and polished on the 3rd floor. There is a 30 percent sales tax exemption for overseas visitors who show a passport and travel ticket.

Markets and shopping centres

Australians love a bustling market, and Adelaide's are excellent.

Brickworks Markets
South Rd., Thebarton ☎ *352 4822* ♿ 🖵 ✱

This complex, to the NE of the city, is a combined market and family-entertainment centre. It has more than 200 stalls, shops, a beer garden, mini-golf, bumper boats, kiddie cars and other novelty rides. The Markets are open Fri-Sun and hols 9am-5pm, and the leisure park Mon-Thurs 9am-5pm, Fri and Sat 9am-9pm, and Sun 9am-7pm.

Central Market
Grote St. Map 12E2 ♿ 🖵

Well worth a visit. The stalls in this colourful, comprehensive market sell

fruit, vegetables, fish, meat, delicatessen food, craft work and jewellery . . . almost anything. Open Tues 7am-6pm, Fri 7am-10pm, Sat 7am-1pm.

Gallerie Shopping Centre
20 Gawler Pl. through to 200 North Terrace ☎ *223 1699. Map 12D3* ♿ 🖵

Three floors of 60 shops that include the **R. M. Williams** (Australian bushmen's clothing) store and the **Australian Broadcasting Corporation Shop** (records, books and posters). There are also 14 international food outlets (dine-in or take-away).

Sports goods

Sporting-equipment stores are something of an Adelaide speciality. This is, after all, the city of Sir Don Bradman.

Rowe and Jarman Sports Store

99 Grenfell St. ☎ *223 5666. Map 12D3* AE ⊕ ⊙ VISA
An excellent shop for sporting equipment and clothing, known around the world for its cricketing supplies. Other sports are also well catered for, with a good selection of tennis gear and the popular locally-made Mr Tim's Silver Fleece rugby tops.

Adelaide environs and South Australia excursions

Many of Adelaide's attractions begin at the edge of the city: the wine valleys, the beach resorts, towns with a flavour of the past, and the bushland reserves among them. The following excursions are within relatively easy reach of Adelaide. The more remote parts of SA are described briefly in a separate final section.

The **Royal Automobile Association of South Australia** (*41 Hindmarsh Sq.* ☎ *223 4555*) offers reciprocal membership to members of affiliated auto clubs. Visitors should bring along their overseas membership card. The RAA offers touring advice, maps and travel agency services. It has also published a particularly useful book for visitors, *Tours From Adelaide*, which details more than 20 excellent round trips from the city.

Day and half-day bus tours to most of the region's points of interest are available from **Briscoes Coach Holidays** (*101 Franklin St.* ☎ *212 7344* ● *87152*). **Ansett Pioneer** (*111 Franklin St.* ☎ *51 2075/216 5452*) also offers similar air-conditioned bus tours.

Details and bookings for extended tours to all parts of the state can be obtained through the **South Australian Government Travel Centre** (*18 King William St.* ☎ *212 1644*).

Excursions from Adelaide

Adelaide Hills

Few cities can have such a magnificent backdrop as the Adelaide Hills, part of the tree-clad Mount Lofty Range and just 20mins from the centre of Adelaide itself.

There are many ways to explore their charms, but one leading to many delights is the drive that begins by travelling SE from Adelaide onto the Glen Osmond Rd. Follow this through to **Mt. Barker Rd.**, where, preserved in the median strip, there is an old tollhouse and gate used more than a century ago.

Climb on past the **Eagle-on-the-Hill**, once a staging post and now a hotel, up to the small town of **Crafers**. David Crafer opened the **Sawyer's Arms Hotel** here in 1839; it was reputedly used by bushrangers who held up travellers in the hills.

Drive on to the 711m (2,333ft) summit of **Mt. Lofty** for a dramatic view across Adelaide and the coast. Then enjoy a short detour into the **Cleland Conservation Park** (☎ *339 2572* ▨ ✱ ⊶ ≼ *open 9.30am-5pm*), one of Adelaide's favourite picnic spots. This vast reserve has koalas (handling and viewing 2–4pm), kangaroos, emus, wombats, dingoes, wallabies and native birds. From here you can travel on to **Norton Summit** to meet up with the Montacute Scenic Route that will wind you back into Adelaide.

But the Adelaide Hills call for detours. Take them to find the **Birdwood Mill**, an old flour mill that has been converted to a museum, with an excellent collection of old cars and motorcycles. Find the lane that leads into **Bridgewater**, and visit **Gumeracha** and see the biggest rocking horse in the world, 18.3m (21½ft) high, at **The Toy Factory** (*Mannum Rd.*) The Hills hold many surprises for the dogged explorer.

The Barossa Valley

The Barossa was named in 1837 by Adelaide's founder, Colonel William Light, after a valley he knew in Spain. It became home for immigrants from Silesia and Prussia in the 1840s, who quickly realised its potential for farming and winemaking. Their heritage is evident today in the Lutheran churches, the stone restaurants, the bakeries and, of course, the names of the winemakers.

The Barossa Valley, which is Australia's most famous wine-making district, is only 55km (34 miles) NE of Adelaide. It is a broad, shallow valley with more than 40 wineries scattered across it, many of them open daily for wine-tasting and sales.

To drive to it take the Main North Rd. from Adelaide up to **Gawler**, turn right at the Barossa Valley Hwy sign and drive on to **Rosedale**. From here you follow a circular route that takes in the towns of **Tanunda**, **Angaston**, **Nuriootpa** and **Seppeltsfield**.

Around Easter every odd-numbered year the Barossa Valley Vintage Festival is celebrated, a week-long carnival of wine, folk-dancing and German brass-band music.

A little farther to the N is the **Clare Valley**, another great wine-making area and, like the Barossa, well worth imbibing.

Hahndorf

28km (18 miles) SE. Getting there: by car, via South Eastern Freeway, then turn off N.

The fascinating town of Hahndorf, a little bit of old Germany in the Australian bush, is well worth a visit. Hahndorf was settled by Germans fleeing from Silesia in 1839 and named after Captain Dirk Hahn, the man who commanded the ship that brought the immigrants to their new land. The original stone cottages are still in use. The visitor walks by such buildings as the **Hahndorf Academy**, **Hahndorf Inn**, the **German Arms Hotel** and the **Lutheran Church**. It is touristy, but charming. The festival of Schutzenfest is celebrated in the town each Jan.

Hahndorf Bavarian (*145a Main St.* ☎ *(08) 388 7921* ▢).

Victor Harbour

84km (52 miles) s. Getting there: by car, via Main South Rd. to Old Noarlunga, the McLaren Vale, Willunga and Mt. Compass, and across the Hindmarsh River. Bicycle rental: Causeway Kiosk, Victor Harbour ☎ *(085) 52 1838.*

Victor Harbour is one of SA's most fascinating coastal resorts and is the largest town on the Fleurieu Peninsula. Linked to it by a long causeway is **Granite Island**, which provides fine views of Encounter Bay. Victor Harbour offers a superb base for fishermen, safe beaches for swimmers, and some exciting waves for surfers.

The island, a wildlife sanctuary, is reached either by an energetic stroll or by a horse-drawn tram, which operates daily 10am-4pm. On one side of the island are fairy penguins and many species of sea bird; at the top of the island the careful visitor can enjoy the company of the shy rock wallabies. Dusk is the best time to view the penguins, when they waddle in from the sea to the rookeries.

Victor Harbour's other prominent landmark is **The Bluff** at Rosetta Head. This 100m-high (328ft) rock formation, which dominates the skyline to the w of the town, was used as a lookout for the Encounter Bay Whaling Station in the 1830s. When a whale was sighted a flag was raised.

Apollon Motor Inn (*Hindmarsh Rd. Victor Harbour, SA, 5211* ☎ *(085) 52 1755* ▮▯); the **Victor** (*Albert Pl., Victor Harbour, SA, 5211* ☎ *52 1288* ▮▯) faces the bay.

The **Glacier Rock** (*13km (8 miles) from Victor Harbour on Inman Valley Rd.* ☎ *(085) 58 8202* ▮▯) has excellent views.

West Beach
Directly to the w of the city, along Burbridge Rd.
The West Beach Reserve is a playground that contains many playing fields, two golf courses, a boating lake, a boat ramp and sailing club. On the reserve is a large modern caravan park and, adjacent to this on Military Rd., **Marineland** (☎ *356 7555, open Wed-Sun 10.30am-4pm*), which holds Australia's largest enclosed aquarium. Seals and dolphins perform in the pools here, and there is a fairly regular "Big Top Show". In the pleasant picnic grounds the pelican is the star of a children's zoo.

Farther afield

Coober Pedy and the Outback
960km (600 miles) NW. Getting there, by car, via Stuart Hwy.
Much of the northern part of SA is semi-desert. It is made up of stony plains, salt pans and sandhills, and the terrain is extremely harsh. This, of course, is still pioneering country; rugged, inhospitable, deadly . . . and yet often uncannily beautiful.

Although the Outback is an intriguing place for the adventurer, it can also be hazardous to visitors unused to the extremes found here. Before driving or venturing into this country seek specialist advice in Adelaide. Better still, travel with one of the well-known safari tour operators who know the territory and its rules.

Coober Pedy, which stands in a lunar landscape of sandy ridges, is famous for its fine opals and for the fact that the majority of its inhabitants live underground. The miners' cavelike homes, often luxurious and magnificently furnished, keep naturally cool although temperatures above ground may be unbearable. The town's name is taken from the Aboriginal *Kupa* (white person) and *Piti* (burrow) – hence *Kupa Piti*: white man's burrow.

Opal Air (☎ *352 3337*) has 3hr flights from Adelaide to Coober Pedy as well as 2-to-3-day air-and-motel-accommodation tours. **Treckabout Safaris** (*30 Berryman Drive, Modbury* ☎ *(08) 264 3770*) offers tours into the Outback. Transport from Adelaide is by air-conditioned 4-wheel-drive vehicle and at night you camp out under the stars. All meals are included, and the equipment is first class. For tours from Coober Pedy, contact **Coober Pedy Tours** (*Main St.* ☎ *(086) 72 5333*).

Underground Motel (*P.O. Box 375, Coober Pedy, SA, 5273* ☎ *(086) 72 5324* ▮▯); **Opal Inn Hotel-Motel** (*Main St., Coober Pedy, SA, 5273* ☎ *(086) 72 5054* ● *80630* ▮▯18).

146

The Eyre Peninsula

This is part of the "West Coast Country", the first land in SA ever seen by European eyes. The Dutch explorer Peter Nuyts sailed just this far before returning w in 1627.

The Eyre Peninsula itself was named after the explorer Edward John Eyre, who was the first to cross Australia overland from E to w. The major centres on the peninsula are **Whyalla**, which rejoices in approximately 300 days of sunshine per year, and **Port Lincoln**, a tuna-fishing port overlooking Boston Bay, and there are many small coastal resorts. Together with the bush country and rich wheatlands, they make this a fine place for a quiet get-away.

Kendall Airlines (*150 North Terrace* ☎ *212 1144*) provides 2-day air tours to Port Lincoln, including motel accommodation. Useful addresses are **Whyalla Tourist Centre** (*3 Patterson St., City Plaza, Whyalla, SA, 5600* ☎ *(086) 45 7428*) and **Port Lincoln Tourist Office** (*Civic Hall, Tasman Terrace, Port Lincoln, SA, 5606* ☎ *(086) 82 3255* ☎ *80493*).

The Flinders Ranges

Getting to the Flinders Ranges takes you travelling in the footsteps of the pioneers. It is hard, exhilaratingly spectacular country. This was where the first Europeans came, unprepared, abandoning homes and often hope as the fierce droughts and unforgiving land made their lives a misery.

The Ranges, some 350km (220 miles) N of Adelaide, are dramatic peaks beloved of film-makers, artists and bushwalkers. Native birds and animals abound here, and in some locations there are Aboriginal rock paintings to be appreciated.

Treckabout Safaris (*30 Berryman Drive, Modbury* ☎ *(08) 264 3770*) provide a 4-day minibus tour, including meals and motel accommodation, from Adelaide to the Flinders Ranges. It includes a visit to **Wilpena Pound**, **Leigh Creek**, **Gammon Ranges** and **Arkaroola**.

Kangaroo Island

There are more than 100 islands off the South Australian coast. Kangaroo Island, a peaceful resort some 113km (71 miles) SW of Adelaide, is, at 145km long by 50km wide (91 by 31 miles), the biggest of them all.

The main town is **Kingscote**. There is some farming, but a large part of the island is taken up by the **Flinders Chase National Park**. There are camping sites and bushwalking tracks aplenty, and the island beaches are a delight to swimmers, surfers and fishermen. The island is a wildlife paradise: seals cavorting on its surf-splashed rocks, fairy penguins, abundant kangaroos, koalas, goannas, and emus "drumming" you away from their territory.

A vehicle ferry sails from Port Adelaide to Kangaroo Island every weekday, but the journey takes more than 6hrs. Perhaps a better idea would be to take the 40min air trip. **Lloyd Aviation** (*38 Currie St.* ☎ *212 5722*) has a day trip. It begins with a 7am flight from Adelaide Airport, features breakfast at Island Resort, Kingscote, and then a bus tour around Kangaroo Island. You return at 6.15pm.

The Murray River

Australia's greatest river, the Murray, completes its last 650km (400 miles) through SA. Once it was a major trading route to the interior; today its main purpose seems to be recreational.

The Murray is there for all to enjoy . . . fisherman, poet, artist or swimmer. Explorers can rent one of the self-drive houseboats from the fleets based at **Murray Bridge** or **Mannum**, or elsewhere along this majestic river. They are easy to pilot, well maintained, comfortable, and you can tie up at night wherever you wish.

For those who would have it easier, there is a paddle-wheeler cruise from Murray Bridge aboard the *Proud Mary*, her passengers living in luxury as she steams upriver past huge gums, willows and river cliffs. Nothing can be quite so relaxing.

Murray River cruises can be booked through the **South Australian Government Travel Centre** (*18 King William St.* ☎ *212 1644*).

Mt. Gambier

455km (284 miles) SE. Getting there: by car, via Princes Hwy.
Mt. Gambier, the bustling and prosperous halfway point between Adelaide and Melbourne, is famous for its lakes and, in particular, its unusually vivid Blue Lake. The city is built on the slopes of an extinct volcano, which has three craters; in the main one lies the Blue Lake. Its average depth is 77m (253ft), but in parts it sinks to about 200m (655ft). The lake is used as Mt. Gambier's main water supply.

The Yorke Peninsula

The Yorke Peninsula, with its distinctive "leg" shape, was originally settled by the Narungga people, who took advantage of its abundant sea foods. In 1859 copper was discovered near the present town of Kadina, and in came the Cornish miners.

Today the peninsula is largely devoted to cereal crops and sheep-farming. The biggest attraction, however, is "Australia's Little Cornwall", the three towns of **Moonta**, **Kadina** and **Wallaroo**. Every second May (on odd years) the region holds a biennial festival, the Kernewek Lowender, to celebrate its Cornish heritage.

Tasmania

The visitor to Tasmania might well feel that the island is no part of Australia, such is the contrast with the mainland. There are many similarities with the British Isles, and the early settlers must have had the same impression, judging by the names of towns: Richmond, Kingston, New Norfolk, Devonport, Perth, Swansea, Derwent, Cambridge. . . . Much of the island resembles England, but parts are reminiscent of Scotland and others are unique.

Tasmania crams great scenic variety into a relatively small area (by Australian standards), from soft, gentle fields, some with hedgerows of hawthorn (may) around Launceston, to the savage and untamed (for once the cliché is accurate) beauty of the Gordon River, in the state's northwestern World Heritage-listed region.

Tasmanians, while friendly, betray that insularity often seen in island people. To be fair, they have rather been neglected by the rest of Australia and in many ways pay the penalty for being a small and isolated state in a federal system. Since World War II Tasmania has seen far fewer changes than the rest of Australia.

There is a faint suspicion therefore that Tasmanians distrust "mainlanders" and somehow prefer to keep themselves to themselves. Some hoary old jokes persist on the mainland about inbreeding among Tasmanians, who have a reputation for extreme parochialism – no mean achievement in a nation that embraces the parochial.

Yet Tasmanians patently welcome overseas tourists. The island is far more tourist-oriented than any other part of Australia. The economy relies heavily on the tourist dollar, partly because Tasmania did not share significantly in the postwar industrialization that transformed the mainland.

More than 40 percent of the island is covered in forest, and forestry plays a major part in the economy. Mining – mainly zinc, aluminium, iron ore, copper and tin – and basic mineral-processing such as smelting, are also major industries. There are few large manufacturing plants, and the lack of a substantial industrial base has led to higher-than-average unemployment in recent years, enhancing, if anything, the importance of tourism.

Much of the island is extremely isolated, and transport and communications can be difficult. The sw is true wilderness, with few, if any, roads through the heavily timbered, mountainous country. Tasmania tends to divide along a N-S line, the two major centres of population, Hobart and Launceston, being at opposite ends of the island. The N coast facing Bass Strait and the mainland is quite densely populated and has several towns, including Devonport (where the ferry *Abel Tasman* docks with cars and passengers from Melbourne after its overnight journey), Burnie, Wynyard and Ulverstone. Inland, Launceston, on the Tamar River estuary, dominates the region.

In the s, Hobart, the capital, is one of the world's most picturesque cities, set against a backdrop of Mt. Wellington, snow-covered for two, sometimes three, months of the year, and the Derwent Estuary – which, as yachting enthusiasts are quick to point out, has more sailable area than Sydney harbour. It is also, of course, the most southerly Australian city, and on winter days when the wind roars in from the Antarctic one is keenly aware of that fact – though summers are often superb.

Hobart, the second site of European settlement in Australia (in 1803), is fortunate in having largely escaped the developers, and has retained more of its heritage than any other major Australian city. Some parts, like Battery Point, have changed little in more than 150yrs. Yet while it retains a strong sense of its distinctive place in Australia's short history, Hobart has been unafraid to take risks. The decision by the state government to sanction Australia's first legal casino, which opened in 1973 at the Wrest Point Hotel overlooking the Derwent River, was considered highly daring. It is also one of the few cities in the world where the largest ships can tie up within a few hundred metres of the main shopping centre. That sense of intimacy makes it quite unlike any other Australian state capital.

Launceston, Tasmania's second city, is equally "English" in appearance and feel. Situated in the valleys formed by the South and North Esk Rivers, which join to become the Tamar River, Launceston is surrounded by rolling hills, small fields divided up by hedgerows, and numerous villages, many with Georgian and Regency mansions. There are also extensive public and private gardens that enhance the rural setting. The recent opening of the Launceston Country Club-Casino has helped to attract increasing numbers of visitors from the mainland, particularly from Melbourne.

It is sad, then, to reflect that such a beautiful island had such an inauspicious beginning. Tasmania, the site of some of the most tyrannical penal settlements Britain ever ruled, had a record of brutality rarely equalled in Australia. One settlement, Port Arthur, ironically quite enlightened by the standards of its day, is now Australia's most important historical site.

Even more deplorable than the cruelty meted out to the convicts was the attitude of the early British settlers to local Aborigines, a very different people from their mainland cousins. After a mere 70yrs' contact with Europeans the Tasmanian Aborigines were extinct, victims of disease and of avaricious settlers who hunted, shot and poisoned them in their hundreds, seeing them as vermin and competition for the available land. Today there are few traces of Tasmania's savage past other than several ruins and some frankly horrific stories.

The huge scale of the mainland states demands a focused approach to planning by the visitor, but in contrast Tasmania's relative compactness allows a more comfortable approach. It is possible to plan a trip, of reasonable duration, that can take in all or most of the island, and this section is geared to a generally *Tasmanian* overview. Introductory essays discuss practical matters: how to get to Tasmania, getting around the island, accommodation, eating out, nightlife and shopping. A special feature spotlights Tasmanian wildlife. There are city gazetteers for both Hobart and Launceston, followed by a selection of excursions that quarter the island. The section ends with suggested tours and tour operators.

Getting there

A pleasant way to reach the island is to take the ferry from Melbourne to the northern port of **Devonport**, an industrial town of 21,000 people. Devonport is situated at the southern end of the **Cradle Mountain/Lake St Clair National Park**, a favourite with bushwalkers and wilderness lovers. Recommended below are a convenient hotel and the popular *Taswegia* shop.

The *Abel Tasman*, a 19,200-tonne ferry, plies between the mainland and Tasmania three times a week in each direction, carrying 440 cars and 850 passengers in mini-liner comfort. It has three restaurants, a large bar, a disco, children's playroom and coffee shop. Accommodation is all-cabin for the overnight journey. The boat leaves Melbourne and Devonport at 6pm and arrives at its destination at 8.30am the following morning. Sailing days: Melbourne-Devonport Mon, Wed and Fri, and Devonport-Melbourne Sun, Tues and Thurs. Book well ahead for the busy Dec-Apr period.

The major airlines, **Ansett** and **Australian Airlines**, and the regional **East-West Airlines**, fly to Tasmania from both Melbourne and Sydney. Ansett flies to Hobart, Launceston, Wynyard and Devonport; Australian to Launceston and Hobart; and East-West to Hobart, Devonport, Burnie and Wynyard.

Gateway Inn

16 Fenton St., Devonport, Tas., 7310 ☎ *(004) 24 4922* ▦ ☀ *59187* ▦
66 rms ▭ ⟺ AE ⊕ ⊙ VISA

Location: Near town centre. A medium-sized motor inn, the Gateway, like scores of good-quality motor inns or motels in Australia, offers acceptable self-contained accommodation and a licensed dining room. Convenient for an overnight stop.
♿ ▣ ♟ ♨

Taswegia

57 Formby Rd. ☎ *(004) 24 8300* ✱ ⊙ VISA

Situated on the waterfront and open every day, Taswegia has a unique collection of fully working printing equipment dating back to 1852, centred around ten presses, including an Albion of 1852 from the Ballarat gold fields. The shop specializes in reprinting old documents and charts from the convict era, and also has an excellent range of Tasmanian gifts, including printed fabric, woodcrafts, ceramics and pottery, reproduction prints and books.

Getting around

The tourist trade in Tasmania is very much geared to the self-drive concept, and many holiday packages include a self-drive car in the price. Campervans are a popular alternative to cars: camping and caravan sites are of a good standard, and in some places it is possible to camp out in the bush. All the major car-rental companies are represented in Tasmania, which has a good network of main roads between major centres.

Tasmania now has no passenger rail services, the last line having closed in the 1970s, but there are good bus services. A regular daily service links Hobart with Launceston via the Midland Hwy, and then continues along the N coast to Smithton, stopping at Devonport, Burnie and Wynyard. An alternative service links Hobart and Launceston, travelling along the E coast, and another service connects Hobart with Burnie via the W coast. An open ticket available from **Tasmania Redline Coaches** (*96 Harrington St., Hobart* ☎ *(002) 34 4577*) gives 14 days' unlimited travel.

Light aircraft can be chartered for sightseeing and other journeys, in Launceston, Hobart (at Cambridge aerodrome, near Hobart's main aerodrome), Evandale, Devonport, Wynyard and Queenstown. In addition, **Airlines of Tasmania** operates scheduled services between Hobart and Launceston, Queenstown, Strahan, Devonport, Wynyard, Flinders Island and King Island.

Accommodation

Tasmania offers a greater variety of accommodation than any other part of Australia, ranging from top-class hotels and casinos to traditional English-style bed-and-breakfast guesthouses, with ample choice in the medium-price range. Several hotel/motel chains, such as the **Four Seasons** group, have state-wide networks. There is also a scheme called Host Farms, involving "living in" with a family.

Colonial Accommodation is a name given to private bed-and-breakfast accommodation, in anything from an old cottage to a stately country home. Look for signs outside saying "Colonial Accommodation." An example is **Prospect House** in *Richmond* (see *Hobart sights*), a beautifully proportioned Georgian house built c.1830 and classified by the National Trust, which has ten double rooms for guests, in a convict-built barn set in the courtyard, among 12ha (30 acres) of ground. A full or continental breakfast is served, and, unusually for this kind of accommodation, there is a licensed restaurant, specializing in game dishes.

Fifteen houses involved in the scheme have formed themselves into the **Colonial Accommodation Association**. Bookings can be made through any branch of the Tasmanian Government Tourist Bureau, through Ansett and East-West Airlines, or directly.

Ordinary public houses throughout Tasmania offer good, clean accommodation, though in most cases without private facilities. However, prices are low and often include a hearty breakfast. Another increasingly popular style of low-budget accommodation is the self-catering holiday, which usually means renting a self-contained house or cabin, sometimes on a farm.

The **Host Farm** scheme involves staying as the guest of a farming family, either in the main home or in a cabin on the property. Guests can join in farm activities. A booklet explaining the idea and listing the farms is published by the **Country Accommodation Association of Tasmania**, available through branches of the Tasmanian Government Tourist Bureau, who can also take bookings.

Most caravan sites have on-site caravans to rent on a per-night or longer-term basis, for really economical accommodation.

Eating out in Tasmania

Tasmania is fish country. This provides a chance to eat the finest scallops, lobsters, tuna and fresh trout to be found in Australia or, as some islanders insist, in the world. For they are surrounded by some of the best fisheries imaginable and by some of the finest trout rivers and lakes in Australia.

Supplementing this natural wealth, there is now a fish farm for Atlantic salmon, which delivers fresh salmon to restaurants on the island and to selected outlets in Sydney and Melbourne. Reportedly its produce compares well with the best Scotch or Canadian salmon.

For a small state, Tasmania has some excellent restaurants, particularly in Hobart and Launceston. In rural areas standards can best be described as patchy.

Nightlife

With the notable exception of Hobart's Wrest Point Hotel-Casino and the Country Club-Casino near Launceston, nightlife in Tasmania centres largely on the home and on such simple pleasures as dining out.

There are, it is true, discos in both main cities, usually attached to public houses, which open and close and change names with the usual frequency. Consult the *Hobart Mercury* or *Launceston Examiner* newspapers for the latest picture.

The **Wrest Point Hotel-Casino** in Hobart has several nightspots within the hotel complex. The **Ten O'Clock Club** has a programme of live entertainment, music and dancing in a traditional cabaret setting. **Regines** is a more relaxed disco-style nightspot, with live bands from Tues-Sat. There is a resident pianist in the **Birdcage** bar, and jazz on Sun in the **Riverview** lounge.

The **Country Club-Casino** near Launceston offers pretty much the same format, but on a smaller scale. The **Ten O'Clock Club** features cabaret, with guest artists, live music, and dancing Tues-Sat; **Regines** has disco music, with some live music Tues-Sat; and in the **Lania** bar a resident pianist plays nightly.

Try to catch the excellent Tasmanian Symphony.Orchestra, which has a touring programme around the state.

Shopping

Shopping in Tasmania has one big disadvantage: prices are anything up to 10 percent more expensive than on the mainland because most goods have to be transported across Bass Strait.

However, despite its population of only ½ million, Tasmania boasts a large number of craft shops and galleries, and is building a reputation for the quality of its crafts, particularly in woodworking media. Woollen goods manufactured on the island are excellent, both in quality and value. And items made from local woods, particularly the rare Huon pine, make unusual gifts and souvenirs.

Tasmania can be a happy hunting ground for antique collectors. There are many old country homes, and by Australian standards the island has a long history. Antique dealers are licensed by the state government, but shoppers still need to know what they are looking at and for. Dealers can arrange transportation of antiques either to the mainland or overseas.

Shopping hours conform with the rest of Australia.

Tasmanian wildlife

Because of its isolation from the mainland, Tasmania's flora and fauna are distinctive and sometimes unique. Keep your eyes peeled, for there is much of interest. Some highlights are described opposite briefly.

Tasmanian Devil A small, smelly, dark-brown-to-black, nocturnal creature, reputed to have the most powerful jaws of any beast of its size. Unpredictable and vicious when cornered.

Tasmanian Tiger Probably extinct, but may still survive in some remote parts. A marsupial, about the size of a large dog, striped across the length of its body. At the point where the tail joins the body has a strong resemblance to a kangaroo. If you see anything resembling this description report it to the National Parks and Wildlife Service (look in the telephone book).

Fish The island is famed for its fishing, in particular for freshwater **trout, bream** in the river estuaries, and **tuna** offshore. Superb **Atlantic salmon** are bred in a fish-farm.

Trees Several unique species give Tasmania its special look and feel. The **Huon pine**, found in only a few areas, mainly the NW and SW, grows extremely slowly – about 120mm (4.7ins) a century. Other species include **celery-top pine, Tasmanian blackwood, King Billy pine, sassafras** and **wattle**.

Honey Tasmania is a major producer, and **leatherwood**, from the W, is unique. White beehives are everywhere. Leatherwood trees have white waxy flowers from Dec-Mar.

Hobart

STD code: 002. Airport ☎ 48 5041; Ansett ☎ 38 0800; Australian ☎ 38 3333; East-West ☎ (008) 11 2411/(002) 38 0200 (toll-free numbers). Car rental: Avis ☎ 34 4222; Budget ☎ 34 5222; Hertz ☎ 34 5555. Tasmanian Government Tourist Bureau: 80 Elizabeth St., Hobart, Tas., 7000 ☎ 30 0211. American Express Travel Service: Websters Travel, 60 Liverpool St., Hobart, Tas., 7000 ☎ 38 1200. Royal Automobile Club of Tasmania (RACT): Corner of Patrick St. and Murray St., Hobart, Tas., 7000 ☎ 38 2200.

The Tasmanian Tourist Bureau can provide information about hotels, sights and tours, and publishes an excellent, free series of leaflets, *Let's Talk About . . .* , covering attractions in the city and environs. The National Trust too has leaflets listing its properties region-by-region, and the Department of Tourism publishes a very full twice-yearly calendar of events.

Sights and places of interest in and around Hobart

Allport Library and Museum of Fine Arts
91 Murray St. ☎ 30 7484 ⊡ ♿ *Open 9.30am-5pm. Closed Sat, Sun.*

Housed in the State Library, the museum and library have a collection of fine and rare books, a large collection of paintings and prints, and a collection of antique furniture, ceramics, glass and silver.

Anglesea Barracks ★
Davey St. ☎ 21 2205 ⊡ *✗ compulsory. Open Tues: tours start 11am.*

The headquarters of the Australian Military Forces in Tasmania, Anglesea Barracks is the oldest military establishment in Australia still occupied by the army. Many of the original Georgian buildings have been preserved and restored. Free guided tours of the barracks take in the guardhouse, hospital, military jail, the original officers' mess, the old drill hall dating back to the early 19thC, and the other ranks' barracks.

Battery Point ★
◀€

One of the best-preserved areas of any Australian city and the oldest part of Hobart, Battery Point is a lived-in, vital area that has largely escaped being "restored", or overwhelmed by souvenir shops. It was first settled in 1804 and takes its name from the battery of guns established in 1818 on the promontory of land overlooking the Derwent Estuary.

Battery Point's architecture is nearly all Georgian and early Victorian, many buildings dating back to the 1830s and '40s. The oldest is the **signal station** used to relay messages to Mt. Nelson near the mouth of the river, mainly announcing the arrival of ships. Old taverns and inns lend the area an almost Dickensian atmosphere. Many of them have been converted into art galleries, antique shops and restaurants. Among the finest streetscapes is **Arthur's Circus**, a perfectly preserved group of single-storey cottages around a central grassed roundabout. **St George's Anglican Church** (built 1836–37)) in Cromwell St., a fine example of Georgian church architecture, is known as the "Mariners' Church" and has some fine boxed pews.

This is very much walking territory, for its charm lies in discovering little nooks and crannies that you would miss on four wheels.

Botanic Gardens ★
Domain Rd. ☎ 34 6299 🅿 ♿ ✗ ✱ ▣ ⇌ ◀◀ *Open Nov-Mar 8am-6.30pm, Apr, Sept-Oct 8am-5.30pm, May-Aug 8am-4.45pm.*

Every Australian city has its botanic gardens. Hobart is no exception. Established in 1818 and situated on 13ha (32 acres) of high ground overlooking the Derwent, Hobart's gardens are small compared to most mainland equivalents, but therein lies their special charm. The gardens have several world-class features, such as a fine tropical glasshouse, a cactus house, a fuchsia house and a herb garden. The conservatory, with its magnificent floral display, changed four times a year, should not be missed. Look out too for the floral clock, the rose garden, and numerous fountains and water features. There is an easy-access area for disabled people.

Constitution Dock
Davey St. ⇌

This is the finishing point for the annual classic blue-water ocean yacht race, the Sydney-to-Hobart, which starts from the mainland on Boxing Day (Dec 26). Following the race it is the scene of much revelry, but at other times it is a quiet place where fishing boats and private sailing craft tie up. Constitution Dock is within a few hundred metres of the **Elizabeth Street Pier**, where large ships dock, and **Brooke Street Pier**, where ferries leave for the eastern shore and pleasure craft depart for cruises in the Derwent Estuary.

Lady Franklin Gallery
Lenah Valley Rd., Lenah ☎ 28 0076 🅿 ✗ ⇌ *Open Sat, Sun 2-4.30pm. Closed Mon-Fri.*

The gallery, home of the Art Society of Tasmania, is housed in a Greek-revival building constructed in sandstone in 1842, under the sponsorship of Lady Franklin, the Governor's wife. Today it houses a display of paintings by members of the society, many of them Tasmania's leading artists, and a library of art books.

Maritime Museum of Australia ★
Secheron House, Secheron Rd., Battery Point ☎ 23 5082 ▦ *Open Mon-Fri, Sun 1-4.30pm, Sat 10am-4.30pm.*

Hidden away down a cul-de-sac in Battery Point, the Maritime Museum is a fascinating collection of models, paintings, artifacts and memorabilia from Tasmania's maritime past. The museum is in **Secheron House**, overlooking the Derwent Estuary.

Parliament House ★
Morrison St. 🚻 *Public access but no guided tours.*

Tasmania's Parliament House is one of the oldest buildings in Hobart, built between 1836–41 to a design by John Lee Archer in a style described as colonial Regency. Its situation at the end of Murray St. opposite the wharves betrays its origins: it started life as the Customs House, and its cellars, which still show the broad, arrowed bricks in the vaulted ceiling, used to be the bond store. It became the home of the State Parliament in 1856. The building is fronted by a spacious garden planted with trees, and colourful flowerbeds in summer, well patronized on fine days by office workers eating their lunch.

Port Arthur Historic Site ★
About 100km (63 miles) SE ☎ *50 2107* 🚻 *(museum only)*
✗ *at 9.30am, 11.30am, then hourly to 3.30pm* 🍴 ⚓ ♿ *Site open at all times. Museum open 9.30am-4.30pm. Guided bus tours leave Tasbureau, 80 Elizabeth St.* ☎ *34 6911 for details.*

This is probably the single most significant historical site in Australia. Port Arthur, established in 1830, was once the major penal settlement of Van Diemen's Land, as Tasmania was originally called, and operated until 1877 when it was abandoned and the remaining convicts were sent to jail in Hobart. More than 12,000 convicts passed through the settlement. The regime was extremely strict and harsh – witness the so-called model prison, based on rules of solitary confinement and silence, with its tiny one-man cells and a chapel where prisoners could not see one another.

The major points of interest are the **chapel**, never consecrated; the **model prison**; the **asylum**, with its visitor reception centre, video display tracing the history of Port Arthur, and museum; the **penitentiary**, **hospital**, **guardhouse** and **magazine**; and the **government cottages** where visitors were accommodated. The penitentiary, the largest building in the settlement, started life as a flour mill before being converted to house convicts.

Much of Port Arthur was damaged in bushfires during 1897, but the extensive remaining ruins give a vivid outline of what prison life was like 150 or more years ago.

Postal and Telecommunications Museum
19-21 Castray Esplanade ☎ *20 7262* 🚻 *Open Mon-Fri 8am-5pm, Sat 9am-noon. Closed Sun.*

An extensive display traces the history and development of postal and telegraphic services in Tasmania. It can be combined with a visit to *Salamanca Place*, 100m (110yds) away.

Richmond ★
26km (16 miles) NE.

This is the site of the oldest bridge still standing in Australia, built by convicts in 1823–25. Richmond and its bridge were important in the 19thC. They enabled heavy horse traffic to travel faster between Hobart and the E coast, and later to *Port Arthur*. Today the bridge is still used to cross the Coal River. There are alarming bows in its structure, but it is quite sound, much work having been done to ensure its survival.

Richmond, a classified historical town, has much else to offer. It claims the country's oldest Roman Catholic church, **St John's** (1836). A Catholic school has operated in Richmond since 1843, and the restored old **school room** is behind the church. **Richmond**

Gaol (_open to visitors_) predates Port Arthur, construction having started in 1825.

There are more than 40 buildings of historical interest, including many fine private houses in classic Georgian style. Most noteworthy are the **Court House** (1825); the **Granary**, now home to an art gallery and a boutique selling mohair; the **Old Post Office and General Store** (started in 1826), which served as the local post office from 1832–1973 and is the oldest surviving postal building in Australia; **St Luke's Church of England** (1834); and **James Gordon's House** (1831), a fine colonial Georgian house built by Captain James Gordon, the district magistrate, who gave his name to the Gordon River on the w coast of Tasmania.

Risdon Cove Historic Site ★
Bowen Park Grasstree Hill Rd., East Risdon ☎ 30 6031 ▨ ♿
Barbecue facilities ⚓ _Open 9.30am-4.30pm._

This is the site, on the eastern shores of Hobart, of the first recognized European settlement in Tasmania, in Sept 1803, abandoned in 1804 in favour of Sullivans Cove, the present site of Hobart. Risdon Cove consists of ruins in varying states of decay, some being only outlines of foundations, dotted around the cove area. The whole site has been landscaped, and there is an impressive visitors' centre.

Risdon Cove is significant in the overall picture of Tasmania's development. Study the models in the visitors' centre for an excellent idea of what the area looked like more than 180yrs ago.

Runnymede House ★
61 Bay Rd., New Town ☎ 28 1269 ▨ **✗** ⚓ _Open 10am-4.30pm. Closed Mon, Christmas Day, Good Friday, July. Ring bell at front door to gain admission._

A beautifully proportioned and preserved house in the suburb of New Town, Runnymede was built in 1844 by the lawyer and reformer Rober Pitcairn, a leading advocate of the abolition of penal transportation. It is a single-storey house in the late-Georgian style, set in an English-style garden. The house was occupied until the late 1970s, when the National Trust took it over, and much of the furnishing is original. At one time the house stood on the shore of New Town, but the land in front has since been reclaimed from the sea.

Salamanca Place ★
Every Georgian warehouse in this superbly preserved line, dating from the late 1830s, is still in use. Some survive as warehouses; others have become cafés, restaurants, art galleries or shops. Today there is grass where once there would have been cargo stacked from ships unloading on the waterfront opposite. Saturday is market day, and people come from miles around to sell and buy anything from fruit and vegetables to handcrafted leather work and bric-a-brac. Buskers (sometimes the Tasmanian Police pipe and drum band) perform, adding a festive note to the activities.

Salamanca Place is virtually an extension of _Battery Point_, and the two areas can be visited together.

Shot Tower ★
Channel Hwy, Taroona ☎ 27 8885 ▨ 🅿 ⚓ ♨ _Open 9am-5pm._

The tower offers unsurpassed views across the Derwent Estuary. It was built in 1870 and was used to make musket balls and shot. Extensively restored, the 60m-tall (197ft) tower is now a museum and art gallery. A short continuously-running video explains its history.

Tasmanian Museum and Art Gallery ★
5 Argyle St. ☎ 23 1422 ☎ *Open 10am-5pm. Closed Christmas Day, Anzac Day, Good Friday.*
The museum possesses a good collection of stuffed native animals including the Tasmanian Devil and the now almost certainly extinct Tasmanian Tiger. Elsewhere the emphasis is on Tasmanian Aborigines and early colonial life.

The art gallery has six galleries devoted to the permanent collection, plus a series of special exhibitions throughout the year. The permanent exhibition has works mainly by Australian and prominent Tasmanian artists, and by early convict painters and colonial painters (those not born in Australia but who did much work there). The permanent collection features such noted Australian artists as William Dobell, Sidney Nolan and Frederick McCubbin.

Tasmanian Transport Museum
Anfield St., Glenorchy ☎ 23 1392 ☎ ✿ *Open Sat, Sun 1-5pm. Closed Mon-Fri.*
A must for bus, train and tram buffs. The museum, complete with a tram and a railway station, is crammed with memorabilia from an earlier transport era.

Theatre Royal
29 Campbell St. ☎ 34 6266. Open for performances: see press.
Australia's oldest surviving theatre, Hobart's Theatre Royal celebrated its 150th anniversary in 1987. The external walls and the stage are largely orginal. The theatre's acoustics are excellent and the Regency decor adds charm and intimacy to the small auditorium.

Van Diemen's Land Folk Museum
Narryna, 103 Hampden Rd., Battery Point ☎34 2791 ☎ ☎ *Open Mon-Fri 10am-5pm, Sat 11am-5pm, Sun, hols 2-5pm.*
Housed in **Narryna**, one of Hobart's oldest houses, built c.1836, the museum, the oldest of its type in Australia, has a fine collection of furniture, china, silver, paintings and other articles from the early days of the colony.

Hotels

Four Seasons Downtowner
96 Bathurst St., Hobart, Tas., 7000 ☎ 34 6333 ▭ ☎ *58074* ▮
107 rms ➤ ▭ ▣ ⊕ ▣ ▥
Location: *Western edge of city.* This represents the best in modern motor-inn accommodation. Service is good, the rooms spacious, reception and service are friendly and efficient, and the hotel is small enough to retain a personal touch.
♿ ▤ ☂ ☎

Four Seasons Westside
150 Bathurst St., Hobart, Tas., 7000 ☎ 34 6255 ▭ ☎ *58228* ▮

139 rms ➤ ▭ ▣ ▣ ▥
Location: *Western edge of city.* A larger brother to the *Four Seasons Downtowner*, this is similar in concept and style, offering good-quality, unpretentious accommodation in generously large rooms. The **Silver Skillet** (see *Restaurants*) and an excellent, inexpensive bistro provide a choice of food and price.
♿ ▤ ☂ ☎

Hatchers Hobart ♣
40 Brooker Ave., Hobart, Tas., 7000 ☎ 34 2911 ▭ ☎ *58010* ▮

42 rms ⬛ AE ⬤ ⬤ VISA
Location: Convenient for the city.
Situated on a busy roundabout,
Hatchers can be noisy at times, but
offers reasonably priced, centrally
located accommodation. A restaurant
on the top floor has excellent views
over Hobart and the Derwent.
⬤ ⬛ ⵗ

Hobart Pacific Motor Inn
Kirby Court, West Hobart, Tas.,
7000 ☎ *34 6733* IDD ☎ *58129* ☎
60 rms AE ⬤ ⬤ VISA
Location: 2km (1¼ miles) from centre.
A good, average motor inn, part of
the Flag Inn chain, the Hobart
Pacific provides decent, clean
accommodation.
⬤ ⥱ ⬛ ⵗ ⚓

Lenna Motor Inn of Hobart
20 Runnymede St., Battery Point,
Hobart, Tas., 7000 ☎ *23 2911* IDD
☎ *58190* ☎ *50 rms* ⬡ ⬛ AE ⬤
⬤ VISA
Location: Ideal for exploring Battery
Point. This is a two-storey 19thC
mansion, to which 50 rooms have

been added, tastefully and entirely in
keeping. The surroundings may be
old-world, but the service and
facilities are certainly not.
⬛ ⵗ ⚓

Wrest Point Hotel-Casino
410 Sandy Bay Rd., Sandy Bay,
Tas., 7000 ☎ *25 0112* IDD
☎ *58115* ⊗ *25 1481* ☎ *278 rms*
⬡ ⬛ AE ⬤ ⬤ VISA
Location: On a small promontory
jutting out into the Derwent River.
This was Australia's first legal
casino. Its unmatched location
provides superb views from rooms in
the 17-storey tower – but note that
the two other wings do not share the
view, and only the tower is air-
conditioned, a strange omission. The
standard throughout is superb. The
casino is suitably exciting and
glamorous, but like the hotel retains
a sense of intimacy. The **Cabaret**
Room attracts top-flight
international acts, and **The Point**
Revolving Restaurant (see
Restaurants) can be recommended.
⬤ ⥱ ⬛ ⵗ ⬡ ⵕ ⬡ ⚓

Restaurants

Dear Friends
8 Brooke St., The Waterfront
☎ *23 2646* ☎ ⬡ ⬥ ⵗ AE ⬤
⬤ VISA *Last orders about 10pm.*
Closed Sat lunch, Sun, Mon
lunch.
A sense of style pervades this
refurbished flour mill, built in 1863.
Waiters are dressed in long white
aprons. The food is *nouvelle cuisine*
adapted to local conditions, with a
strong leaning towards Tasmanian
fish.

Milan's Seafood Restaurant
7 Beach Rd., Sandy Bay ☎ *25*
2180 ☎ ⬡ ⬥ ⵗ ⬡ ⵦ AE ⬤
⬤ VISA *Last orders about 10pm.*
Closed Sun.
Housed in an elegant old mansion in
Hobart's premier suburb of Sandy
Bay, Milan's offers a huge range of
local seafood, including locally
caught lobster.

Mr Wooby's ⬡
Rear of 65 Salamanca Pl. ☎ *34*
3466 ⬡ ⬡ ⬡ *Last orders*
1.30am. Closed Sun, Mon dinner.
Ideal for a light lunch or dinner and a
cup of coffee: the blackboard menu
offers hot quiche, home-made
sausages, savoury crêpes, pizza, *tacos*
and vegetarian pies, and there is
usually at least one home-made soup
on the menu. Theatre bills and

programmes decorate the walls. Far
from elegant, but genuinely friendly.

Mures Fish House
5 Knopwood St., off Montpelier
Retreat, Battery Point ☎ *23 6917*
⬡ ⬡ ⬥ ⵗ ⬤ VISA *Last orders*
10pm. Closed Sat lunch, Sun
lunch.
If you don't like fish, forget Mures.
For this Hobart institution rates as
one of the best fish restaurants in
Australia. It is hidden away in a
Georgian house, built in 1849, in a
little cul-de-sac in Battery Point:
knock on a brass doorknocker to gain
admittance. The decor is simple:
high-backed wooden chairs, and a
flower on each table. But the menu is
imaginative, with regular dishes,
including Tasmanian-reared Atlantic
salmon (at a price . . .), and varying
fish specials. A must for anyone who
loves fish – but be sure to book
ahead.

The Point Revolving Restaurant
Wrest Point Hotel-Casino, 410
Sandy Bay Rd., Sandy Bay ☎ *25*
0112 ☎ ⬡ ⬥ ⬡ ⵗ ⬥ ⵦ AE
⬤ ⬤ VISA *Last orders 9.30pm.*
From the top of the tower at the
Wrest Point (see *Hotels*), The Point
offers unrivalled views across Hobart
and the Derwent: the moon reflected
on the water on a calm evening

should bring out the poet in even the hardest heart. Fortunately both food and service match the view. The menu may be unadventurous, but the dishes are all impeccably prepared, some at the table. The restaurant revolves at a sedate pace, about once an hour.

Sakura Japanese Restaurant
85 Salamanca Pl. ☎ _23 4773_ ▥
▭ ▬ ♉ Ⓐ Ⓔ Ⓞ Ⓒ Ⓥ _Last orders 11.30pm. Closed lunch, Sun, Mon._
Highly recommended by Japanese visitors and businessmen, this restaurant is housed in one of the old warehouses on _Salamanca Place_ (see _Sights_). It is part of the Japanese Seamens Club opened in 1974 to cater to visiting tuna-fishing fleets from Japan, and is now open to the public.

Silver Skillet
Four Seasons Westside, 156 Bathurst St. ☎ _34 6255_ ▥ ▭ ▬
♉ ➳ Ⓐ Ⓔ Ⓞ Ⓒ Ⓥ _Last orders 9.30pm. Closed lunch, Sun._
Silver service plus a "traditional" menu – the Silver Skillet succeeds admirably in its deliberate appeal to long-valued standards. Part of the _Four Seasons Westside_ (see _Hotels_).

La Suprema Pasta House
255 Liverpool St. ☎ _31 0770_ ▥
▭ _Last orders 10-10.30pm. Closed Sat-Tues lunch. BYO licence._
Indulge in some fine home-made pasta in this casual, busy restaurant. Recommended: _fettuccine_ with _fegatini_ (chicken livers) sauce; good veal dishes too. It's vital to book ahead.

Shopping

Distinctively Tasmanian crafts, jewellery, locally-made clothes . . . the following is a representative cross-section of the best shops in Hobart. The main shopping area is bounded by Liverpool, Murray, Elizabeth and Collins Streets; at its centre is the modern **Cat and Fiddle Arcade and Square.**

Aspect Design
79 Salamanca Pl. ☎ _23 2642_ ⅋
✾ Ⓐ Ⓔ Ⓞ Ⓥ
In an old warehouse in _Salamanca Place_ (see _Sights_), resident craftspeople can be seen at work: a goldsmith, a silversmith and a glassblower. Also displayed for sale is the work of some 90 artists and craftspeople. Recommended.

Huon Pine Shop
18 Criterion St. ☎ _34 5171_ ▣
A wide range of gifts made from Tasmania's unique Huon pine and other local woods. The pine's light weight and colour make it an ideal wood for working, and some first-class, imaginative gifts can be purchased. Special orders are taken.

Skin Rugs Tasmania
35 Morrison St. ☎ _34_

_8142/34 9523_ Ⓐ Ⓔ Ⓞ Ⓥ
A wide selection of opals from triplets to the expensive black opals gives this shop one of the best ranges in the state. There is also a vast selection of sheepskin and kangaroo-skin products, from rugs to coats and boots. There's knitwear too, much of it locally made, and other souvenirs of Tasmania.

Spinning Gum
236 Sandy Bay Rd., Sandy Bay (in the Mayfair Shopping Centre)
☎ _23 6891_ ✾ Ⓞ Ⓥ
Owner Graham Wilson's shop has become a mecca for craftspeople throughout Tasmania, who send their work to the shop for sale. It specializes in Tasmanian woodcrafts, pottery, fabrics, blown glass, soaps and scents, and leather goods. Open every day.

Launceston
☎ _STD code: 003. Airport_ ☎ _91 8288; Ansett_ ☎ _31 7711; Australian_ ☎ _31 4411. Car rental: Avis_ ☎ _31 1633; Budget_ ☎ _34 0099; Hertz_ ☎ _31 2099. Tasmanian Government Tourist Bureau: Corner of St John St. and Paterson St., Launceston, Tas., 7250_ ☎ _32 2101. American Express Travel Service: Corner of Charles St. and Cimitiere St., Launceston, Tas., 7250_ ☎ _31 2411. Royal Automobile Club of Tasmania (RACT): Corner of York St. and George St., Launceston, Tas., 7250_ ☎ _31 3166._

The Tasmanian Tourist Bureau publishes a useful series of leaflets entitled *Let's Talk About . . .*, available from any Tasbureau outlet. One of the best is *Let's Talk About the Cataract Gorge and Cliff Grounds Reserve*. The National Trust also has a helpful guide to its properties in the Launceston region.

Sights and places of interest in and around Launceston

Cataract Gorge ★
Gorge Rd. ☎ *31 5915* 🚠 *for chairlift* ⧫ 🅿 🚗 ◀ *Chairlift operates mid-Aug to mid-June 9am-4.30pm, mid-June to mid-Aug Sat, Sun only 9am-4.30pm.*

The gorge, situated on the western edge of Launceston, is carved out of softer rock by the South Esk River and provides spectacular views, floral walks and hiking tracks. The chairlift across the gorge is said to have the longest central span in the world, at 308m (1,010ft); the crossing takes about 6mins.

A large area, the **First Basin**, worn away by the river before it rushes down the cataract to feed into the Tamar River, is Launceston's favourite picnic spot and recreational area. Facilities include swimming and paddling pools. Overlooking the First Basin is the dramatically located *Gorge Restaurant* (see *Restaurants*). A visitors' information centre, occupying a former bandstand, provides background information on the gorge and exhibits local flora and fauna.

The city end of the gorge is sometimes floodlit; good views can be obtained from Kings Bridge or Cataract Walk. For times of floodlighting contact the **Town Hall** (*John St.*) or the **Tasmanian Government Tourist Bureau**.

Clarendon House ★
Clarendon, near Nile, 28km (18 miles) s ☎ *98 6220* 🚠 🅿 🚻 🚗 *Open Sept-May 10am-5pm, June-Aug 10am-4pm. Closed Christmas Day, Good Friday.*

Among the finest examples of colonial Georgian architecture in Australia, Clarendon is a large 3-storey house of fine proportions, built 1836–38, situated in a parkland setting with an English-style garden and kitchen garden enclosed by a wall. The house has been restored and furnished in the style of the 1830s and '40s, and is maintained by the National Trust.

Clarendon was built by the Englishman James Cox, a merchant who amassed a fortune from wool, meat and grain. He lived, in effect, the life of an English country squire, founding the village of Lymington, now renamed Nile, and endowing its church. He died in 1866 and was buried in the family vault in St Andrew's Church at *Evandale*.

Entally House ★
Bass Hwy, Hadspen, 15km (9½ miles) sw ☎ *93 6201* 🚠 ♿ *on ground floor* 🚗 *Open 10am-12.30pm, 1-5pm. Closed Christmas Day.*

Entally House, built c.1820, is possibly the most gracious of Tasmania's 19thC mansions. Situated on the outskirts of the historic town of Hadspen, it was built by Thomas Reibey II, who played a leading part in the development of Tasmania. His son, the first Archdeacon of the Church of England at Launceston, later left the Church and became for a short period Premier of Tasmania. Entally House contains some fine and valuable antiques. The gardens, like the house itself, are beautifully maintained.

Evandale Village ★
20km (12½ miles) s.
Evandale is classified as an historic town and is as nearly as perfect a Georgian village as you are likely to see in Australia. Many of the buildings have remained astonishingly untouched, forming some perfectly preserved 19thC streetscapes.

At **Nile**, 8km (5 miles) beyond Evandale, are two remarkable Georgian buildings, **St Andrew's Church of England** and *Clarendon House*.

Franklin House
Franklin Village, 6km (4 miles) s ☎ 44 7824 🖭 ⬛ 💷 ⬛
Open Sept-May 9am-5pm, June-Aug 9am-4pm. Closed Christmas Day, Good Friday.
This is another charming colonial Georgian house, the first house purchased by the Tasmanian National Trust. It was built in 1838 for Britton Jones, an early Launceston brewer, with two storeys and an attractive porch. The interior timberwork is noteworthy in consisting entirely of NSW cedarwood. A restaurant attached to the house, called the **Hollies**, is open for lunch and for morning and afternoon teas.

Penny Royal World ★
147 Paterson St. ☎ 31 6699 🖭 ⬛ ✳ ⬛ *Open 9am-4.30pm. Gunpowder Mill closed July 19-Aug 1.*
Situated on the western edge of Launceston, this imaginative attraction combines re-creations of 19thC industries: a gunpowder mill, a cannon foundry, an arsenal, a watermill, a windmill and a corn mill. A canal system and a lake have been created inside the complex, plied by large-scale model sailing ships, big enough to carry real passengers; and a model sloop, the *Sandpiper*, fires its cannons daily. A full-size paddle steamer, the *Lady Stelfox*, built of Huon pine, cruises up the Tamar River, sailing on the hour from 10am-5pm.

Other attractions include a millwright's shop, a wheelwright and a blacksmith. A gift shop sells English pottery, Welsh woollen goods and bags of stoneground wholemeal flour produced on the premises. See too *Penny Royal complex* in *Hotels*.

Waverley Woollen Mills ★
Waverley Rd., Waverley ☎ 39 1106 🖭 ⬛ ✗ *compulsory* ⬛ ⬛ *Tours 9am-4pm. Showrooms open 9am-5pm.*
One of several woollen mills in Launceston, Waverley Mills were established in 1874 and process wool from fleece to finished product, much of the work being carried out on old-fashioned machinery. A showroom attached to the mills features a range of quality garments. They are situated in Waverley, about 4km (2½ miles) E of the centre.

Hotels

Colonial Motor Inn ❦
31 Elizabeth St., Launceston, Tas., 7250 ☎ 31 6588 🎟
● *58667* 🖭 *64 rms* ⬛ ⬛ 🅰🅴 ⬛
🆎 🆅🅸🆂🅰
Location: Convenient, though not central. A first-class motor inn, offering a wide range of facilities at a competitive price.
& ⬛ 🍸 ⚓

Four Seasons Great Northern
3 Earl St., Launceston, Tas., 7250 ☎ 31 9999 🎟 ● *58877* 🖭 *115 rms* ⬛ 🅰🅴 ⬛ 🆎 🆅🅸🆂🅰
Location: Handily placed for the main attractions. The Great Northern is a comfortable establishment with two restaurants, and courteous and attentive staff.
& ⬛ 🍸 ⚓

Launceston Country Club-Casino
*Country Club Ave., Prospect
Vale, Tas., 7250* ☎ 44 8855 Ⓜ
⊕ 58600 ☒ 43 1880 ▥ *104 rms*
▂ ⊐ ⧆ AE ⊕ ⊙ VISA

*Location: Set in its own extensive
grounds, 8km (5 miles) SW.* This is
built in the style of a Deep South
mansion in the USA. Somehow it
lacks the style of its Hobart sister
establishment, Wrest Point, yet the
accommodation is excellent and all
facilities are first-class. The setting,
among English-style lawns and
formal gardens, with a water spout
and a bridge over an artificial creek,
is nicely designed and laid out. Ideal
If you aspire to nothing higher than a
good meal, a flutter at the tables and
a comfortable bed for the night, this
hotel will suit you admirably.
& ⇌ ▤ ¥ ⚓ ⚲ ✓ ⛵ ⛷

Penny Royal complex
*145 Patterson St., Launceston,
Tas., 7250* ☎ 31 6699
⊕ 58605 ▥ *68 rms* ▂ ⧆ ⊕ ⊙
VISA

*Location: On western edge of
Launceston.* The accommodation
section of the Penny Royal tourist
complex consists of three motels: the
Penny Royal Watermill, and the
Penny Royal Village, which
incorporates the **Penny Royal
Gunpowder Mill**. They all offer
good motel accommodation,
combining old-world decor with
modern facilities, and easy access to
the attractions of *Penny Royal
World* (see *Sights*). The Penny
Royal Gunpowder Mill tariff
includes admission to the
Gunpowder Mill.
▢

Restaurants

Burgundys
O'Keefes Hotel, 124 George St.
☎ 31 5422 ▥ ▣ ▬ ▬ ¥ ▂ AE
⊕ ⊙ VISA *Last orders 9pm.
Closed lunch, Sun, Mon.*
Worth a visit just to see the splendid
genuine Tasmanian antiques. But the
food is good and hearty too.

Gorge Restaurant
*Cataract Gorge Cliff Grounds,
Gorge Rd.* ☎ 31 3330 ▥ ▢ ▬
¥ ▂ ⧆ AE ⊕ ⊙ VISA *Last
orders about 9.30-10pm. Closed
Sun dinner.*
Excellent food in a splendid location,
among the lawns and trees of the
spectacular *Cataract Gorge* grounds
(see *Sights*). The menu is strong on
local seafood and game, and the
atmosphere is warm and intimate.

Quill and Cane
*Colonial Motor Inn, 31 Elizabeth
St.* ☎ 31 6588 ▥ ▢ ▬ ¥ ▂
AE ⊕ ⊙ VISA *Last orders 9pm.
Closed Sun lunch.*
Attached to the *Colonial Motor Inn*
(see *Hotels*), this is, for a motel, a
surprisingly imaginative restaurant.

Shrimps
72 George St. ☎ 34 0584 ▥ ▢
▬ ▂ AE ⊕ ⊙ VISA *Last orders
about 9pm. Closed Sat lunch,
Sun.*
Seafood, naturally, is the speciality
here, prepared with some style.
Shrimps also serves Tasmanian
wines, for some obscure reason hard
to find in most restaurants on the
island. Housed in a National Trust-
classified Georgian building in the
heart of Launceston.

Terrace Restaurant
*Launceston Country Club-Casino,
Country Club Ave., Prospect Vale*
☎ 44 8855 ▥ ▢ ▬ ¥ ▂ ⧆
AE ⊕ ⊙ VISA *Last orders 9.30pm.*
The main restaurant at the
Launceston Country Club-Casino
(see *Hotels*), the elegant Terrace, all
wood panelling and brass light
fixtures, aspires to high standards,
matched by the excellent food but
rather let down by the patchy
service. However, the wine list is
nicely balanced and the view, across
well-manicured lawns and formal
gardens, relaxing.

Shopping
The central mall and surrounding streets comprise the major
shopping area. But some of the arts and crafts shops are spread
throughout the city. *Emma's Arts* is a leading example.

Emma's Arts
78 George St. ☎ 31 5630 ⚒ AE ⊙ VISA
Emma's Arts stocks only work by Tasmanian craftspeople and artists, and
carries a wide range of handcrafted gifts with a particular emphasis on local
woods. There is also a selection of oils and watercolours painted by
well-known local artists.

Tasmania excursions

Touring Tasmania is relatively easy. There are few options. Basically, you can travel from Launceston to Hobart or vice versa, depending on your city of arrival, via either the w coast, the E coast or through the heartland. Each option offers a wide variety of scenery, from mountains and wilderness to spectacular seascapes.

For speed and good highway conditions the best route is through the centre, using the Midland Hwy, which is mostly a first-class road. The route also offers several side trips, such as a visit to Evandale, near Launceston.

The w coast route passes through spectacular wilderness country, such as the Lake St Clair National Park, with the option of an excursion to *Strahan* (see below) and a boat trip up the Gordon.

The E coast route, through towns like St Helens, Scamander and St Marys, follows the coast closely for much of the journey, providing some spectacular sea views. It also passes close to the Freycinet National Park, famed for its red granite outcrops and excellent bushwalking, combined with swimming and sunbathing on some fine, uncluttered beaches. This route is described in *Planning* – see *Route 4*.

The two following excursions are ideal for motorists. The **Royal Automobile Club of Tasmania** (*corner of Murray St. and Patrick St., Hobart* ☎ *(002) 38 2200; corner of York St. and George St., Launceston* ☎ *(003) 31 3166*) sells maps and can recommend routes.

The Midland Highway

This is the easiest route, skipping most of the mountainous areas. It is an excellent road, well surfaced, with gentle bends, and has several opportunities for side trips.

Leaving Launceston heading s, the first detour is to the historic town of *Evandale* (see *Launceston sights*), to the E of the main highway. The turn-off is at Breadalbane, about 13km (8 miles) from Launceston. The detour rejoins the Midland Hwy about 10km (6 miles) farther along.

The next 60km (38 miles) or so pass through rich farmland and rolling countryside, until the road nears the town of **Ross**, which is worth a short detour. Built on the banks of the Macquarie River, the town used to be an important stopping place for stagecoaches on the Hobart-Launceston route. The bridge at Ross, built in 1836 by convict labour, has carvings by the convict artist Daniel Herbert, which were so much admired that they earned him a pardon. **Church St.** has many notable buildings including **Scotch Thistle Inn,** now a restaurant, but first granted a licence in 1830.

Next the highway passes through the village of **Oatlands,** on the shore of Lake Dulverton. Historic buildings of note include the courthouse, jail, flour mill and several churches.

Melton Mowbray, at the junction of the Midland and Lake Hwys, was named in 1843 after the English town of the same name. In the immediate area are several homesteads that are over 100yrs old. The highway then passes through Kempton, Bagdad, Mangalore and Brighton, crossing the Derwent at **Bridgewater Junction,** to the N of Hobart.

The west coast route

Between Hobart and Launceston the w coast route encounters some of the most spectacular scenery on the island.

Leaving Hobart NW on the Lyell Hwy, the road follows the

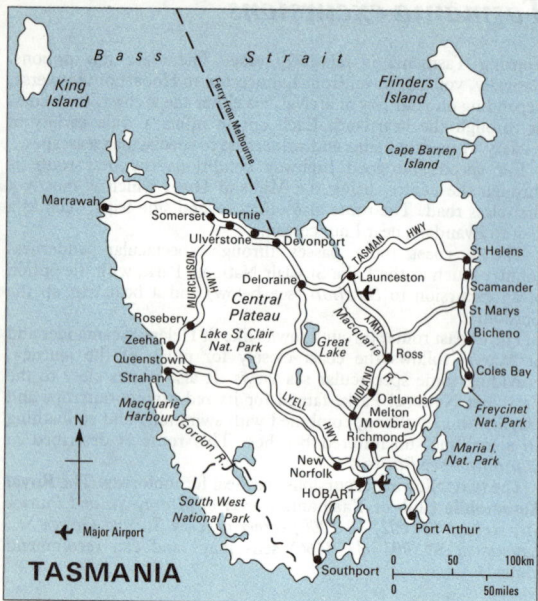

TASMANIA

Derwent for about 20km (12½ miles), passing several paper and pulp mills and the Cadbury chocolate factory at **Claremont.**

New Norfolk, the first largish town on the route, was settled in 1807 by convicts brought from Norfolk Island off the Queensland coast. It is notable for Australia's oldest church building, **St Matthew's Church of England,** and for one of the oldest continuously licensed pubs in the country, the **Bush Inn,** which dates back to 1815.

The road next crosses the **Mt. Field National Park,** a popular skiing area, which covers 16,000ha (39,500 acres). The scenery is spectacular: rugged mountains, an area of alpine plateau, and lakes in the lower regions.

The highway takes a sharp turn due W at the small township of Bronte as it heads towards **Queenstown,** a mining town since the 1880s, surrounded by a moonlike landscape caused by copper smelting, now stopped, which killed all the vegetation. The huge open-cut copper mine can be visited.

Here the road detours to *Strahan* (see below), a distance of 42km (26 miles), which is the gateway to the Gordon River.

From Strahan, either retrace the route to Queenstown and then take the Zeehan Hwy to Zeehan, or take the minor road to Zeehan that follows the coast for some kilometres before striking inland.

From Zeehan the Murchison Hwy passes through **Rosebery,** a mining town. At **Williamsford,** 7km (4½ miles) S, zinc is extracted.

The road then passes through fairly mountainous country before reaching the coast at **Somerset.** From there, travel E, following the coast. By Tasmanian standards, the road becomes busy as it passes through a series of coastal towns such as Burnie, Penguin, Ulverstone and the ferry port of Devonport, before heading inland to Launceston.

Strahan and the Gordon River

On **Macquarie Harbour**, into which flows the **Gordon River**, lies **Strahan**, the only town on Tasmania's rugged w coast. The entrance to the Harbour, known as **Hell's Gates**, was so named by convicts who in the 19thC helped carve out something from nothing on this inhospitable coast.

A pleasant if isolated community, Strahan has manifestly benefited from the worldwide interest aroused by the Hydro Electricity Commission of Tasmania's proposal some years ago to dam the Gordon River. The environmentalists' blockade of the river and the ensuing arrests, including that of the British botanist David Bellamy, forced the Commonwealth Government in 1982 to intervene. The area was added to the World Heritage List, allowing Canberra to treat the matter as a foreign-affairs issue.

The area has many attractions. The town has some magnificent beaches, and there are impressive sand dunes on the ocean beach; good surfing and surf-fishing can also be found near the harbour entrance. Macquarie Harbour itself offers good wind-surfing, sailing and waterskiing.

And then there is the Gordon River, which, though perhaps thrust into the limelight in recent years, has actually been a popular tourist attraction since the late 19thC. Three jet-powered boats and a seaplane are based at Strahan to take tourists up the Gordon River. Keeping up his family tradition, boat operator Rex Kearney today runs two of the three boats (details are given below), just as in the 1890s his grandfather guided tourists up the river.

Navigable, though not for very large craft, for 42km (26 miles) from its mouth in Macquarie Harbour, the river is a true wilderness. Trees grow down to and actually into the water, and on all sides it is virtually untouched by man. In places the riverbed reaches a depth of more than 42m (138ft), punctuated by cataracts and towering cliffs. No effort should be spared to see this great spectacle.

At the mouth of the Gordon River is **Sarah Island**, a few hectares of land with no fresh water, used as a penal settlement for the worst prisoners until it was abandoned in 1833 for the model prison conditions of *Port Arthur* (see *Hobart sights*). The outlines of some of the buildings erected by the inmates can still be seen. The structures failed the test of time, for the brackish water used in the mortar ate away the lime. Most Gordon River cruises include a short stop at the island.

Along the banks of the Gordon River are some of the few remaining stands of Huon pine, found only in Tasmania. Extremely slow-growing, its value to woodworkers was soon recognized by early settlers, who cut the trees down in large numbers, so that today few survive. Some Huon pines along the river's banks started growing before the birth of Christ.

Gordon River cruises
Cruises on the jet-powered boats *James Kelly II* and *Wilderness Explorer* depart daily at 9am from Aug 25-Dec 31 (Christmas Day at 2pm) and from Mar 16-June 1. Two cruises a day depart at 9am and 1.30pm from Jan 1-Mar 15. At most times reservations are advisable (*from Scenic Gordon and Hell's Gates Charters, P.O. Box 38, Strahan, Tas., 7468 ☎ (004) 71 7187/71 7281*).

Cruises on the *Gordon Explorer* jet-powered cruiser depart daily at 9am and 3pm in summer and at 9am only in winter. Precise dates vary – contact the operator for details. Reservations are usually advisable at most times (*from Morrisons Tourist Services, The Esplanade, Strahan, Tas., 7468 ☎ (004) 71 7179*).

All three boats are fully licensed and serve tea and coffee and light refreshments.

From the air

Wilderness Air (_Strahan Wharf, Strahan, Tas., 7468_ ☎ _(004) 71 7280_) operates a single-engined floatplane, based at Strahan, over the wilderness region – one of the best ways of seeing the Gordon and surrounding area. River height and weather permitting, the plane lands on the river. There is no scheduled service, and flights are by previous arrangement only.

☎ Four Seasons Strahan Motor Inn

Jolly St., Strahan, Tas., 7468 ☎ _(004) 71 7160_ ☻ _59030_ ⬛⬜ _50 rms_ ⬛ ⬛ AE ① ⓒⒹ VISA

Location: On high ground overlooking Strahan's harbour. Basic rustic charm, with a range of Tasmanian wood used throughout. The restaurant is no more than average – the choice in Strahan is limited, so there is little incentive to improve. But there are excellent views from most of the self-contained suites.

⬛ ⬛ ⬛ ⬛ ⬛

Tasmanian tours and tour operators

Much of Tasmania is wilderness country, and a number of companies specialize in tours of the remote regions by 4-wheel-drive vehicle and on foot. There are also, of course, conventional tours of a more sedate nature by bus.

Some words of warning are in order about Tasmania's wilderness regions, which are subject to extremely heavy rainfall. Weather conditions can change so suddenly and dramatically that in the highland regions people have died of exposure, even in summer. Sensible clothing should always be worn – reputable tour operators working in the wilderness areas will recommend what to wear. It is also inadvisable for tourists unfamiliar with the bush to venture alone into some of the more remote, untamed areas, where it is easy to get lost.

Those caveats apart, a trip into one of the wilderness regions under the eye of an experienced guide can be most rewarding.

Below are given a selection of tour operators. The **Tasmanian Government Tourist Offices** (or **Tasbureau**, as they are also known) can offer guidance on the best sort of tour to suit particular needs and can arrange reservations for most tour operators. Main addresses are given under _Hobart_ and _Launceston_.

For 4-wheel-drive tours, **Bushventures 4 WD Tours** (_171 Summerleas Rd., Kingston, Tas., 7150_ ☎ _(002) 29 4291/66 3427_) – tours to wilderness areas and to the World Heritage-listed Franklin River region.

For guided tours, **Lottah 4 WD** ("_Lottah_", _Nubeena, Tas., 7184_ ☎ _(002) 50 2173/50 2254_) – tours of the Tasman Peninsula, visiting such historic sites as _Port Arthur_ (see _Hobart sights_), and venturing also off the beaten track.

For hiking tours, **Craclair Tours** (_P.O. Box 516, PO Devonport, Tas., 7310_ ☎ _(004) 24 3971_) – escorted hiking tours of up to 8 days visiting wilderness regions, such as Cradle Mountain.

For cruises, **MV Commodore 1** (_inquiries_ ☎ _(002) 34 9294/25 2794_) – cruises around Hobart harbour, lasting 2hrs, usually with morning and afternoon departures.

For bus tours, **Tasmanian Redline Coaches** (_Hobart terminal_ ☎ _(002) 34 4577; Launceston terminal_ ☎ _(003) 31 9177_) – scheduled passenger services, and tours and charters. The company has terminals in all major towns and cities. Bookings can also be made through Tasmanian Tourist Offices.

For scenic flights, **Par Avion** of Cambridge aerodrome near Hobart (*P.O. Box 300, Sandy Bay, Tas., 7170* ☎ *(002) 48 5390*) offers a range of scenic flights and in season has a daily flight, weather permitting, to the sw wilderness area. There are also scenic flights to *Port Arthur* (see *Hobart sights*).

Victoria

Victoria's compactness – it is the smallest of the mainland states, with a land area of 227,600sq.km (84,884sq. miles), only 3 percent of the Australian total – means its major attractions are readily accessible. Yet there is greater variety here than anywhere else on the continent. For example, a motoring trip down the Murray River (which forms the border between Victoria and NSW), from, say, Mildura to Albury, would provide an excellent and representative cross-section of the state.

Victoria, and particularly Melbourne, is where the ruling elite of Australia makes its home. Don't take too seriously all those stories about this being a completely classless society: a short stroll down Melbourne's Collins St., or a visit to Toorak, Australia's most exclusive suburb, soon dispels any such myth. Victorians have a superior air, and the "squattocracy" – descendants of the early settlers who squatted on the land and then lobbied the authorities to recognize their claims – have a code of conduct as rigid as any upper-class group in the world.

Much of the early wealth was based on land, and many large estates remain in the hands of descendants of those pioneers who claimed the land more than 120yrs ago. Such families consider themselves the cream of society, much like their counterparts elsewhere, and they have provided some of the nation's leading politicians and entrepreneurs.

Melbourne very much reflects this sense of continuity and adheres to many of those old-fashioned virtues beloved by conservatives everywhere: Church, school and family (though not necessarily in that order). An old cliché – that in Sydney people ask you the size of your bank balance, in Adelaide what church you attend, in Brisbane whether you'd like a beer, and in Melbourne what school you went to – reflects pretty fairly on the values of Melburnians and Victorians. The most prestigious private schools in the country are in Victoria – and Geelong Grammar counts the Prince of Wales among its old boys.

And yet, despite this innate sense of superiority, Victoria feels acutely that in the postwar period it has lagged behind the brasher NSW and its, to Victorian eyes, rather vulgar capital, Sydney. Melbourne was the federal capital from 1901–27, and its current second-rank status is not readily accepted. Yet somehow all efforts to emulate Sydney's style belie Victoria's solidly respectable image; Melbourne never quite achieves Perth's laid-back feel or Sydney's fast-lane vibrance; and unlike Sydney, Melbourne still seems to be influenced more by London than by Los Angeles, although today that is changing.

Victoria forms the base for many large companies in long-established sectors such as engineering, mining and industrial farming. Newer high-tech enterprises almost exclusively choose Sydney, as do most of the new wave of overseas banks. If anything this sectoral split emphasizes differences between Victoria and its arch rival to the N. Melbourne continues its traditional role as Australia's financial capital; and its reliance on the traditional industries of banking, insurance and stockbroking reinforces the city's conservative image and fosters in its citizens an air of gravity and reserve.

Victoria abounds in contradictions. It is conservative, but has a reputation for radical politics. It includes more than 50 nationalities in its population of 4,164,700 (in June 1986), though in many of its attitudes – for example, its intense preoccupation with Australian Rules football and almost total disregard of the nationally more popular soccer – the state is remarkably insular. Melbourne feels itself superior to Sydney, but worries disproportionately about what its rival is up to.

Such rivalry is not easy for outsiders to understand, for it is intense and sometimes bitter.

During the gold rush of the 1850s and 1860s Melbourne was the fastest-growing city in the British Empire. Then it probably boasted more public houses and bordellos per head of population than any other English-speaking city. It was quite common to see drunken miners light Havana cigars with banknotes and marry prostitutes they had met only a few hours before.

There followed, inevitably, a moral reaction, compounded by a disastrous slump in land prices. From this catastrophe grew an urge for respectability, giving rise to the temperance (and kindred) movements, who achieved so much power that the city soon acquired the reputation of being the home of "wowsers", or killjoys.

Money from the gold rush fuelled a huge building boom and underpinned the growth of great landed families, who made their fortunes out of feeding the miners flooding into the colony. These families built substantial mansions that still adorn inner suburbs such as South Yarra, Toorak and St Kilda.

Much of Melbourne's elegance stems from its physical layout and a tradition of genuine municipal pride. The central city area is laid out on a grid pattern with main thoroughfares running straight and wide. Narrower one-way streets, bearing the diminutive of the major street (e.g., Bourke St. and Little Bourke St.) run parallel. Many of the major streets are linked by arcades of chic shops.

But though Melbourne is a fine city it can also be incredibly stuffy and pompous. Older men are still inclined to wear three-piece suits in winter, complete with London-made overcoats. Until recently, women were not allowed into such places as the members' stands at most horse-racing tracks. The city also has the most hidebound gentleman's club in the country, the Melbourne Club. One British knight recently remarked that such clubs no longer existed even in London.

Rural Victorians are as conservative in their attire and politics as their city cousins. The annual Royal Melbourne Show, held in Nov, sees the moleskin-attired farmers, all with compulsory hat, and their sensibly-dressed wives descend for their annual encounter with city life.

The arcades, the green-and-gold trams (the newer ones sport a sort of municipal orange), coupled with a large Mediterranean immigrant population, contribute to the distinctly European flavour. Melbourne is the third-largest Greek-speaking city in the world and has one of the country's largest Italian communities, reflecting its intensely cosmopolitan makeup.

Above all, it is a city of parks and gardens. One-fifth of the central area is made up of parkland – one of the largest ratios of open space to built-up area of any city of comparable size in the world. There is a sense of spaciousness, mitigating the impact of the high-rise buildings of recent years. And if Melbourne lacks the stunning beauty of Sydney's harbour or Perth's handsome Swan River, it possesses a sense of quiet, unassuming style that other world cities find hard to match.

Melbourne

Maps 8–11 ☎ *STD code: 03. Airport: Tullamarine* ☎ *338 2211. Railway stations: for country services, Spencer Street* ☎ *62 3115; for suburban services, Flinders Street* ☎ *617 0900. Car rental: Avis* ☎ *663 6366; Budget* ☎ *320 6333; Hertz* ☎ *699 8899. Victorian Government Travel Centre: 230 Collins St., Melbourne, Vic., 3000* ☎ *602 9444. American Express Travel Service: 505 St Kilda Rd., Melbourne, Vic., 3004* ☎ *267 3711. Royal Automobile Club of Victoria (RACV): 123 Queen St., Melbourne, Vic., 3000* ☎ *607 2211.*

Orientation

Melbourne, the most southerly of Australia's mainland capital cities, lies largely around the saucerlike rim of Port Phillip Bay. To the s it stretches for 60km (38 miles) through a series of beachside suburbs such as Brighton, Hampton, Black Rock and Beaumaris, the urban sprawl petering out at Frankston, at the end of the suburban railway line. To the e – residentially popular and generally the more expensive side – the Dandenong Ranges more or less mark the physical limit of the built-up area. And to the w, flat and comparatively cheap land encourages continuing industrial development.

Melbourne has been slowly reaching out along the western fringe of Port Phillip Bay towards the town of Geelong, a process accelerated by the opening in 1978 of the West Gate Bridge across the Yarra River, making that side of the bay much more accessible.

The northern part has escaped most of the burgeoning postwar development that swallowed up orchards and small farmsteads in the eastern and southern areas, and mostly dates back to the early 20thC or even before.

Seeing the city

Melbourne is an easy city to negotiate. The centre has wide, pleasant, treelined main thoroughfares, and most of the postwar suburbs have wide, straight main roads.

The **Victorian Government Tourists' Bureau (VICTOUR)** (*230 Collins St.* ☎ *602 9444*) can answer most questions about Melbourne and Victoria. The **Melbourne Tourism Authority** (*80 Collins St.* ☎ *654 2288*), a free-enterprise organization funded by city business, is a valuable source of information about the state capital.

Melbourne has an extensive and efficient tramway system, convenient for journeys up to about 10km (6 miles). There is also a well-developed suburban rail system.

The **Metropolitan Transit Authority** (popularly styled the "Met"), which runs the trams, trains and buses and coordinates most of the privately owned bus lines, issues free maps showing the city transport network, available from main railway stations, tram depots and bus garages. There is a 24hr transport information service (☎ *617 0900*) for train and tram times.

The city is divided by the Met into ten neighbourhoods, within which fares are based on periods of time. For example, a 2hr ticket gives unlimited use of trams, trains and buses within a given neighbourhood. Daily Travelcards allow unlimited use of all three systems across the Metropolitan area.

A useful guide is *Melways Street Directory*, which shows tram routes and stop numbers, as well as railway stations. **Victour** also supplies metropolitan transport maps.

Trams

Melbourne's trams, once objects of scorn when every other city was converting to buses, are now a source of pride. Quiet and pollution-free, they set Melbourne apart from Australia's other major cities.

Tram tours depart from the intersection of Collins St. and Exhibition St. every Tues and Thurs at 11.30am. The trip lasts 3hrs and includes all the major sights on the tram routes. (*Tickets* ☎ *654 8629, or through any branch of the RACV*).

Buses

The **City Explorer Bus** leaves on the hour from outside Flinders Street station every day except Mon, between 10am and 4pm. The red double-decker bus offers a first-class tour of the city's sights, and you can disembark where you wish.

Cycling

Melbourne has more than 100km (over 60 miles) of designated bicycle paths. Cycling is easy in this fairly flat city, particularly in the cooler spring and autumn seasons. At weekends bicycles can be rented on the Yarra Bank on Alexandra Ave., opposite the Botanic Gardens. Rental is from Sat noon–dusk and Sun 10am–dusk. Many suburban bicycle shops also rent out bicycles.

A book, *Melbourne Bike Tours*, describing 20 cycle tours, is published by the State Bicycle Committee and is sold at larger newsstands and camping shops.

For the indulgent, **Pedicabs** (☎ *890 2991*) will send around a two-person modern version of a rickshaw and take you for a pedal-powered tour of the city – but avoid peak hours.

On foot

Melbourne is also good for walkers. **Melbourne Heritage Walks** (☎ *241 1085*) has a choice of six guided walks lasting about 1½hrs that explore historic Melbourne. Tailor-made walks can be organized.

River and bay cruises

The Yarra River, running through the centre of Melbourne, provides fascinating views of the city. **River Cruises** (☎ *654 1233*) leave from Princes Bridge near Flinders Street station, and from the quay at the World Trade Centre. The trips take in the port area, pass under West Gate Bridge (the longest in the southern hemisphere), and go past the Botanic Gardens and Como Island in the Yarra.

The large catamaran *Spirit of Victoria* cruises around Port Phillip Bay, leaving Station Pier, Port Melbourne, Wed-Sun in summer at 11am, taking in several stops and returning at 5pm. On Thurs nights in summer there are disco cruises. (*Bookings during holiday periods and for disco cruises at Station Pier, or at level 5, 459 Collins St., or* ☎ *62 6997.*)

Sights and places of interest

Arts Centre of Victoria ★
100 St Kilda Rd. ☎ *611 1566. Map 11D4* 🔄 ᕤ *✗ of concert halls and theatres by arrangement (ask at the centre)* 🖵 ⌒ *National Gallery open 10am-5pm; closed Mon except hols. Performing Arts Museum open Mon-Sat 11am-6pm, Sun noon-6pm.*

Three large buildings on treelined St Kilda Rd. beside the Yarra River form the focal point for the arts in Melbourne. They house the National Gallery of Victoria, the Melbourne Concert Hall, three theatres, the Performing Arts Museum and several restaurants, all linked by lawns, gardens and walkways.

Designed by Australian architect the late Sir Roy Grounds and completed in 1968, the **National Gallery** is constructed in local bluestone, with a moat lapping the sides of the building echoed by water running betweeen two sheets of glass at the entrance. The gallery, built around three courtyards, houses an extensive collection of Australian paintings by, among others, Tom Roberts, Frederick McCubbin, Russell Drysdale, Sidney Nolan, Arthur Streeton, and more recent figures such as Jeffrey Smart and Jon Balsaitis. Sculptures exhibited in the courtyards include Sir Henry Moore's *Seated Figure*. Among the fine European collection are Picasso's *Weeping Woman*, works by Turner, Tiepolo's *Banquet of Cleopatra* (one of the centre's highlights), engravings by Durer and watercolours by Blake.

The much newer **Concert Hall** can seat 2,677 (considerably more than the Sydney Opera House) and is designed primarily for symphonic performances; it is equipped with highly advanced acoustic facilities. A feature of the stunning interior design is Sir Sidney Nolan's monumental *Paradise Garden*, comprising 1,320 individual paintings in 220 panels.

The theatre building is topped by a metal spire, a poor-man's Eiffel Tower, considerably foreshortened by cuts in the building budget. It is divided into three theatres: the 2,000-seat **State**, home of the Australian Opera, the Victorian State Opera and the Australian Ballet; the 880-seat **Playhouse**, used for much of the year by the Melbourne Theatre Company; and the multipurpose 420-seat **Studio**, a centre for experimental theatre.

The **Performing Arts Museum** houses a fascinating and exhaustive collection of theatre memorabilia. Tours of the concert hall and theatres leave at 10.30am and 4pm and last about 1hr, and on Sun there are 1½hr backstage tours.

Beaches

Melbourne, situated as it is on Port Phillip Bay, is blessed with fine, sheltered, sandy and safe beaches within easy reach of the city – in many cases just a tram-ride away. There are also some fine surf beaches within comfortable driving distance, on the ocean side of the Mornington Peninsula s of the city. From the eastern side the closest surf beach is **Point Leo**; from the southern suburbs **Rye** ocean beach offers the easiest-to-reach surf.

Because of the way the Mornington Peninsula narrows close to the entrance to Port Phillip Bay, the best of both worlds can be found at such beachside towns as **Rye**, **Sorrento** and **Portsea**. All these have safe bay beaches on one side and open-ocean surf beaches only a 10min drive away on the other side of the narrow strip of land. Melburnians call the bayside beaches "front" beaches and the ocean ones "back" beaches. So if someone says they are going to Portsea back beach, they mean the ocean.

Close to the city, about 5km (3 miles) from the centre, **St Kilda** beach (much maligned by the Prince of Wales after a swim there some years ago) has long been popular, as has **Elwood** beach, about 3km (2 miles) farther s. St Kilda is easily accessible by train or tram and is a favourite place for city workers rushing to grab a lunchtime or after-work swim. Although a decade ago it probably deserved its reputation as a dirty beach, great strides have since been made towards cleaning up all Melbourne's inner-city beaches. Throughout summer the Environment Protection Authority publishes regular press reports on the condition of the beaches.

Melbourne's attempt to introduce a European flavour to the city, the Bourke Street Mall is reminiscent of Amsterdam, an impression reinforced by the trams that run along the centre of the pedestrian mall. It runs from one block from Elizabeth St. to Swanston St.

After a shaky beginning – no one believed it would work with trams running down the centre – the mall is now an established favourite with Melburnians and visitors. There are several rest areas, with seating and enormous potted plants. The entire surface of the mall has been levelled and laid in herringbone-pattern brickwork. Most days, street entertainers regale shoppers with music, from Bach to Springsteen.

Captain Cook's Cottage
Fitzroy Gardens, off Wellington Parade, East Melbourne.
Map 11C4 ▩ ✦ *Open 9am-5pm.*
In 1934, to mark Melbourne's centenary, a private citizen, Sir Russell Grimwade, financed the transportation of the cottage from the village of Great Ayton, Yorkshire, England, and its re-erection in the *Fitzroy Gardens*. The ivy covering the cottage was grown from a cutting taken at Great Ayton. Cook, however, never lived in the cottage: it was merely the home of his parents.

Carlton
Map 10A3.
The inner suburb of Carlton, Melbourne's substantial Italian quarter, is one of the most entertaining and stimulating areas of the city, particularly on Sun morning when Lygon St., 3km (2 miles) N of the city, turns into a fashion parade as the locals sport their best finery, some on foot, others cruising in their cars. It is all very crowded, noisy, and immensely enjoyable. Carlton is lively at nighttime too, for it has one of the largest concentrations of restaurants and cafés in Melbourne.

The best way to soak in the atmosphere and excitement is on foot. Start at the beginning of **Lygon St.**, where it extends from Russell St. in the city centre, and walk N past the Downtowner Motel on the right. This is the Italian heart of Carlton, alive with bistros and cafés (the scenes when Italy won the World Cup soccer championship in 1982 had to be seen to be believed). Each Nov the Italian community of Carlton holds a street festival, the Lygon Street Festa, lasting a week and including street theatre, folk dancing, music and general Italian-style carnival fun.

But the area has more than just a strong Italian identity, and has become increasingly popular among young business executives and students as a place to live. As a result prices have soared. Carlton was built in the 1860s-'80s and has some fine examples of Victorian colonial architecture. Try to detour down **Grattan St.** and **Elgin St.**, which both cross Lygon St., and along some of the minor streets off these two main thoroughfares. Here you will find some architectural gems: single-fronted Victorian cottages of one and two storeys with ornate lace balcony ironwork, most of them lovingly restored in the 1960s to their original condition.
Drummond St., running parallel to Lygon St. a block to the E, is arguably the best-preserved 19thC street in Melbourne and must not be missed; one block E are **Carlton Gardens** (see *Gardens*) and the *Exhibition Buildings*.

The campus of Melbourne University, two blocks to the w of Lygon St., is a mix of building styles and periods and has some neo-Gothic buildings of merit. The campus grounds are crisscrossed by pedestrian streets.

Lygon St. crosses Princes St. at **Melbourne General Cemetery**, worth a stroll for fascinating insights into the hardships of early colonial life: note the many graves of children. Adjacent is **Princes Park**. Then turn right into Princes St. and walk four blocks to Nicholson St. for a tram to the centre.

Leaflets suggesting walking and driving tours, published by the Carlton Association, are available from the **National Trust Bookshop** (*Tasma Terrace, Parliament Pl.* ☎ *654 4711*).

Chinatown ★
Little Bourke St. Map 10B3 ✿

A somewhat strained attempt was made in the mid-1970s to create a tourist-type Chinatown in a short section of Little Bourke St., a narrow one-way street, by adding a couple of kitsch Chinese-style arches and generally upgrading the area.

At first the district was a source of cheap lodgings for the Chinese who in the 1850s flocked to Victoria during the gold rush; but gradually the boarding houses were replaced by Chinese businesses. Today the area houses some of Australia's finest Chinese restaurants, the *Museum of Chinese Australian History*, a Chinese Methodist Church, the Chinese Masonic Society and numerous Chinese stores, emporiums and businesses.

City Square ★
Map 10C3.

The city fathers' earnest attempt to give Melbourne this focal point has proved successful up to a point, though only time will reveal the true value of such an expensively created piece of open space. The City Square has been the subject of more plans and proposals than any other comparable piece of real estate in Melbourne. At present it comprises a mix of water races and waterfalls, glass canopies, trees and conversation alcoves; a graffiti wall is provided for would-be artists. Yet despite the good intentions, the City Square seems to lack heart, although it is becoming the focal point for rallies, demonstrations and marches.

Como House ★
Como Ave., South Yarra. Map 8D2 🚾 ✿ *Open 10am-5pm.*

This is the headquarters of the National Trust. Designed by Arthur Johnson, the two-storey mansion, with a wide colonial verandah, is one of the finest surviving examples of early colonial architecture designed on the grand scale. All the rooms opened to the public are furnished in the Victorian style of the house's heyday. The oldest part, dating from 1847, is the kitchen wing, which has staff quarters, a laundry and stables. Highlight of the interior is the white and gold **ballroom**, the focal point for social life in Mebourne in the Victorian and Edwardian eras.

Como House is set in a landscaped garden, distinguished by several enormous magnolia trees. The garden was developed with advice from the botanist Baron Ferdinand von Mueller, who was responsible also for planning Melbourne's *Royal Botanic Gardens*.

Exhibition Buildings ★
Nicholson St., Carlton ☎ *663 5000. Map 10A3* ⚹ *(Nicholson St. entrance best)* 🍴 🚻 *Open: depending on exhibition.*

A magnificent example of Victorian architecture, reflecting all the confidence of the era, the Exhibition Buildings were erected by

173

David Mitchell (father of Dame Nellie Melba, the world-famous soprano) for the vast 1880 International Exhibition. Here, on May 9 1901, Australia's first Federal Parliament was opened by Prince George, the future King George V. The occasion was marked by the celebrated proposal by Australia's first prime minister, Sir Edmund Barton: "A continent for a nation and a nation for a continent."

The Western Annexe of the Exhibition Buildings housed the Victorian State Parliament from 1901–27, after it gave up its magnificent Spring St. home for the use of the Federal Parliament while the design for the new Federal Parliament House was selected and built in Canberra.

Situated in **Carlton Gardens**, the Exhibition Buildings are flanked by gardens and an ornamental pond on the s side, and are still used today for conferences, exhibitions and trade fairs. Because of their timber construction, they have the unfortunate reputation of being one of Melbourne's worst fire risks.

Fitzroy Gardens

Among Melbourne's glorious gardens, the Fitzroy Gardens, laid out in 1850, are deservedly popular. Children enjoy the model Tudor village and, nearby, an old tree whose trunk was carved with tiny fantasy creatures by Australian sculptress the late Ola Cohn. *Captain Cook's Cottage* is also located here. Together with other city parks, the gardens play host in summer to a programme of free entertainment which ranges from open-air theatre to pop concerts and is claimed to be the largest entertainment scheme of its kind in the world.

Gardens

Melbourne's gardens are its greatest treasure. No other state capital has such quantity or variety, and few world cities have such a high proportion of open space.

Brightest of its jewels are the *Royal Botanic Gardens*, 2km (1¼ miles) s of the city centre and easily accessible by tram. They are situated in the middle of the **King's Domain Gardens**, which unlike the Botanic Gardens are not enclosed. In the centre of the King's Domain is *La Trobe's Cottage*, the state's first Government House.

Closer to the centre are the *Fitzroy Gardens*, 1km (½ mile) away to the E, which date back to 1850. Adjoining them are the **Treasury Gardens**, handily placed for politicians seeking respite from the affairs of state: the Victorian *Parliament House* is a short walk away. The gardens are bound by Spring St., Treasury Place and Lansdowne St.

Oldest of Melbourne's gardens are the **Flagstaff Gardens** on the NW fringe of the city proper, bound by King St., William St. and La Trobe St. They rise gently from La Trobe St., and are terraced down to King St. Paths wind through stands of lovely elms and oaks.

Carlton Gardens, on the NE fringe of the city centre, have as their centrepiece the *Exhibition Buildings*. The gardens, which have some fine oaks and elms, make a striking sight in autumn when the leaves change colour.

Royal Park, N of the city, has part of its area given over to the *Royal Melbourne Zoo*. Much of the remaining space is used for sports playing areas. The park was the departure point for the ill-fated Bourke and Wills expedition in 1860: a cairn marks the spot, off The Avenue. Farther afield is the **Yarra Bend Park** in the suburb of Kew, about 5km (3 miles) E of the city, an extensive natural bushland park beside the Yarra River. Rowing boats and canoes can be rented and the area is ideal for picnics and barbecues.

La Trobe's Cottage ★
King's Domain Gardens, Birdwood Ave. ☎ 654 5528. Map 11E4 ☒ & by prior arrrangement with curator ✱ Open 11am-4.40pm. Closed Fri.

This cottage was prefabricated in England and brought to Australia by Charles La Trobe, who was appointed Lieutenant-Governor of Victoria in 1851, a post he held for 3yrs. In effect it was Victoria's first Government House. The cottage has been restored and furnished in the style of the period and still contains many of its original furnishings. It is a National Trust property.

Law Courts and Supreme Court Library
Lonsdale St. ☎ 603 6111. Map 10C2 ☒ ✿ in court. Open to public during sitting of courts, commencing 10am.

Grouped around a cobbled courtyard, these Classical buildings, dating from 1885, are a fine example of Victorian civic architecture. A noteworthy feature is a rotunda, and the central library is topped by a vaulted dome. The Law Courts are open to the public during most trials.

Meat Market Craft Centre
Corner of Courtney St. and Blackwood St., North Melbourne ☎ 329 9966. Map 8C2 ☒ & 💻 ✱ Open 10am-5pm.

Formally one of Melbourne's meat markets, the centre houses craftspeople, including potters, fabric printers, weavers, silversmiths and others. It was set up by the Victorian Ministry for the Arts to form the centre for crafts in the state. The programme of exhibitions and demonstrations changes regularly, and there are craft shops, workshops and a resource and information centre. Most work shown is available for sale. The building itself is an excellent example of a Victorian produce market, now tastefully and imaginatively refurbished for its new role. At its rear is the **State Craft Collection.**

Melbourne Cricket Ground ★
Batman Ave. Match-day inquiries ☎ 654 6066. Map 11C5 ☒ & ✗ of ground, library, gallery and museum (2hrs) every Wed 10am 💻 ✱ ⬢ Ground open for viewing if no match in progress Mon-Fri 9am-5pm.

In size the greatest cricket ground in the world, the Melbourne Cricket Ground (MCG) has witnessed many famous epic struggles. Here was staged the first international cricket match in 1862 and the first test match between England and Australia in 1877. In 1956 it was the main stadium for the Olympic Games.

The MCG was established on its present site in 1853. Today it has a capacity of 120,000 and holds the world record for attendance at a one-day cricket match (78,000 in 1982 for Australia v. West Indies), as well as the highest attendance for a single day of a full test match (90,800 in 1961, again for Australia v. West Indies).

It is also the home of Australian Rules Football, that spectacular hybrid of rugby and Gaelic football. It is common to see crowds of 50-60,000 for club games at the MCG, and every Sept the Grand Final attracts 120,000 spectators here.

The **Australian Gallery of Sports** (*at main entrance to MCG ☎ 654 8922 ☒ open Wed-Sun 10am-4pm*), opened in 1986, contains a display of Australian sports memorabilia. The separate **Australian Museum of Sport** (☎ *654 6066* 🎫 *open Wed-Sun 10am-5pm*) is also at the ground.

Montsalvat

Hillcrest Ave., Eltham ☎ 439 7712. Map 8B3 🎫 ♿ ☕ (weekends) ✱ 🚗 Open Mon-Fri 10am-5pm, Sat, Sun 11am-5pm.

In 1934 architect and philosopher Justuf Jorgensen, whose defiantly Bohemian lifestyle once outraged conservative Melbourne, started an artists' colony at Eltham, then virgin bushland but now an outer suburb of Melbourne, about 18km (11 miles) NE of the city centre. All the buildings were designed by Justuf, in a style described by his son Sigmund Jorgensen as Provincial French Gothic. They comprise the **Great Hall, chapel** and **living quarters**. The floor of the Great Hall and some other parts of the complex are made of Welsh slate slabs once used by sailing ships as ballast on the voyage from Britain. Some of the windows were recovered from buildings being demolished in Melbourne.

Today Montsalvat is operated as a trust and is home to some 20 artists. Their work is available for purchase. Occasional varied concerts are held in the Great Hall and include supper with wine. Look in *The Age* newspaper for details.

Museum of Chinese Australian History

22 Cohen Pl. ☎ 662 2888. Map 10B3 🎫 ✱ Open Mon, Wed, Fri 10am-4.30pm, Sat, Sun noon-4.30pm. Closed Tues, Thurs.

A replica of Ling Xing Gate facing Heaven Palace in Nanjing, in China's Jiangsu Province, forms the entrance to this *Chinatown* museum. Exhibits and audiovisual aids outline the history of the Chinese in Australia and their contribution to the nation's culture and development, and the museum houses the **Sun Loong** (dragon) of the Melbourne Chinese community. There is no attempt to gloss over the early bitter resentment felt towards the Chinese in Australia, nor some of the extremely unpleasant racism practised against the Chinese community.

Museum of Victoria and State Library ★

328 Swanston St. (entry also from Russell St.) ☎ 669 9888. Map 10B3 🎫 ♿ access via La Trobe St. entrance, then through library to museum ☕ ✱ Museum open 10am-5pm. Children's Museum open during school hols 10am-5pm, during school term Mon-Fri noon-5pm, Sat, Sun 10am-5pm. Library open Mon-Fri 10am-10pm, Sat, Sun 10am-6pm.

An amalgamation of the **National Museum of Victoria** and the **Science Museum**, this new hybrid is clearly a success. As befits a nation of sports lovers, a highly popular exhibit (in the former National Museum) is the racehorse **Phar Lap**, world-famous and the subject of a feature film, who died in the USA in the 1930s after winning countless races in Australia. The science section includes Australia's first aircraft and car and many working models, with much emphasis laid on education. For example, **Experilearn**, the children's department, explains scientific principles, such as the transmission of light and the phenonomenon of light reflection, using assorted media and practical demonstrations, including echo tubes and a distortion room.

The separate **Children's Museum** is designed to appeal to

children between the ages of five and 12. A major attraction is the opportunity offered for "hands on" experience on a three-dimensional display of the human body, which explains in simple terms how the body works. Now deservedly popular, it caused a controversy when first opened.

Old Melbourne Gaol

Russell St. ☎ *663 7228. Map 10B3* 🚇 *Open 10am-5pm.*
This finely preserved bluestone building of 1845 is a ghouls' delight, notably for its collection of death masks of executed prisoners. Here the renowned bushranger Ned Kelly was hanged in 1880, making his departure from this world with the immortal words, "Such is life." The gallows where Kelly was hanged still remain. A triangle to which prisoners were strapped for floggings and numerous other items of prisoner paraphernalia have also survived. Several cells are laid out in the fashion of the Victorian era, complete with dummy prisoners clad in arrow-marked garb.

Parliament House ★

Spring St. ☎ *651 8911. Map 11B4* 🔲 *✗ compulsory* ✻ ◁€
Tours start Mon-Fri 10am, 11am, 2pm, 3pm when State Parliament not in session.
Before Parliament House was opened in Canberra in 1927, this was the meeting place for the Federal Parliament. Today it houses Victoria's Legislative Assembly and the Legislative Council (the upper house).

Described by the late Sir John Betjeman as one of the finest examples of Victorian architecture, the Neoclassical structure is superbly sited looking down Bourke St. The plans called for "a magnificent classic design for a building of colossal proportions surmounted by a tower 256ft high." The original design included a dome and N and S wings, though these are unlikely ever to be completed. The Parliamentary Library was completed in 1860, Queen's Hall and the Vestibule in 1879, and the w façade, with a grand flight of steps and a colonnade, in 1892.

The outer walls and foundations are made of stone from the Grampians mountain range (about 240km (150 miles) to the w of Melbourne). **Queen's Hall** was intended to be as nearly as possible the length and width of the House of Commons in London. The **Council chamber** has fine gold-leaf decoration covering a vaulted ceiling; the red benches and carpet again echo the style and character of the Parliament in Westminster. The **Assembly chamber,** more utilitarian, is still imposing, and the grand **Parliamentary Library** has a splendid glass chandelier. All told, this is an emphatically impressive experience.

Polly Woodside and Maritime Park ★

Corner of Normanby Rd. and Phayer St., South Melbourne ☎ *699 9760. Map 10D2* 🚇 🅿 ✻ 🚃 *Open Mon-Fri 10am-4pm, Sat, Sun noon-5pm.*
The 648-ton restored barque *Polly Woodside*, built in Ireland in 1885, had by 1897 rounded Cape Horn no fewer than 16 times on the England to South America run. Later she was sold to a New Zealand concern and renamed *Rona*, plying the Tasman Sea between Australia and New Zealand and later working the passage through the Pacific to the USA. By 1962 she was the only survivor of the 120 sailing ships that as recently as 1930 still carried coal around the coast of Australia. She was saved from an ignominious end by enthusiasts who in 1972 started restoring the old ship.

Today the *Polly Woodside* is run by the National Trust and is the only full-rigged ship still afloat in Australia. She forms part of a maritime display housed in buildings beside the barque, which is moored in an old water-filled dry dock. The display includes a good collection of relics, photographs and other memorabilia of the days of sail.

Ripponlea ★
192 Hotham St., Elsternwick ☎ 523 9150. Map 8C3 ▨ Open 10am-5pm.
The landscaped gardens of Ripponlea are the outstanding attraction of this National Trust house, built between the late 1860s and 1887. The 6ha (15 acres) of gardens feature an ornamental lake with a series of bridges, a fernery, a grotto, stands of English elms and other European trees, and vast expanses of sweeping lawns – a fine example of the early colonists' urge to re-create the style and ambience of the English country gentleman. Designed in the Romanesque style by Joseph Reed for wealthy businessman Frederick Sargood, using intricate polychromatic brickwork, the house originally contained 15 rooms, which over 20yrs or more grew to today's total of 33. Ripponlea was given to the National Trust in 1963.

Royal Botanic Gardens ★
Birdwood Ave., South Yarra ☎ 63 9424. Map 11E5 ⊡ ৬ ▣ ✿ ◁‹ Open Mon-Sat 7am-sunset, Sun, hols 8.30am-sunset.
One of the great gardens of the world, yielding first place only to London's Kew Gardens, covering 35ha (88 acres), the Royal Botanic Gardens are home to more than 12,000 species of native and non-native plants. The site beside the Yarra River was selected by Governor Charles La Trobe in 1845, and the gardens as they look today were shaped by Dr Ferdinand von Mueller (later Baron Sir Ferdinand von Mueller, appointed Government Botanist in 1852) and the landscape artist W. R. Guilfoyle.

Today they form a tranquil setting for a picnic or walk, with acres of sweeping lawns, flowerbeds, specimen trees and an ornamental lake (home to families of ducks, moorhens and black swans), all within an easy 10min tram ride from the city centre. The lake is popular with children, who enjoy feeding the birds and spotting eels swarming in its waters. The **Tennyson lawn** features four English elms more than 120yrs old. Adjoining it is the **National Herbarium** (*not open to the public*), a research centre housing a vast collection of herbs and other plants.

A special explanatory leaflet indicating walks around the gardens is produced each year and is usually available at most of the major gates.

Royal Melbourne Zoo ★
Elliott Ave., Parkville ☎ 347 1522. Map 8C2 ▨ ৬ ✗ (free) ▣ ✿ ➸ Open 9am-5pm.
Among the oldest zoos in the world, housing more than 3,000 animals, Melbourne Zoo has been substantially upgraded with a number of walk-through animal compounds that provide a first-class view of the animals. The enclosure for big cats is spanned by a bridge that gives the feeling of being physically *in* with the animals: an interesting sensation at feeding time. . . . Another highlight is the walk-through butterfly enclosure. There are excellent displays of wombats, emus, kangaroos, platypuses, echidnas and reptiles. The zoo has also pioneered work with artificial insemination of rare species: the gorilla Mzuri, born by artificial insemination, is a major attraction.

St James Old Cathedral ★
King St. (at corner of Batman St.) ☎ *329 6133. Map **10**B2.*
This is Melbourne's oldest church, started in 1839. Designed by
Robert Russell, Melbourne's first city architect, it was originally
sited at the corner of William St. amd Little Collins St., but in
1913–14 was moved stone by stone to its present site. The
building, of sandstone and bluestone, is a charming example of
early colonial workmanship. The main entrance has a display of
old prints and photographs. Note the old enclosed box pews, and a
font from the London church of St Katherine Cree.

St Kilda Upper Esplanade ★
*St Kilda. Map **8**D2.*
The Upper Esplanade has become a traditional Sunday favourite
among local craft lovers and bargain hunters. Most of the work
displayed is in ceramic, leather or wax; woodwork and paintings
also stand out. In any case, the characters who make up the
Sunday morning scene are an entertainment in their own right.

St Patrick's Cathedral ★
Albert St. ☎ *662 2233. Map **11**B4 ♿ (disabled ramps in
Cathedral Pl.). Open 6am-6pm.*
The tallest church in Australia, William Wardell's St Patrick's
Cathedral is a massive bluestone building surmounted by a spire
104m (340ft) high. Its grandeur reflects Melbourne's strong Irish
Roman Catholic connection.

St Paul's Cathedral ★
Flinders Lane ☎ *63 3791. Map **10**C3. Open 7am-6pm.*
Melbourne's fine Gothic-style Anglican cathedral, built in 1891, is
regrettably hemmed in by modern city buildings, though it
provides a fine landmark from across the Yarra River. The water
cascade and modern glass-canopied shopping arcade of the *City
Square* adjoin the cathedral close, the square's pond pleasingly
reflecting the traditional cathedral.

Shrine of Remembrance ★
*St Kilda Rd. Map **11**E4 ▣ ◁€ Open Mon-Sat 10am-5pm, Sun
2-5pm.*
The shrine, approached from St Kilda Rd., Domain Rd. or
Birdwood Ave., is the most imposing war memorial in the country.
The foundation stone was laid on Armistice Day 1927, and St
Kilda Rd. was realigned to give a continuous line s through from
Swanston St. Inside, each year, at the 11th hour on Nov 11,
sunlight strikes the **Stone of Remembrance**.
  Public subscription financed the construction of the shrine, as
the enormity of Australia's losses in the Great War dawned – of an
all-volunteer army of 400,000, Australia had suffered casualties
totalling nearly 200,000 either killed or wounded, one of the
highest per capita of any of the combatant countries. Today the
shrine forms the focus of Melbourne's Anzac Day
commemorations.

Sidney Myer Music Bowl
Alexandra Ave. ☎ *617 8211, 617 8332. Map **11**D4 ♿*
The Bowl, as it is affectionately known, is a huge sound-shell, able
to seat 2,000 people under cover and up to 100,000 on the
surrounding lawns of the **Kings Domain**. The bowl can be
approached through the gardens from either St Kilda Rd. or
Alexandra Ave. In winter, part of the stage is frozen over for

public ice-skating, and it is the home of the annual Christmas Eve "Carols by Candlelight" show.

Contact the *Arts Centre* for bookings and details of performances, ranging from pops to classics, or look in the metropolitan press.

Treasury Building ★
Corner of Spring St. and Treasury Pl. Map 11B4.
A Neoclassical structure of fine proportions, built in 1857, the Treasury Building is situated in Spring St., a block away from *Parliament House*. Adjacent are the **Treasury Gardens**, a quiet oasis in a busy part of the city, and the small open space of the **Gordon Reserve**, with its statue of the defender of Khartoum, General Charles Gordon.

Victoria Racing Museum
Gate 22, Caulfield Racecourse, Station St., Caulfield ☎ 572 1111. Map 8D3 ⊡ ▰ Open Tues, Thurs 10am-4pm. Closed Fri-Mon, Wed.
A must for all who love the sport of kings, the Victoria Racing Museum is dedicated to preserving the history of horse racing in Australia. The museum, the only one of its kind in the country, was opened in 1981 by Queen Elizabeth II. Statues of winning jockeys welcome visitors.

Williamstown
Map 8D2.
Williamstown has been a backwater for several decades, chiefly because until the opening in 1978 of the West Gate Bridge across the Yarra River it was a roundabout journey from the city by road (although there is a good train service). This comparative isolation has enabled the area to escape much of the postwar development that transformed other inner suburbs of Melbourne.

To catch the atmosphere of Williamstown – the whiff of the sea, the comings and goings of the boating fraternity who inhabit the area – it is essential to explore it on foot.

The best way to get there is to take a train from Melbourne to Williamstown Pier station, then start walking w down Nelson Parade. To your right is the **Royal Australian Naval Dockyard**, which has built several of the RAN's destroyers. The dockyard building itself, dating from 1874, is a fine example of local bluestone industrial architecture. Opposite the dockyard is the **Prince of Wales Hotel**, an imposing building with fine cast-iron balcony decorations, built in the 1850s.

Farther along is the **Gem Pier**, to which is moored a World War II **minesweeper**, HMAS *Castlemaine* (*open Sat, Sun 10am-6pm*), now a maritime museum. The **Customs House** (1874), with its twin porticos, is a fine example of civic building. On the reserve – an area of lawn in front of Gem Pier – is the **Tide Gauge House** (built 1869), formerly an automatic device for gauging the tide.

Continuing past Gem Pier, you come to the continuation of Nelson Parade, which here changes its name to The Strand. Here too is the Williamstown Yacht Club jetty and a ramp for launching boats. Retrace your steps to Williamstown Pier station and take a train two stops to North Williamstown. This is the home of the **Williamstown Railway Museum**, which has an extensive collection of steam engines, carriages and rolling stock (*open Sat, Sun, hols 2-5pm*).

Williamstown also has a **historical museum**, on the corner of Melbourne Rd. and Electra St. (*open Sun 2-5pm*). Reach it by walking up Parker St., which turns off Nelson Parade and crosses Electra St. It has a good collection of old model ships, and pictures from Williamstown's 19thC heyday.

Young and Jackson's Hotel
Corner of Swanston St. and Flinders St. ☎ *63 3884. Map 10C3* 🍺 *Open normal pub hours. Restaurant open Mon-Sat lunch and dinner.*

One of the most famous public houses in Australia, Young and Jackson's occupies a special place in the hearts of Melburnians. It is situated on a corner opposite Flinders Street railway station, Melbourne's main commuter terminus, and *St Paul's Cathedral*. During World War II Australian soldiers from Melbourne promised to meet here for a drink if they made it back alive, and its central location makes it still a popular meeting place.

Why Young and Jackson's should command so much affection is a mystery. Inside, the pub is largely nondescript, apart from a large oil painting of a nude, *Chloe*, of dubious merit and the subject of much moral outrage over the years. Many efforts have been made to have her removed; but she still reigns supreme.

Accommodation

Melbourne has seen a boom in hotel building since the mid-1970s, transforming it from an accommodation desert with only a handful of first-class hotels into a city offering world-standard accommodation supplemented by a good selection of inexpensive hotels and motels.

As in all cities, location very much governs price. Many of the major new hotel developments have been located in the central area. Notably, the new *Hyatt*, *Menzies at Rialto*, *Regent* and *Regency* have all recently been located in the city proper. However, a number of more modest hotels and motels have also sprung up on the fringes of the city, offering excellent accommodation at an economical price.

Those wanting first-class accommodation of international standard naturally will look for a city-centre hotel. More budget-conscious travellers can achieve substantial savings by moving 4 or 5km (2-3 miles) out of the centre; but as most areas are served by trams the distance is unlikely to present a problem. Two inexpensive areas are **Carlton** and **St Kilda Rd.**, near the centre and with frequent tram services.

Reservations are advisable at most times, and are essential during busy periods such as Easter, Christmas and the week of the Melbourne Cup horse race, run on the first Tues of Nov.

Most larger hotels ask guests for a credit-card imprint.

Australia ♣
266 Collins St., Melbourne, Vic., 3000 ☎ *63 0401* ☎ *30988. Map 10C3* ▥ *88 rms* ⇌ ≡ ▣ ① ⓒ
▨

Location: Right in the heart of the city. 30yrs ago this used to be *the* place to stay, and it retains a certain faded charm that appeals to many visitors. There is nothing rushed or exotic here, but good, solid comfort and service. The Australia is ideally placed for shopping and has its own first-class arcade just underneath.
▱ ⅋ ⚒

Hilton International
192 Wellington Parade, East Melbourne, Vic., 3002 ☎ *419 3311* ▥ ☎ *33057* ⓧ *419 5630. Map 11C5* ▥ *391 rms* ⇌ ≡ ▣
① ⓒ ▨

Location: Beside Fitzroy Gardens, opposite Jolimont railway station. This has the best outlook of any hotel in Melbourne, and is only a 5min stroll from elegant Collins St. In its showpiece **Cliveden Room** restaurant (see *Restaurants*), the Hilton has retained a link with the elegant old mansion it displaced, furnishing it with a fine selection of antiques. **Juliana's** nightclub has a fashionable clientele and features top international acts (see *Nightlife*), and the **Tapestry Lounge** has a resident pianist to accompany cocktails.

Hyatt on Collins

123 Collins St., Melbourne, Vic., 3000 ☎ *657 1234* **IDD** ☏ *38796* ℞ *63 3491. Map 11C4* **////** *580 rms* ➡ ⊐ 𝖠𝖤 ⊙ ⊙ 𝖵𝖨𝖲𝖠

Location: Near Parliament House, at top end of Collins St. The new (1986) Hyatt has a classic façade, a 34-storey tower rising up behind, and a striking exterior of gold glazing. Inside, marble is much in evidence. The exclusive **Regency Club** occupies the top four floors, with personalized service, a lounge, complimentary breakfasts and a serviced bar. There is also a fully equipped business centre. A fashionable food court, **Collins Chase**, with eight food outlets and two bars, provides a wide choice of meals from 7.30am.

Kingsway Motel ✿

Corner of Park St. and Eastern Rd., South Melbourne, Vic., 3205 ☎ *699 2533. Map 10E3* ☐ *40 rms* ➡ 𝖠𝖤 ⊙ ⊙ 𝖵𝖨𝖲𝖠

Location: On southern fringes of centre. This is one of a group of inexpensive hotels and motels just outside the centre that offer good, comfortable accommodation without the big-city price tag. A small motel with basic facilities, it is well placed for tram services into the city (about 10mins away), and is within walking distance of St Kilda Rd., Albert Park Lake and public golf course, and the *Royal Botanic Gardens* (see *Sights*). Another 10min tram ride will take you right to the excellent beach at Albert Park.

Menzies at Rialto

495 Collins St., Melbourne, Vic., 3000 ☎ *62 0111* **IDD** ☏ *136189* ℞ *62 0111 ext. 1646. Map 10C2* **////** *243 rms* ➡ ⊐ 𝖠𝖤 ⊙ ⊙ 𝖵𝖨𝖲𝖠

Location: At western end of city, just over a block away from Spencer Street railway station. The Menzies is part of the twin-tower Rialto complex, at 242m (794ft) Australia's tallest building. The hotel is built around a courtyard with twin wings of nine and five storeys respectively; the base was built in 1890. Mixing the old and the new, it still offers all the facilities

of a top-class hotel. The rooms are of a generous size, and the hotel is well placed for the World Trade Centre in Spencer St.

Noahs Melbourne ✿

186 Exhibition St., Melbourne, Vic., 3000 ☎ *662 0511* **IDD** ☏ *32779* ℞ *663 6988. Map 10B3* **////** *288 rms* ⊐ 𝖠𝖤 ⊙ 𝖵𝖨𝖲𝖠

Location: At eastern end of centre, a block away from Parliament House. Noahs is a modern 23-storey building, ideally positioned in an exciting part of the city with easy access to entertainment. Theatres and cinemas are within easy walking distance, and *Chinatown* (see *Sights*) is just around the corner. The standard is generally good without quite reaching top international class.

Old Melbourne ✿

5 Flemington Rd., North Melbourne, Vic., 3051 ☎ *329 9344* **IDD** ☏ *32057* ℞ *328 4870. Map 8C2* **////** *212 rms* ➡ ⊐ 𝖠𝖤 ⊙ ⊙ 𝖵𝖨𝖲𝖠

Location: In North Melbourne. The image is of an old English coaching inn: outside lighting, decor and balconied rooms, overlooking a paved central courtyard, echo this theme. Convenient for Melbourne University campus, Royal Park, and the Italianate suburb of *Carlton* (see *Sights*) – and on the way to the airport.

Parkroyal

562 St Kilda Rd., Melbourne, Vic., 3004 ☎ *529 8888* **IDD** ☏ *152242* ℞ *525 1242. Map 11E4* **////** *219 rms* ➡ ⊐ 𝖠𝖤 ⊙ ⊙ 𝖵𝖨𝖲𝖠

Location: Halfway along St Kilda Rd. travelling S from city. The outlook – onto a wide, treelined road, lined with gardens, some decent office buildings and a few remaining old mansions – suits those not needing to be in the heart of the city. The Parkroyal is a stark white building, but a canopied entrance offers a warm welcome, and there is attentive service for arriving guests. Only a short walk away are the Albert Park public golf course and lake, where sailing boats can be rented. The hotel can arrange tennis at a nearby public court.

President Melbourne

63 Queens Rd., Melbourne, Vic., 3004 ☎ *529 4300* **IDD** ☏ *30987*

51 1042. Map **11F4** ▭ *103 rms*
🚗 🚅 AE ⓐ ⓒ VISA

Location: Opposite Albert Park Lake.
This is a popular business hotel, with
a superb view across parkland. A
public golf course is nearby, and the
hotel is a 10min tram ride from the
centre. Standards are high without
being too lavish.
🦽 🚅 ⵙ 🍴 🐎 ⵖ ⚓ 👙

Regent
25 Collins St., Melbourne, Vic.,
3000 ☎ *63 0321* ⅢⅮ ● *37724*
63 4261. Map **11C4** ⅢⅡ *325 rms*
🚗 🚅 AE ⓐ ⓒ

Location: Near Parliament House, at
top end – the "Paris end" – of Collins
St. A hotel on the grand scale, the
Regent occupies 16 storeys of the
50-storey Collins Tower building.
Views across Port Phillip Bay, the
city and Melbourne's generous
parklands are superb, and there are
good views of Government House,
the *Melbourne Cricket Ground*
(see *Sights*) and many other
landmarks. The hotel lobby is at
ground level, function rooms are on
the first floor, and rooms on floors
34-50 are reached by a glass lift in a
transparent shaft. The building,
among the most imaginative of
Melbourne's modern structures, is
created around a central space,
surrounded by shops facing into the
centre; choirs and carol singers
perform here. Service is always
impeccable.
🦽 🚅 ⵙ 👙

Rockmans Regency
Corner of Lonsdale St. and
Exhibition St., Melbourne, Vic.,
3000 ☎ *662 3900* ⅢⅮ ● *38890*
663 4297. Map **10B3** ⅢⅡ *186*
rms 🚗 🚅 AE ⓐ ⓒ VISA

Location: Eastern end of centre, a block
away from Little Bourke St. and
Chinatown. This small boutique
hotel, the brainchild of Irvine
Rockman, has a genuinely friendly,
intimate and very individual
atmosphere. Rockman persisted
when warned that people did not
want smaller hotels and that this was
quite the wrong part of town, but the
Regency now has occupancy rates
that are the envy of many larger
hotels. The hotel is a tribute to
Rockman, who supervises in person.
🦽 ⵙⵕ 🔲 ⵙ 🐎 ⚓

Southern Cross
131 Exhibition St., Melbourne,
Vic., 3000 ☎ *63 0221* ⅢⅮ ● *30193*
63 2119. Map **10B3** ⅢⅡ *426 rms*
🚗 🚅 AE ⓐ ⓒ VISA

Location: Eastern end of centre, a block

from Parliament House. Opened in
1962, this was one of Melbourne's
original first-class hotels. Its 1960s
exterior now looks somewhat dated,
but recently major renovation and
upgrading were undertaken. The
hotel has first-class facilities for
conventions (a speciality) and hosts
many long-established functions and
balls. Set in pleasant surroundings, it
has an excellent shopping arcade as
part of the street-level entry area.
🦽 ⵙⵕ 🔲 ⵙ 🍴 ⵔ ⵖ ⚓ 👙

Spencer Motel ♣
44 Spencer St., Melbourne, Vic.,
3000 ☎ *62 6991* ⅢⅮ ● *37544.*
Map **10D2** ▭ *96 rms* 🚗 🚅 AE
ⓐ ⓒ VISA

Location: Almost opposite Spencer
Street railway station. In the
unfashionable end of town, the
Spencer offers good, basic budget
accommodation in a convenient
location. There are no frills, but then
the price is remarkably modest.
🔲

Victoria ♣
215 Little Collins St., Melbourne,
Vic., 3000 ☎ *63 0441* ⅢⅮ ● *31264*
63 9678. Map **10C3** ▭ *520 rms*
🚗 🚅 ⵕ AE ⓐ ⓒ VISA

Location: Very central, between Russell
St. and Swanston St. Old-fashioned
and staid, but this popular hotel has
modern business facilities.
Comfortable basic accommodation
without frills or fancy decor, and the
restaurant serves good, wholesome
food. Not all rooms have private
facilities, so when booking specify a
room with a bath or shower. Just the
place for the tourist on a budget.
🔲 ⵙ 👙

Windsor
103 Spring St., Melbourne, Vic.,
3000 ☎ *63 0261* ⅢⅮ ● *30437*
654 5183. Map **11B4** ⅢⅡ *173*
rms 🚗 🚅 AE ⓐ ⓒ VISA

Location: Opposite Parliament House.
Melbourne's (indeed, Australia's)
last remaining "Grand" hotel is listed
by the National Trust. Always a
favourite with politicians and
Victoria's wealthy rural landholders,
it feels like a very traditional, elegant
British hotel. Excellent meals are
served in the impressive **Grand**
Dining Room (see *Restaurants*).
An elegant, tall Victorian building
built in 1883, it was extensively
modernized after its purchase by the
state government. 19thC furnishings
and colour schemes were retained,
with gold-leaf work on ceilings and
black marble fireplaces.
🦽 🔲 ⵙ 👙

Eating out in Melbourne

Melbourne has the greatest selection and some of the finest restaurants in Australia. A bold statement, perhaps, but one repeatedly borne out by awards and by plaudits from food writers and gastronomic experts.

At the last count Melbourne had 1,800 places to eat and there were 2,500 in the entire state of Victoria. Of Melbourne's total, 1,500 are licensed to Bring Your Own liquor (BYO) – a sign you will see everywhere. It allows restaurant patrons to drink with their meal without the costs usually associated with a fully licensed establishment. The rules governing such matters as the ratio of toilets to customers, air conditioning and parking are far stricter for a fully licensed restaurant than for a BYO and increase overheads markedly. The hygiene rules governing both categories are the same, though, and high.

The eating-out selection in Melbourne ranges from international-class cuisine to a simple dish in a Chinese restaurant in Little Bourke St., in the Chinatown district. In between it is possible to eat virtually every sort of cuisine including Russian, Vietnamese, Lebanese, Afghan, Japanese, Nepalese and Greek. In Melbourne, you name it, and you can probably eat it.

Most restaurants in Melbourne, humble or prestigious, are usually full on Fri and Sat nights, so book ahead.

Bundy's Tavern ✿
Olinda Rd., Monbulk ☎ *756 6122*
◻ ▦ ▬ ⑥ ▨ *Last orders
llpm. Closed Mon, Tues. BYO
licence.*
It is worth the 40km (24-mile) trip from the centre to sample the friendly, relaxed atmosphere at rustic Bundy's, situated in the *Dandenongs* (see *Environs*). The food – like chef and owner Les Kovassy – is Hungarian and portions are hearty. On Thurs, families with children are enticed by the reduced-rate 3-course meal, which usually means a full house. There's a large open fire in winter.

Cliveden Room
Corner of Wellington Parade and Clarendon St., East Melbourne
☎ *419 3311. Map 11C5* ▦ ◻ ▬
▦ ⑥ ⑩ ▨ *Last orders
11pm. Closed Sun.*
The Cliveden Room at the *Hilton* (see *Hotels*) is widely acknowledged to be one of Melbourne's best hotel dining rooms. The decor, imaginative and tasteful, features some fine antiques. The menu is cautious but interesting, with a good selection of traditional dishes. A Hilton speciality is superb smoked salmon, sliced at the table. The ideal place for a special night out.

Empress of China ✿
120 Little Bourke St. ☎ *663 1883.
Map 1083* ◻ ◻ ▦ ▦ ⑥ ⑩
▨ *BYO licence.*
Melbourne is blessed with a large number of excellent Chinese restaurants, particularly in the Little Bourke St. area. This popular Cantonese restaurant gives good service, prices are reasonable and the menu is extensive. Seafood is their speciality: be sure to try the crystal prawns.

Florentino ✿
80 Bourke St. ☎ *662 1811. Map
1083* ▦ ◻ ▼ ▦ ⑥ ⑩ ▨ *Last
orders midnight. Closed Sun.*
Florentino maintains a thoroughly traditional approach, and the Italian food, served with panache by black-tied waiters with long white aprons, is consistently good. The restaurant can get crowded, so it is advisable to book.

Gourmand ✿
604 Station St., Box Hill ☎ *890
8788. Map 8C3* ▦ ◻ ▬ ▦ ⑥ ⑩
Closed Sun, Mon. BYO licence.
Situated in Box Hill, an eastern suburb 16km (10 miles) from the city, this has a good reputation. Run by an Austrian, Peter Scheiber, its menu offers Germanic dishes (including venison) and lighter dishes that reflect recent eating trends. Decor is "junk shop antique".

Grand Dining Room at the Windsor
115 Spring St. ☎ *653 0653. Map
11B4* ▦ ◻ ▬ ▬ ▼ ▦ ⑥ ⑩
▨ *Last orders 10.45pm. Closed
Sun.*

The *Windsor* (see *Hotels*) is the last of the great traditional hotels. Its restaurant, the Grand Dining Room, oozes tradition, with silver service, white table linen, first-class staff and an excellent menu that changes with the seasons. A carvery-style meal is available at lunchtimes, usually with at least two roasts and poultry, an extensive cheese table and some deliciously tempting desserts. Unmissable.

Mietta's

7 Alfred Place ☎ *654 2366. Map 11B4* ▥ ▭ ⊟ Ⓐ Ⓔ Ⓓ ⒱ *Last orders 10.30pm, Sun 8pm.*
Mietta's serves some of the most imaginative food in Melbourne, in the somewhat cavernous former Naval and Military Club building. The owner, Mietta O'Donnell, has built a formidable reputation here for good food. Downstairs there is a lounge where coffee and liqueurs, light meals and lunches are served. The formal restaurant is upstairs in what used to be the ballroom; here, chef Jacques Reymond shows his talents best. Sauces are his speciality.

Petty Sessions

459 Collins St. (entrance in William St.) ☎ *614 3854. Map 10C2* ▥ ▭ ⊟ ⬛ Y Ⓐ Ⓔ Ⓓ *Closed Sat lunch, Sun, Mon dinner.*
This is popular with the legal professional (as the name implies) and businessmen. Though, like the customers, the decor is conservative, owners Richard Frank and Edouard Demaneuf have reorganized the menu to reflect changing tastes. Traditional French, *nouvelle cuisine*, and a vegetarian menu on Thurs, are offered, with, in each category, three choices of starter, main course and dessert. Food and service are first-class and very professional.

Potter's Cottage ✿

Jumping Creek Rd. (near Ringwood Rd.), Warrandyte ☎ *844 2270. Map 9B4* ▯ ▭ ⬛ ⬟ Ⓐ Ⓔ Ⓓ *Closed dinner Sun-Thurs. BYO licence.*
Though some way out of town, this is handy for several of the day trips suggested in *Environs*. Charmingly situated beside the Yarra River at Warrandyte, it is part of a craft centre (see *Environs*). The building, long and low with a wide verandah and slate floors, is homely. The menu changes constantly: choose from hearty dishes such as individual beef casserole, or lighter ones such as

quail salad and smoked trout mousse. There's usually live music – pianist, trio or guitarist – on Fri and Sat nights: be sure to book.

Rosati ✿

95 Flinders Lane ☎ *654 7772. Map 10C3* ▯ ▭ ▭ Y Ⓐ Ⓔ Ⓓ ⒱ *Last orders midnight Mon-Sat, 10.30pm Sun.*
Handy for people exploring the city centre, this vast establishment seats 500. The menu is predictable but the food is well presented and the service first-class. The emphasis is on Italian, but there is also steak, chicken and so on. It's a good place too for morning coffee breaks or afternoon tea. The decor is impressive: the name set in mosaic in Venetian glass over the entrance, a bright, airy atmosphere inside and, as a centrepiece, a large bar.

Slattery's Cafe ✿

219 King St. ☎ *67 1360. Map 10C2* ▯ ⬛ Ⓐ Ⓔ Ⓓ *Closed Sun, Mon. BYO licence.*
Thoroughly unpretentious, like its owner, Slattery's style is simple. Photographs by Geoff Slattery himself, formerly a distinguished sports writer, decorate the wall. The food is always imaginative and changes constantly. Prices are very reasonable, considering the high quality.

Stephanie's

405 Tooronga Rd., East Hawthorn ☎ *20 8944. Map 8C3* ▭ ⬛ ⬛ Ⓐ Ⓔ Ⓓ *Last orders 9pm. Closed Sun.*
Stephanie's is one of the grandest restaurants in Melbourne, and certainly rates as one of the finest, the service and attention to details like table settings being unsurpassed. It is housed in an ornate former mansion in the suburb of East Hawthorn. Much of Stephanie Alexander's food is simple but prepared with a flair that raises it above the mundane. The menu is mostly French Provincial.

Two Faces

149 Toorak Rd., South Yarra ☎ *266 1547. Map 11F5* ▥ ▭ ⬛ Y Ⓐ Ⓔ Ⓓ ⒱ *Last orders 10.30pm. Closed Sun.*
One of Melbourne's top restaurants, this has maintained a high standard for more than 20yrs. It is owned and run by Hermann Schneider, who was trained in the best European tradition. The service is impeccable, the decor subdued and the food superbly traditional. There are

conservative dishes such as grilled porterhouse steak, and daily specials like roast squab with preserved kumquats and blackcurrants. The wine list is both excellent and extensive.

Uccello's ♥
102 Canterbury Rd., Blackburn ☎ *877 6949. Map 9C4* ▢ ▢ AE ⊙ ⊙ *Last orders 11pm.*

Another of those delightful surprises: a good Italian restaurant in an unlikely place, 18km (11 miles) from the centre, far from the gastronomic mainstream – yet it's impossible to find a table here on Fri or Sat evening without having booked. It is efficiently and pleasantly run by an

Italian family. Children are always welcome. Spaghetti Marinara is highly rated, and there is a good selection of pasta, veal, steak and chicken dishes.

The Willows
462 St Kilda Rd. ☎ *267 5252. Map 8D2* ▦ ▢ ⏁ AE ⊙ ⊙ *Last orders midnight. Closed Sun.*

Housed in a National Trust-classified building on St Kilda Rd. – one of the best settings in Melbourne. First-class service, crisp table linen, classic pink-and-white decor and a sense of space. The cooking is traditional French; game and beef are specialities.

Nightlife and the arts

In Melbourne the arts flourish, bolstered by an excellent symphony orchestra, ten mainstream theatres, scores of smaller fringe theatres, the open-air *Sydney Myer Music Bowl* (see *Sights*), the **Sports and Entertainment Centre** in Richmond, for ice shows, pop concerts and so on, and the **Festival Hall** in West Melbourne, which also stages pop concerts.

Since 1986 the city has been one of three sites for the annual springtime **Spoleto Festival of Three Worlds**, shared with Spoleto, Italy and Charleston, West Virginia, USA. The programme includes opera, dance and ballet, music, drama and arts exhibitions.

Melbourne's reputation as a place where nothing happened after 9pm has been shattered in recent years as the city wholeheartedly embraced the disco, nightclub and theatre-restaurant. Now there are more than 40 discos and nightclubs, ranging from local pub discos playing well-worn records to the sophisticated *Juliana's* at the Hilton, with its full-blown sound system.

The nightclub and disco scene is fluid and fast-moving, and it is advisable to check out the rise and fall of various establishments and which ones are considered trendy at any given time. If you lack local contacts, your hotel desk and concierge should help.

For computerized theatre and concert bookings contact **BASS (Best Available Seating Service)** (☎ *11500, or at branches of Myer department store*). The best daily guide to arts and entertainments is *The Age*.

Arts Centre of Victoria
100 St Kilda Rd. ☎ *information 11 566, bookings 11 500. Map 11D4* ⏁ AE ⊙ ⊙ ▨

Focal point for the arts in the city (see *Sights*), the Arts Centre is home or host to some of Australia's leading performance companies. The Melbourne Symphony Orchestra plays at the **Concert Hall** during the "Red Series" season, Apr-Oct. The **State** theatre hosts the Australian Ballet Company June-July and Oct-Nov, the Australian Opera Company March-May and the Victorian State Opera July-Aug and Nov-Dec. The Melbourne Theatre Company, more

or less the city's repertory company, performs at the **Playhouse**, and at the **Athenaeum** (*188 Collins St.* ☎ *654 4000*) and the **Russell Street Theatre** (*19 Russell St.* ☎ *654 4000*). Melbourne's Playbox Theatre Company performs in the intimate multipurpose **Studio**.

Impression
536 Swanston St., Carlton ☎ *347 4020. Map 10A3* ⏁ ⊙ ▯ AE ⊙ ⊙ ▨ *Open Tues-Sun 8pm-1am.*

A fun disco in the inner suburb of Carlton, with plenty of mirrors, lights and colours. Theme nights are the policy here.

Inflation
60 King St. ☎ *62 4117. Map 10C2*
Y ○ ⚌ AE ⊙ CD VISA *Open*
Wed-Mon 9pm-4 or 5am.

Inflation, only a few doors away from the *Underground*, is aimed at the younger set, with a hard-rock disco, a video bar, a restaurant, a cocktail bar and an attractive rooftop garden.

Juliana's
Hilton Hotel, 192 Wellington Parade, East Melbourne ☎ *419 3311. Map 11C5* Y ○ J AE ⊙ CD VISA *Open Tues-Sat 7pm-3am.*

This very classy nightspot, part of the *Hilton* (see *Hotels*), features live bands and disco, and also visiting international entertainers. It has a first-class restaurant.

The Last Laugh Theatre Restaurant
64 Smith St., Collingwood ☎ *419 8600. Map 8C2* Y ⚌ AE ⊙ CD VISA *Open Wed-Sat, dinner 7.30-9.30pm, show starts 9.30pm.*

Zany, irreverent and unique, this is one of the best-known, longest-established Australian theatre-restaurants, for two decades a nursery for scores of successful entertainers. Here you will see original Australian humour – and, you never know, perhaps a future star.

Nero's Fiddle Theatre Restaurant
454 Whitehorse Rd., Mitcham ☎ *874 8065. Map 9C4* Y ⚌ AE ⊙ CD VISA *Shows Wed-Sat start 7.30pm.*

Shows in the music hall tradition, with predictable jokes, harmless innuendo and opportunities for the audience to join in. Good, unpretentious food, quick service, and drinks aren't too expensive. An ideal place to go with a crowd.

The Palace
Lower Esplanade, St Kilda ☎ *534 0655. Map 8D2* Y ○ J AE ⊙ CD VISA *Open Mon-Sat 8pm-2am.*

The Palace has class, aiming, with such touches as valet parking for guests, to appeal to an upmarket clientele. A first-class restaurant and live bands and a disco make it ideal for a good night out.

Ticki and John's Theatre Restaurant
169 Exhibition St. ☎ *663 1754. Map 10B3* Y ⚌ AE ⊙ CD VISA *Open Tues-Sat* ☎ *for times.*

Among Melbourne's flourishing theatre restaurants, this has become an institution. There's reasonable

food, and the entertainment, in the review tradition of comedians and sketches, can be fun. As Fri and Sat evenings are usually booked months in advance, it may be easier to go during the week.

21st Century Dance Club
1 Davey St., Frankston ☎ *783 7311* Y ○ ⚌ AE ⊙ CD VISA *Open Wed-Sat 8pm-3am.*

Situated in a beachside dormitory town well s of Melbourne, this is well worth the trip for the sheer assault on the senses. The plush, spacious interior reflects the fortune spent by owner John Finch in converting a former bowling alley into a top-class entertainment centre; the computer-controlled lighting system alone cost A$800,000. There's room for 1,000 people, but there are always queues at weekends.

The Underground
22 King St. ☎ *62 4701. Map 10D2* Y ○ J ⚌ AE ⊙ CD VISA *Open Tues-Sat 9pm-4am or later.*

One of Melbourne's classiest nightspots. Eight bars (with a 24hr licence), a large disco and an "alternative dance" floor – so it should meet most tastes. There is also a piano bar, a private function room, a restaurant and a live theatre. The old warehouse sports relics and signs from former railway stations, trams and tram depots. Gaining entry can be simple: if the doorman likes the look of you, in you go.

The Venue
17 Upper Esplanade, St Kilda ☎ *534 5179. Map 8D2* Y ○ J ⚌ AE ⊙ CD VISA *Open Fri, Sat 8pm-3am.*

Three floors of non-stop entertainment, with live bands, discos and coffee lounges. Elegantly and spaciously laid out, with usually a corner to hand where you can retreat for a quiet chat. As each floor has its own bar there is no need to queue for a drink.

York Butter Factory Disco
62-66 King St. ☎ *62 0111. Map 10C2* Y ○ ⚌ AE ⊙ CD VISA *Open Tues-Sat 8pm-3am.*

Plenty of mood here in this lovely old 19thC former butter factory. The ground-floor disco and restaurant attracts the not-so-rich younger set with its reasonable entrance fee, free house wine on Fri, and free admission on Tues and Wed and before 9.30pm on Sat. The upstairs bistro restaurant serves very fair meals.

Shopping

Often called the shopping capital of Australia, Melbourne has some of Australia's finest department stores, as well as a number of speciality shops of high standing.

Retailing power lies with the department stores – and one, *Myer*, stands alone. The old slogan, "Myer is Melbourne", is in many ways still true. In 1985 Myer was taken over by G. J. Coles, the Melbourne-based supermarket-and-variety-store chain. The new group now accounts for about 20 cents in every retail dollar spent in Australia and is the fifth-largest retailer in the world. Myer's major city store is in Melbourne's shopping heart, the *Bourke Street Mall* (see *Sights*). There are also Myer stores at the major regional shopping centres that dot the outer suburbs.

The central shopping area declined as the suburban sprawl, fuelled by the postwar immigration programme, grew apace, encouraging major retailers to concentrate on stores located in huge suburban shopping centres. These offer complete one-stop shopping and easy parking. But the central area has fought back. The Bourke Street Mall was one successful answer. Fri-night late shopping, introduced in the 1970s, has also helped regenerate the city centre.

Among the joys of shopping in Melbourne are the arcades that crisscross the centre. The major ones are **Block Arcade**, which runs off Collins St. and is renowned for its smart boutiques; **Royal Arcade,** between Bourke St. and Little Collins St.; **Australia Arcade,** running between Collins St. and Little Collins St. and with several coffee lounges and light-snack outlets; and **Centrepoint Mall** and **The Walk**, both in the Bourke Street Mall.

There are some excellent conventional, high-street-style shopping centres in the inner suburbs, notably at South Yarra, Toorak Village, Prahran, High St. in Armadale and Smith St. in Collingwood.

The **High St. in Armadale** is renowned for antiques. Scores of shops are concentrated into one length of street, many importing antiques direct from Great Britain and Europe. There are also several exclusive dress and menswear shops.

Shopping hours are Mon-Thurs 9am-5.30pm, Fri 9am-9pm and Sat 9am-noon.

Australiana

Antipodes (*22 Toorak Rd., South Yarra* ☎ 266 5749 AE ⊕ ⊙ VISA) has a big selection of Australian souvenirs. The policy of **Thingummybob** (*58 Ross St., Toorak* ☎ 241 6719 AE ⊕ ⊙ VISA) is to carry only Australian-made products. At the **Australiana General Store** (*1227 High St., Armadale* ☎ 20 2324 AE ⊕ ⊙ VISA) there's kitchenware, giant soft-toy kangaroos and rocking horses.

Beauty salons and hairdressers

The major department stores have excellent salons in their city stores. Long-established is **Frederic Muller Hairdressing** (*100 Collins St.* ☎ 63 4173/63 6593 ⊙ VISA), very exclusive but very good. **Edward Beale** (*3rd floor of Sportsgirl fashion shop, 240 Collins St.* ☎ 63 9761 ⊙ VISA) appeals more to the younger set.

Books and records

Kenneth Hince (*623 Glenhuntly Rd., South Caulfield* ☎ 523 7711 AE ⊙ VISA) has a fine selection of antique and hard-to-find books. **Collins Booksellers** (*city stores: 86 Bourke St., 115 Elizabeth St. and 401 Swanston St.* ☎ 654 3144 *for all three branches* ⊙ VISA), with three city stores and 11 suburban stores, is hard to beat for everyday book needs. **Brashs** (*108 Elizabeth St.* ☎ *654 6544* AE CB CD VISA) has a wide selection of tapes and records, with 24 branches and an outlet at almost every major shopping centre.

Department stores

Melbourne has some of the largest department stores in Australia: *Myer* in Bourke St. claims to be the biggest in the country.

David Jones
310 Bourke St. (entrance in Bourke Street Mall) ☎ *669 8200. Map 10C3* & 🖵 AE CB CD VISA
Very upmarket, and renowed for imaginative displays, using fresh flowers and even a pianist. David Jones carries top brand names, especially in men's and women's fashions.

Georges
162 Collins St. ☎ *63 0411. Map 10C3* & 🖵 ✱ AE CB CD VISA
An unashamedly elite store with the best international designer names. Renowned for children's clothes and window displays. Stocks fine china, glassware and kitchen accessories.

Myer Melbourne Ltd
314 Bourke St. and 295 Lonsdale St. ☎ *66111. Map 10C3, 10B3* & 🖵 ✱ AE CB CD VISA
It is almost impossible to avoid shopping at Myer when in Melbourne: the store dominates the centre and advertises everywhere. This classic store, solid and reliable, sells nearly everything and has an outstanding food hall. There is a Myer store in nearly every major regional shopping centre around the city and in the larger country towns.

Fashion

Australian women are highly fashion-conscious. Melbourne has good representatives in every sector of the market. Though boutiques and fashion chain-stores have made inroads, large stores such as *David Jones* and *Georges* have also held their own.

Country Road
271 Bourke St. ☎ *63 4067. Map 10C3* & AE CB CD VISA
Excellent-quality, fashionable clothes aimed at the upper end of the mass market. There are ten suburban branches, nearly all for both men and women.

Hemden Tailored Shirts
1024 High St., Armadale ☎ *509 0933. 423 Little Collins St.* ☎ *67 8844. Map 8D3, 10C3* AE CB CD VISA
Handmade shirts in exclusive fabrics; also classically designed women's clothing. Expensive, but the workmanship is likely to be unsurpassed.

Henry Buck
320 Collins St. ☎ *67 9951. Map 10C3* AE CB CD VISA
Outfitters to the professions, Henry Buck stocks well-known names such as Daks, Aquascutum, Van Heusen and Church's Shoes, and the best European, American and Australian brands.

Katies
284 Bourke St. ☎ *663 2711. Map 10C3* AE CB CD VISA
Another big chain offering inexpensive clothes for women on a tight budget. More than 20 suburban branches.

Najee
149 Swanston St. ☎ *66334. 90 Elizabeth St.* ☎ *63 9836. Map 10C3* AE CB CD VISA
A big 1980s men's fashion success story, Najee's clothes and accessories, locally designed and mostly locally made, are aimed at stylish young executives. 12 branches around Melbourne.

Sportsgirl
240 Collins St. ☎ *653 9111. Map 10C3* & 🖵 AE CB CD VISA
Top quality but conservative women's clothes aimed at the top end of the mass market, plus accessories such as handbags, stockings, jewellery and shoes. Window displays are imaginative and eye-catching. 17 suburban branches.

Sussan
Walk Arcade, Bourke St. ☎ *63 2744. Map 10C3* CD
Inexpensive clothes for the working girl: more than 30 suburban branches. Stores are bright and cheery. Good-value clothes, and nothing too avant-garde.

Jewellers
There are several good chain jewellers such as **Proud** and **Edment**, who in addition to city stores have extensive networks of suburban branches selling affordable jewellery and silverware. Better-class jewellers tend to have only one or two branches: *Hardy Brothers* is a good example.

Hardy Brothers
338 Collins St. ☎ *67 8461. Map 10C3* AE ① ⑥
Melbourne's most exclusive jewellers and silversmiths stock the best in jewellery, porcelain and glassware, including Waterford, Royal Worcester, Orrefors and Caran d'Ache, plus fine antique silverware and jewellery.

Pamamull's Jewellers
Shops 47 and 44, Lower Plaza, Southern Cross Hotel, Exhibition St. ☎ *63 4761/654 5906. Map 10B3* AE ① ⑥ VISA
A wide selection of loose opals such as solid blacks, reds and greens, rough-cut and specimen stones, as well as opal jewellery. (Australia has 90 percent of the world's opals.)

Markets
One of the joys of living in Melbourne is the proliferation of markets both in the city and suburbs. They have proved so popular that several suburban markets have been enlarged or completely rebuilt in recent years. Price competition is intense and real bargains can be had – but be on your guard, for some of the goods are cheap . . . and nasty.

Prahran
Commercial Rd., Prahran. Map 8D2.
Mainly fruit and vegetables, but there are some fish and meat outlets and other stalls selling cosmetics, sunglasses and such.

Queen Victoria
Corner of Peel St. and Victoria St., North Melbourne. Map 8C2.
One of the largest markets (under one roof) in the world, where you can buy virtually every exotic and ethnic food, from Camembert to rollmops and kiwi fruit to custard apples, plus a vast range of other goods. Especially popular on Sun, when take-away refreshment stalls offer anything from hot dogs to *dim sims* (a kind of Australianized Chinese meat roll eaten with soy sauce).

South Melbourne
Corner of Cecil St. and Coventry St., South Melbourne. Map 10E3.
Essentially a food market, but other items are also sold. Rooftop car park.

Shopping centres
Melbourne is ringed with suburban shopping centres afloat in seas of parked cars. Most are first-rate and offer virtually all the facilities and services available in the city, but are geared almost exclusively to the car and are unpleasant if you try to get by with public transport.

   Doncaster Shoppingtown, one of the largest in the eastern suburbs, has a branch of **Myer** department store, a large supermarket, more than 100 speciality shops on two floors, and a twin-screen cinema. **Box Hill Central and White Horse Plaza**, built over Box Hill railway station, is one of the few shopping centres connected to public transport.

Jam Factory
500 Chapel St., South Yarra ☎ *240 0537. Map 8D2.*
The former Henry Jones IXL jam factory has been imaginatively converted into a modern 50-shop centre, selling mainly women's fashions. Constructed around a central courtyard area, with a glass roof. Coffee lounges serve snacks, and browsing is fun.

Melbourne environs

Not all Melbourne's many attractions are in the immediate city area. The *Dandenong Ranges* to the E, for example, make an ideal spot for a picnic or barbecue, with some magnificent scenery and lovely bush walks. To the W, *Werribee Park* is another popular picnic spot, with extensive grounds and tennis and golf nearby.

This section offers highlights that are easily reachable in a half-day's drive there and back. A chat with your hotel porter will probably uncover more options.

Dandenong Ranges ★

50km (31 miles) SE of Melbourne. Map 9E4 ❉ ◁ Getting there: by car, via Burwood Hwy; by train, to Belgrave; also bus tours from Melbourne.

The range of densely forested hills known as the Dandenongs (or sometimes as the Blue Dandenongs) may be compared to the Vienna Woods or the Bois de Boulogne, in being a favoured recreation area for Melburnians. In large part they are a National Park, having a mix of native bushland and private garden, and they are home to some of the world's largest hardwood trees, such as the mountain ash. Spectacular tree ferns grow there to prodigious sizes, fed by heavy rainfall nearly double that of Melbourne.

The highest point is **Mt. Dandenong**, 471m (1,545ft) high, which has a panoramic view of Melbourne and Port Phillip Bay, with a restaurant at the summit and extensive viewing areas equipped with telescopes. Numerous craft and art galleries are to be found among the hills, which over the years have developed a reputation as an artists' haven.

There are many points of interest in "the Hills", as Melburnians are apt to call the Dandenongs. The **William Ricketts Sanctuary**, near Mt. Dandenong, is administered by the Forests Commission and exhibits open-air works by the eponymous sculptor, whose art uses Aboriginal themes. The **National Rhododendron Gardens**, near Olinda, have a first-class display of rhododendrons and other specialized plants. Tulip farms, a joy in spring, abound around the Silvan area. Between Belgrave and Emerald Lake, **Puffing Billy**, a narrow-gauge steam train, runs at weekends and during school holidays (*timetable available from Metropolitan Transit Authority or at most railway stations*).

The hills are rich in exotic birdlife – even, sometimes, the elusive lyrebird, famed for its spectacular tail. The year-round popularity of the hills for picnics and barbeques leads to many of the birds, such as galahs and parrots, being tame enough to eat out of your hand. Try if possible to visit the hills during the week, for the narrow roads get busy at weekends.

 Recommended: **Bundy's Tavern** (see *Restaurants*).

Gulf Station ★

Yea Rd., Yarra Glen, 50km (31miles) NE of Melbourne ☎ 730 1286 ▦ ❉ ↝ Open Wed-Sun 10am-4pm. Getting there: by car, through Lilydale, then look for Yarra Glen turnoff on left, 5km (3 miles) on.

Gulf Station provides a rare taste of life as it must have been for the early colonists. The Bell family settled on this land during the 1850s and established a prosperous farm. When the last of the Bells died in the 1950s the farm was still run very much as a 19thC enterprise. The National Trust then assumed responsibility for the property, and has since restored it to its 19thC condition. The farmhouse is built of vertical slabs of local timber, as are the farm buildings, which include a milking shed, barn, butcher's shop, slaughterhouse and woolshed. There is also a schoolhouse where the Bell children were taught.

Hanging Rock and Woodend ★
80km (50 miles) NW of Melbourne ⇚ Getting there: by car, via Calder Hwy to Mt. Macedon or Woodend; by train, to Woodend, then taxi to Hanging Rock.

This is familiar as the setting for the film *Picnic at Hanging Rock*, about a party of young girls who mysteriously disappear while on a school picnic. The rock and surrounding region has been a popular destination since the 1870s. In the 1880s many large houses were built on the slopes of **Mt. Macedon**, many of them sadly destroyed in the 1983 Ash Wednesday bushfires, which devastated much of the mountain. So resilient is the Australian bush that most of the Ash Wednesday scars have since vanished.

Hanging Rock itself is a strange, massive outcrop of volcanic origin, quite easily climbed, although the track should be noted carefully. There are barbecue facilities with a refreshment kiosk and toilets at the base.

Nearby **Woodend** nowadays is a quiet country community, but in the gold-rush era it marked an important stopping point on the way to the Bendigo gold field. The stone bridge over Five Mile Creek, built in 1862, is noteworthy, as are the *Bentinck Hotel* (see below) and the bluestone Anglican church.

⌦ ▭ **Bentinck Hotel** (*Carlisle St., Woodend* ☎ *(054) 27 2330* ▮▮▮▮) was once a large country house. The open log fires in winter give the feel of an old-fashioned English country house. Advance booking essential. BYO-licensed dining room.

Healesville Sanctuary (Sir Colin MacKenzie Sanctuary) ★
Badger Creek Rd., Healesville, 65km (41 miles) NE of Melbourne ☎ (059) 62 4022 ▭ & ▯ ✴ ⬤ Open 9am-5pm. Getting there: by car, via Maroondah Hwy; by train, to Healesville, then taxi.

One of the "must see" sights around Melbourne, the sanctuary, situated 5km (3 miles) SE of the town of Healesville, houses one of the finest collections of Australian wildlife in the country. The sanctuary was founded in the 1920s by Sir Colin MacKenzie, an expert on Australian fauna. In 1944 it became the first place in the world to breed the duck-billed platypus in captivity.

Most of the sanctuary is open-plan. Kangaroos and wallabies live in free-range enclosures, allowing visitors to get near to the animals and even to touch them. Emus wander around freely, stealing brazenly from picnic tables. All the enormous aviaries are of the walk-through variety, which allows the birds to live in an environment as near as possible to their natural habitat. There are excellent displays of nocturnal animals, and at certain times it is possible to see the duck-billed platypus swimming in a glass-sided tank. There is also an extensive collection of snakes, koalas, wombats, cassowaries and water birds.

Potter's Cottage
Jumping Creek Rd. (near Ringwood Rd.), Warrandyte, 30km (18 miles) NE of Melbourne ☎ 844 3078. Map 9B4 ▭ ═ ✴ ⬤ Gallery open Mon-Fri 10am-4.30pm, Sat, Sun 10am-5pm.

Getting there: by car, via Eastern Freeway – take Thompsons Rd. exit, following signs to Templestowe; Thompsons Rd. becomes Parker St., then Andersons Rd., then Warrandyte Rd.

Potter's Cottage was opened in 1958 by a group of potters to promote Australian studio pottery, and has since developed into a popular weekend destination for locals and visitors. The gallery, where the potters' work is exhibited and sold, stands beside the Yarra River in an attractive bush setting at Warrandyte. Both gallery and restaurant (see *Restaurants*) are timber-built.

Several other arts and crafts galleries can be found in **Warrandyte** itself, which is surrounded by **Warrandyte State Park**. Here, on Anderson's Creek, gold was first discovered in Victoria in 1851: a cairn marks the spot.

The State Park borders the Yarra River and is heavily timbered bushland. It is made up of three separate reserves. One of these, the **Pound Bend Reserve**, w of Warrandyte, has a tunnel hacked through the river valley's side by goldminers in the 19thC, intending to divert the river so that the dry riverbed could be sluiced for gold.

Werribee Park ★

K Rd., Werribee, 35km (22 miles) w of Melbourne ☎ 742 2444 ⬛ grounds ⬛ mansion ♿ 🖳 ➹ ⤴ ⬝/ Grounds open 10am-8pm (summer), 10am-sunset (winter). Mansion open 10am-4.45pm. Getting there: by car, via Princes Hwy; by train, to Werribee, then taxi.

Werribee Park is an impressive estate whose centrepiece is a large, 60-room mansion, **Chirnside**, built in the 1870s in Italianate style for the Chirnside brothers, who established a pastoral empire to the w of Melbourne. A two-storey building of local bluestone, Chirnside was designed by London architect James Henry Fox. No expense was spared, and the mansion is resplendent with gold leaf, mosaic floors and fine ornamentation.

The garden of Werribee Park was laid out by the curator of the *Royal Botanic Gardens* (see *Sights*); a lake surrounds an island, which features a grotto. Outbuildings contemporary with the mansion, such as shepherds' huts, a dairy and woolsheds, still survive.

Victoria excursions

For motoring tourists Victoria could hardly be easier. Distances are fairly manageable, and much of interest and beauty lies between the major centres. The following excursions are selected from the best the Garden State has to offer. For more ideas, see *Routes 1* and *2* in *Planning*.

The Mornington Peninsula

240km (150-mile) round trip. Allow 2 days. Recommended stop: Sorrento.

The mornington Peninsula is often called Melbourne's playground. A southern extension of the city's bayside suburbs, it divides Port Phillip Bay from Westernport Bay, to the E. An overnight stop is recommended, for though it can be seen in a long day, some of the best sights would have to be missed. Traffic jams are likely along the coastal roads during summer holidays and at weekends.

Driving s through St Kilda junction, take the Nepean Hwy, following signs for Frankston. The highway passes through **Brighton**, one of the most expensive suburbs; take a detour w just to glimpse the scale and opulence of some of the houses.

Just past Brighton, at a place called **Half Moon Bay**, look out for HMAS *Cerberus*, the hulk of an ironclad battleship, flagship of the Victorian navy in the late 19thC and thought to be the only surviving ironclad.

Frankston, back on the Nepean Hwy, is a dormitory town at the end of the railway line, 41km (26 miles) s of the city, with an excellent shopping centre and a pleasant beach, good for fishing. Continue through **Mornington**, home base for many competitors in the Sydney-Hobart blue-water and Melbourne-Devonport w coast classics. Take time to walk along the pier to see these fine yachts.

Several bayside towns, such as **Mt. Martha** and **Safety Beach**, follow. At **Dromana**, with its backdrop of **Arthur's Seat**, a high point rising steeply from the coast to 305m (1,000ft), a chairlift up Arthur's Seat affords a spectacular view of the bay as far as Melbourne. More small resorts, such as McCrae, Rosebud, Rye, Blairgowrie and Sorrento, lead to Portsea at the end of the peninsula.

Sorrento, a lovely old town with many well-preserved buildings and a small museum, is the site of the first European settlement in Victoria, in 1803. There is a memorial to the leader, Colonel Collins. Overlooking Sullivan's Bay are several graves of early settlers. Near the pier is an excellent **aquarium** (*open every day in summer*).

Portsea is the playground for Melbourne's rich, who live close to the beach in large, secluded houses. On the s side of the peninsula is **London Bridge**, a rocky part of the cliff, worn away and separated, with a hole straight through the centre that resembles a bridge – hence the name. The surf beach at Portsea is one of the best within easy reach of Melbourne; but beware of the strong riptide (in summer the beach is patrolled by lifeguards).

The extreme end of the peninsula, controlled by the federal government, encompasses a quarantine station and an army officers' training college. The quarantine station has existed since the 19thC, when many early immigrant vessels buried their dead there.

Return from Portsea on the Old Melbourne Rd., which runs parallel to the Nepean Hwy and passes through some lovely coastal bushland, rejoining the Nepean Hwy at **Rye**. Continue to **Rosebud West**, then turn right onto Boneo Rd. towards Flinders. The road passes near **Cape Schanck**, 4km (2½ miles) s, a most spectacular point looking across Bass Strait, with a lighthouse that can be visited most weekends at certain times. A walk e along **Cape Schanck Coastal Park** to **Bushrangers Bay** repays the effort.

Flinders is a charming fishing village on Westernport Bay, opposite **Phillip Island**, with one licensed hotel, a motel, a caravan park and a few shops. Sample the fine bread from **Flinders Bakery** in the main street, which uses a wood-fired 19thC oven.

The main road back to Melbourne passes **Point Leo**, about 8km (5 miles) on, which has an excellent surf beach that is patrolled. The road bypasses Hastings and feeds into the Mulgrave Freeway, via Dandenong back into Melbourne.

 Sorrento has several hotels and motels. Among them is the **Koonya** (*Nepean Hwy* ☎ *(059) 84 2281* ▢), offering comfortable accommodation and an excellent restaurant (*see below*). Nearby is the **Oceanic** (*Ocean Beach Rd., 1.5km (1 mile) from Sorrento* ☎ *(059) 84 1417* ☐), a 12-unit motel.

The restaurant at the **Koonya** (*see hotel above*) serves delicious locally caught fish. In Flinders, the **Bakery Restaurant** (*in front of Flinders Bakery, in the main street* ☎ *(059) 89 0291* ▮▮) provides superb home-cooked food.

The Great Ocean Road, Portland and Hamilton
725km (450-mile) round trip. Allow at least 2 days.
Recommended stops: Port Fairy, Hamilton.

The Great Ocean Rd., which starts just outside Torquay, 23km (14 miles) s of Geelong, is about 180km (112 miles) long and presents some of the most spectacular coastal scenery in Australia. Built during the Great Depression as a make-work scheme, the road demanded great engineering skill, frequently having to be carved out of almost sheer cliffs.

Take the Princes Hwy to the port of **Geelong**, 74km (46 miles) sw. This is Victoria's second largest city (population 125,279), important for grain export and major oil refineries. Beyond Geelong look for the sign to **Torquay** and the Great Ocean Rd. Torquay and nearby **Bells Beach** have some of the finest surf in Australia.

The road follows the coast through several picturesque villages such as **Aireys Inlet** and **Fairhaven** until it reaches attractive **Lorne**, with its backdrop of the Otway Ranges, a popular watering place since the 19thC. The 1983 Ash Wednesday bushfire licked the outskirts of Lorne and the population had to be evacuated to the beach for several hours.

From Lorne the road continues along the coast for 45km (28 miles) until **Apollo Bay**, a pleasant resort town, then turns inland and meanders through the **Otway National Park**, rejoining the coast again at **Princetown**.

Some magnificent views open up on the ocean-hugging stretch to **Port Campbell**. From Port Campbell to Warrnambool the coast is the graveyard of scores of sailing vessels, wrecked as they sailed down Bass Strait. Just before Port Campbell is **Loch Ard Gorge**, a tiny inlet where the sailing ship *Loch Ard* was wrecked in 1878 with the loss of 50 lives; there were only two survivors. A sad little cemetery overlooks the gorge, which can be viewed from specially constructed platforms. Some days after the shipwreck a packing case washed up in the gorge was found to contain a life-size Minton pottery peacock, destined for the Melbourne Great Exhibition of 1880.

At **Warrnambool**, a city of 21,414 people, the main attraction is the **Flagstaff Hill Maritime Museum** (*open 9.30am-4.30pm*), a faithful re-creation of a 19thC seaport similar to many that dotted the coast before large vessels concentrated trade into a few centres. The museum is based on an old lighthouse and on fortifications erected in 1887 against a putative Russian invasion; 60-pounder muzzle-loading guns remain in place. The *Loch Ard* Minton peacock is displayed here.

Stay on the Princes Hwy for Portland, stopping at **Port Fairy**, a well-preserved fishing village, settled by sealers in the 1820s. Some of the oldest houses in Victoria, dating back to the 1840s, are open for viewing. At the mutton bird rookery, near the mouth of the Moyne River, watch the nightly return of the huge flocks, each bird unerringly finding its own nest – a hole in the ground – in the dark.

From Port Fairy head for **Portland**, said to be the site of the first permanent settlement in Victoria, in 1834. (Port Fairy also claims that title: the argument revolves around the word "permanent".) Modern Portland's landmark is its huge aluminium smelter.

Now turn inland, heading northwards 76km (48 miles) on the Henty Hwy towards **Hamilton**, an important rural centre that styles itself the "Wool Capital of the World". Hamilton's fine **art gallery** (*Brown St., open Tues-Fri 10am-5pm, Sat 10am-noon, 2-5pm, Sun, hols 2-5pm*) started with a local farmer's donation of an extensive collection of Mediterranean pottery, antique porcelain and silver, now housed in the downstairs Shaw Gallery. There are also fine Chinese ceramics from the Sung, Ming, Ching and Tang dynasties covering a period of about 1,600yrs from AD95, and several good examples of Chinese lacquer work. Upstairs is an important collection of Tibetan, Indian, Nepalese, Chinese and Indian artifacts, mostly dating from the 16th-18thC, though some go back to the 13thC. There are works by Australian artists, and etchings and watercolours by English artist Paul Sandby.

From Hamilton, take the Hamilton Hwy to Geelong (passing through some of the best sheep-rearing country in the world), then on to Melbourne.

The **Lady Julia Percy Motel** (*54 Sackville St., Port Fairy* ☎ *(055) 68 1800* ☐) is comfortable: BYO restaurant with à la carte menu. The **Caledonian Motel** (*Thompson St., Hamilton* ☎ *(055) 72 1055* ☐) is simple, welcoming and has a restaurant.

The Murray Valley

1,350km (850-mile) round trip, including short side trips from Mildura. Allow at least 3 days, preferably 4. Recommended stops: Echuca, Mildura, St Arnaud.

The Murray River (the "Mighty Murray"), a vital lifeline for Victoria, NSW and South Australia, forms, with the Darling River, the largest river system in Australia. The Murray Valley is also an important resort area.

Head NW on the Calder Hwy towards Bendigo, then NE towards Echuca on the Midland Hwy, which after 47km (30 miles) joins the Northern Hwy at Elmore.

Echuca is a well-preserved town at the junction of the Murray, Campaspe and Goulburn Rivers. Once Australia's largest inland port, Echuca collected vast amounts of wool from sheep stations strung out along the Murray and its tributaries. Echuca's river boats helped open up large areas of the Outback, and by 1895 there were 105 steamers and 110 barges and boats registered.

The **Port of Echuca** (*open 9.15am-5pm*) has been restored to its former glory. The **Star Hotel** (built 1867) acts as the port information centre, where you can buy tickets to visit the wharf and the **Bridge Hotel** (1858), where travellers quenched their thirst while waiting for the pontoon ferry. Obtain tickets here too for the Star Hotel itself, which has an underground bar to provide a welcomely cool resting place out of the sun; the hotel was delicensed in 1897, and a tunnel from the bar is believed to have been used as an escape route by illegal drinkers. The **wharf**, built in 1864 out of red gumwood, was at one time nearly 1km (over ½ mile) long, and is constructed on three levels to accommodate the massive rise and fall of the Murray. A visit to the wharf includes a continuous 10min audiovisual explanation of the river trade and of the history of Echuca and the surrounding area. Also part of the display are the paddle steamers *Pevensey* and *Adelaide*; cruises can be taken on another paddle steamer, *Canberra* (☎ *(054) 82 2141 for bookings and information*).

Other attractions include the **Bond Store** (*open 9am-5pm*), built in 1859, where goods were stored awaiting payment of customs duty to the three states along the Murray River; the **Echuca Historical Society Museum** (*open Sat, Sun, hols, school hols 1-4pm*), formerly the police station and lockup (built 1867), which displays original charts of the river and numerous old photographs of Echuca; and the **Coach House Carriage Collection** (*open 9.30am-5pm*), housing 35 restored horse-drawn coaches from all over the world.

Just outside Echuca, off the Murray Valley Hwy, to the SE, is the excellent **Tisdall winery** (*14 Cornelia Creek Rd., open for cellar-door sales Mon-Sat 10am-5pm, Sun noon-5pm*). Qantas chose Tisdall wines in 1986 for serving in-flight.

From Echuca head NW along the Murray Valley Hwy, approximately following the river towards Swan Hill, about 160km (100 miles) away. On the way is **Kerang**, centre of a rich farming area. Several lakes are skirted, including Lake Charm and Lake Boga, both good for watersports. At Lake Boga is **Best's winery** (*open for cellar-door sales*).

Swan Hill was a busy river port in the 19thC and, like Echuca, is now a major resort, with excellent fishing and boating facilities. The big attraction is the **Pioneer Settlement** (*open 8.30am-5pm; nightly light-and-sound tour*), a re-creation of a river town, tracing the story of the riverland pioneers from 1830. The old paddle steamer *Gem* marks the entrance to the centre; another one, *Pyap*, takes visitors on 1hr river cruises (*depart 10.30am, 2.30pm*). Swan Hill also has a reputable **military museum** (*open 9am-5pm, hols, school hols 8.30am-5.30pm*).

The Murray Valley Hwy follows the river NW until Lake Powell, then heads NW to join the Sunraysia Hwy at Hattah. Alternatively the Murray can be crossed at **Robinvale** and the Sturt Hwy taken in NSW, crossing back into Victoria at Mildura – the more direct route.

Mildura (population 15,763) is the centre of the Sunset Country, famed for red soil, brilliantly blue skies and magnificent sunsets. Try to spend two days there, for the area has much to offer. Mildura's importance began when two brothers, George and William Chaffey, introduced irrigation to the region, following their success with similar projects in California. Today it is the centre for a prosperous dried-fruit industry and for wine-making.

Several paddle steamers work out of Mildura. The *Rothbury*, *Avoca* and *Melbourne* offer day trips from Mildura wharf, and the *Coonawarra* and the *Murray Explorer*, a modern luxury craft, offer extended cruises lasting up to five days.

There are numerous other places of interest. The **Mildura Arts Centre** (*open Mon-Fri 9am-4.30pm, Sat, Sun 2-4.30pm*) comprises an art gallery and a theatre; the gallery is housed in Rio Vista, formerly home of William Chaffey. In its collection, based on the R. D. Elliott collection of works by British and Australian painters, is Sir Jacob Epstein's *Eve Dervich*, executed in 1924. At the **Mildura Co-operative Fruit Company Limited** (*open 9am-noon, 1-4pm, closed Sat, Sun*) you can watch citrus grown in the area being handled at the packing-shed door. And **Merbein**, 15km (9 miles) W of Mildura, is the home of **Mildara Wines**, one of the largest Australian producers (*self-guided tours Mon-Fri 8-11.15am, 1-4.15pm; open for cellar-door sales Mon-Fri 9am-5pm*).

The route back to Melbourne follows the Sunraysia Hwy. At first this passes through the **Mallee** country, an arid, semi-desert region famous for spectacular sunsets and home of the strange mallee fowl, which can be seen at the **Wathe Fauna Reserve** (*Lascelles*). After Lascelles the countryside rolls with vast wheat fields.

From Ballarat, take the Midland Hwy to Melbourne. The complete journey from Mildura, a distance of 557km (348 miles) can be managed in one day. Alternatively, stop in **St Arnaud**, an old gold-mining town containing several buildings with fine cast-iron lacework decoration: the **Botanical Hotel** is an excellent example. There is good fishing near St Arnaud in the **Avoca River** and **Teddington Reservoir**.

In Echuca, the **Steam Packet** (*corner of Leslie St. and Murray Esplanade* ☎ *(054) 82 3411* ⬜) is handy for all the attractions: old-fashioned charm in a National Trust-classified building. On the Northern Hwy, 4km (2½ miles) s, is the **Red Carpet Inn** (☎ *(054) 82 4244* ⬜), a good motel.

In Mildura, **The Grand** (*Seventh St.* ☎ *(050) 23 0511* ⬛⬜) is a comfortable, well-appointed old-world hotel. In St Arnaud, try the **St Arnaud Motel** (*5 Ballarat Rd.* ☎ *(054) 95 1755* ⬜).

Echuca has several first-class restaurants. **The Bridge Hotel** (*High St.* ☎ *(054) 82 2247* ⬛⬜) has a seasonally changing à la carte menu. The **Steam Packet** (*see hotel above* ☎ *(054) 82 3411* ⬜) specializes in steaks; BYO licence. **The Cock 'n' Bull** (*17-21 Warren St.* ☎ *(054) 82 4287* ⬛⬜), in an idyllic setting beside the Campaspe River, also serves steaks; BYO licence.

In Mildura, **The Grand** (*see hotel above*) has an excellent set menu; there is also a bistro. In St Arnaud, the **St Arnaud Motel** (*see hotel above* ⬛⬜) has a BYO-licensed restaurant.

The Golden Triangle
Round trip of about 330km (206 miles). Allow at least 2 days. Recommended stops: Ballarat, Bendigo.

Victoria's so-called golden cities, Ballarat and Bendigo, were the foundation of Victoria's (and Australia's) wealth in the 19thC. Anyone hoping to understand how modern Australia was forged should make a point of visiting them. Between them they claim some of the finest Victorian buildings in Australia.

For **Ballarat**, take the Western Hwy, passing through the suburbs of Deer Park and heading w (via Bacchus Marsh). The city, Victoria's largest inland conurbation, has a population of 62,000. Its vital part in Australia's development into a democracy centres upon the 1854 Eureka Stockade rebellion, a short-lived uprising against an oppressive administration and the gold-mining licensing system.

Gold was first discovered in the Clunes region near Ballarat in 1851. Within 3mths some 8,000 people were on the diggings between Ballarat and Buninyong; 4yrs later the influx had swelled to 100,000, turning the area into a lunar landscape in the frantic hunt for gold. This gold rush led to an alarming reduction in the population of Melbourne, and immigrants poured in from the USA, Britain and elsewhere.

A shuttlebus (with commentary) takes 1hr to view the major attractions. Take a ride too on the remaining old public tramway system (*operated by enthusiasts at weekends and during school hols*), which circles **Lake Wendouree**, site of the rowing contests in the 1956 Olympics. The adjoining **Botanic Gardens** contain an avenue of busts of every prime minister since Federation.

Sovereign Hill (☎ *(053) 31 1944 for bookings and information on on-site accommodation; open 9.30am-5pm*) is an accurate working re-creation of a mid-19thC gold township, located on the site of the Sovereign Quartz Mining Company. Near the summit, the company sank a shaft, which still survives, to a depth of 216m (709ft). Here you can pan for gold and be guaranteed to find a speck, ride an authentic Cobb and Co. stagecoach, visit the town's shops, see a live music hall and watch a smithy at work.

The **Eureka Stockade** is marked by a memorial of the uprising; a diorama explains the events leading up to it. Opposite is an exhibition (*open 9am-5pm*) with a moving tableau of the dramatic events of 1854. The **Gold Museum** (*open Sat-Thurs 10am-5pm, Fri noon-5pm*) recounts gold's effects on society since prehistory.

Ballarat Fine Art Gallery (*open 10.30am-4.30pm, closed Mon*) has one of the finest collections of Australian paintings, including work by Eugene von Guerard, Walter Wither, Lionel Lindsay, E. Phillips Fox, William Dobell, Sidney Nolan, Aaron Sherritt, Russell Drysdale and Fred Williams.

A walk through the city reveals several outstanding Victorian buildings, lovingly maintained and renovated. When the mighty McDonald's hamburger chain sought to open a branch here, the city council eventually persuaded the company to restore rather than demolish the old building on its site and to develop it in keeping with its surroundings – the first time McDonald's had ever departed from its universal format.

Leaving Ballarat, take the Midland Hwy N to **Castlemaine**, another old gold-mining town with a fine Classical **market** (*open for viewing 10am-5pm*) that resembles a church basilica, built in 1862. Then continue to Bendigo, about 40km (25 miles) N on the Midland Hwy.

Bendigo (population 52,700) is the other great regional goldfield town. Gold was discovered here in the same year (1851) as at Ballarat. The gold fields became known as the Bendigo Diggings, and the town that grew up nearby was known as Sandhurst, changed to Bendigo in the 1890s. During the gold rush thousands of Chinese flooded into the Bendigo Diggings, causing severe racial tension. Bendigo today retains its long association with the Chinese, and a major attraction is the **Joss House** (*open 10am-5pm*), constructed of handmade bricks in the 1860s. One of the finest Chinese dragons in the country parades annually through the city as part of the Chinese New Year celebrations.

Other attractions include a guided tour of the **Central Deborah Mine**, built in 1909 and closed in 1954, providing a view of operations above and below ground; the vintage **"Talking Tram"** (*departs hourly Sat, Sun 9.30am-5pm from Central Deborah Mine*), with a taped commentary on points of interest around the city; and **Bendigo Art Gallery** (*open Mon-Thurs 10am-5pm, Fri-Sun, hols 2-5pm*), built in 1887, an outstanding regional gallery with an important collection of Australian and European paintings.

From Bendigo the route s back to Melbourne along the Calder Hwy passes through rich farming country. A detour w of about 17km (10½ miles) is worthwhile to visit **Maldon**, another gold-mining township that has recently developed into a centre for crafts. The town has some outstanding streetscapes.

The Calder Hwy continues through **Mt. Macedon**, which suffered badly during the 1983 Ash Wednesday bushfires (a side-trip to *Hanging Rock* – see *Environs* – and **Woodend** is possible here), and passes Tullamarine airport on the way back into Melbourne.

🐚 ⚞ Ballarat has some good hotels and motels. Recommended: the **Bell Tower** (*Western Hwy, 6km (4 miles) w from city centre* ☎ *(053) 34 1600* **Ⅲ**), with excellent facilities including swimming pool, sauna, spa, tennis courts and restaurant.

In Bendigo, the **Shamrock** (*corner of Pall Mall St. and Williamson St.* ☎ *(054) 43 0333* ▮▮▯) combines comfort and history. The ornate building, built in 1897 and classified by the National Trust, counts among former guests singer Dame Nellie Melba and cricketer Sir Donald Bradman. The delightfully old-world restaurant even has waiters in full evening dress.

Western Australia

Mountains of iron, fields of gold and diamonds, valleys of wine, the most intricate wild flowers, the hardiest of creatures, lush green pastures and wild scrub desert . . . Western Australia, the country's largest state, appears rich in all but population.

Only 1.4 million people live here, one million of them clustering around the handsome capital of Perth on the Swan River. The grandness of scale of the land itself is overpowering. WA, which occupies almost a third of the continent, is three times the size of Texas or as large as Western Europe, and the 400,000 who live outside Perth are scattered in small towns and remote settlements over an area of some 2.5 million sq.km (965,000sq. miles). Here native and visitor alike may grasp the vast size of Australia, the true experience of isolation, and feel something of what it is like to live in frontierland. Little quite shakes the soul so much as spending one day among the ebullient, zinc-creamed, sun-worshipping crowd on Perth's Cottesloe Beach, and the next in the emptiness of the red dust and spinifex wilderness outside Kalgoorlie.

Perth claims the title of "the most remote capital in the Western world". Its "neighbour", Adelaide, is 2,700km (1,700 miles) to the E; the Indonesian capital of Jakarta is closer than the Australian federal capital of Canberra. For Australians on the E coast, it can be cheaper to fly to Hawaii for a holiday than to Perth; for those in the W, Singapore or Bali may seem a more economical destination. But Western Australians have turned their isolation into a challenging sort of virtue, looking with some condescension to the "Eastern States", as they somewhat disparagingly refer to them, and particularly to that mass of politicians in the ACT, "the Wise Men from the East". Sandgropers – the nickname they have happily accepted – believe they are blessed with the best and are determined, it seems, to prove it. In sports, entertainment and big business, Western Australians manifest an aggressive dynamism that others in Australia, and indeed the world, find hard to match.

The landscape of WA is infinitely varied. The state's climate ranges from temperate in the sw, through Mediterranean between Perth and Geraldton, to subtropical beyond the Pilbara. Much of the interior, however, is arid wilderness, marked only by exotic rock formations, rugged red gorges and shimmering salt lakes.

Evidently at first glance it did not appear a hospitable place in which to settle. The first Europeans known to have landed in WA were 17thC Dutch seamen, blown off course by the Roaring Forties on their way from Holland to Batavia (present-day Jakarta). Englishman William Dampier, a pirate who became a Royal Navy officer, explored the coast of "New Holland" in 1688 and 1699, but his report to the British government was so unfavourable that the Colonial Office lost all interest. It was only when the French began showing the flag in Australian waters, at the beginning of the 19thC, that the British felt that perhaps the time had come to act. So in 1826 Major Lockyer was sent from the

E to establish the settlement of King George's Sound (now known as Albany). Then, 2yrs later, the British decided to form a colony around the Swan River, which had been partly surveyed by the French in 1801. On May 2 1829, Captain Charles Fremantle, commander of HMS *Challenger*, raised the British flag at the head of the Swan River and took possession of the territory. A month later, Captain James Stirling (later to become the first governor of WA) arrived aboard the ship *Parmelia* with settlers; on Aug 12 1829, he founded Perth in a simple ceremony near the city's present Town Hall.

Today the state's financial wealth derives largely from its immense mineral deposits. Barely a week seems to pass without another vein of rare stone, yet another mountain of ore being discovered. The Hamersley Range of the Pilbara is among the world's largest sources of iron ore. Huge deposits of oil and natural gas have been found off the NW coast. One of the world's richest diamond fields is in the Kimberleys. And gold, first discovered in the 1890s around Kalgoorlie and Coolgardie, is mined now throughout the state – as are silver, nickel, lead and zinc.

There is danger, of course, in simply daubing the vivid main features of this broad landscape. The picture is of earthy reds and browns – a huge quarry for the world – with tycoons, miners, oilmen, engineers, muscled sportsmen and obstinate adventurers appearing like so many Lowry stick-figures trapped in an unnatural sandy plain. But WA is far from this caricature; and certainly not all its pleasures are crudely hedonistic. In frontierland such as this there is always room for subtleties, though it lies with the individual to seek out and paint in these other riches. They may take the form of a meeting with a green sea turtle in the Exmouth Gulf; an unexpected chat about poetry with a fisherman in a pub; a lonely wind whistling through abandoned, rusting goldmining equipment at Boulder; a sudden face-to-face with a frill-necked lizard; being dive-bombed by a frisky pelican; or finding yourself sailing nervously among dolphins. Every view is a different one – and you might suddenly find you are *truly* alone for the first time in your life.

The light, the colours are memorably vivid in WA. In the w the sky truly seems a deeper blue, as though the more subtle shades had been reserved for the northern hemisphere alone. So it is all the more magical when the wild flowers here bloom and break the artist's rules, showing far more delicate shades of colour. WA claims to have the world's largest collection of native wild flowers – more than 6,500 species – and in spring, from about Sept 1 onwards, they dramatically change the landscape. Delicate the wild flowers may be in appearance, but they are all hardy survivors, well attuned to the harsh conditions of climate and territory. The most popular, attracting thousands of visitors to WA each year, are kangaroo paws, distinctively shaped plants with bizarre plumes, of which there are 12 species in varying colour combinations: red and yellow, green and black, and red and green, this last adopted as WA's floral emblem. Most of the plush carpet of flowers spreads through the sw of the state, in and around the forests and rolling grasslands. There are leschenaultias, delicately petalled in blue, violet, scarlet and yellow, and dampiera, named after the English buccaneer and appropriately coloured in various shades of ocean blue. In the drier northern reaches, the visitor may witness the remarkable transformation of a sandy wilderness into vast, rich red-and-black fields of the Sturt desert pea.

But if the wild-flower season in WA is one of Australia's better-kept secrets, the secret of WA's fine wines is fast becoming known throughout the country, and even overseas. For many years the state's wineries were overshadowed by the excellent quality of the wines produced in the Hunter Valley in NSW, the Barossa Valley in South Australia and the N of Victoria. Only the white Burgundy produced in the Swan Valley, just 30mins' drive from Perth, received acclaim. In the past 10-15yrs, however, there has been a rapid growth in the number of vineyards in the state. The Margaret River winemakers, in the SW, have produced Chardonnays and Cabernet Sauvignons to delight the most perceptive palate.

WA itself is a blend of the raw and the sophisticated. Perth, one of the most attractive modern cities in the world, offers every facility and comfort a traveller might want. Yet within hours the true adventurer can escape to quite another world.

Flanked by the Indian Ocean and the broad stretches of the Swan River, Perth to many eyes is Australia's most attractive city, probably its cleanest, and certainly the sunniest, with an average 8hrs of sunshine a day. In winter the average temperature is 18°C (65°F), in summer 29°C (84°F); everyday dress is generally light and casual. As the interior heats up each day in summer, it draws cool sea air from the Indian Ocean. This cooling sea breeze, usually from the SW, is known by locals as the "Fremantle Doctor".

Perth is a city of modern steel-and-glass office towers, traffic-free shopping malls, uncluttered freeways, lakes and parks. Residential areas lie within minutes of the central city blocks, and half a dozen cars ahead of you at the traffic lights amounts to a traffic jam. Remarkably clean ocean beaches fringe the city's western reaches, offering both exhilarating swimming and excellent sea-fishing from man-made groynes.

Although the capital has grown fast, it never seems overcrowded. The boom in construction work and the influx of big business that followed the America's Cup yachting trophy into the city led to financial journalists tagging it "Dallas Down Under". But the name doesn't quite ring true. Certainly wheeling and dealing do go on in Perth; but the place itself still hardly mirrors the hard edge of all that that entails; and the delights of small-town life are still everywhere to be found. The people are warm, open, usually friendly, occasionally blunt; they are curious about visitors, eager to converse and happy to share. Theirs is a young city still growing into its clothes.

To capture one pleasing flavour of Perth, wander through Kings Park in spring; from this splendidly conserved bush-and-parkland you can enjoy a fine view across the Narrows Bridge and down the Swan River. Take advantage of the free city Clipper buses; take a ferry or a cruise boat on the Swan, a bus to Nedlands to sip a Swan beer or two in a beer garden, then a taxi home via riverfront Dalkeith to see how the country's moguls live. . . . Perth's pleasures need not come expensively.

In recent years the focus in WA has switched somewhat away from the capital, down the road (or river) to the port of Fremantle. In 1983 businessman Alan Bond and The Royal Perth Yacht Club brought to WA the America's Cup, the "Auld Mug" awarded in perhaps the greatest regatta of all, and in 1986-87 the challengers raced on the ocean off Fremantle. After months of tacking and talking, Dennis Connor and the San Diego Yacht Club regained the prized trophy for the USA.

Before that, however, the port city had gone through a multimillion-dollar facelift that turned a somewhat sleepy arts-and-crafts and fishing harbour into a cosmopolitan centre that genuinely bubbles with atmosphere. Fremantle, with new restaurants and boutiques peppering the sympathetically restored historic buildings, has emerged as Perth's recreation spot. There are old maritime streets to wander in, hundreds of craft stalls to browse over, and a place in the sun where you can watch the fishing boats jostle with the yachts. Young people flock in on summery evenings to eat pasta and drink *cappuccini* in terraced cafés . . . the influences are visibly, relaxingly Mediterranean.

Beyond Perth and Fremantle lies the sheer enormity of WA. Visitors often find it difficult to understand just how far away those places are that seem to beckon on the map. What looks like a 3hr drive might turn out to take three days. One of the more remote and yet fascinating points on the coast is Broome, once the pearling capital of the world – 2,230km (1,394 miles) N of Perth! Sydney is 3,400km (2,125 miles) – or a 65hr rail journey aboard the Indian-Pacific – away. From the N to the S of WA is roughly equivalent to the distance from Oslo in Norway to Madrid in Spain.

Simply, to those who go W in Australia, the advice is stark: plan your expedition with extreme care – and expect to lament the lack of time. . . .

Perth

Maps 14-15 ☎ *STD code: 09. Airport* ☎ *277 9022 (domestic), 478 8770 (international); Ansett* ☎ *323 1111; Australian* ☎ *323 3333. Railway stations: for country services* ☎ *326 2222; for suburban information* ☎ *325 8511. Car rental: Avis* ☎ *325 7677/277 1729 (airport); Budget* ☎ *322 1100/277 9277 (airport)/481 1004 (chauffeur drive); Hertz* ☎ *321 7777. Western Australian Holiday WA Centre: 772 Hay St., Perth, WA, 6000* ☎ *322 2999. American Express Travel Service: 51 William St., Perth, WA, 6000* ☎ *322 1177/426 3777. Royal Automobile Club of Western Australia (RACWA): 228 Adelaide Terrace, Perth, WA, 6000* ☎ *421 4444.*

Orientation

Perth, the most isolated and arguably the most attractive of Australia's mainland capital cities, flanks the broad, final stretches of the Swan River, with its western suburbs licked by the surf of the Indian Ocean. The city is 19km (12 miles) inland from the seaport it embraces, Fremantle. Around the northern stretch of its riverfront are the luxurious palaces of the rich and famous. To the S, in suburbs such as Welshpool and Kwinana, its heavy industry is concentrated. To the W and N is the suburban sprawl and the clean ocean beaches that make this such a pleasant city in which to live. In the NE, 11km (7 miles) from the centre of the city, is Perth Airport, and more suburban homes, stretching as far inland as the Darling Range.

The heart of downtown Perth is Hay St. It runs parallel to the other main business and shopping streets: Murray St. and Wellington St., and elegant St George's Terrace, which runs from the W, following the Swan River, but becomes Adelaide Terrace as it moves E. Kings Park overlooks the city and the two main bridges, the Causeway, which is E of Barrack Street Jetty, and the Narrows, which is to the W.

Seeing the city

The centre of Perth is easy for the walker to get around, though not quite so convenient for the unwary visiting driver. Signposts and street signs are good on the highways and underpasses around the city, but somewhat eccentric within the busy shopping area. Nevertheless, the state of the roads is generally excellent, and as long as you keep an eye out for the tricky one-way streets there should be no trouble at all. One great advantage that Perth does have over Sydney and Melbourne is that parking is cheap and never far away, and traffic snarls are a rarity.

Perth's public transport system is clean, cheap and efficient and can put most of the sights of interest within easy reach.

Clipper buses
Among the most delightful surprises are the free city **Clipper buses** for shoppers. They circle the centre of Perth and run every 10mins, Mon-Fri 7.30am-5.30pm, Sat 9-11.30am, from specially marked bus stops. Red, Blue and Green Clipper buses operate on other city routes and are also free.

Ferries
The **Metropolitan Passenger Transport Trust (MTT)** operates ferry boats daily, from 6.45am-7.15pm, from Barrack Street Jetty to Mends Street, South Perth (convenient for those visiting the Zoo).

Buses
The Perth central business district and suburban areas are well-connected by MTT buses. The buses, which are comfortable and punctual, have designated departure points in the city, but elsewhere can be hailed at signposted stops. The passenger pays the bus driver; tickets are valid for 2hrs and can also be used on MTT trains and ferries.

For further MTT information on timetables or routes for Clippers, ferries or buses ☎ 325 8511 from 6am-9pm, or visit the **MTT Information Service** (*125 St George's Terrace*).

Trains
Suburban trains operate from Perth to Fremantle, Midland and Armadale from 5.30am-1am on weekdays, with reduced services at the weekends and on public holidays. Interstate and Kalgoorlie trains leave from Perth Railway Terminal, East Perth; suburban and Bunbury trains from City station, Wellington St., Perth.

Taxis
Meter-operated taxis are to be found at hotels, transport terminals and taxi ranks around the city. Or you can simply hail them in the street. Vacant cabs have an illuminated sign on the roof. Where multiple hiring occurs (and the first customer makes the decision on this) only 75 percent of the metered fare is payable. The main taxi companies include **Black & White Taxis** (☎ *328 8288*), **Swan Taxis** (☎ *322 0111*) and **Green & Gold Taxis** (☎ *328 3455*).

Bus tours
Perth offers a remarkable selection of half-day and full-day sightseeing bus tours covering the sights in and around the city. Most of them depart from the Hay Street Coach Rank on the corner of William St. For details, contact the **Holiday WA Centre** (*772 Hay St.* ☎ *322 2999*).

River cruises
Swan River sightseeing cruises are available from Barrack Street Jetty. There are several operators:

Boat Torque ☎ 325 6033
Captain Cook ☎ 325 3341/325 2041
Golden Swan Cruises ☎ 325 9916
Jolly Jumbuck Cruises ☎ 325 3793
Met. Transport Trust ☎ 325 8511/425 2525
Swan River Cruises ☎ 325 3793
WA Wine Cruises ☎ 325 6033

On foot

Escorted walking tours of Perth and Fremantle are available, including personalized excursions for small groups or individuals. Details are obtainable from the **Holiday WA Centre** (*772 Hay St.* ☎ *322 2999, or at corner of High St. and Henry St., Fremantle* ☎ *430 5555*).

For disabled people

Many Perth hotels, restaurants, cinemas and shops have facilities for disabled people, though not all cater for severely handicapped people or for those in wheelchairs. The Australian Tourist Commission recommends that advance notice be given wherever possible to ensure the best possible assistance. A useful series of pamphlets, *Accent On Access*, is available from the **Department for Youth, Sport and Recreation** (*Perry Lakes Stadium, Wembley* ☎ *387 9700*) or from **ACROD Access And Mobility Committee** (☎ *382 2017*).

Sights and places of interest

Alan Green Conservatory

Corner of William St. and The Esplanade ☎ *425 3153. Map 15C4* ⊡ *Open Mon-Sat 10am-5pm, Sun, hols 2-6pm.*

For those inspired by Western Australia's wild flowers, this is something a little different. Here, a short walk from the main shopping arcades, is a rare and remarkable collection of exotic plants. These tropical flowers have been raised within the controlled environment of this small pyramid-shaped glasshouse on the lawns of The Esplanade.

Art Gallery of Western Australia ★

James St. ☎ *328 7233. Map 15B4* ⊡ & 🐾 *(restricted to certain exhibits: ask at inquiries desk)* ✗ *Open 10am-5pm (including most hols), Anzac Day 1-5pm. Closed Christmas Day, Good Friday.*

The somewhat austere exterior of the building belies what is held within. The gallery was opened only in 1979, since when it has acquired a broad range of significant international and Australian works. In recent years there has been a renewed interest in early Australian art throughout the country, and WA is fortunate to have particularly fine paintings by Frederick McCubbin, Tom Roberts and Arthur Streeton. Other Australians – Nolan, Boyd, Lindsay, Dobell, Drysdale and Blackman – are also well represented.

The gallery is proud of its collection of European sculpture, which includes works by Henry Moore, Rodin, Greco, Renoir and Hepworth. And do not miss the gallery's Aboriginal carvings and paintings, nor its unique collection of works from Southeast Asia and the Indian Ocean.

Barracks Archway

St George's Terrace. Map 14C3 ⊯

An odd architectural curiosity, this – a strange but fascinating brick monument, in front of *Parliament House*, left as a memorial to the early colonists of the state. The Archway was all that was retained when the headquarters of soldier-settlers of the enrolled Pensioner Forces was demolished in 1966. The Tudor-style edifice was built in the 1860s in Flemish bond brickwork to the design of Richard Roach Jewell, the Colonial Superintendent of Works.

Government House

St George's Terrace ☎ 325 3222. Map 15C4. Gardens open several days each year: telephone for dates and times.
This, the official residence of the Governor of Western Australia, was built between 1859–64 in the romantic Tudor-Gothic style of architecture much favoured by nostalgic early settlers in the mid-19thC. The gardens would have possibly created further nostalgia for English occupants of the house, for they offer a unique example of informal landscape design from the Old Country. In 1979 the **Western Australian Native Garden** was added as a permanent memorial to the state's 150th anniversary.

Government House, which was built with convict labour, caused a financial scandal, having cost the equivalent of A$30,000, double the original estimate. Today it is used to entertain members of the Royal Family and for state occasions. Both house and gardens have been classified by the National Trust of Australia.

Governor Kennedy's Fountain

Mounts Bay Rd. Map 14C2.
Finding suitable fresh water was always a major problem for the early colonists. This small stone structure at the base of Mt. Eliza was built in 1861 to enclose a permanent spring in the park. The fountain provided Perth with its first public water supply.

Kings Park ★

Kings Park Rd., West Perth ☎ 321 4801. Map 14C2 ▣ & ⚹ (free guided bush tours Apr-Oct) ▤ ✱ ☎ ◄ Bicycles can be rented.
Perth can thank its pioneers for their foresight in establishing this magnificent piece of land so close to the city as a recreation area. An energetic 20min walk up the hill from St George's Terrace takes you to it and to the most spectacular views of both the city and the Swan River.

Today it encompasses 404ha (998 acres), much of which remains largely bushland. Locals tend to outdo one another on what wild creatures can be found here (raise an eyebrow if they start talking about bunyips), but you are quite likely to see skinks, lizards and a variety of birdlife . . . if not a few fellow trekkers.

Not all of the park has been left "native". There are broad expanses of lawn, avenues of trees, 12ha (30 acres) of botanic gardens, carefully cultivated flowerbeds and drifts of wild flowers. **Kings Park Restaurant** caters for diners, and there is a refreshment kiosk for those who want to picnic on the park's grassy slopes. A lookout tower provides panoramic views of Perth and the suburbs; but photographers seem to take many of their best shots near the park's war memorial, looking across the yacht-speckled Swan towards the distant Darling Range.

London Court

Between Hay Street Mall and St George's Terrace. Map 15C4 ✱
A kitschy shopping arcade whose decorative mock-Tudor façade never fails to fascinate photographers. London Court, best-known of Perth's many arcades, was built in 1937 by Claude de Bernales, an entrepreneur who made his fortune mining gold around Kalgoorlie. Its dubious attractions include statues of Sir Walter Raleigh and Dick Whittington and, at the Hay St. end of the Court, medieval knights who joust as the clock strikes the quarter-hour. At the terrace entrance St George and the Dragon perform similar battles with Time. The shops themselves, trapped

in narrow and intricately carved woodwork, sell jewellery,
T-shirts, souvenirs and refreshments.

Museum of Childhood ★
*160 Hamersley Rd., Subiaco ☎ 381 1103 ▣ ♿ ✗ ♣ ➘ Open
Mon-Fri 10am-3pm, Sun 2-5pm. Closed Sat.*
This charming museum was created for children, but with adults
in mind. It holds the treasure of many childhoods, and on display
are wax and wooden dolls of the 19thC, clockwork toys from
before World War I, and nursery furniture from the Victorian era.
Director Brian Shepherd recommends a guided tour, but says that
for all visitors "the emphasis is on hospitality".

Among the museum's exhibits are a large collection of
traditional Japanese toys, Indian toys, and 150 items from the toy
box of a local archbishop's children. Most prized, however, is the
original manuscript for a child's alphabet, drawn up by William
Makepeace Thackeray in 1833.

Ocean beaches
The Perth metropolitan area is blessed with no fewer than 19 sandy
ocean beaches, spreading from South Fremantle to Mullaloo in the
northern suburbs. **Cottesloe, City Beach, Scarborough** and
Trigg Island are among the most popular and, remarkably, the
cleanest. All are close to the city and are patrolled by surf
life-saving clubs. The beaches are generally safe for all swimmers,
although there is often a small surf in which the unwary can be
dumped. For surfers, Scarborough and Trigg hold the best waves.
Swanbourne, between Cottesloe and City Beach, is for those who
prefer swimming *au naturel*. Don't forget the suntan lotion!

Old Gaol and Courthouse
*Francis St. ☎ 328 4411. Map 15B4 ⊡ Open Mon-Thurs
10.30am-5pm, Fri-Sun 1-5pm, hols 9.30am-5pm. Closed
Christmas Day, Good Friday.*
Behind the *Western Australian Museum* is a Georgian-style
stone building, built in 1856, that served as Perth's original prison.
The architect was R. R. Jewell and the jail and courthouse, a fine
example of early colonial architecture, were constructed with
convict labour. In Apr 1888 the last prisoner was removed from
the Perth prison and put in nearby Fremantle Gaol; in Nov that
year the gallows were also moved to Fremantle. Extensively
restored, and the old cells contain early dental and pharmacy
equipment and intriguing reminders of Perth's pioneering days.

Old Mill
*Narrows Bridge, South Perth. Map 14D3 ▣ ♣ Open Sun,
Mon, Wed, Thurs 1-5pm, Sat 1-4pm. Closed Tues, Fri.*
A modest "museum" in a spectacular location on the Swan River.
This flour mill was built in 1835 and, now restored, displays many
relics from the early days of settlement.

Old Perth Boys' School
*139 St George's Terrace ☎ 321 2754. Map 15C4 ⊡ Open
10am-3pm. Closed Sat, Sun.*
Convicts ferried the limestone up the Swan River from Rocky Bay,
near Fremantle, for the building of this somewhat quaint early
school building. Pupils from the Government school, founded in
1847, were able to move into it from an old courthouse in 1854.

The school was designed by William Sandford, Colonial
Secretary and Director of Education, in a style that, with its long,

narrow windows and steeply pitched gables, was obviously influenced by the Gothic ecclesiastical architecture of the 19thC. Today it serves as the headquarters in WA of the National Trust.

Parliament House
Harvest Terrace, West Perth ☎ *222 7222. Map 14B3* 回 ₺
🖾 *in parts (ask first)* ✗ ➳ *Open 8.30am-5pm. Closed Sat, Sun.*

Look w and past the *Barracks Archway* at the end of St George's Terrace and you will see the predictably impressive architecture of Parliament House. Here the state's politicians gather to deal with WA (rather than federal) legislation.

For individuals or small groups 10-15min tours are available throughout the week; for larger, organized groups there are 1hr conducted tours of both Houses of Parliament. But tours depend on Parliamentary sessions, so do be sure to telephone and check for times. Historical detail and explanations of parliamentary procedure are provided on the tours.

Perth Concert Hall
St George's Terrace ☎ *325 3399. Map 15C4* ₺ ⊒ *Open Mon-Sat for viewing when not in use.*

The Perth Concert Hall was opened on Australia Day (Jan 26) 1973, mainly as a place for symphony concerts. But opera, chamber music and folk music performances have also been staged here successfully, and art exhibitions are held in the rooms and corridors surrounding the main theatre. The hall, whose somewhat austere exterior is transformed for concerts by artfully placed lights, also contains a restaurant, a tavern bar and cocktail lounge.

Round House
Arthur Head (between Cliff St. and Fleet St.), Fremantle
☎ *335 6422* 回 *Open Wed, Thurs 11am-4pm, Fri 10.30am-4.30pm, Sat, Sun 10.30am-12.30pm, 1.30-4.30pm. Closed Mon, Tues.*

The Round House, the oldest surviving public building in WA, is in fact not round, but a 12-sided establishment that stands imposingly like a fortress over Fremantle Harbour. It was designed by the colony's first civil engineer, Henry Reveley, as a jail for minor offenders, and was completed in Jan 1831. Today its history is on display in paintings, photographs and documents, and visitors can see the cells where convicts were chained during the night.

St George's Cathedral
St George's Terrace. Map 15C4 ₺

The present Anglican cathedral was designed by Edmund Blacket and built on the site of an earlier cathedral. (In the 1840s this had replaced a wood-and-rushes church hurriedly erected by the first settlers in time to hold Christmas services in 1829.) The foundation stone was laid in 1880 and the church itself was consecrated in 1888, 5yrs after the death of the architect. Notable interior features include an impressive wrought-iron **chancel screen**, erected as a memorial to the city's first two bishops.

Stirling and Supreme Court Gardens
Corner of St George's Terrace and Barrack St. Map 15C4 回
❉

These attractively laid-out gardens are a favourite lunchtime spot for Perth's city workers, who picnic beneath the huge Norfolk

Island pines. The land on which they stand, close to where the city was founded, was set aside in 1829 for botanic gardens. In 1845 the area was officially proclaimed public gardens; in 1899 they were officially opened.

University of Western Australia
Crawley, 5km (3 miles) w ⬤ ◁€

An international competition in the 1920s produced the distinctive Mediterranean style of architecture seen in the University of WA. Few manmade structures merge so charmingly with the landscape as do these pleasing sandstone and orange-tiled buildings in the riverside suburb of Crawley.

Visitors may wander through much of the grounds, which stretch down towards the Swan River. During the Festival of Perth, the university's theatres (which include a small but charming stage in sunken gardens) are often open for public performances. Nearby is the headquarters of the **Royal Perth Yacht Club**, until early 1987 the home of the America's Cup.

Western Australian Maritime Museum ★
Cliff St., Fremantle ☎ *335 8211* ▣ *(but small donation requested)* ⅃ ✗ ⬛ ⚹ *Open 1–5pm. Closed Christmas Day, Good Friday.*

The maritime museum, an imposing 2-storey building in the Georgian style, is among the finest of Fremantle's remarkably handsome restored buildings. But it also houses a wealth of Australian naval history, most notably a reconstruction of the stern of the 1629 Dutch wreck *Batavia*. An archway from the *Batavia*, as well as relics and pictorial displays from other ships wrecked off the WA coastline, is also on display. Suitably nautical gifts and souvenirs are available from the museum's shop.

Western Australian Museum
Francis St. ☎ *328 4411. Map* **15B4** ▣ ⅃ ⬛ ⚹ *Open Mon-Thurs 10.30am-5pm, Fri-Sun, Anzac Day, Boxing Day 1–5pm, other hols 9.30–5pm.*

The museum includes a spectacular marine gallery that contains among its exhibits a 25m (82ft) blue whale skeleton; Aboriginal artifacts and paintings; a very popular collection of veteran and vintage cars and motorcycles; and the 11-tonne **Mundrabilla meteorite**:

Zoological Gardens
Labouchere Rd., South Perth ☎ *367 7988. Map* **14F3** ▣ ⅃ ⬛ ⚹ ⬤ *Open 10am-5pm. Ferry from Barrack St. to South Perth, or bus from city.*

In a relaxing parklike setting across the river, the zoo has an extensive collection of exotic and native animals and birds. Always popular are the koalas and always fascinating the numbats, the official fauna emblem of WA.

Accommodation

Perth and Fremantle have an abundant supply of good, clean hotels, motels and other accommodation. Before the America's Cup returned to American hands, an enormous amount of building took place in anticipation of a boom in tourism.

For visitors seeking budget-style accommodation (from A$50 and below), the **Holiday WA Centres** (*772 Hay St., Perth* ☎ *322 2999, and corner of High St. and Henry St., Fremantle* ☎ *430 5555*) have useful accommodation listings. They also have details for those who would like to stay in a private home or on a working farm. The overseas offices of the **Australian Tourist Commission** have similar accommodation listings on request.

Ansett International

10 Irwin St., Perth, WA, 6000
☎ 325 0481 ⅢⅢ ☎ 92999 ⓕ 323 2902. Map **15C4** ⅢⅢ 232 rms ⌷
⌷ ⒶⒺ ⓞ ⓞ ⱽⁱˢᵃ
Location: Conveniently central. This flourishing top-of-the-range luxury hotel has been modernized with great success since it changed its name . from the Gateway a few years ago. It is owned by Ansett Transport Industries, the company that runs and manages both the Gateway in Adelaide and Hayman Island, off Queensland. It contains the pricey but excellent **Irwin** restaurant, a bistro and three bars. Valet parking for guests.
⌷ ⌷ ⌷ ⌷ ⌷ ⌷ ⌷ ⌷

Chateau Commodore

Corner of Victoria Ave. and Hay St., Perth, WA, 6000 ☎ 325 0461 ⅢⅢ ☎ 92872. Map **15C5** ⅢⅢ 133 rms ⌷ ⌷ ⒶⒺ ⓞ ⓞ ⱽⁱˢᵃ
Location: Only a short walk from main shopping centre. A smartly efficient hotel with clean, spacious rooms, though be sure to ask for one with a reasonable view. The hotel's main dining room, **Isabella's**, is a pleasant if unadventurous European-style restaurant. The **Birdrock Cafe** offers hearty breakfasts.
⌷ ⌷ ⌷ ⌷

Criterion

560 Hay St., Perth, WA, 6000
☎ 325 5155. Map **15C4** ⅢⅢ 61 rms ⌷ ⌷ ⒶⒺ ⓞ ⱽⁱˢᵃ
Location: Opposite Town Hall. An old-fashioned, well-worn Victorian-style establishment, and probably the most conveniently placed of Perth's budget-priced hotels. Bedrooms are compact, though they have high ceilings, fashionable before the days of air conditioning. As well as several bars, the Criterion has a dining room offering inexpensive, hearty dinners.
⌷

Fremantle Esplanade ♥

Marine Terrace, Fremantle, WA, 6160 ☎ 430 4000 ⅢⅢ ☎ 96977 ⓕ 430 4539 ⅢⅢ 141 rms ⌷ ⌷ ⒶⒺ ⓞ ⓞ ⱽⁱˢᵃ
Location: Splendidly located near Fremantle's fishing harbour. This elegantly restored hotel, spacious, cool and peaceful, was a favourite of the well-heeled international yachties who attended the America's Cup

races off Fremantle. Reopened in May 1986, it features fine smorgasbord meals in the atrium and seafood specialities in its **Spinnakers** restaurant. There is also a boutique and gift shop and, for those who want to shake the salt from their sandals, a popular disco.
⌷ ⌷ ⌷ ⌷ ⌷ ⌷ ⌷ ⌷

Merlin

99 Plain St., Perth, WA, 6000
☎ 323 0121 ⅢⅢ ☎ 95823 ⓕ 325 8785. Map **15D6** ⅢⅢ 369 rms ⌷
⌷ ⒶⒺ ⓞ ⓞ ⱽⁱˢᵃ
Location: In the less crowded, eastern stretch of fashionable Adelaide Terrace. A luxurious and large, if slightly overpowering, hotel with friendly management and staff and spacious rooms. The easy shopping clustered around the atrium compensate for the uncanny feeling of being a figure in an architect's drawing. But the Merlin has 24hr room service and some useful extras (among them tennis and squash courts, and a small library for business executives). It has first-class restaurants: **The Langley** offers classic European dining; **Princess Jade** provides Cantonese and Malaysian dishes.
⌷ ⌷ ⌷ ⌷ ⌷ ⌷ ⌷

Miss Maud ♥

97 Murray St., Perth, WA, 6000
☎ 325 3900 ⅢⅢ ☎ 93176. Map **15C4** ⅢⅢ 52 rms ⌷ ⌷ ⒶⒺ ⓞ ⓞ ⱽⁱˢᵃ
Location: Usefully situated close to the busy heart of city shopping. Miss Maud Edmonston, the Swedish proprietor of this clean, friendly and unpretentious hotel, is famous for her coffee and pastry shops. The hotel serves a particularly hearty smorgasbord in its restaurant.
⌷ ⌷

New Esplanade

18 The Esplanade, Perth, WA, 6000 ☎ 325 2000 ⅢⅢ ☎ 93327. Map **15C4** ⅢⅢ 74 rms ⌷ ⌷ ⌷ ⒶⒺ ⓞ ⓞ ⱽⁱˢᵃ
Location: Overlooking The Esplanade, with fine views across the Swan and Kings Park. This is a bright, modern and sensible hotel, superbly located. The award-winning **Room With A View** restaurant features European-style cuisine, with local specialities (such as the dhufish) prominent on the menu. It's a restful dining spot

overlooking the river, and a favourite of local romantics.
📺 ❖ ⚰ ⚓ ⛵

Observation City Resort Hotel
The Esplanade, Scarborough, WA, 6019 ☎ *245 1000* 🖥 *95782* 🄿 *245 1345* ▥▥ *336 rms* 🛏 ⊟ 🅰🅴 🔘 🔘 🆅🆂🅰

Location: On one of Perth's favoured Indian Ocean beaches. An extraordinarily sited new luxury hotel. Observation City, one of the many enterprises of America's Cup magnate Alan Bond, boasts that this is "where golden sands meet silver service". Among its four restaurants, the **Ocean Room** specializes in French fare (the pressed duck is a speciality). Relaxed and friendly, the hotel offers, among other things, a convenient recreation room for holidaying families. A courtesy bus links the hotel to Perth, Fremantle and the airport.
🔥 ⊠ ⚐ 📺 ❖ 🐾 ﾞ ⚰ ⚓ ⛵

Orchard ❦
Corner of Milligan St. and Wellington St., Perth, WA, 6000 ☎ *327 7000* ▥▥ 🖥 *95050* 🄿 *322 4174. Map* **14B3** ▥▥ *279 rms* 🛏 ⊟ 🅰🅴 🔘 🔘 🆅🆂🅰

Location: Near Perth Entertainment Centre. The Huang family, who run this clean, modern and friendly hotel, have a similar establishment in San Francisco. Two restaurants are attached to the hotel, and there are a total of seven – Chinese, Japanese, Italian, seafood etc. – within the complex of shops and offices in which it stands. 24hr room service.
🔥 ⊠ ⊟ ❖ 🐾 ⚰ ⚓ ⛵

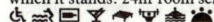

Parmelia Hilton ❦
Mill St., Perth, WA, 6000 ☎ *322 3622* ▥▥ 🖥 *92365* 🄿 *481 0857. Map* **14C3** ▥▥ *275 rms* 🛏 ⊟ 🅰🅴 🔘 🔘 🆅🆂🅰

Location: In the heart of Perth's central business district. A first-class hotel offering the familiarity of a Hilton plus unexpected warmth in service from general manager Fernand David's efficient staff. The Parmelia has been a favourite of visiting interstate executives since the early 1970s. In 1979 it was taken over by the Hilton chain and has managed to hold its own against a barrage of newcomers. Rooms are spacious and well-equipped (at least two phones, a room, hair dryer, cocktail bar etc.) and relaxingly furnished. The hotel itself is decorated with a valuable collection of European *objets d'art.* The **Garden Restaurant**, under executive chef Anton Muhlbock, has

gained an enviable reputation for its seafood dishes.
🔥 ⚐ ⊟ ❖ 🐾 ⚓ ⛵

Perth Ambassador
196 Adelaide Terrace, Perth, WA, 6000 ☎ *325 1455* ▥▥ 🖥 *95799* 🄿 *325 6317. Map* **15C5** ▥▥ *171 rms* 🛏 ⊟ 🅰🅴 🔘 🔘 🆅🆂🅰

Location: Just an invigorating walk away from city centre. A newish hotel decorated in soft, pastel colours. Service is congenial. Its Chinese restaurant, the **Majestic**, serves Singaporean-style dishes and is said to be one of Perth's top three.
🔥 ⊟ ❖ 🐾 ⚰ ⚓ ⛵

Perth Parkroyal
54 Terrace Rd., Perth, WA, 6000 ☎ *325 3811* ▥▥ 🖥 *92316* 🄿 *221 1564. Map* **15D5** ▥▥ *99 rms* 🛏 ⊟ 🅰🅴 🔘 🔘 🆅🆂🅰

Location: Overlooking Langley Park. Every room in this intimate, immaculately clean hotel offers a fine view over the Swan. Its restaurant, **The Royal Palm**, presents monthly food promotions (New Orleans/ Cajun, Scandinavian etc.).
⚐ ⊟ ❖ 🐾 ⚰ ⚓

Princes Plaza
334 Murray St., Perth, WA, 6000 ☎ *322 2844* 🖥 *95000* 🄿 *481 2105. Map* **14B3** ▥▥ *167 rms* 🛏 ⊟ 🅰🅴 🔘 🔘 🆅🆂🅰

Location: In a very competitive, busy part of the city centre. A pleasant and efficient hotel. Its main restaurant, the **Society**, has won the coveted local Gold Plate Award for its European-style menu.
🔥 ⊟ ❖ ⚓

Sheraton Perth
207 Adelaide Terrace, Perth, WA, 6000 ☎ *325 0501* ▥▥ 🖥 *92938* 🄿 *325 4032. Map* **15C5** ▥▥ *396 rms* 🛏 ⊟ 🅰🅴 🔘 🔘 🆅🆂🅰

Location: Overlooking the Swan River. Decorated in cool, restfully good taste, this sensitively run, well-managed hotel incorporates all the facilities travellers require.
🔥 ⚐ ⊟ ❖ 🐾 ⚓

Transit Inn
37 Pier St., Perth, WA, 6000 ☎ *325 7655* ▥▥ 🖥 *92739* 🄿 *325 7655. Map* **15C4** ▥▥ *121 rms* 🛏 ⊟ 🅰🅴 🔘 🔘 🆅🆂🅰

Location: Near to central business district. This pleasant hotel is another favourite among visiting executives. Its main restaurant, **Ruby's**, has a romantic, old-world atmosphere and is remarkably popular.
⚐ ⊟ ❖ 🐾 ⚓

Eating out in Perth

There is no doubt that, for its size, Perth enjoys an extraordinary number of restaurants. There are more than 600 in and around the city, ranging from the woeful to the wonderful.

The food available to them is generally first-rate – with the seafood excelling. Dhufish, kingfish, crayfish (rock lobster), prawns and crabs are fresh and delicious. Well worth trying, if and when available, is the local delicacy marron, a freshwater crayfish that is similar, albeit tastier, to the yabbies found in the eastern states. Fresh fruit and vegetables are plentiful and tasty.

WA produces an excellent range of red and white table wines, with the Margaret River estates proving particularly popular. Its local beer, Swan Lager, is crisp and invigorating and, arguably, rivals the Melbourne-based Fosters Lager as the country's tastiest brew.

Perth and Fremantle have good restaurants to cater for all tastes – French, Indonesian, Swiss, Spanish, Portuguese, Jewish, Yugoslav, Chinese, Thai, Japanese, Indian, Vietnamese, Greek, Dutch and Lebanese among them. The Italian restaurants, many of them situated in and around the Northbridge area of Perth (just over the railway line from the city centre), are particularly fine.

Much of the improvement to Perth's dining-out scene has occurred since the early 1970s. Because there is such a demand for restaurant staff, the service in some restaurants is not always as smooth as that to be found in, say, Sydney or Melbourne. But the situation is fast-changing. And in friendliness, the Western Australians are second to none.

Adelphi Steak House
Mill St. ☎ *322 3622. Map 14C3*
▥▯�}⁋☒▬ AE ⊕ ⊚ VISA
Closed Sat and Sun lunch.
An unpretentious, friendly, well-established restaurant within the *Parmelia Hilton* complex (see *Hotels*), specializing in hearty, tender steaks. For those who want something lighter, the grilled fish is particularly pleasing. On quiet nights the service can be a little too casual.

Emperor's Court
66 Lake St. ☎ *328 8860. Map 15B4* ▥▯➁⁋AE⊕⊚VISA
Closed Sat and Sun lunch.
There are many above-average Chinese restaurants in Perth; quite possibly this is the best, recently named the finest in the state by the national news magazine *The Bulletin*. The Emperor's Court offers both Cantonese and hotter, spicier Szechuan dishes.

The Establishment ♣
35a Hampden Rd., Nedlands
☎ *386 5508* ▥ ▯ *Last orders 10pm. BYO licence.*
The choice of the city's in-crowd, The Establishment, close to the University of WA, is small and highly in demand. The emphasis is on the careful preparation of French-style and Australian dishes. Highly recommended.

Fast Eddy's
Corner of Hay St. and Milligan St.
☎ *321 2552. Map 14C3* ▯ ▯
BYO licence.
A burger restaurant, open 24hrs a day, 7 days a week. As well as a full range of filling hamburgers, the menu includes breakfasts, steaks, sandwiches and many other light meals. Fast Eddy's also serves ice-cream sundaes guaranteed to silence the noisier, younger members of the family.

Hana of Perth
Mill St. ☎ *322 7908. Map 14C3*
▥▯⁋AE⊕⊚VISA *Last orders 10.30pm. Closed lunch, Sun.*
This traditional Japanese restaurant offers mouth-watering *shabu shabu*, *sukiyaki*, *tempura* and *sashimi*. The Hana has four private *tatami* rooms, seven "semi-private" booths, and tables that overlook its garden. *Sushi* and *sashimi* are available at the *sushi* bar or at the table.

Harbour Lights (Lombardo's)
Boat Harbour, Mews Rd., Fremantle ☎ *430 4344* ▥▯▬ ⁋ ◁ AE⊕⊚VISA *Last orders 10pm.*
An excellent place to watch the world sail by, this elegant seafood restaurant overlooks Fremantle's Mediterranean-style fishing harbour.

Enjoy the crayfish (rock lobster), king prawns, dhufish and snapper and many, many other fruits of the sea.

Matilda Bay ♣
3 Hacket Drive, Crawley ☎ *386 5425* ▥ ▭ ➤ ➤ ◁ ⓐⓔ ⊕ ⓒⓓ ⓥⓘⓢⓐ *Last orders 10pm. Closed Sat lunch, Sun.*
The Matilda Bay is one of Perth's long-time favourites, situated only 10mins from the city and close to the University of WA and the Royal Perth Yacht Club. It is cool, airy, elegant and serves an excellent French-Californian cuisine. The views across the Swan River towards the city are spectacular. Service is first-class.

Ord Street Cafe ♣
27 Ord St., West Perth ☎ *321 6021. Map* **14B2** ▥ ▭ ➤ ◁ ⊕ ⓒⓓ ⓥⓘⓢⓐ *Last orders 10.30pm. Closed Sun.*
With an ever-changing menu, chef Glen Davies has helped make this one of the busiest dining spots in the city. *The Bulletin* presented it with a "best food in Perth" award. The pleasant garden setting is a bonus.

Oyster Beds
26 Riverside Rd., East Fremantle ☎ *339 1611* ▥ ▭ ➤ ➤ ◁ ⓐⓔ ⊕ ⓒⓓ ⓥⓘⓢⓐ *Last orders 10pm. Closed Sat lunch.*

This river restaurant-on-stilts has for at least 15yrs enjoyed the reputation of serving the area's finest seafood. Service may sometimes be a little sluggish, but the food is well worth waiting for, and the dhufish and crayfish are invariably excellent. On a balmy summer's night you can dine outdoors and watch the tourist and fishing boats chug by.

The Plum
99 Francis St. ☎ *328 5920. Map* **15B4** ▥ ▭ ⓐⓔ ⊕ ⓒⓓ ⓥⓘⓢⓐ *Last orders 11.15pm. Closed Mon; Tues and Wed lunch; Sat lunch; Sun. BYO licence.*
A Victorian-style restaurant whose four main burgundy-coloured rooms are decorated with period art and memorabilia. Log fires (in winter), lace tablecloths and velvet drapes, soft lighting and music all add to the atmosphere. There's a choice of French and "international" dishes, with a set price for lunch.

River Room
207 Adelaide Terrace ☎ *325 0501. Map* **15C5** ▥ ▭ ➤ ➤ ◁ ⓐⓔ ⊕ ⓒⓓ ⓥⓘⓢⓐ *Last orders 10.30pm. Closed lunch.*
Part of the *Sheraton Perth* (see *Hotels*), this is an elegant restaurant that serves the finest European-style food. It is a favourite dinner-dance spot for those celebrating a special occasion.

Nightlife and the arts
The city of Perth seems to go to sleep early, concentrating its entertainment and relaxation around the home. In the past the nightlife was indeed sparse. But recently there have been changes – more big international shows, more theatre, more clubs – and, for the visitor who looks around, the city's nightlife is varied and offers something to suit most tastes.

For those who enjoy dancing until just before dawn, there are many discos in the city and the suburbs. Among the better known are **Juliana's**, part of the *Parmelia Hilton* (see *Hotels*) and of the international chain of discos; **Clouds** (*207 Adelaide Terrace* ☎ *325 0501*), part of the *Sheraton Perth* complex (see *Hotels*); and **Tomorrow** (*99 Adelaide Terrace* ☎ *323 0121*), in the *Merlin* (see *Hotels*). For younger travellers, favourites include **Gobbles** (*613 Wellington St.* ☎ *322 1221*), **Beethoven's** (*418 Murray St.* ☎ *321 6887*) and **Pinocchio's** (*393 Murray St.* ☎ *321 2521*).

A particularly lively area for both restaurants and nightclubs is **Northbridge**, a short walk from the city centre, down William St. and over the railway bridge.

The pubs and wine bars are always changing, but worth checking are the **Brewery Alehouse** (*149 Stirling Hwy, Nedlands*), which sells beer from all over the world, as well as its own private brew; **O'Connors Wine House Restaurant** (*Hay St., West Perth* ☎ *321 5495*); and the English pub-styled **Cock and Bull** (*123 Rokeby Rd., Subiaco* ☎ *381 8400*).

Burswood Casino
Great Eastern Hwy, Rivervale
☎ *362 7777* ⛾ ⇌ *Open 24hrs.*
The new Burswood Casino, on the
other side of The Causeway that
leads into Perth, is the third largest
in the world, with 140 gaming tables
and facilities spread over an area of
75,000sq.ft. Blackjack, baccarat,
mini baccarat, roulette, big and small
craps, keno, the Australian game
two-up – all are played at Burswood.
There are also restaurants (AE) (CB)
(CB) (VISA)), cocktail bars and a lounge-
cabaret area within the complex. The
casino is part of the **Burswood Island
Resort**, which, when completed, will
include a 412-room hotel, an
entertainment and convention
facility, a huge exhibition/sports
complex, an 18-hole golf course and
landscaped gardens.

The Entertainment Centre
Wellington St. ☎ *information
322 4766, bookings 322 4766.
Map 14B3* ⛾ AE CB CB VISA
Perth's prime centre for large-scale
extravaganzas featuring the world's
most popular entertainers seats
8,000, thus ensuring that the big
stars that once bypassed the West
Coast now include it in their
schedules. Big attractions staged
here have included the Miss
Universe Contest, figure skaters
Torvill and Dean, Disney on Parade,
a major tennis tournament and the
Bolshoi Ballet.

Gloucester Park
Nelson Crescent, East Perth
☎ *information 325 8822,
bookings 325 8822. Map 15C6* ⛾
⇌ *Open for race meetings (see
local newspapers for details),
generally Fri nights.*
The "Night Trots" offers a pleasant

way to have a flutter or two on WA's
trotting or pacing horses. Under the
lights on a balmy evening, Gloucester
Park is a colourful delight. There are
bars, on-course betting, and
restaurants that range from fast-food
to elegant.

His Majesty's Theatre
Corner of Hay St. and King St.
☎ *information 322 2929,
bookings 321 6288. Map 14C3* ⛾
⇌ AE CB CB VISA
"The Maj" offers theatregoers a
glimpse into the past. This
splendidly restored Edwardian
theatre retains the decor of the 1920s
with the innovations of the 1980s. It
is now the home of the WA Opera
Company and the WA Ballet
Company, but is also used for Gilbert
and Sullivan productions and plays.
Both Pavlova and Dame Nellie
Melba appeared at the theatre; a
downstairs tavern and restaurant,
Nellie's, is named after Australia's
famed opera star. Guided tours are
available.

Hole in the Wall Theatre
Hamersley Rd., Subiaco ☎ *381
2733* ⛾
This theatre has gained an enviable
reputation for its mix of modern and
classical plays. Among the most
popular productions are those by
up-and-coming Australian writers.

Perth Concert Hall
5 St George's Terrace ☎ *325
3399. Map 15C4* ⛾ ⇌ AE CB CB
VISA
The main hall for symphony
concerts, this is the home of the
Western Australia Symphony
Orchestra and has seating for 1,900.
The building includes a restaurant,
tavern and cocktail bar.

Shopping
Probably the most novel aspect of Perth for visitors is the many
shopping arcades that wind through the city. They offer the banal
with the intriguing, the curious with the kitsch. But look around,
for there are bargains to be found. Modern department stores, like
Myer (*corner of Murray St. and William St.*), **Aherns** (*between Hay
St. and Murray St., near Barrack St.*) and **Boans** (*246 Murray St.*)
are efficient and well-stocked, but it is in the markets and off the
beaten track that you will find the gifts or specialities that can only
be found in WA.

In Perth, the visitor can buy a high-quality diamond that has
been mined, cut and polished in WA. These gems, which include
unique pink diamonds, come from the Argyle Diamond Mine in
the remote and rugged Kimberley region. There are also shops
that specialize in that most beautiful of Australian stones, the opal.
Other jewellers specialize in pearls retrieved from the waters off
Broome in the far N of the state.

For jewellery, sports goods and folkcraft shops, a trip to the near-city suburb of **Claremont** is worthwhile. **Fremantle** – and particularly the attractive **Bannister Street Mall** – offers a range of shops specializing in everything from wool and leather goods to crafts and Aboriginal artifacts. There is also the excellent *Fremantle Markets*.

Most shops and arcades are in the area bounded by St Georges Terrace, William St., Murray St. and Barrack St. A favoured starting point for any shopper's expedition in Perth is *London Court* (see *Sights*), the arcade that links St George's Terrace with the **Hay Street Mall,** right in the heart of the city's shopping district. The arcade itself offers mainly simple souvenirs and gifts, but it can be the start of a pleasant and profitable stroll. From here, you are only a browse or two away from **Piccadilly Arcade** (between Hay Street Mall and Murray St.), both of which are well worth visiting.

Shopping hours are 8.30am-5.30pm Mon-Fri and 8.30am-noon on Sat. Late-night shopping is on Thurs.

Perth's main post office (and poste restante) is the **GPO** (*3 Forrest Pl.* ☎ *326 5211*). It is open Mon-Fri 8am-5pm. After-hours service (stamp sales only) is available Mon-Fri 5-7pm, Sat 9am-noon and Sun 9am-noon.

Aboriginal art
If your purchase is old or of a sacred nature, it is advisable to inquire whether an export permit is needed.

Aboriginal Art Gallery
242 St Georges Terrace. Map 14C3 ☀ AE ⊕ ⊛ VISA
Government-authorized marketing outlet for authentic items of Aboriginal culture. Among the items on sale here are bark paintings, boomerangs, spears and other weapons, carvings and basketware.

Australiana
As well as the usual tourist nicknacks, usually imported from Southeast Asia, widely available in shopping centres and department stores, Perth has a selection of quite individual shops selling authentic Australian artifacts.

Purely Australian
London Court, Hay Street Mall, City Arcade (map 15C4) and Perth Airport AE ⊕ ⊛ VISA
Superb hand-knitted woollens with unique Australian designs, T-shirts and sweatshirts, blackboy wood and jarrah wood gifts, jewellery, stationery and books . . . and a fairly comprehensive selection of souvenirs you will find throughout WA.

Puritan Man
343 Stirling Highway, Claremont (near Bayview Terrace) ☎ *384 3434* AE ⊕ ⊛ VISA
An attractive shop that sells colonial and Oriental antiques, contemporary arts and crafts, and museum-quality folkcrafts. There's a peaceful courtyard where you can relax over coffee.

Timothy's Toys
Croke Lane, Fremantle ☎ *336 1982* ☀
Handcrafted wooden toys, designed and made in this Fremantle workshop, make ideal gifts for all ages.

Fashion
Shoes in Australia can be intimidatingly expensive or poorly made. A shop, however, where you can guarantee colourful and

fashionable women's shoes is **Tamekas Footwear Boutique** (*1222 Hay St., West Perth* ☎ *321 7976* 🆎 🔾 🔾 🕮). For women's swimwear, casual clothes, evening and day wear (with specialist fittings and speedy alterations) there is **Thompsons** of West Perth (*1267 Hay St., West Perth* ☎ *321 8007* 🆎 🔾 🔾 🕮). And for men's clothes, formal, casual or practical, there are many fine outlets. Below are some examples.

John Buzza
Corner of Howard St. and St Georges Terrace ☎ *325 8377. Map 15C4* 🆎 🔾 🔾 🕮
Classical men's outfitters, stocking a fine line of quality casual gear, both imported and Australian. Some excellent outfits for armchair sailors. First-class service.

Leather Life
75 Barrack St. ☎ *325 5186. Map 15C4* 🆎 🔾 🔾 🕮
The place for sheepskin and lambskin wear, from jackets to boots, slippers to coats.

R. M. Williams
Carillon Centre, Hay Street Mall. Map 15C4 🆎 🔾 🔾 🕮
Akubra hats, moleskin strides, fine leather boots and all the other trappings to turn you into a dinki-di Aussie drover. This is where the Stock Exchange graziers get outfitted!

Jewellers
Superb stones and jewellery are an Australian speciality. WA itself is a prime source, making Perth a good place for purchasing jewellery. Below are two distinguished city outlets.

Broome Pearl Traders
23 Rokeby Rd., Subiaco ☎ *381 6431* 🆎 🔾 🔾 🕮
The pearls are, of course, from Broome in the N, the erstwhile "pearling capital of the world", most of them grown by marine biologist Bill Reed. Goldsmith Alan Linney uses them to make outstanding jewellery. Service here is particularly good.

Opal Centre
Shop 1-6, St Martin's Arcade, off London Court ☎ *325 8684. Map 15C4* 🆎 🔾 🔾 🕮
Opal, formed millions of years ago from a mixture of silica in water, is known as "the fire in the stone". Here it is easy to see why. The store's brilliant collection of opals comes from Coober Pedy (South Australia) and Lightning Ride (New South Wales). There is normally a special discount for overseas visitors who can show an airline ticket and passport; ask the staff for details. The staff here speaks Japanese, Malay, French and German.

Markets and food centres
Australians love a good, bustling market. *Fremantle Markets* is the best example in Perth and Fremantle. Look too at Perth's food centres, which are groups of kitchens sharing communal dining tables and chairs – a Singaporean idea. Good examples include the **City Centre Market** (*Hay Street Mall*) and the **Citipak Food Market** (*895 Hay St.*).

Fremantle Markets
Corner of South Terrace and Henderson St., Fremantle ♿ 🖃 ♣
These excellent markets were originally built in 1897, but were remodelled and reopened in 1975 with 150 or so stalls. Here you can find jewellery, clothing, fresh fruit, pottery, leather, and home-made pickles . . . all you might need and a lot more. Open 8.30am-9pm Fri, 8.30am-1pm Sat and 11am-5pm Sun.

Perth environs and Western Australia excursions

The excursions described in this section cover places of interest within relatively easy reach of the city of Perth. Following them is a separate section on four main regions of WA.

Details (and bookings) for extended tours to all parts of the state can be obtained through the **Holiday WA Centre** (*772 Hay St.* ☎ *322 2999*).

Excursions from Perth

Armadale
One-day self-drive excursion. Tour operators offer trips that take in the highlights.
Take the Albany Hwy SE towards Gosnells. Shortly before you reach the town, 20km (12½ miles) from Perth, turn off left to the **Cohunu Wildlife Park** (*Mills Rd.* ☎ *(09) 390 6090, open Mon-Fri 10am-5pm, Sat, Sun 10am-5.30pm*), a sanctuary that has 16ha (40 acres) of bushland in which Australian birds and animals can thrive in natural settings. Cohunu has the biggest walk-through aviary in the southern hemisphere as well as a large collection of wild flowers.

Travel on towards Kelmscott and back onto the Albany Hwy. Nearby, on Canns Rd., is the **Elizabethan Village**, a full-scale Tudor replica that includes a copy of Shakespeare's birthplace. At **Armadale** itself, the attraction is a village of another era. **Pioneer World** (☎ *(09) 399 5322, open 10am-5pm*) celebrates the life of the country's settlers with its re-creation of an early Australian town. The focus is two 19thC streets, in which shop assistants in period costume go out of their way to provide a feeling of authenticity. Visitors can pan for gold, watch "traditional craftsmen" at work, buy opals and pearls, join in a sing-song in the pub, and play "two-up".

If the Elizabethan Village (see above) isn't all too much for you, you can eat traditional olde English fare at the **Poet's Arbour Restaurant** (☎ *(09) 399 3166* ◼).

Avon Valley
The three main towns, Toodyay, Northam and York, are all within 100km (63 miles) of Perth and ideal to explore either in a single day or over several one-day trips.
The "Valley For All Seasons" is a comfortable day's drive from Perth. Drive E through Guildford to Midland, then take the Great Northern Hwy (Route 95) N for a few kilometres before turning right onto the Toodyay Rd.

Toodyay (pronounced Too-gee), 85km (53 miles) NE of Perth, was one of the first inland towns settled back in the colony's early days. Much of its history has been charmingly retained. It was in the rugged bushclad hills SW of Toodyay that WA's most notorious bushranger, Moondyne Joe, roamed. The **Toodyay Tourist Centre** (*Connor's Mill, Stirling Terrace*) has a floor devoted to his life and times. In Sept this town of 800 commemorates his passing, in the Moondyne Joe Festival.

Follow the Avon River through the undulating farmland and bush country to **Northam**, 27km (17 miles) SE of Toodyay. Northam, the second largest *inland* town in WA with a population of only 8,500, is the commercial centre for this rich agricultural district. It is also the home of what has become a classic white-water event for canoeists in Australia, the Avon Descent. Northam's less energetic attractions include stately white mute swans. These aristocratic birds, rare in Australia, can be seen from the pedestrian **Suspension Bridge** that crosses the Avon near the town centre.

Leaving the town, you can drive s direct to York on the main York Rd. Alternatively, take the scenic drive that follows the Avon through **Spencer's Brook**, 10km (6 miles) s of Northam, stopping for a drink at the 100yr-old **Spencer's Brook Tavern** before completing the final 25km (16 miles) to York.

Once the Wild West town of the colony, **York** was a bustling centre for the diggers in the gold rush of the 1890s. Today this picturesque town has been carefully renovated and restored to remind visitors of its wealthy past. A good example is the **York Town Hall**, once WA's largest. For motoring enthusiasts, the **York Motor Museum** (☎ *(096) 411 288*) houses more than 150 classic and vintage cars, motorcycles and some horse-drawn vehicles. The Perth-York Vintage Car Rally is held over 2 days each Nov.

After York, it's a 97km (59-mile) journey w along the Great Southern and Great Eastern (Route 94) Hwys back to Perth through fertile, restful countryside.

In Northam: the **Byfield House Restaurant** (*30 Gordon St.* ☎ *(096) 22 3380* ◼️▯), for Victorian elegance, or **The Colonial Restaurant** (*197 Duke St.* ☎ *(096) 22 1074* ◼️▯), for old-world charm (and Northam's only licensed restaurant). In York, the **Castle Hotel** (*Avon Terrace* ☎ *(096) 41 1007* ▯), built in 1835 (and licensed since 1851), serves counter lunches.

El Caballo Blanco

60km (38 miles) E. Getting there: by car, via Great Eastern Hwy; by bus, contact booking office at Centerway Arcade, Hay St. ☎ *321 9729.*

The Spanish connection with WA may be difficult to fathom, but this entertainment park, whose stars are its Andalusian dancing stallions, has been one of the state's most popular attractions for years. The "ranch" complex includes an adventure playground and water slides, a Spanish restaurant, and picnic-barbecue facilities. There is also a variety of horse-drawn carriages at the **Bodeguero Carriage Museum** and a chairlift that takes visitors to the top of **Mt. Bodeguero**.

The Hills

Explore the foothills of the Darling Range if you have a day to spare, and a car. The Hills run N-S, about 20km (12½ miles) E from Perth, and have some particularly pleasant picnic spots and lesser-known tourist attractions.

To get there, take the Guildford Rd. E from Perth through Guildford and Midland and drive onwards along the Great Eastern Hwy (Route 94). As you travel towards Mundaring, you will see on the left, about 26km (16 miles) from Perth, the entrance to the **John Forrest National Park**, the state's first national park. It contains an open eucalypt forest, good bushwalking, scenic views, spring wild flowers and a natural swimming pool for children.

Farther along the highway, on the right, is the **Old Mahogany Inn**, where you can enjoy morning tea. At **Mundaring**, stretch your legs again and explore one of the many trails that wind through the area's unique jarrah forest. Leave the highway here and drive along the Mundaring Weir Rd. until you get to the weir itself. In this wild bushland setting, you can prepare a picnic-barbecue or simply visit the splendidly restored **Mundaring Weir Pub**.

Along the road is the **O'Connor Museum**, which records the history of the provision of water from this area to the Eastern Goldfields. From here, take a scenic drive along Mundaring Weir Rd. through the Hills to **Kalamunda**, then drive on to **Gooseberry Hill National Park** for spectacular, panoramic views of Perth to the w. Then follow the **Zig-Zag**, once an old railway line, down to the base of the hill.

Return to the city, either by turning back towards Midland and the Great Eastern Hwy or by working your way to the Albany Hwy.

Mandurah

74km (46 miles) s. Getting there: by car, via Cockburn Rd. (Route 12) from Fremantle, then Mandurah-Fremantle Coast Rd.; by bus, from Fremantle railway station.
Life in Mandurah, one of WA's favoured resorts, revolves around the Murray and Serpentine Rivers, the attractive Peel Inlet and the Harvey Estuary. The magnificent waterways, rich in blue manna crabs, prawns and whiting, are a magnet to fishermen from all over Australia.

The sizeable town (population 16,500) also boasts 40km (25 miles) of clean, sandy Indian Ocean beaches, and caters for diving enthusiasts, windsurfers, surfers, waterskiers and canoeists . . . as well as family swimmers.

But really this is paradise for the amateur fisherman. Rent a boat with outboard motor and some tackle, buy some bait from the locals, and chug up river to what seems a likely spot. A cast or two and the tailor fish will be queuing up to get into the frying pan. Guide the boat around the estuary and you are likely to have a couple of dolphins as escorts, while a curious pelican swoops across the bows.

For accommodation, contact the **Mandurah Tourist Bureau and Travel Centre** (*5 Pinjarra Rd., Mandurah, WA, 6210* ☎ *(095) 35 1155*).

The Pinnacles

260km (163 miles) N. Getting there: by car, via Brand Hwy, turning w to Cervantes a few kilometres s of Badgingarra; by tour bus, from Perth or Cervantes.
The Pinnacles, in the **Nambung National Park**, are limestone formations, the fossilized remains of an ancient forest. Today they stand as eerie windswept golden statues in a desert landscape.

The risk of sand drifts makes the road to the Pinnacles often unsuitable for conventional vehicles. Visitors are urged to join the 4-wheel-drive or air-conditioned bus tours that journey either from Perth or the fishing village of Cervantes into the park. In Perth, contact **Pinnacle Tours** (☎ *364 2603*).

Rottnest Island

Off the coast, 20km (12½ miles) w. Getting there: by sea, Boat Torque Cruise Ferries ☎ 325 6033 (Perth)/335 7181 (Fremantle); by air, Rottnest Airlines ☎ 478 1322. General information: Rottnest Island Board, Rottnest Island, WA, 6161 ☎ (09) 292 5044 ● 95033.
Rottnest is the resort that Western Australians once tried to keep

to themselves. No wonder! This delightfully relaxing island, carefully administered and kept as uncommercial as possible, seems to offer a cure for all the ills of boisterous city life.

There are no private landowners on Rottnest and no private motor vehicles. A small bus provides regular tours of the 11km by 5km (7 by 3 miles) island, but most visitors throw caution to the wind and, provoking muscles almost forgotten, rent a bicycle to get around (☎ *(09) 292 5043*).

Rottnest was named (in translation "Rats Nest") by the Dutch mariner William Vlamingh in 1696 after he mistook for large rats the small rock wallabies that inhabit the island. These unique, endearing marsupials, known as quokkas, roam the island today, tame and well-fed by visitors.

A high-speed ferry takes about 40mins from Fremantle to reach the island; or it is a 10min flight from Perth Airport. Rottnest has a wide range of accommodation, but, over holiday periods and long weekends, it is generally heavily booked. So, if anything longer than a day trip is being considered, it is wise to insure well in advance that you have a place to stay.

Relaxing it may be, but there is much that can be done on Rottnest. There are salt lakes to wallow in, pitted limestone cliffs to explore, picturesque bays with clear turquoise-blue water, and long, white, sandy beaches.

For swimmers, there are plenty of safe beaches, with no sharks or rip tides to worry about. Skin-diving gear is available for hire: on Rottnest you can explore some of the most southerly coral, or the numerous wrecks that can be found on the reef surrounding the island. There is exhilarating surfing, boating and fishing (with crayfish awaiting those who can catch them on the reefs by hand!)

Golf, tennis, bowls and volleyball are available for the energetic. For those less so, there are plenty of places in which to sunbake; the **Quokka Arms** will provide refreshingly chilled drinks in its beer garden overlooking Thomson Bay; and there are glass-bottom boats for a relaxing cruise over the coral.

The **Rottnest Hotel** (☎ *(09) 292 5011* ■) has both hotel and motel rooms, with daily or weekly tariff; **The Rottnest Resort Lodge** (☎ *(09) 292 5026* ■) offers hotel or motel accommodation. Cottages, villas and tents, for those who wish to cater for themselves, are available through the **Rottnest Island Board** (☎ *(09) 292 5044*).

Swan Valley

20-30km (12½-19 miles) NE. Getting there: by car, via Guildford Rd., then Great Northern Hwy; by bus or train, from Perth, Guildford or Midland; by boat, daily cruises from Barrack Street Jetty.

East of Perth, below the Darling Range, the Swan River winds its way through a maze of vineyards and small farms. This is the Swan Valley, which since the 1830s has been producing quality wines.

The Swan Valley covers an area of 104sq.kms (40sq. miles). There are 30 commercial wine producers today; many of the smaller, family vineyards produce under 90,000 litres per vintage, but the larger wineries, such as **Houghton's, Sandalford** and **Valencia**, produce up to 1.5 million litres.

A pleasant and economical way to see the valley is to take a river cruise from the Barrack Street jetty. The boats set off at about 9.45am on a 5hr round trip that includes wine on board, a visit to a vineyard, the chance to sample and buy some of the best wines, lunch ashore, and a look at some of the more scenic reaches of the River Swan.

Yanchep/Atlantis Marine Park
52km (33 miles) N. Getting there: by car, via Wanneroo Rd.
(Route 60); by bus, Ansett Pioneer Tours departs Wed-Sun
12.30pm for Atlantis Marine Park – book through Holiday
WA Centre.

Yanchep, an easy drive N of Perth along the Wanneroo Rd. and
through Wanneroo itself, offers another reasonable day trip.

At **Yanchep National Park** (☎ *(095) 61 1661*) the visitor can
join a guided tour of well-lit limestone caves, or walk around the
lake, where a colony of black swans are forever posing for the
photographers. There are also koalas, wallabies and native birds in
the park – and bushwalks along the **Yanjidi Trail**. For disabled
people, there is the **Boomerang Gorge Nature Trail**. After the
fresh-air exercise, refreshment can be obtained from the
picturesque **Yanchep Inn**.

A short drive away is the **Atlantis Marine Park** (☎ *(095) 61
1600, open 10am-4.30pm*), which is off Sovereign Drive, Yanchep
Sun City. This oceanarium-aquarium features performing seals,
sea lions and dolphins and, to delight the young, a fine family of
non-performers that includes penguins, turtles and swans.

Farther afield

The Holiday WA Centre in Perth can provide details for a wide
range of tours to the regions below and, indeed, to all places
throughout WA. Accommodation varies greatly and should be
booked well in advance wherever possible. Further suggestions are
given in *Planning* – see *Routes 6* and *7*.

The Kimberley

This is the northernmost part of the state, an expanse of land larger
than California, three times the size of England, yet with a
population of less than 10,000. It is rugged and spectacularly
beautiful, one of the hottest places on earth, magnificently wild
and, for the careless or unwary, ruthlessly unforgiving. The best
time to visit is from Apr-Nov, when there are warm, sunny days
and comfortable tropical evenings.

The **West Kimberley** is one of the oldest geological areas on
earth, with rocks estimated at some 2,500 million years old. Time
and weather have carved awesome gorges and mountain ranges;
crystal-clear pools are sheltered by towering cliffs. This is
awe-inspiring country.

The port of **Broome**, about 2,200km (1,375 miles) N of Perth,
was once the centre of the world's pearling industry. Settled in the
1800s, it is today the home of a polyglot community – a mixture of
Malays, Filipinos, Japanese, Chinese, Aboriginals and white
Australians. Well worth considering here is a cruise of the
Kimberley coast aboard a restored pearling lugger. The cruises
range from 2hr trips to extended charters (*bookings and further
details from Broome Tourist Bureau* ☎ *(091) 92 1176*).

Derby, 2,366km (1,479 miles) NE of Perth, is near the mouth of
the Fitzroy River and, because of its location, has become the
administrative centre for the Kimberley. It has a population of just
over 3,000. Tides in the adjoining **King Sound** rise twice daily to
levels of up to 11.8m (39ft) . . . an impressive feat of nature that
can be observed from a 550m (600yd) steel jetty. But, more
important, Derby is the perfect starting point for visitors to
explore the remarkable Gorge country of the Kimberley – **Geikie
Gorge**, with its huge cliffs and waters abounding in freshwater
crocodiles, barramundi, sharks, sawfish and stingrays, and

Windjana Gorge and **Brooking Gorge**. 4-wheel-drive tours are available from Derby (*bookings and details: Derby Tourist Bureau* ☎ *(091) 91 1426*).

There is much to see in the East and West Kimberleys – including the second largest meteorite crater in the world at **Wolf Creek**, 1km (1,100yds) in diameter and 49m (160ft) deep; Australia's largest man-made lake, the **Ord River Dam**; the **Argyle Diamond Mines**; and the "lost world" of the **Bungle Bungle Mountains**. Though a popular tourist region, it is largely undeveloped, and much of it is still only being truly "discovered" today.

Ansett WA (☎ *(09) 478 9222*) offers 5-night fly-and-stay packages to Broome, Derby and Kununurra, which feature accommodation and return air travel from Perth. A rented Avis 4-wheel-drive Toyota Land Cruiser can be added to the package.

East Kimberley Tours (*Box 537, Kununurra, WA, 6743* ☎ *(091) 68 2213/(091) 68 7882*) organize 7-day adventure safaris through the region. These include return airfare from Perth, an experienced bushman as a guide, a 4-wheel-drive vehicle, tent accommodation and all meals.

The Midwest and Northwest

The Midwest, which occupies almost a quarter of the state's total area, extends from the Batavia Coast in the w to the Northern Territory border in the e. **Geraldton**, 424km (265 miles) n of Perth, is the main town (with a population of 18,000) and is an excellent base from which to explore. It is the centre for the multimillion-dollar rock lobster (crayfish) industry.

Skywest (☎ *(09) 478 9898*) has day flights to Geraldton that include a local tour and meal. There are also weekly *Midwest Explorer* flights, which include a bus tour to the beach resort of **Kalbarri**, overnight accommodation, and a journey inland with refreshments on a farm property.

Farther n is the **Gascoyne Region**, with Carnarvon as its main centre. Bananas, pineapples, beans, tomatoes and melons are grown here. Other important local industries are wool from the vast sheep stations and commercial fishing for prawns and scallops. This region, which takes in **Shark Bay**, **Exmouth**, **Monkey Mia** and **Coral Bay**, is tempting for the adventurous traveller. Off the coast, the dazzling blue sea abounds with mackerel, snapper, kingfish, tuna and, for game fishermen, sailfish and marlin. VIP big-game fishing safaris from Exmouth can be arranged through the Holiday WA Centre in Perth.

n of the Gascoyne region is the **Pilbara**, rich in massive iron and mineral deposits. **Port Hedland**, **Dampier**, **Onslow**, **Wittenoom** and **Marble Bar** (whose average daily maximum temperature is 35.67°C or 96.2°F) are its main centres. **East-West Airlines** (☎ *(09) 478 9888*) and **Amesz Adventure Charters** (☎ *(09) 271 2696*) can arrange week-long camping tours of the Pilbara.

The Southwest

Rolling green hills, forests carpeted in wild flowers, meandering rivers, and a patchwork of orchards . . . the Southwest is indeed one of the most attractive and unspoiled parts of Australia. There are trout and marron (freshwater crayfish) in its streams, barely touched sandy beaches on its rim. The vineyards of Margaret River produce some of the country's finest wines – and where better for picnicking than among the karri trees, some soaring to 80m (262ft)?

There are good roads throughout the region, and mostly

accommodation is comfortable, clean and conveniently accessible. Many tours and excursions, by rail, bus or air, are available and can be organized from Perth. Examples:

Westrail (☎ *(09) 326 2690*), the state's rail and bus service, offers a 3-day *Southern Highlights* tour taking in the forests, wineries and coastline, from Perth to Bunbury, Busselton, Margaret River, Bridgetown, Pemberton and Manjimup.

Parlorcars (☎ *(09) 325 5488*) runs a 3-day bus tour, *Margaret River Magic*, that takes in the ocean scenery, the tall timber, vineyards and a marron farm.

The Goldfields

Some 600km (375 miles) E of Perth is **Kalgoorlie**, centre of the Goldfields, a town almost as rich in history as it has been in gold. Paddy Hannan, an Irish-born prospector, first discovered gold here in 1893. His strike set off a gold rush and created the impetus for the development of WA as a whole. Kalgoorlie, which has a population of 23,000, is still the centre for mining and has a "frontier" feel to it even today. From "Kal" and **Boulder**, its twin town, the visitor can travel to the nearby "ghost towns" of **Coolgardie**, **Gwalia** and **Broad Arrow**, all deserted after the precious metal "cut out". Many air, rail and bus tours to the Goldfields can be arranged in Perth. Examples:

Skywest (☎ *(09) 478 9898*) offers a 3-day, 2-night *Diggers Delight* air package that includes gold-detecting, the game of "two-up", a tour of Kalgoorlie/Boulder and the ghost towns, and a visit to the **State Battery** (the gold treatment plant).

Westrail (☎ *(09) 326 2690*) provides a series of rail-bus tours that include transport aboard WA's fastest train, "The Prospector". *Goldrush Explorer*, a 3-day, 2-night package, includes the rail trip and accommodation in Kalgoorlie.

Australian wildlife

Nature has crammed Australia with an extraordinarily diverse range of animals, birds, plants and creatures of the sea – an inheritance so richly rewarding that the tourist or new arrival may initially be surprised by the blasé attitude of many native Australians to the beautiful, colourful and often bizarre creatures about them.

The visitor need not feel so restricted. The rainforests of the N, the wild flowers of Western Australia and the rugged lake district of Tasmania offer their own unique pleasures. And in the Great Barrier Reef, Australia has a haven for marine life of almost every shape, size and colour.

Fauna

Australia is famous for its **marsupials**. There are more than 170 species in the country, classified into 13 "families" of which the largest is the **kangaroo**. More than 45 species thrive here, including the smaller **wallabies**. They are all herbivorous, but can be found in a complete range of habitats throughout Australia. They range in size from the big Red Kangaroo, which may be over 2m (6½ft) tall, to the small Rat Kangaroo, about 30cm (12ins). Visitors who want to see kangaroos in the wild, rather than in the wildlife sanctuaries near the major cities, should plan a trip that takes them away from cultivated farmland and towards the bush. The best time for sighting 'roos, and if you're lucky their young, the joeys, is at sunrise or nearing sunset. There are numerous locations, often signposted as a warning to motorists, around each state capital.

Other marsupials include the **koala** (often and wrongly called the koala bear), the **possum**, the **numbat**, the **marsupial mole**, the **bandicoot**, the **wombat**, the **Tasmanian devil**, and the **thylacine**, or **Tasmanian tiger** (now generally considered extinct).

That unique Australian marsupial, the koala, is one of the country's best-known and most popular animals. Its natural habitats are the forests and woodlands, where it spends its time almost exclusively up a particular species of eucalypt, living contentedly drowzy on a nutritious but mildly narcotic gum leaf. Wombats live in burrows and are known by graziers for their stubborn attitude to fence-poles; rather than detour around one, the wombat simply claws underneath until it collapses.

Australia contains the world's only two **monotremes**, those animals that lay eggs instead of giving birth to their young and are regarded as primitive links between reptiles and mammals. One of these is the **duck-billed platypus**, which is found in freshwater areas of eastern Australia but is shy and difficult to see outside a wildlife sanctuary. When the body of this animal was first taken from the colonies to London at the end of the 18thC, it seemed so bizarre that it was dismissed by many as a fake, a trick that had been sold to gullible travellers. The other monotreme is the **echidna**, or **spiny ant-eater**, a porcupine-like animal that grows to about 45cm (18ins) in length.

Australia's **crocodiles**, found in the estuaries and freshwater lakes of northern and northeastern Australia, have acquired some notoriety in recent years not only because of the Paul Hogan film but also because of several fatal attacks on people in Queensland and the Northern Territory. There are two types: the generally nocturnal **estuarine crocodile**, which grows to 7m (23ft) in length and has been responsible for the attacks on humans, and the **freshwater crocodile**, which grows to about 3m (10ft) and is considered harmless. From 1972 the crocodiles have been protected, but a rise in the number of attacks has brought several calls for a broad culling.

Australia has about 450 of the world's known species of **lizard**, the largest of which, the **Perentie goanna**, grows to 2.5m (8ft). There are more than a hundred species of **snake**, only a few of which are really dangerous to man. However, two of the snakes likely to be encountered in the most populated areas of the eastern seaboard, the **brown** and the **tiger** snakes, have respectively the second and fourth most poisonous venom of any snake in the world. The highly poisonous **taipan** is Australia's biggest venomous snake, growing to about 2m (6½ft) in length. Antivenom is available at most major hospitals.

Among imported animals, **camels** are still to be found wild in the Northern Territory.

Flora

Legislation protects Australia's wild flowers as well as the country's wildlife. Native species may be bought in plant nurseries, but it is generally forbidden to pick Australian flowers in the forest or bush. One seen everywhere is **acacia**, which includes about 700 species of Australian **wattle**. The **golden wattle**, *acacia pycnantha*, is featured on the Australian coat of arms and is the country's floral emblem. Among other well-known native plants is the **waratah**, with its vivid scarlet flowers.

Although the overseas visitor may notice many familiar European and American trees in Australian cities, native **eucalypts** make up about 90 percent of the country's forests and a large proportion of the woodlands. **Baobabs**, only found in the arid country of the NW of Western Australia and in the Northern Territory, have huge bottle-shaped trunks in which moisture is stored. Another spectacular tree is the **Moreton Bay fig**, a sprawling rainforest plant that grows to 40m (131ft) in height and sends the "tentacles" that make up its trunk in all directions.

Birds

Particularly to Europeans accustomed to a more subdued palette, much of Australia's birdlife appears to have been painted by an artist with a manic desire to experiment with every colour in the rainbow. And outside the cities, the shattering din of early-morning birdcalls will astound the first-time visitor.

There are some 700 species of birds in Australia, about 400 of which live within the island continent. Others are migratory, spending a part of the year in the country and the remainder overseas. To the bird-lover, the treasures of Australian flight are its **cockatoos** and **parrots**, of which there are 60 species. Among the more prolific cockatoos are the **gang-gangs** of southeastern Australia, the pink-and-grey **galahs** and the white-and-yellow-plumed **sulphur-crested cockatoo**. Another colourful species of parrot to be found in the E of the country is the **rosella**, which lives in forests and woodlands, where it nests in the hollows of trees. At the other end of the scale from such friendly small parrots as the native **budgerigar** is the **emu**, the second-largest bird in the world. It can grow up to about 1.4m (4½ft) tall; like the ostrich and its native relative the **cassowary** it does not fly, but can run at speeds of up to 40kph (25mph). The **southern cassowary**, which has a vivid blue neck and a flat, black, horny crown on its head, grows up to about 1.5m (5ft) tall and can be found in northeastern Queensland.

Australia has ten species of **kingfisher**, the best known of which is the **kookaburra**, whose unique call resembles human laughter. Kookaburras are found throughout eastern Australia. Over the years, they have also been called "laughing jackass", "the bushman's clock" and "ha ha pigeon". Other familiar natives include the **frogmouth**, a nocturnal bird with flat, crumpled bills surrounded by bristles, and **bellbirds**, which are so called because of their pinging, chimelike calls.

One family of birds, the **diggers**, has devised a unique way of adapting to the harsh climate, incubating its eggs by burying them in mounds of soil and decaying vegetation. The **scrub fowl**, **brush turkey** and **mallee fowl** are all diggers.

Finally, Australia has its **black swans**, which have been known to Europeans since Dutch explorer Willem de Vlamingh first saw them in 1697, near what was later to become Perth. These large, elegant birds with distinctive red beaks breed in colonies, unlike the white swans, which live in pairs.

Fish

There are about 20 "families" of **shark**, most having representatives in Australian coastal waters. Their presence, particularly along the eastern seaboard, is a good reason for swimmers to frequent patrolled or protected beaches. Great whites, blue pointers, tiger sharks and **whaler sharks** have attacked people, and **hammerhead sharks** have come under suspicion. On the other hand, Australians also regularly attack the local sharks, eating shark meat as "flake" in their fish 'n' chips.

There are some 3,000 different species of fish in Australian waters. In and around the coral reefs that bracket Australia from both oceans is a multitude of exotic, brilliantly coloured fish. But it is in the colder waters that commercial fishermen catch such fish as snapper, flounder, trevally and John Dory. The best-known of Australia's freshwater fish is the barramundi, although this Aboriginal name is given to several species. The most common use is for the giant perch, a restaurant delicacy; it grows to 1.8m (6ft) long and can weigh 50kg (10lbs). The Murray cod, Murray perch and Tasmania's trout are also among the country's finest food and sporting fish.

Marine life to stay well away from? Rays are plentiful in Australian waters, their tails often armed with serrated spines that can inflict painful wounds. Avoid the highly poisonous porcupine fish, bluebottles (the jellyfish also known as the Portuguese man-of-war) and the blue-ringed octopus (in or out of the water). These are to be found in waters ranging from warm-temperate to tropical. And it is wise not to handle the crown-of-thorns starfish, whose poisonous spines can become embedded. The crown-of-thorns, which feeds on coral polyps, infested large areas of the Great Barrier Reef in the 1970s, causing great concern and sparking off several scientific investigations.

And things that bite and crawl. . . .
Everything thrives in the Australian climate, including some insects and crawly creatures that endear themselves only to producers of television wildlife documentaries.

There are about 1,700 species of spiders – cobweb, sheet-web and orb-web weavers. They include the redback, which is poisonous and related to the black widow spider of North America, and the Sydney funnel-web, an aggressive and venomous spider that lives in a funnel-shaped web over a shallow burrow.

Australia also has about 1,500 species of ant. In the N of Australia, termite mounds are a familiar sight; they are built up to 7m (23ft) high.

An immediately noticeable pest is the fly. There are more than 6,250 species, the house variety and biting bush-flies among them. Their presence is responsible for the too-familiar wave across a person's face that has become known as "the Australian salute".

Far more attractive to the visitor are the 11,000 species of butterflies and moths that thrive in Australia. Witchetty grubs, which are a delicacy to tribal Aborigines and may be offered to the visitor in some parts, are the larva of the large cossid moth.

Australian wine

The Australian wine industry has come a long way from the days of Emu sherry and now can claim recognition as a serious producer of quality wines comparable with many older-established producers. Moreover, Australian wine is surprisingly cheap by world standards.

Australia and the grape go back to the very beginnings of European settlement, vine cuttings being among the specimens brought out with the First Fleet. Despite its long history the industry has only begun to be taken seriously outside Australia in the past 10-15 years, although at home good wine has been appreciated by a select few for many years.

The advent, more than 20 years ago, of the wine cask (or bag in a box, as it is known in Britain), claimed as an Australian invention, brought wine to the masses, and consumption started to take off. More than 60 percent of Australia's consumption is now "cask" wine, usually made from Sultana grapes grown in irrigated areas such as the Riverina of NSW and the Sunraysia area of northwestern Victoria.

Despite the wine snobs who despise cask wine, which could be truly called Australia's *vin ordinaire*, it has allowed wine drinking to become an everyday habit in very many Australian homes. Retailing for between A\$6 and A\$7 (£2.60-£3) the 4-litre cask represents outstanding value and, for the price, excellent quality – certainly far superior to *vin ordinaire* drunk in France.

The cask-led wine boom now means that Australians consume 21.4 litres per head a year, well ahead of countries like Britain and the USA but still way behind such nations as France and Italy. However, it is for quality that Australian wines are now making a name for themselves.

In the late 1940s and 1950s few people believed that Australia could produce anything other than indifferent fortified wines and that the climate was too hot for the production of quality table wine. Technology and research enabled Australia to overcome that problem. The wine industry then had a naming problem – and a belief that Australian-produced wine had to correspond to a French wine type. Hence "Australian claret" or "Australian Burgundy". Now, however, Australian wine is being labelled and sold on its merits by grape varieties, and the era of the "varietal" wine has arrived.

Most good-quality wines have labels that carry a wealth of information, including grape type, alcohol by volume (a legal requirement in most states), and grape sugar level at harvest, as well as a brief description of the type of wine and what food it would partner best.

In the past two decades there has been an enormous increase in the number of small or so-called "boutique" wineries run by dedicated experts or self-taught *vignerons*. These wineries have been in the van of developing varietal wines and matching grape types to regional climates and in some cases even micro-climates.

The boutique wineries have grown up in such areas as the Yarra Valley, about 50km (30 miles) N of Melbourne, and in the Hunter Valley of NSW, as well as the Barossa and Clare valleys of South Australia. The Margaret River area sw of Perth in Western Australia has emerged as one of the most exciting new wine regions, producing some magnificent reds as well as fine white wines.

This pioneering work has not been confined to the boutique wineries, and some of the older established wineries, like Brown Bros of Victoria NE, have made great strides in cool fermentation techniques.

South Australia is the leading wine-producing state. Most of the state's production is concentrated in an area around Adelaide. The Barossa Valley, starting about 50km (30 miles) NE of the city, is the most famous of the state's wine districts. It was settled by German migrants in the 1840s and retains a distinctly Germanic air about it. There are more than 35 wineries in the vallery, nearly all open for tasting. Farther N of the city is the Clare Valley, an area of rolling hills and farmlands spotted with fine wineries.

The odd man out in South Australia is the Coonawarra district in the extreme SE of the state and isolated from the other major wine regions. A narrow strip of volcanic soil about 10km (6 miles) long, the so called terra rosa, produces arguably some of Australia's finest red wines. A good Coonawarra Cabernet Sauvignon can hold its own with some of the finest products of Bordeaux.

The Hunter Valley, which starts about 200km (125 miles) N of

Sydney, has a justifiable reputation as one of the country's leading regions. Its full-blooded reds are much in demand. The Hunter Valley has achieved great results with its small plantings of Semillon grapes, but as these white wines are much sought after they can be hard to find. They are well worth the effort.

Australia's wine industry is full of surprises and contradictions. For example, wine from heavily irrigated areas has tended to lack class, yet the "Sauternes" produced by De Bortolis of Griffith in the NSW Riverina irrigation area have been favourably compared with the products of Château Yquem.

The other delight is, of course, the civilised habit that Australian wineries have of offering prospective customers a taste of their latest product. The cellar-door sales and tasting are a tradition, and some wineries are more generous than others – a trap if one is driving.

Sparkling wine, it should be noted, is now so inexpensive as to be almost an everyday drink. All the better makes are produced by the traditional *méthode champanoise*.

The interest shown by such world-famous names as Rémy Martin, who have acquired interests in Australian producers, and recent international awards in London and other centres, are sure signs that the local industry has come of age.

Sport in Australia

"Sport to many Australians is life and the rest a shadow. . . . To play sport, or watch others play, and to read and talk about it is to uphold the nation and build its character," wrote Donald Horne in *The Lucky Country*.

Horne's analysis was written in the 1960s, but there is no reason to suppose that his findings are any less true today. Australians are close to being fanatical about playing sport, and, as spectators, take to all forms of it. Take the America's Cup (which Australia did in 1983 to end 112 years of American domination). Interest in the Cup became a national passion when *Australia II*, skippered by John Bertrand, beat the American entry *Liberty*, skippered by Dennis Conner, and the nation was transfixed again by Connor's gutsy recovery of the trophy in the stiff breezes off Fremantle four years later.

Horseracing

Australia's love of horseracing is perhaps best illustrated by the way it reacts to its most famous race, the Melbourne Cup, which began in 1861 and is held on the first Tuesday in November at Melbourne's Flemington Racecourse. The Cup, the highlight of Victoria's Spring Racing Carnival and a public holiday in Melbourne, is considered one of the most colourful races in the world by turf enthusiasts. It draws a crowd of more than 100,000, attracts some of the most bizarre fashions seen outside a Fellini movie, offers more than a million dollars in prize money, and around the country everything stops while it is run.

There are currently more than 450 flat- and harness-racing tracks throughout Australia; the better-known include Rosehill, Randwick and Warwick Farm in NSW, Caulfield and Flemington in Victoria, Eagle Farm and Albion Park in Queensland, Victoria Park in South Australia, Elwick in Tasmania, and Ascot and Belmont in Western Australia.

Visitors may note TAB (Totalizator Agency Board) shops, with windows for computerized betting on race meetings, in all cities.

The state-controlled betting organization, TAB, is comparable to New York State's off-track betting system. Its original totalizator, or pari-mutuel machine, and the photo-finish camera used on the tracks were both invented in Australia.

Cricket

The great summer sport in Australia is cricket, both for spectators and for players. Australian fanaticism for the game is only matched by that among the followers of its greatest rivals, the West Indies and England. The fierce rivalry with the English probably goes back to 1882, when "the colonies" won their first cricketing match "back home" in England. From that arose The Ashes, an urn containing the ashes of a burned cricket stump. These now remain permanently in the Members' Pavilion at Lord's Cricket Ground in London, but the term "The Ashes" has come to stand for cricket's ultimate prize. Rivalry between the two countries reached its peak in 1933, in "The Bodyline Series". The English, facing what promised to be an unassailable performance from Australia's greatest batsman, Don Bradman, decided to bombard the Australian batsmen with short-pitched deliveries.

The series created a great anti-English sentiment. Politicians in both countries became involved; Australian unionists called for a boycott of British goods. Ultimately, "bodyline" changed the game. The rules were modified and batsmen began padding their bodies against future bowling onslaughts. England won the Ashes that year, but Australia, under the brilliant leadership of Bradman, bounced back in the next series.

Cricket was raised to full professional status, and nudged rudely into the TV Age, with World Series Cricket, which was launched by Australian magazine and television magnate Kerry Packer in the 1970s. WSC, inspired perhaps by what had been happening in televised sport in the USA, introduced such innovations as floodlit night cricket, coloured kit and big incentives for star performers like bowler Dennis Lillee. The changes caused shudders among cricketing "purists" on both sides of the globe.

Football

Australians enjoy four kinds of football, each with a passion verging on the religious. Amateur Rugby Union is played enthusiastically throughout the country; professional Rugby League is the main spectator sport in Queensland and NSW; soccer, although increasingly popular in schools, is still mainly favoured by immigrants; and Australian Rules, a spectacular game said to stem from Gaelic football, attracts the biggest crowds and is played in Western Australia, South Australia, Tasmania and Victoria.

Tennis and other sports

Between 1956 and 1970 there were ten all-Australian Wimbledon finals. In the 1960s and 1970s Australian tennis champions included Ken Rosewall, Lew Hoad, Roy Emerson, Neale Fraser (now coaching the Australian Davis Cup squad), Rod Laver and John Newcombe; and in 1987 Pat Cash triumphed memorably at Wimbledon. Australia has also produced a number of world-ranking women players, including that supreme player Margaret Court, who won at Wimbledon in 1963, and the skilfully graceful part-Aboriginal player Evonne Goolagong, winner in 1971 and 1980.

In sports such as swimming and golf, Australia is hardly less pre-eminent, with fine facilities from its pools and tracks to some of the most delightfully landscaped courses imaginable. There have been notable successes too in motor-racing, cycling, sailing, and in the increasingly competitive international surfing events.

Special information

Sport for the participant

Australians, it seems, are game for anything that moves, provides a challenge, calls for stamina, needs a stopwatch, and allows the ecstasy of victory. And there may be a special need to be satisfied Down Under. When you live so far away, it can be comforting to make the rest of the world stand up occasionally and take notice.

The spin-off of Australia's sporting excellence is that sporting facilities are generally excellent and extensive and cost often a fraction of what visitors can expect to pay in their own country. This, coupled with a benign climate, makes Australia, to use that well-worn cliché, a sportsman's paradise. Virtually every town or small community has its tennis courts, and golf courses too are surprisingly plentiful. For example, a country town of 8,500 people about 200km (125 miles) NE of Melbourne typically has 20 lawn tennis courts, more than half a dozen squash courts, a golf course and numerous other facilities.

Sport in country areas is even more important than in the cities, as it is the hub of social activity. Although tennis courts in Australia are frequently leased or owned by clubs, facilities are usually available for visitors under the status of temporary membership or on a simple hire basis as a member's guest. There are also many public courts usually owned by the local municipality. Hotels, if they do not have their own tennis courts, can usually arrange for guests to hire local courts.

Public indoor tennis courts have mushroomed in state capital city suburbs in recent years. They are easy to hire during the day, but it may be hard to get a court in the evening without booking some days ahead. Squash is also extremely popular, and there are courts for hire in most suburbs, again more easily during the day than in the evening.

Golf is a game enjoyed by all classes of Australian society. By world standards it is inexpensive. Japanese visitors find the cost of golf in the country so cheap that a few games can go a long way to paying for their air fare when compared to green fees payable in their own country.

Australian courses are among the finest in the world. Around Melbourne, for example, is a sandy belt of land near Port Phillip Bay that boasts some of the finest courses anywhere. These so-called sandbelt courses are a delight. Many municipalities have their own public courses of a high standard and charge reasonable green fees, around A$5-A$10.

Increasingly visitors to Australia are heading N to the Great Barrier Reef for skin diving (some of the best in the world), sailing through the reef islands, and big-game fishing for marlin, which attracts the wealthy and famous. In Queensland, with its subtropical-to-tropical climate, you can waterski, wind surf, sail, skin dive, swim, surf and fish to your heart's content. Wind surfers, surf boards, canoes or pedal craft and so on can be hired at most resorts, in Queensland and around the country.

For the adventuresome, cross-country horse riding in the Australian Alps in Victoria and NSW is increasingly popular, particularly since the film *The Man from Snowy River* made the area better known to visitors and locals alike. And skiing in the Snowy Mountains of NSW is becoming increasingly popular.

Virtually all the equipment needed for the more common sports can be hired in Australia, so there is no need to burden yourself with equipment. All that is really needed for a sporting holiday in Australia is plenty of enthusiasm, particularly if playing against the locals. For Australians like only one thing more than playing, and that's winning.

Index

Within this index are listed towns and other places of interest covered in this book; major entries, important sights and general categories such as hotels, restaurants and places nearby form sub-entries. Important sights and places of interest are also listed separately, both under their common names and in general categories such as Museums or Beaches. Important artists, novelists etc. are also listed. Specific hotels, restaurants and shops are not indexed individually but are easily located within *A to Z* entries.

Page numbers in **bold** indicate the main entries; page numbers in *italic* refer to illustrations and two-colour maps.

Index

Index

Index

Index

Index

Index

AUSTRALIA

1

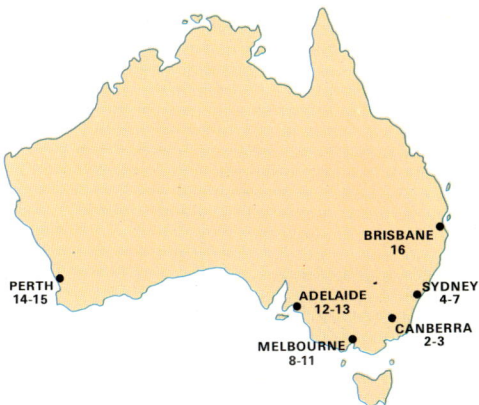

BRISBANE
16

PERTH
14-15

ADELAIDE
12-13

SYDNEY
4-7

CANBERRA
2-3

MELBOURNE
8-11

LEGEND

City Maps

- ▬ Major Place of Interest
- ▬ Other Important Building
- ▬ Built-up Area
- ▬ Park
- ✝ † Named Church, church
- ☾ Mosque
- ✡ Synagogue
- ✚ Hospital
- *i* Information Office
- ✉ Post Office
- ✋ Police Station
- 🅿 Car Park
- → One Way Street
- ▦ Stepped Street

Environs Maps

- ■ Place of Interest
- ▬ Built-up Area
- ▬ Wood or Park
- ═○═ Freeway (with access point)
- ═ ═ Freeway under construction
- ▬ Main Road
- ▬ Secondary Road
- ▬ Other Road
- ▬▬► Railway
- ✈ Airport
- 𝒳 Good Beach

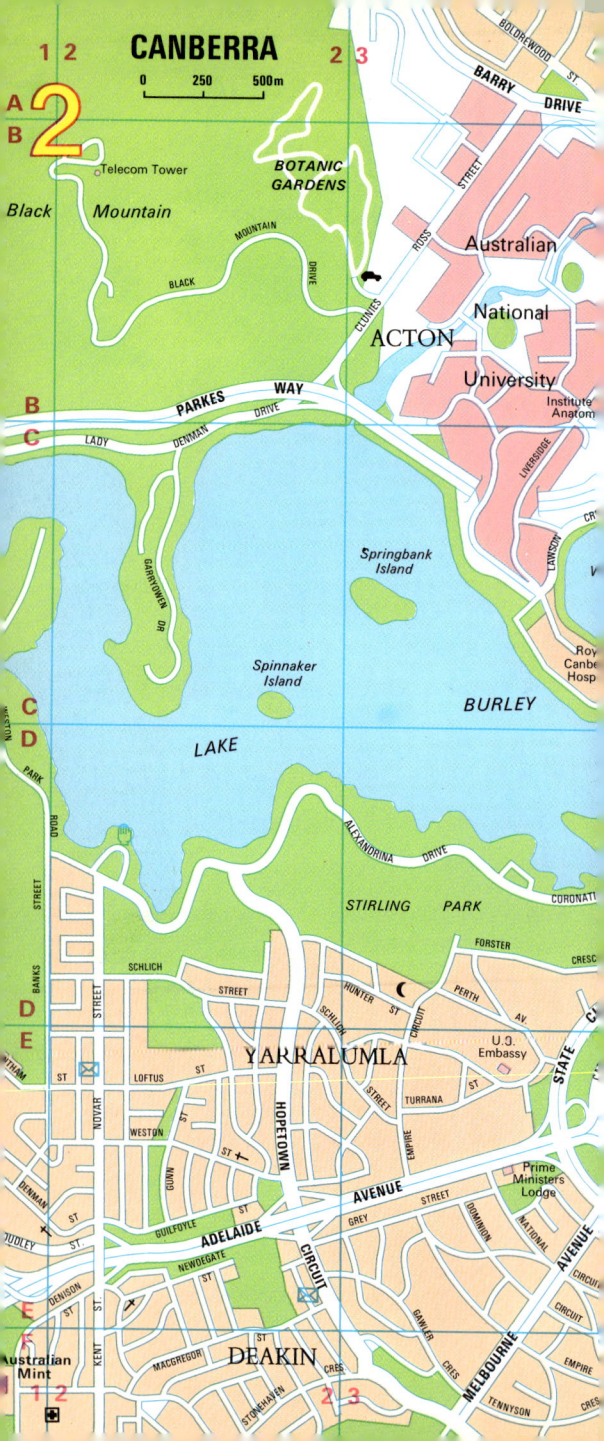

CANBERRA

0   250   500m

A
B

2

1 2 · · · 2 3

Telecom Tower

BOTANIC GARDENS

Black Mountain

MOUNTAIN

BLACK

DRIVE

BOLDREWOOD ST

BARRY DRIVE

STREET

ROSS

CLUNIES

ACTON

Australian National University

Institute Anatom

B

PARKES WAY

DRIVE

LADY

DENMAN

GARRYOWEN DR

LIVERSIDGE

LAWSON

CR

V

C

WESTON

Springbank Island

Spinnaker Island

LAKE

BURLEY

Roy Canbe Hosp

C
D

PARK ROAD

STREET

ALEXANDRINA DRIVE

CORONATI

STIRLING PARK

FORSTER CRESC

BANKS STREET

SCHLICH

STREET

SCHLICH

HUNTER

CIRCUIT

PERTH AV

D
E

STREET

NTHAM

ST

LOFTUS ST

NOVAR

WESTON

GUNN ST

ST

GUILFOYLE

YARRALUMLA

HOPETOWN

STREET

TURRANA

EMPIRE

U.O. Embassy

STATE

Prime Ministers Lodge

ADELAIDE

AVENUE

GREY

STREET

DOMINION

NATIONAL

AVENUE

CIRCUIT

DENMAN

ST

DUDLEY

ST

DENISON ST

NEWEGATE

CIRCUIT

E
F

Australian Mint

KENT ST

MACGREGOR

ST

DEAKIN

STONEHAVEN

CRES

GAWLER

CRES

MELBOURNE

CRES

EMPIRE

TENNYSON

1 2 · · · 2 3

BRADDON

MASSON ST

GIRRAHWEEN 4 5

ST

STREET

FARRER

LIMESTONE

ST

CHISHOLM

5 6

ST

3 A B

GOULD ST

MOORE

ST

ELOUERA

ELDER

ST

AVENUE

NORTHBOURNE

AVENUE

WATSON

DRIVE

COOYONG ST

LONSDALE

ST

TORRENS

DONALDSON

ST

DONINGONA

Questacon
Science Centre

QUICK

ST

RUDD ST

ALINGA ST

BALLUMBIR

BUNDA

AVENUE

AVENUE

ST

UNIVERSITY CLARK

AV.

Civic
Centre

i

AINSLIE

TRELOAR

Australian
War Memorial

NARCISS

LONDON

VERNON
Law
Courts

CIRCUIT

AKUNA

ST

ST

CURRONG

ST

CHURONG

RIMATTA

GUREE

ST

Reid
Park

ST

FAIRBAIRN
AV.

B
C

CITY

my
nce

EDINBURGH
AV.

CIRCLE

CIRCUIT

CONSTITUTION

REID

CORANDERRK

AMAROO

ANZAC

PARADE

CRESWELL

BLAMEY

CAMPBELL

ry
inal
asin

PARKES

WAY

St John
the Baptist

AVENUE

ST

BLAMEY
CRES.

COMMONWEALTH
PARK

Regatta Point
Planning Exhibition

ROFELIA

RUSSELL

DR.

GRIFFIN

Captain Cook
Memorial

Blundell's
Cottage

Central
Basin

PARKES

WAY

C
D

AVENUE

National
Library

PLACE

Aspen
Island

KINGS
PARK

Australian
American
Memorial

COMMONWEALTH

DRIVE

KING

LANGTON

PARKES

PARKES

EDWARD

ST

High
Court

Carillon

National
Gallery

KINGS

MORSHEAD

DR.

RIVE
tish
assy
dian
assy

KING GEORGE TERRACE

TERRACE

BOWEN

AVENUE

GREVILLE
PARK

D
E

cle

QUEEN VICTORIA TERRACE

Parliament
House

G.P.O.

PLACE

AVENUE

East
Basin

lew Parliament
House
der construction)

KINGS

BARTON

BLACKALL

ST

BOWEN

DR.

Bowen
Park

BRISBANE

AVENUE

PITAL

CRES.

STATE

CIRCLE

CIRCUIT

YORK
PARK

NATIONAL

SYDNEY
AV

MACQUARIE

PARK

TELOPEA

WENTWORTH

MUNDARING

ORREST

HOBART
AV

CANBERRA

AV.

Serbian
Church

MANUKA

TELOPEA

GILES

HOWITT

AVENUE

MILDURA

E
F

COLLINS
PARK

CIRCUIT

FURNEAUX

ST

4 5

CIRCLE

KINGSTON

OXLEY

LEICHHARDT ST

Canberra
Railway Station

5 6

SYDNEY ENVIRONS

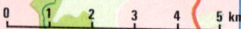

KOALA PARK

Pennant Hills Park

Ku-ring-gai Nat. Park (

0   1   2   3   4   5 km

Windsor

4

1   2   3

Cheltenham

30

A

Baulkham Hills

Epping

28

Carlingford

28

40

Northmead

Eastwood

55

30

33

North Parramatta

Dundas

Ryde

40

B

Ermington

40

Putney

32

PARRAMATTA

Glades

C

Merrylands

F4

Parramatta

33

Western   Freeway

Auburn

Concord

Guildford

33

Lidcombe

32

STRATHFIELD

rfield

Ashfie

Camden, amphelltown

Regents Park

Enfield

C

31

Hume   Highway

D

31

Yagoona

33

Campsie

Canterb

54

BANKSTOWN

BANKSTOWN

Punchbowl

Milperra

54

Bexley

55

Revesby

D

Riverwood

55

E

East Hills

55

Hurstville

33

Military Reserve

Princes Hig

61

Alfords Point

Lugarno

Blakehurst

Georges   River

Oyster Bay

Sylvania

E

Menai

1

F

64

1   2

3

Cari

Sutherland

Gymea

↙ Royal Nat. Park

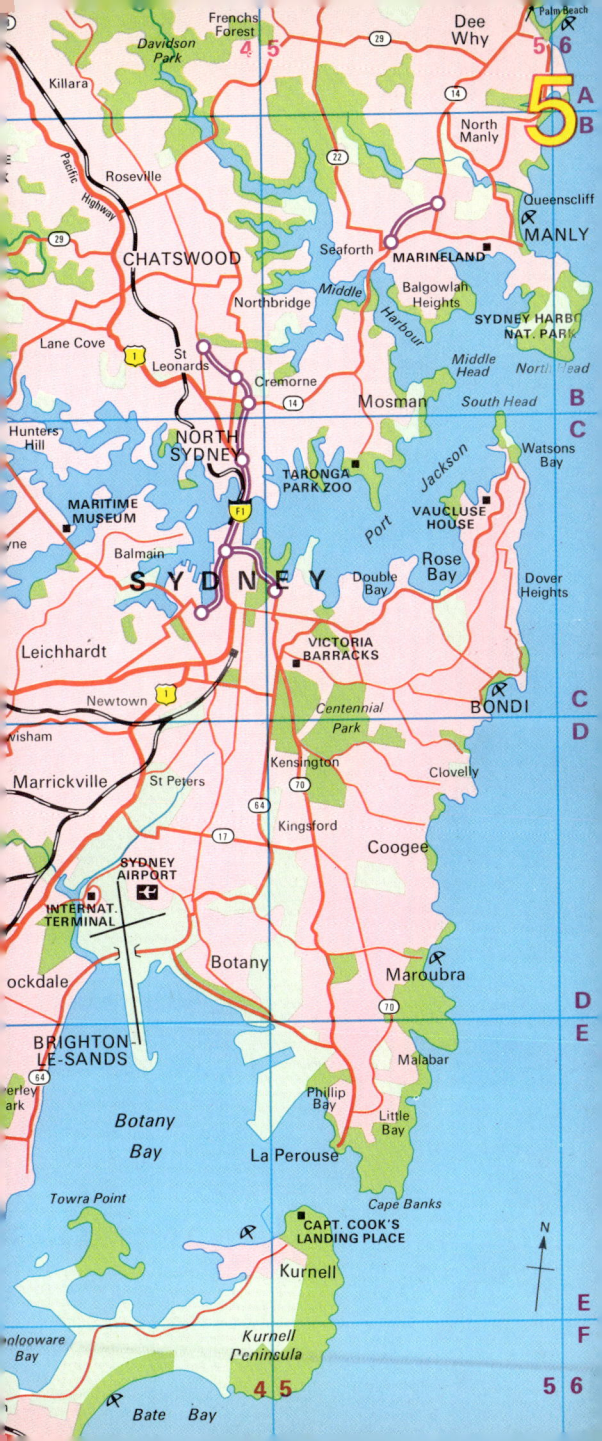

4 5
5 6

5

A

B

Frenchs Forest

Davidson Park

Dee Why

29

14

Killara

North Manly

Roseville

Pacific Highway

22

29

CHATSWOOD

Seaforth

MARINELAND

Queenscliff

MANLY

Northbridge

Balgowlah Heights

SYDNEY HARBO NAT. PAR

Middle Harbour

Lane Cove

1

St Leonards

Cremorne

Middle Head

North Head

Hunters Hill

NORTH SYDNEY

14

Mosman

South Head

B

C

TARONGA PARK ZOO

Jackson

Watsons Bay

MARITIME MUSEUM

F1

Port

VAUCLUSE HOUSE

Balmain

SYDNEY

Double Bay

Rose Bay

Dover Heights

Leichhardt

VICTORIA BARRACKS

Newtown

1

Centennial Park

BONDI

C

D

isham

Kensington

Clovelly

Marrickville

St Peters

70

Coogee

64

Kingsford

17

SYDNEY AIRPORT

INTERNAT. TERMINAL

Botany

Maroubra

ockdale

70

D

E

BRIGHTON-LE-SANDS

Malabar

64

erley ark

Phillip Bay

Little Bay

Botany Bay

La Perouse

Cape Banks

Towra Point

CAPT. COOK'S LANDING PLACE

N

Kurnell

nlooware Bay

Kurnell Peninsula

E

F

Bate Bay

4 5
5 6

SYDNEY

Pier One

Sydney
Harbour
Bridge

Bennel

0 100 200 300 400 500m

6

A
1 2
2 3
3

Sydney

Cove

THE
ROCKS

MILLERS
POINT

TOWNS PL
HICKSON ROAD
WINDMILL ST
ARGYLE PL
ARGYLE ST
KENT ST
HIGH ST
FORT ST
LOWER
BRADFIELD
CUMBERLAND ST
GLOUCESTER
HARRINGTON
GEORGE STREET

Observatory

BRADFIELD HIGHWAY

CIRCULAR QUAY

Passenger
Terminal

Maritime
Services
Board

6 5 4 3 2 1

Circular Quay
Station

Darling

Harbour

B

C

CAHILL EXPRESSWAY

CIRCULAR QUAY

Customs House

PITT ST
LOFTUS ST
YOUNG STREET
PHILLIP STREET
MACQUARIE STREET

MACQUARIE
PLACE

State Gove
Offic

GROSVENOR
ST

BRIDGE STREET

BENT ST

LANG
JAMISON ST

Australia
Sq. Tower

O'CONNELL ST
BLIGH ST

CHIFLEY
SQUARE

HUNTER ST

Wynyard
Station

WESTERN DISTRIBUTOR

MARGARET ST
ERSKINE ST
KENT
SUSSEX
CLARENCE
YORK
GEORGE STREET
PITT ST
CASTLEREAGH

CITY

Martin
Place
Station

C

D

MARTIN PLACE

G.P.O.

KING ST

M.L.C.
Centre

St
James

St James
Station

STRAND
ARCADE

David
Jones

Centrepoint

Archibald
Fountain

HYDE

KING STREET
MARKET STREET

Queen
Victoria
Bldg

Hilton
International

ELIZABETH STREET
COLLEGE

DRUITT ST

Town Hall

PARK STREET

Town Hall
Station

PARK

St Andrews
Cathedral

D

E

BATHURST STREET

PITT
CASTLEREAGH STREET

Museum Station

Anzac
Memorial

LIVERPOOL STREET

WHITLA

DIXON STREET
PIER ST
GEORGE STREET

CHINATOWN

GOULBURN

Power House
Museum

MACARTHUR
ULTIMO

Entertainment
Centre

CAMPBELL

WENTWORTH
COMMONWEALTH

Paddy's
Market

HAY STREET

Belmore
Park

RESERVOIR

ALBION ST

E

F

1 2

MARY ANN ST
RD

Museum of
Applied Arts
& Sciences

BARLOW ST

2 3

Central Railway
Station

EDDY AV.

ANN

SURR

dney pera ouse

Mrs. Macquaries Point

Mrs Macquaries Chair

Garden Island Naval Dockyard

vernment House

Farm Cove

THE DOMAIN

MRS MACQUARIES RD

Woolloomooloo Bay

Capt. Cook Dock

B C

servatorium of Music

ROYAL BOTANIC GARDENS

THE

Elizabeth Bay

CRES

WHARF RD

BROADWAY

WYLDE ST

McELHONE

STREET

CHALLIS AV

MACLEAY STREET

nt House

THE

ART GALLERY RD

LINCOLN CRES

COWPER

ST

Elizabeth Bay House

C D

Art Gallery of NSW

ilding um)

DOMAIN

NICHOLSON ST

ONSLOW AV

ITHACA RD

GREENKNOWE AV

rar Generals Bldg.

WOOLLOOMOOLOO

SIR JOHN YOUNG CRES

HUGHES ST

VICTORIA STREET

BROUGHAM ST

ORWELL ST

ROAD

WARATAH

Mary's thedral

CATHEDRAL ST

DOWLING ST

KINGS CROSS

PALMER STREET

DARLINGHURST

Kings Cross Station

WARD AV

ROSLYN ST

St Luke's Hospital

RANG ST

AV

FORBES STREET

BAYSWATER RD

D E

WILLIAM STREET

stralian Museum

KINGS CROSS ROAD

CRAIGEND STREET

RILEY ST

CROWN ST

BOURKE STREET

ROAD

SURREY

WOMERAH AV

BARCOM AV

McLACHLAN AV

NEILD AV

LIVERPOOL STREET

DARLINGHURST

BURTON ST

FORBES ST

DARLINGHURST ST

VICTORIA ST

St Vincent's Hospital

GLENVIEW ST

BOUNDARY ST

BROWN ST

LAW

E F

xford

STREET

TAYLOR SQUARE

FLINDERS ST

OXFORD ST

PADDINGTON

GLENMORE ROAD

CROWN ST

RILEY ST

BOURKE ST

NAPIER ST

ORMOND ST

HILLS

4 5 5 6

GERTRUDE ST

ST

ST

ST

ST

LANGRIDGE ST

BRUNSWICK
NAPIER
GEORGE
GORE
SMITH
WELLINGTON
ROKEBY

VICTORIA PARADE

EAST

Brigade
useum

North
Richmond
Station

ALBERT STREET

Parliament
House

St Patrick's
Cathedral

MELBOURNE

GREY STREET

HODDLE ST

Hotel Windsor

MACARTHUR ST

Treasury
Building

Fitzroy Gardens

GIPPS STREET

West Richmond
Station

Model
Village

CLARENDON ST

POWLETT ST

SIMPSON ST

Treasury

STREET

Gardens

Capt. Cook's
Cottage

Collins
Place

Hilton
International

GEORGE STREET

West Richmond
Station

B
C

LANE

WELLINGTON PARADE

WELLINGTON PARADE SOUTH

STREET

Jolimont
Station

ROAD

B

PUNT

C

JOLIMONT ST

VALE ST

**Melbourne
Cricket
Ground**

AVENUE

PARADE

BRUNTON

AVENUE

C
D

en Victoria
Gardens

SWAN STREET

Yarra Park

ROAD

Sydney Myer
Music Bowl

ALEXANDRA

SOUTH

Yarra

PUNT

ks Centre
Victoria

Kings Domain

EASTERN

FREEWAY

KILDA ROAD

LINLITHGOW AV

Government
House

River

AVENUE

Victoria
Barracks

BIRDWOOD

Old
Observatory

ANDERSON ST

D
E

Com
Hous
2km

La Trobe's
Cottage

**ROYAL BOTANIC
GARDENS**

AVENUE

Shrine of
Remembrance

DOMAIN RD

DOMAIN RD

PARK STREET

ST

BROMBY ST

ST

ST

SOUTH

DOMAIN ST

MILLSWYN ST

PARK ST

WALSH ST

YARRA

KILDA ROAD

PUNT ROAD

TOORAK ROAD

E
F

ALBERT ST

QUEENS RD

Albert Park

*Fawkner
Park*

4 5 5 6

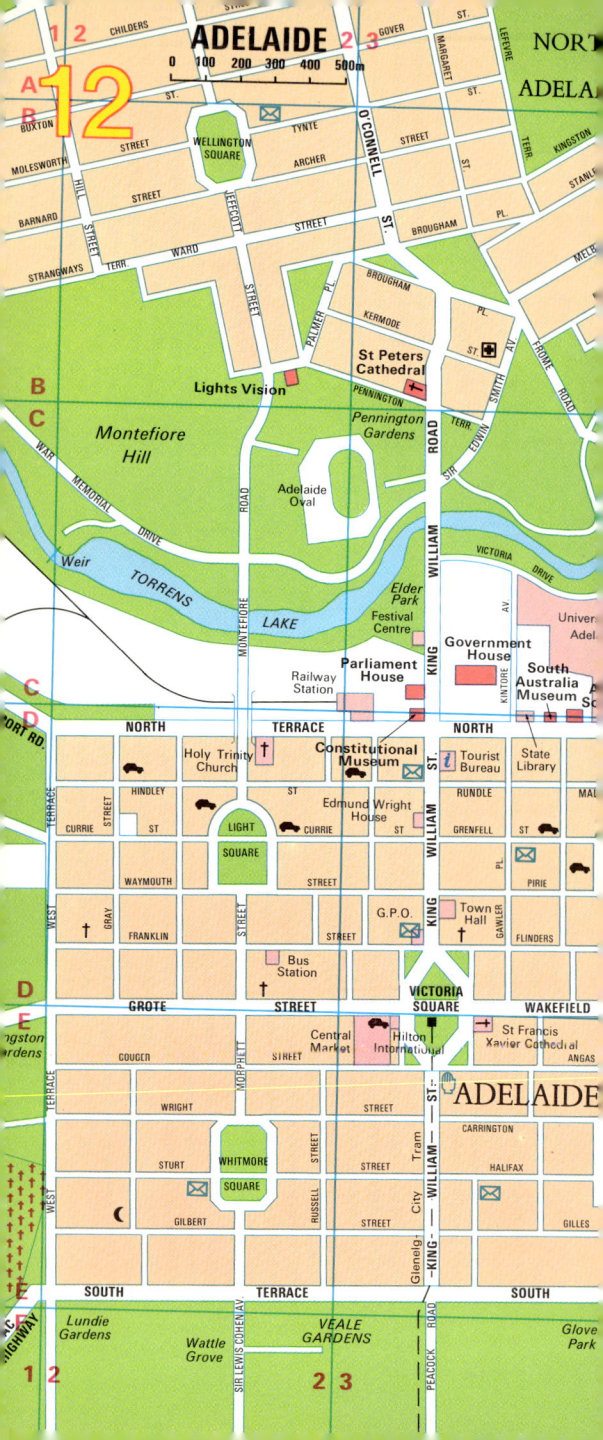

13

A
B

5 6

A
B

GILBERT ST
RIVER STREET
STEPHEN AV.
EIGHTH
SEVENTH AV.

ROSE ST
MANN
PARK TERRACE
River Torrens
SIXTH
FIFTH
ST PETERS
ST
FOURTH
THIRD
SECOND
FIRST AV.
AVENUE TERR.
AVENUE

STREET
STREET
MACKINNON
PARADE
BUNDEYS RD.

RICHMOND
TORRENS
ST.
HATSWELL ST.
COLLEGE ST.
PETERS
HARROW
ROAD

MEMORIAL DRIVE
HACKNEY ROAD
DRIVE

PEMBROKE
ST.
RUGBY
PAYNEHAM
RD.

B
C

logical
dens

BOTANIC
Botanic Park

HACKNEY

MAGILL RD.

CHAPEL ST

NORTH
TERRACE

BOTANIC GARDENS

Royal Adelaide Hospital

STREET
KING
WILLIAM
COLLEGE
STREET
FULLARTON
BEULAH RD.

KENT

C
D

TERRACE
Ayers House
EAST
TERR.

BOTANIC ROAD

RUNDLE ROAD
RUNDLE
PARADE
TOWN
WEST
RD
THE PARADE

RYMILL PARK
DEQUETTEVILLE
FLINDERS
STREET
WAKEFIELD
ST
CHARLES
WILLIAM
STREET

ST
STREET
BARTELS ROAD
TERRACE

FROME
STREET
STREET
EAST
TERR.
EAST

STREET
WAKEFIELD ROAD

D
E

STREET
CARDWELL
STREET
HUTT
TERR.
EAST
KENSINGTON RD.
FULLARTON

STREET
STREET

Victoria Park Racecourse

GRANT AV.
SWAINE AV.
ROAD
DULWICH AV.

E
F

TERRACE
Osmond Gardens
GLEN OSMOND RD.
HUTT RD.

4 5

5 6

F

PERTH

14

A

B

RAILWAY PARADE

0 100 200 300 400 500m

SUBIACO RD

RAILWAY

NEWCASTLE

ABERDEEN STREET

STREET

MITCHELL

CAMBRIDGE ST

FREEWAY

STREET

FITZGERALD

ROBERTS

ROAD

Mueller Park

HAY ST.

THOMAS

MURRAY ST.

WELLINGTON

STREET

STREET

STREET

WEST PERTH

West Perth Stn.

MARKET ST.

JAME

ROE

STREET

RICHARDSON

HAY

COLIN

ST.

STREET

STREET

Entertain Cen

WELLINGTON

KINGS

ORD

VENTNOR

OUTRAM

ST.

STREET

HAVELOCK

STREET

STREET

TER.

ELDER ST.

MILLIGAN ST.

ST.

HAY

PARK

ROAD

Parliament House

Arch

Cloiste

B

C

HARVEST ST.

MALCOLM

MOUNT

SPRING ST.

MILL ST.

Jacobs Ladder

Arboretum

AVENUE

BAY

ROAD

MITCHELL

FREEWAY

Alan Conse

KINGS

PARK

Reservoirs

FRASER

MOUNTS

C

D

LOVEKIN

DRIVE

DRIVE

MAY

DRIVE

War Memorial

Botanic Gardens

BAY

ROAD

Narrows Bridge

FORREST

MOUNTS

BAY

The Narrows

Mill Point

Old Mill

MILL

SOUTH

D

E

KWINANA

POINT

PERTH

ROAD

SCOTT ST.

ESPLA

FREEWAY

BOWMAN ST.

MELVILLE

HARDY

ST.

Windsor Park

E

F

PARADE

RICHARDSON

ST.

Zool Gar

1 2 3

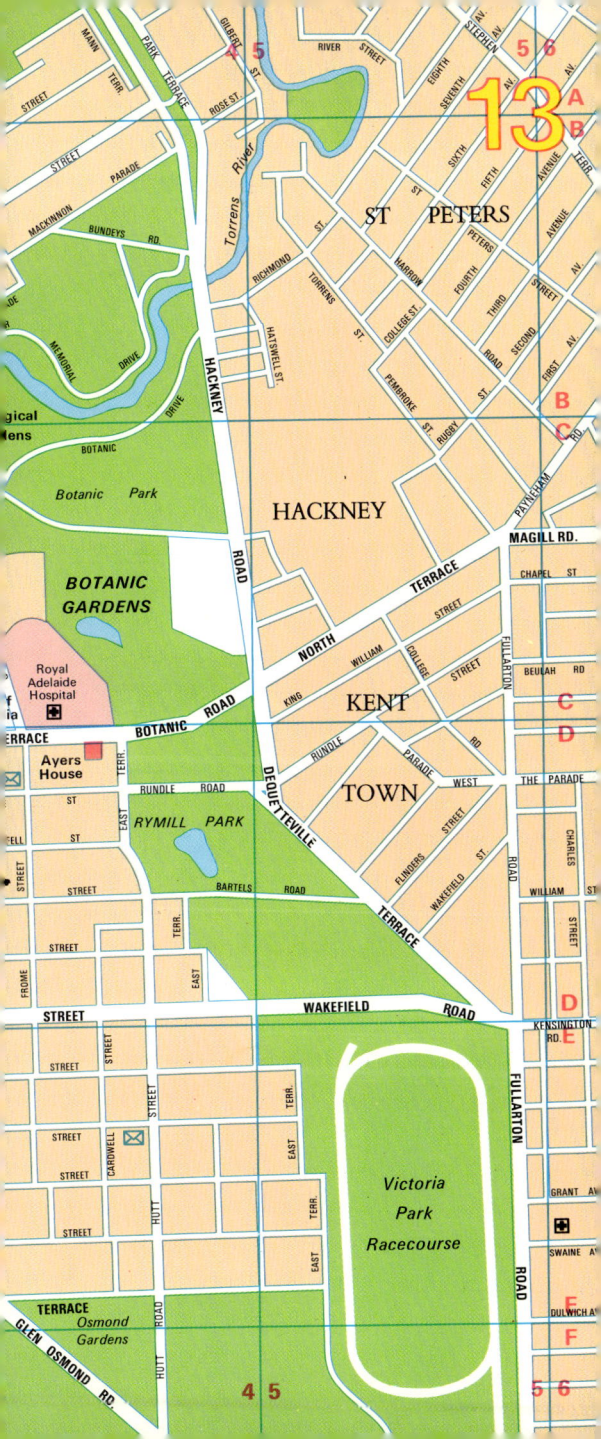

13 A B

5 6

RIVER STREET

EIGHTH AV
SEVENTH
STERLN AV
5 6
A
B

ST PETERS

SIXTH

FIFTH

PETERS

HARROW ST

FOURTH

COLLEGE ST

THIRD

ROAD SECOND AV

PEMBROKE ST

FIRST AV

RUGBY ST

B
C

PAYNEHAM RD

MAGILL RD.

CHAPEL

HACKNEY

NORTH TERRACE

WILLIAM STREET

COLLEGE

STREET

FULLARTON

BEULAH RD

KING

KENT

RD

C
D

ROAD

TOWN

RUNDLE STREET

PARADE

WEST

THE PARADE

FLINDERS STREET

WAKEFIELD ST

ROAD

CHARLES

WILLIAM STREET

BARTELS ROAD

TERRACE

WAKEFIELD ROAD

KENSINGTON RD.

D
E

FULLARTON

FROME STREET

STREET

RYMILL PARK

RUNDLE ROAD

DEQUETTEVILLE TERRACE

EAST TERR.

EAST

HUTT

CARDWELL

Victoria Park Racecourse

GRANT AV

SWAINE AV

ROAD

DULWICH AV

TERRACE

Osmond Gardens

GLEN OSMOND RD.

HUTT ROAD

EAST TERR.

4 5

E
F

5 6
F

BOTANIC PARK

Botanic Park

BOTANIC GARDENS

Royal Adelaide Hospital

Ayers House

BOTANIC ROAD

MEMORIAL DRIVE

HACKNEY ROAD

Torrens River

PARK TERRACE

GILBERT ST

ROSE ST.

RICHMOND

TORRENS ST.

HATSWELL ST.

MANN TERR.

MACKINNON PARADE

BUNDEYS RD.

PARADE

STREET

STREET

4 5

14

A
B
C
D
E
F

1 2 2 3

RAILWAY PARADE

MITCHELL
CAMBRIDGE

ST

NEWCASTLE
Aberdeen
STREET
STRE

0 100 200 300 400 500m

SUBIACO RD

FREEWAY

FITZGERALD

West
Perth
Stn

ROBERTS

ROAD

Mueller
Park

STREET

RAILWAY

MARKET
ST

JAM

ROE

HAY ST.

MURRAY

WELLINGTON

STREET

Entertai
Cent

WEST PERTH

AV.

HAY

STREET

WELLINGTO

ST.

RICHARDSON

ST.

COLIN

STREET

MILLIGAN

HAY

THOMAS

ORD

VENTNOR

OUTRAM

STREET

STREET

HAVELOCK

ELDER
ST.

Parliament
House

KINGS

PARK

ROAD

Arch

HARVEST
ST.

MALCOLM

Cloist

SPRING
ST

MILL
ST

Arboretum

MOUNT

Jacobs
Ladder

ROAD

Alan
Conse

MAY

Reservoirs

FRASER
AVENUE

BAY

MITCHELL

FREEWAY

KINGS
PARK

DRIVE

LOVEKIN DRIVE

DRIVE

War
Memorial

MOUNTS

Botanic
Gardens

ROAD

BAY

The Narrows

Narrows
Bridge

FORREST

MOUNTS

Mill
Point

Old
Mill

MILL

SOUTH

KWINANA

POINT

PERTH

SCOTT ST.

ROAD

FREEWAY

MELVILLE

BOWMAN ST.

HARDY

ESPLA

Windsor
Park

Zool
Gar

PARADE

RICHARDSON

1 2 2 3

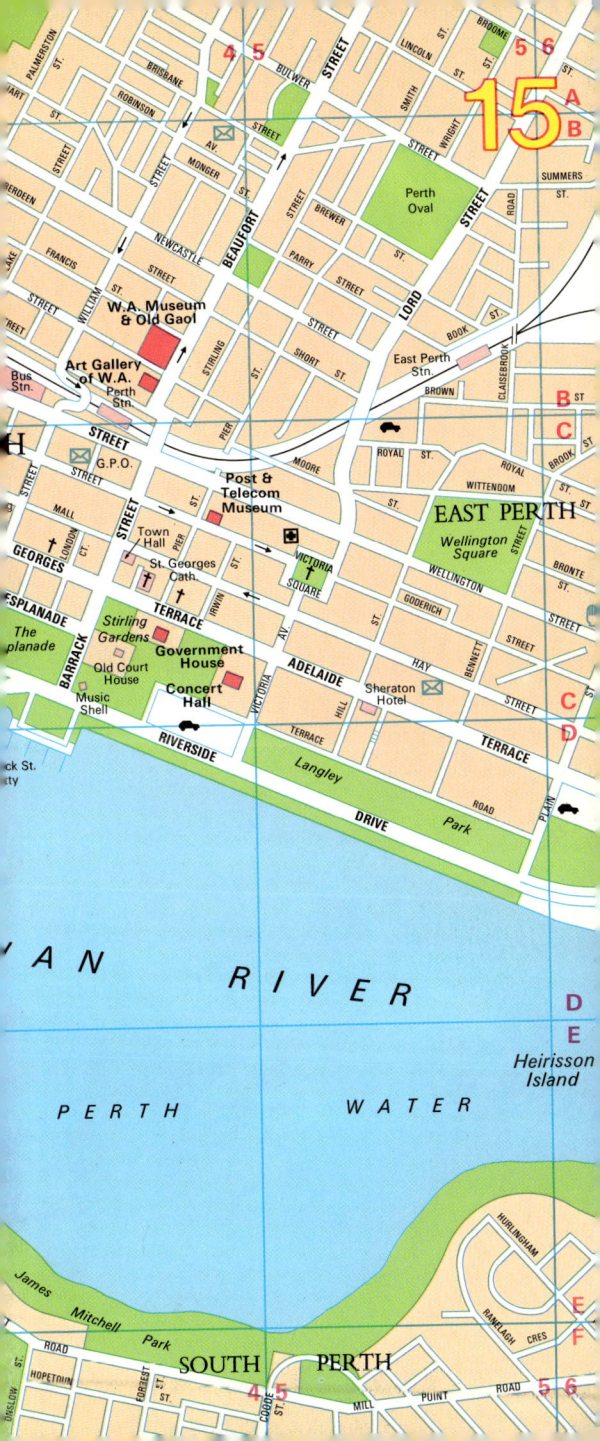

✠ Royal Brisbane Hospital

BRISBANE

Exhibition
Grounds

16

A
B

HERSTON
ROAD

0 100 200 300 400 500 m

TERRACE

BROOKS

ST

ALEXANDRIA

GREGORY

COSTIN

ST

Newste
House

BOWEN
BRIDGE
RD

WATER

ST

TERRACE

CONSTANCE

ST

ST

Municipal
Golf Course

VICTORIA

AVENUE

GILCHRIST

KENNIGO

WARRY

ST

STREET

ALFRED

ST

Brunswick
St Station

BRUNSWICK

PARK

TERRACE

UNION

ST

LOVE

ST

QUARRY

ST

STREET

WATER

ST PAULS

GOTHA ST

GIPPS

WICKHAM

STREET

ST

B

C

GREGORY

FORTESCUE

ST

GLOUCESTER

ST

BARRY PARADE

STREET

STREET

SPRING HILL

BOUNDARY

STREET

ST

STREET

WHARF

LEICHHARDT

ST

ASTOR TERR.

ANN

*ALBERT
PARK*

TERRACE

WICKHAM

BIRLEY

ST

WICKHAM

TER

Central
Station

TURBOT

ST

St Johns
Cathedral

All
Saints

STREET

STREET

ST

STREET

Ferry

Custom
House

C

D

ALBERT

Observatory

Albert St
Uniting

EDWARD

Anzac
Square

CREEK

QUEEN

EAGLE ST

ROMA

STREET

ANN

ST

G.P.O.

John Oxley
Monument

NORTH

City
Hall

ADELAIDE

MALL

ST

STREET

CITY

GEORGE

ST

QUAY

QUEEN

ELIZABETH

CHARLOTTE

ALBERT

ST

ST

ST

Ferry

D

E

Fountain

VICTORIA
BRIDGE

Treasury
Building

STREET

MARY

MARGARET

ST

ALICE

BOTANIC

Queensland
Club

Museum &
Art Gallery

ST

BRISBANE

Parliament House

GARDENS

Queensland
Cultural Centre

South Brisbane
Station

Old Government
House

MELBOURNE

MERIVALE

Expo '88
Site

RIVER

RIVERSIDE

Conservator
of Music

*MUSGRAVE
PARK*

CORDELIA

ST

COLCHESTER ST

EXPRESSWAY

RIVER TERRACE

F

SOUTH BRISBANE

VULTURE

STREET